TREASURY'S WAR

TREASURY'S WAR

❖

The Unleashing of a
New Era of Financial Warfare

JUAN C. ZARATE

PublicAffairs *New York*

PublicAffairs books are available at special discounts for bulk purchases in the
U.S. by corporations, institutions, and other organizations. For more information, please contact the Special Markets Department at the Perseus Books
Group, 2300 Chestnut Street, Suite 200, Philadelphia, PA 19103, call (800)
810-4145, ext. 5000, or e-mail special.markets@perseusbooks.com.

Book design by Mark McGarry, Texas Type & Book Works
Set in Meridien

Library of Congress Cataloging-in-Publication Data
Zarate, Juan Carlos.
Treasury's war : the unleashing of a new era of financial warfare /
Juan C. Zarate.—First edition.
pages cm.
Includes bibliographical references and index.
ISBN 9781610391153 (hardcover)—ISBN 9781610391160 (ebook)
1. United States. Dept. of the Treasury. 2. Terrorism—Finance—Prevention.
3. Money laundering—Prevention. 4. Commercial crimes—Prevention.
5. Finance—Moral and ethical aspects—United States. 6. National security—
United States. 7. Security, International. I. Title.
HJ261.Z37 2013
363.325'170973—dc23
2012051582

FIRST EDITION
10 9 8 7 6 5 4 3

*To my father and mother, who came to this country
believing in the American dream and who showed us
with unconditional love how to live it. And to my wife,
whose support and love made this story possible.*

CONTENTS

Prologue: "The Hidden War"   ix
Introduction: The Modern Megarian Decree   1

Part I: Foundation

1. A New Kind of War   15
2. Financial Footprints   45
3. Nose Under the Tent   67
4. Financial Chokepoints   93

Part II: A New Paradigm

5. Blowfish   127
6. Bad Banks   145
7. "The Mother of All Financial Investigations"   169
8. Resurrection   201

Part III: Financial Furies

9. "Killing the Chicken to Scare the Monkeys"   219
10. The Awakening   239
11. Putting the Genie Back in the Bottle   249
12. Revelation   269
13. The Constriction Campaign   287

Part IV: Adaptation

14. Dusting Off the Playbook   319
15. Learning Curve   357
16. The Coming Financial Wars   383
     Epilogue: Lessons from the Use of Financial Power   423

Acknowledgments   433
Notes   439
Selected Bibliography   465
Index   473
Photo insert between pages 248–249.

Prologue: "The Hidden War"

On October 8, 2012, Iranian President Mahmoud Ahmadinejad publicly bemoaned that the Iranian economy was under direct economic assault, with oil sales cut, bank transfers banned, and the value of the Iranian rial and foreign currency reserves plummeting. He admitted plainly, "The enemy has mobilized all its forces to enforce its decision, and so a hidden war is underway, on a very far-reaching global scale. . . . [W]e should realize that this is a kind of war through which the enemy assumes it can defeat the Iranian nation."[1]

He was right.

Over the past decade, the United States has waged a new brand of financial warfare, unprecedented in its reach and effectiveness. This "hidden war" has often been underestimated or misunderstood, but it is no longer secret and has since become central to America's national security doctrine. In a series of financial pressure campaigns, the United States has financially squeezed and isolated America's principal enemies of this period—Al Qaeda, North Korea, Iran, Iraq, and Syria. Far from relying solely on the classic sanctions or trade embargoes of old, these campaigns have consisted of a novel set of financial strategies that harness the international financial and commercial systems to ostracize rogue actors and constrict their funding flows, inflicting real pain. America's enemies have realized they have been hit with a new breed of financial power. And they have felt the painful effects.

Al Qaeda has found it harder, costlier, and riskier to raise and move money around the world and has had to adapt to find new ways to raise capital for its movement. The documents found in Osama bin Laden's compound in Abbottabad, Pakistan, reflect a terrorist leader and movement in search of new sources of money. This was not a new development—from 9/11 on, the movement struggled to maintain its core financing. In statement after statement— intended for donors and sometimes only for internal consumption— Al Qaeda has admitted that it has been choked financially. In a July 9, 2005, letter to Abu Mus'ab al-Zarqawi, leader of Al Qaeda in Iraq, Ayman al-Zawahiri, then Al Qaeda's number two, asked for money, noting that "many of the lines [of financial assistance] have been cut off."[2]

The campaign against North Korea had direct and immediate impact. In the wake of financial pressure unlike any the regime had seen while under international sanctions, North Korea found its bank accounts and illicit financial activity in jeopardy. A North Korean deputy negotiator at the time quietly admitted to a senior White House official, "You finally found a way to hurt us."

The Iranians, too, have suffered the economic effects of a targeted financial assault. On September 14, 2010, former Iranian president Akbar Hashemi Rafsanjani urged the Iranian Assembly of Experts to take seriously the painful sanctions and financial pressure being imposed by the United States and the international community. "Throughout the revolution," he said, "we never had so many sanctions [imposed on Iran] and I am calling on you and all officials to take the sanctions seriously and not as jokes. . . . Over the past 30 years we had a war and military threats, but never have we seen such arrogance to plan a calculated assault against us." The journalist Moisés Naím has opined that the financial pressures on Iran "are biting, the sanctions are very, very powerful. They are the most sophisticated economic and financial sanctions imposed on a country ever."[3]

All of these assaults against America's enemies derive from a blueprint for financial warfare developed years ago by the United States. This is warfare defined by the use of financial tools, pressure, and market forces to leverage the banking sector, private-sector interests, and foreign partners in order to isolate rogue actors from the international financial and commercial systems and eliminate their funding sources.

This book tells the story of this new era of financial warfare. It began after 9/11, as the US government developed these techniques for use against terrorists, rogue regimes, and other illicit financial actors. These capabilities—which fall between diplomacy and kinetic warfare—would increasingly become the national security tools of choice for the hard international security issues facing the United States. Now, the United States can call upon these techniques to confront its most critical national security threats, from terrorist groups and international criminals to North Korea and Iran.

This is also the story of the small group of officials from the Treasury Department and other government agencies who engineered this new brand of financial power. These strategies were designed under the radar, with the clear mission to revamp the way financial tools were used. They served also to resurrect a Treasury Department that was struggling to remain relevant to national security issues. From the bowels of an emasculated Treasury Department, bureaucratic insurgents—guerrillas in gray suits—envisioned a new national security landscape in which the private sector could be prompted to isolate rogue actors in line with US interests. With the help of bankers and financial institutions, the Treasury Department led a campaign to protect rogues from the financial system. We envisioned a day when the Treasury Department would become central to core national security debates, and that's exactly what happened.

I was privileged to be a part of that Treasury team and to play a role in shaping and executing these strategies. Later, from my privileged perch as deputy national security adviser, I helped my Treasury colleagues deploy these powers, and together we witnessed the growth in Treasury's role as its expertise and influence became increasingly important to national security.

Finding the soft financial underbelly of our country's enemies became our mission. These financial strategies became indispensable to targeting and isolating the North Korean, Syrian, and Iranian regimes and other rogue actors who threatened US national security and engaged in international criminal behavior. This approach remains central to our national security to this day. We redefined the way the US government engages in financial warfare and in the process fundamentally reshaped the role of the US Treasury itself.

We successfully formulated and used these strategies during the administration of President George W. Bush, but since the changing of administrations, President Barack Obama and his team have continued to rely heavily on this brand of financial warfare. The world still faces challenges from rogue states, networks, and actors, but there now exists a well-developed international system to use financial information, power, and suasion to isolate rogues from the legitimate financial system. Though this type of warfare alone cannot solve issues of deepest national security concern, this private-sector-based paradigm gives the United States and its allies the tools and leverage they need to affect rogue actors and their interests in ways that historically would have been considered out of reach.

The story of Treasury's campaigns of financial warfare is not well known, even within the upper reaches of the US government. The role of Treasury, the scope of its powers, and the effectiveness of its strategies were often unseen amid the more visible signs of the global war on terror. When I left the Treasury Department in 2005 to join the National Security Council, I had a conversation with a senior Pentagon official who noted that Treasury should be engaged in the global fight—meeting with its foreign counterparts and urging concerted financial action against America's enemies. I was surprised at the comments, knowing what Treasury had been doing. Treasury was already at war.

But this was a new kind of war—not "shock and awe," but more like a creeping financial insurgency. It was a "hidden war" intended to constrict our enemies' financial lifeblood. And we were succeeding, under the radar.

This book explains how and why this power has worked and what must be done to maintain it in the future. It also raises a wary eye to competitor states like China, or transnational networks, that might use the lessons of the past ten years to wage financial battles against the United States.

The new era of financial warfare that began after 9/11 will continue to evolve into the foreseeable future. It came about because we were able to view the landscape differently than our predecessors. The era of globalization and the centrality of American financial power and influence allowed for a new approach. And, in this sense, Iranian President Ahmadinejad was not mistaken: there was indeed a hidden war striking at the heart of America's enemies—a war that has been expanded and continues to this day on multiple fronts around the world. This is Treasury's war.

Introduction: The Modern Megarian Decree

Money binds the world—now more than ever. It has always been a source of power for nations, companies, and people. It continues to be the lifeblood for terrorist organizations, criminal syndicates, and rogue regimes. Whether it's North Korea producing the world's best $100 counterfeit bills, Al Qaeda paying pensions to the families of its deceased operatives, or Mexican drug cartels in Ciudad Juárez dispensing bribes to gain access to lucrative *plazas*, or smuggling routes, into the United States, money is what fuels the operations of the world's rogues. It pays salaries, buys influence and allegiance, and makes possible the fanciful imaginings of leaders. Budgets and cash flow give them access, capabilities, and global reach to build their organizations, expand their influence, and give life to their personal, political, and ideological ambitions.

Money also creates vulnerabilities. The need for money to survive and operate in the twenty-first century—whether in local economies or globally—creates financial trails that do not lie and dependencies that are hard to hide. In a globalized economy, money flows across borders at a lightning pace and in staggering volumes. With the ease of a phone call or the touch of an app, billions of dollars move every day in myriad ways—via antiseptic wire transfers, the traditional practice of *hawala*, and satchels full of cash. Money is a common denominator that connects disparate groups and interests—often generating new networks of convenience aligned against the United States.

Money is their enabler, but it's also their Achilles' heel.

If you can cut off funding flows to rogue groups or states, you can restrict their ability to operate and force them to make choices—not only budget decisions, but also strategic choices. Al Qaeda's budget, in addition to the payments to families of deceased operatives, covers training expenses for new recruits. Iran's national budget includes a specific line item for its support of terrorist groups such as Hezbollah and Hamas. North Korea enriches its leadership with luxury goods and uses money to maintain both internal order and military and political allegiances. Organized crime groups around the world use their profits to buy influence and access at border crossings and in the halls of governments and to expand their business empires.

Financial strategies are powerful tools that can constrict our enemies' current activities and their strategic reach. Yes, one suicide bombing may cost a terrorist organization less than $1,000, but if that organization cannot pay for all the sophisticated training it would like, cannot adequately maintain its international alliances, and cannot develop all the programs and operations it imagines, then its ultimate impact will be limited. In maximalist terms, we can alter the enemy's behavior by affecting its bottom line.

A small group of us within the US Treasury Department and other areas of the US government recognized this strategic vulnerability of America's enemies after 9/11. We viewed the global battlefield through the lens of dollars, euros, and rials, seeing money as our greatest asset and our enemies' greatest vulnerability. Pursuing this idea, we began to devise means of using money as a weapon against terrorists, rogue regimes, and illicit financial actors. As a result, we are now living in a new era of financial warfare. The ability to undercut and disrupt the financial flows and networks of our enemies gave the United States a different kind of strategic leverage.

This new warfare is defined by the use of financial tools, pressure, and market forces to isolate rogue actors from the international financial and commercial systems and gain leverage over our enemies. As this book will explore, the US government has innovated the use of financial power in the twenty-first century. That is not the end of the story—America's enemies have adapted to the pressure, and our competitors have learned from our example. Financial warfare will continue to develop rapidly—now outside of the control of the United States—and has started to form a central part of international security strategies. This is why it is so important to understand how this type of financial power evolved and to ensure that we preserve the ability to wage financial warfare smartly.

Our techniques, innovative as they are, build on a longer history. Financial power and economic influence have served as weapons since the dawn of warfare. The Greek city-states, the Roman Empire, and even the barbarians used sieges and economic deprivation to weaken their enemies. Eighteenth and nineteenth-century nations relied on blockades and trade warfare. By the late 1990s, broad, country-based trade embargoes and targeted sanctions were used to attempt to affect the behavior of international pariahs.

Perhaps the oldest and best-known example of financial warfare dates back to the Peloponnesian War. In 432 B.C., Athens and Sparta were the two strongest city-states in Ancient Greece, each leading its own competing coalition of allied city-states. Athens was an economic power, influential thanks to its trading system and its advanced navy. Sparta maintained a large and well-trained army.

Conflict erupted between the two over the city of Megara, which at that time was aligned with Sparta. The Athenian politician Pericles proposed that Athens sanction Megara economically. This policy—which became known as the "Megarian Decree"—excluded Megarian merchants from the ports and markets of the Athenian-allied Delian League. The Athenians wanted to avoid a direct military confrontation with Megara, but the Spartans saw the decree differently. Sparta sent word that the decree must be withdrawn, and when the Athenians refused, Sparta declared war—a war that would conclude with Sparta's subjugation of Athens and the end of the Athenian Golden Age.

Trade sanctions and blockades of city-states and key ports persisted for centuries. In the 1500s, the English and other naval and trading powers innovated the use of privateers—privately owned ships—to act as agents of the state under issued "letters of marque." These letters authorized the vessels to attack specific nations' ships in specific geographic zones. As privateering became an increasingly pernicious problem, England installed a standing navy in 1708 to defend its trade routes. This brand of outsourced financial warfare on the high seas was not legally abolished until 1856.

During the American Civil War, economic warfare in the form of naval blockades, privateering, and counterfeiting became an endemic part of the landscape. Counterfeiting grew to be particularly problematic—with estimates suggesting that approximately a third of all currency circulating in the United States at the time was counterfeit.[1] To police the money supply, President Abraham Lincoln ordered the creation of the US Secret Service within the Treasury Department. It was charged with infiltrating counterfeiting rings and shutting down their printing presses—and this remains a core mission of the Secret Service to this day.[2]

As the nature of conflict and international relations changed, the use of sanctions and financial pressure continued to evolve. After World War I, the major powers created the League of Nations to regulate international affairs. The Covenant of the League of Nations specifically formalized the use of economic sanctions as a tool for avoiding conflict, signaling the international community's approval of these methods to change state behavior. Unfortunately, economic sanctions were not only insufficient to prevent war in Europe, but may have actually increased the likelihood of war. The victors of World War I required large amounts of reparations from the losers, bankrupting some and contributing to widespread frustration in Germany that may have led to the rise of extreme nationalist political parties.

During the years prior to World War II, the United States used sanctions against Japan much as Athens had used sanctions against Megara. Concerned about the expansion of Japanese influence throughout East Asia, the United States placed sanctions on the export of aviation fuel, iron, and steel to Japan in 1940. In July 1941, the United States went further, freezing Japanese assets and imposing a licensing restriction on trade with Japan. Just one week before the Japanese attack on Pearl Harbor, the Japanese ambassador to the United States noted, to an American counterpart, "The Japanese people believe that economic measures are a more effective weapon of war than military measures. . . . They are being placed under severe pressure by the United States to yield to the American position; and [they believe] that it is preferable to fight rather than to yield to pressure."[3]

After World War II, economic sanctions would become a tool not merely for use against enemies, but for persuading allies as well.[4] In 1956, Israel, Britain, and France conspired to gain control over Egypt's Suez Canal, striking against Gamal Abdel Nasser's revolutionary Egyptian government.[5] Seeking to rein in the three US allies, the Eisenhower administration threatened to withhold US financial assistance and oil supplies, warning Britain that a run on the pound was possible. The proposed sanctions forced them to capitulate, and Britain and France, and eventually Israel, withdrew their troops.

In 1960, the United States imposed a blockade against Cuba. This blockade became almost total in February 1962 in response to nationalization of American properties by Cuban authorities.[6] Sanctions on Cuban economic and commercial activity continued in full for three decades, and in the 1990s President Bill Clinton expanded the trade embargo by targeting private assistance to potential future Cuban governments as well as by sanctioning foreign subsidiaries trading with Cuba (although he authorized the provision of humanitarian goods in 2000).

By the end of the twentieth century, broad sanctions against some countries, such as apartheid-era South Africa, Saddam Hussein's Iraq, and Muammar el-Qaddafi's Libya, were applied as a way of expressing international opprobrium and attempting to change a country's behavior. They served to constrain the ability of those countries to obtain goods and services, leveraging commercial isolation to change their policies. These strategies, though involving a larger number of countries, followed the classic pattern of states applying sanctions against one another. They updated the idea of blockades and trade-route disruption for a modern age—introducing new versions of the sanction to account for international trade and financing that had the effect of isolating a country's economy.

Yet, by the mid-1990s, there was a growing sense that broad sanctions had become counterproductive. Aloof and repressive regimes seemed perfectly willing to allow their already vulnerable populations to suffer—and often used the sanctions as propaganda to condemn the international community for assaulting and impoverishing their nation. Such sanctions also threatened to become a way for entrenched regimes and their cronies to more easily enrich themselves. Their control of permissible trade and of loopholes in the sanctions allowed them to benefit at the expense of their populations. This was seen plainly in the Iraqi sanctions program through 2003, where humanitarian exemptions, such as those provided for in the Oil for Food Program, gave the ruling regime an opening to profit. As a result, the international community began to lose faith in the idea that sanctions as traditionally applied could be used effectively.

One solution appeared to be to move away from broad sanctions to those that targeted individuals. The Clinton administration used economic sanctions to pressure Serbia from 1993 through 1995, specifically targeting Serbia's leader, Slobodan Milosevic. By seizing the US-based assets of Milosevic and his regime, the United States was able to ratchet up financial pressure on the support network of his government.

In 1995, after pressuring Serbia, the Clinton administration also greatly expanded the use of targeted sanctions against individuals and companies associated with narcotics in Colombia and elsewhere in Latin America. The Treasury's Office of Foreign Assets Control (OFAC), responsible for implementing all US sanctions programs, began targeting hundreds of individuals, companies, and associated properties that were subject to asset freezes and shut them out of the US financial system. Banks not just in the United States but throughout Latin America stopped doing business altogether with individuals labeled by the OFAC as "Specially Designated Nationals" (SDNs), including drug kingpins. Those who appeared on what became known as "la lista Clinton" suffered a virtual financial death penalty. Banks clearly recognized that it was better to continue doing business in the United States than to risk doing business with designated parties. The Clinton administration also twice used executive orders to name terrorist organizations, such as Palestinian terrorist groups, Hezbollah, and Al Qaeda, and their leaders, freezing assets and forbidding US citizens and companies from doing business with them.

The newly minted sanctions of the 1990s offered novel opportunities to focus financial pressure on specific targets. Even so, and in spite of their failings, broad sanctions continued to be the predominant tool. Though the Serbian, Colombian, and anti-drug related policies had proven that targeted sanctions could work, there remained doubts and concerns about the overall effectiveness and sustainability of sanctions as an international tool of statecraft. That would soon change.

After September 11, 2001, the United States unleashed a counter-terrorist financing campaign that reshaped the very nature of financial warfare. The Treasury Department waged an all-out offensive, using every tool in its toolbox to disrupt, dismantle, and deter the flows of illicit financing around the world. The "smart" sanctions of the late 1990s that had targeted rogue leaders and the entities they controlled were now put on steroids to target the Al

Qaeda and Taliban network and anyone providing financial support to any part of that network.

There were three primary themes defining this campaign that shaped the environment and evolution of financial power after September 11: the expansion of the international anti-money-laundering regime; the development of financial tools and intelligence geared specifically to dealing with issues of broad national security; and the growth of strategies based on a new understanding of the centrality of both the international financial system and the private sector to transnational threats and issues pertaining to national security. This environment reshaped the ways in which key actors—namely, the banks—operated in the post-9/11 world.

Reliance on the anti-money-laundering regime permitted an all-out campaign to ensure that funds intended for terrorist groups, such as Al Qaeda, were not coursing through the veins of the international financial system. This focus reshaped the international financial landscape forever, presenting a new paradigm that governments could use to attack terrorists, criminals, and rogue states. It was a paradigm rooted in denying rogue financial actors access to the international financial system by leveraging the private sector's aversion to doing business with terrorists.

In this context, governments implemented and expanded global anti-money-laundering regulations and practices based on principles of financial transparency, information sharing, and due diligence. They applied new reporting and information-sharing principles to new sectors of the domestic and international financial community, such as insurance companies, brokers and dealers in precious metals and stones, money-service businesses, and *hawaladars* (*hawala* is a trust-based money transfer mechanism).

This approach worked by focusing squarely on the behavior of financial institutions rather than on the classic sanctions framework of the past. In this new approach, the policy decisions of governments are not nearly as persuasive as the risk-based compliance calculus of financial institutions. For banks, wire services, and insurance companies, there are no benefits to facilitating illicit transactions that could bring high regulatory and reputational costs if uncovered. The risk is simply too high.

Because of these new strategies, rogue actors who try to use the financial system to launder money, finance terrorism, underwrite proliferation networks, and evade sanctions can be exposed. They can be denied access by the financial community itself. And the sanctions are based on the conduct of the rogues themselves, rather than on the political decisions of governments. It is the illicit or suspicious behavior of the actors themselves as they try to access the international financial system that triggers their isolation. Such an approach was possible because of the unique international environment after September 11. The environment after the terrorist attacks allowed for amplified and accelerated use of financial tools, suasion, and warfare to attack asymmetric and transnational threats.

The twenty-first-century economy is defined by globalization and the deep interconnectedness of the financial system—as seen in the contagion of financial crises like the Great Recession of 2008. The United States has remained the world's primary financial hub, with inherent value embedded in access to and the imprimatur from the American financial system. The dollar serves as the global reserve currency and the currency of choice for international trade, and New York has remained a core financial capital and hub for dollar-clearing transactions. With this concentration of financial and commercial power comes the ability to wield access to American markets, American banks, and American dollars as financial weapons.

The tools the United States applied to tracking and disrupting illicit financial flows—in particular, terrorist financing—were given greater muscle and reach after 9/11. The more aggressive and directed use of these tools amplified their impact and served to condition the environment, making it riskier and riskier for financial actors to do business with suspect customers. The campaign focused on ferreting out illicit financial flows and using that information to our enemies' disadvantage. The military and intelligence communities focused their attention and their collection efforts on enemy sources of funding and support networks. The Treasury Department used targeted sanctions, regulatory pressure, and financial suasion globally to isolate rogue financial actors. Law enforcement and regulators hammered banks and institutions for failing to identify or capture illicit financial activity or failing to institute effective anti-money-laundering systems. The United States leveraged the entire toolkit, and the aversion of the international banking system and commercial environment to illicit capital, to craft a new way of waging financial warfare.

This approach puts a premium on targeting rogues based on their illicit conduct. Interestingly, under the right conditions, this model created a virtuous cycle of self-isolation by suspect financial actors. The more isolated the rogue actors became, the more likely they were to engage in even more evasive and suspicious financial activities to avoid scrutiny, and the more they found themselves excluded from financial networks.

But perhaps the most important insight powering Treasury's campaign was its focus on the financial sector's omnipresence in the international economic system. Financial activity—bank accounts, wire transfers, letters of credit—facilitates international commerce and relationships. The banks are the ligaments of the international system. In Treasury, we realized that private-sector actors—most importantly, the banks—could drive the isolation of rogue entities more effectively than governments—based principally on their own interests and desires to avoid unnecessary business and reputational risk.

Indeed, the international banking community has grown acutely sensitive to the business risks attached to illicit financial activity and has taken significant steps to bar it from their institutions. As the primary gatekeepers to all international commerce and capital, banks, even without express governmental mandates or requirements, have motivated private-sector actors to steer clear of problematic or suspect business relationships. The actions of legitimate international financial community participants are based on their own business interests, and when governments appear to be isolating rogue financial actors, the banks will fall into line. Reputation and perceived institutional integrity became prized commodities in the private sector's calculus after 9/11. Our campaigns leveraged the power of this kind of reputational risk.

In such an environment, the Treasury Department, finance ministries and central banks, and financial regulators around the world used their unconventional tools and influence for broader national security purposes. The old orthodoxy of unilateral versus multilateral sanctions became irrelevant—the strategic question was instead about how to amplify or synchronize the effects of financial pressure with other international actors, including states, international institutions, banks, and other commercial actors.

Transnational nonstate actors and rogue regimes are tied to the global financial order regardless of location or reclusiveness. Dirty money eventually flows across borders. Moreover, in this environment, the banks, as the central arteries of the international financial system, have their own ecosystems, with established regulatory expectations and penalties and a routinized gatekeeping function. With this role come vulnerabilities for America's enemies.

This new brand of financial power was spawned by both design and necessity. We recognized the possibilities this new environment presented for reshaping the way the United States used its financial influence to promote its national security. The strategies that resulted focused squarely on protecting the broader international financial system and using financial tools to put pressure on legitimate financial institutions to reject dealings with rogue and illicit financial actors.

These tools and this approach are no longer new. Economic sanctions and financial influence are now the national security tools of choice when neither diplomacy nor military force proves effective or possible. This tool of statecraft has become extremely important in coercing and constraining the behavior of nonstate networks and recalcitrant, rogue regimes, which often appear beyond the reach of classic government power or influence.

But these rogue actors are already adapting to this kind of financial pressure. It is only a matter of time until US competitors use the lessons of the past decade to wage financial battles of their own—especially against the United States.

More worrisome, our ability to use these powers could diminish as the economic landscape changes. Treasury's power ultimately stems from the ability of the United States to use its financial powers with global effect. This ability, in turn, derives from the centrality and stability of New York as a global financial center, the importance of the dollar as a reserve currency, and the demonstration effects of any steps, regulatory or otherwise, taken by the United States in the broader international system. If the US economy loses its predominance, or the dollar sufficiently weakens, our ability to wage financial warfare could wane. It is vital that policymakers and ordinary Americans understand what is at stake and how this new brand of financial warfare evolved.

This is the story of how a small team at the Treasury Department, in concert with other parts of the US government and the private sector, unleashed this new era of financial warfare—how it took shape, why it became so important to US national security, and how it will continue to be shaped by the changing international economic and security landscape. This group of officials and operatives recognized that the world was entering a new financial and political environment and took advantage of the possibilities it presented. We fashioned strategies that used financial suasion and financial tools to attack our enemies' greatest vulnerabilities, deploying hidden financial campaigns against a range of America's most dangerous and difficult enemies, including Al Qaeda, North Korea, and Iran. In so doing, we undermined the financial infrastructures of those enemies.

What we unleashed was a modern Megarian Decree, with all the financial tools and financial firepower America could muster. In so doing, we redefined the very nature of financial warfare as well as the role of the US Treasury Department in national security. And we did it all without ever firing a shot.

Part I

FOUNDATION

1

A New Kind of War

As our US Air Force C-17 approached Kabul, we were jostled in our jump seats as the pilot corkscrewed down toward the airport to avoid surface-to-air missiles. I looked down the line at our group of Treasury Department officials. We were strapped into the sides of the plane with cargo nets enveloping us. We were clean-shaven, decked out in suits and ties, our briefing books stored away and our briefcases now at the ready. It was November 2002, and our delegation was beginning what would become our "century-hopping" tour of Afghanistan, Pakistan, and India.

In Afghanistan, we were trying to build the government's capacity to counter Al Qaeda and Taliban financing, which originated largely from the poppy trade and was transmitted via the nascent banking sector, cash couriers, and the traditional *hawala* network of traditional moneylenders. In Pakistan, we were trying to partner with the government to dismantle the financial networks coursing through the country via charities, bank accounts, and trusted couriers, funding routes that Al Qaeda and the Taliban had relied upon for two decades. And in India, we would be meeting with the G20 Finance Ministers to push for global controls on movements of illicit financing to terrorist groups, with an emphasis on trying to regulate the hawala networks that bound Central and South Asia to the Middle East, Africa, and the rest of the world. My job was to advise

Secretary of the Treasury Paul O'Neill on terrorist financing and money laundering and to help shepherd our policies along with others.

As we landed in Kabul, the members of the Secret Service's elite Counter Assault Team (CAT) who were traveling with us to protect Secretary O'Neill stood up in the plane. They began to don body armor and load their automatic weapons. The CAT members would be the last line of defense for the secretary against a direct attack. Unlike the men of the classic Secret Service plainclothes protection division, they did not want to blend into the environment. These were big, bulky, ominous-looking security professionals. They spent their training days lifting weights, running, and perfecting their marksmanship. As one of them said to us as they prepared their M5 assault rifles and bulked up with their body armor, "We want people to know we are here."

Suddenly, I, too, felt dangerously conspicuous. My suit and tie seemed wholly inappropriate and out of place, if not outright dangerous. It was almost laughable. I looked at Tim Adams and Rob Nichols, two senior Treasury officials, down the row and wondered what we were doing in Afghanistan. Our thick briefing books full of memos and background papers would be our only protection. Though the fighting in Kabul had ended with the fall of the Taliban regime, we were walking out of the plane into a war zone.

As we exited onto the tarmac—briefcases in hand—the light of dawn had just broken the darkness. The snowcapped Hindu Kush Mountains stood at 15,000 feet like waking giants in the distance. On the side of the airport runway, I saw the tattered remnants of planes—the tails and fuselages of Soviet-era jets with the vivid hammer-and-sickle insignias still visible. I felt as if I had flown back into history.

We joined with Secretary O'Neill on the tarmac and immediately boarded transport helicopters. Flanked by two armed Black Hawks as our escort, we flew over the dusty and destroyed city. Looking down, I imagined the decades of fighting and civil war the people must have witnessed from their mud homes. A little more than a year before this, Al Qaeda and the Taliban had roamed freely in the training camps and towns of this destitute country. We flew through the mountains surrounding Kabul, well beyond the city, and when we landed, the Black Hawks remained in the air, circling overhead for security. Within seconds after stepping off the helicopter, I felt the effects of the altitude and the dryness of the air. There wasn't much visible on the horizon other than dusty mountains. Very quickly, villagers began descending out of nowhere from the surrounding area—a boy with a donkey, small children, and a few men, all curious to see the visitors who had just landed in their midst. We were like aliens landing in a seventeenth-century village.

As I looked around, the reality of the new war we were waging hit me. We were doing battle with many of the same financial networks and support mechanisms that had been developed long ago to support the fight against the Soviet Union in the villages and mountains of Afghanistan. These were financial structures used now by Al Qaeda to drive its global agenda and war against the United States.

Our power and reach had to have an impact well beyond the conventional tactics and strategies—beyond the military and the diplomats to the Treasury Department's power and role. Our financial influence and tools needed to be used to help our friends and allies, and had to be tailored to pressure and impact our enemies' financial networks. And this needed to happen not just in the comfortable, modern banking centers of the world, but in the most remote and underdeveloped corners of the globe. This was a war that required new thinking about the use of financial pressure and influence to undercut the enemy's influence and reach, and we were at the center of it. We had already come a long way since 9/11.

In September 2001, from my desk on the fourth floor of the Treasury building, I could see Reagan National Airport, the Potomac

River, and the Pentagon. I had just started my new job at the
Treasury Department only weeks before, on August 24. In my previous job as a federal prosecutor in the Department of Justice's Terrorism and Violent Crimes Section, I had been blessed early on with
opportunities to work with and learn from the nation's best terrorism prosecutors—Patrick Fitzgerald, George Toscas, and John Lancaster—and had been asked to help with our investigations of the
1998 embassy bombings case, and later, the October 12, 2000, attack
on the USS *Cole* in Aden, Yemen. I had been brought over to Treasury to serve as senior adviser for all things international to the new
undersecretary for enforcement in the department, Jimmy Gurulé.

The undersecretary for enforcement had enormous statutory
responsibilities, overseeing all of Treasury's law-enforcement agencies, including the US Customs Service; the Secret Service; the
Bureau of Alcohol, Tobacco, and Firearms; the Federal Law Enforcement Training Center (FLETC); and the Treasury Executive Office
for Asset Forfeiture (TEOAF), as well as Treasury's coordination
with the IRS's Criminal Investigative Division. Treasury agents
made up about 40 percent of federal law-enforcement personnel,
and they investigated all manner of financial crimes—from money
laundering and counterfeiting to financial fraud and tax evasion.

A well-respected former prosecutor and law professor, called an
"inspired choice" for the job by Senator Orrin Hatch, Gurulé also
had oversight of the agencies responsible for managing all of the US
government's sanctions, through the Office of Foreign Assets Control, and overseeing application of the Bank Secrecy Act (the
requirements for banks to file currency transaction and suspicious
activity reports). Since assuming the office, Gurulé had been intent
on increasing Treasury's focus on money laundering at home and
globally—a focus that would prove relevant to the campaign to
come.

On 9/11, Gurulé and his Treasury spokesperson, Tasia Scolinos,
sat with a reporter from the *Wall Street Journal*, previewing the
launch of the Bush administration's first National Money Launder-

ing Strategy, to be signed by the secretary of the treasury, the attorney general, and the secretary of state and published publicly the next day. This strategy was intended to be the focus of Gurulé's tenure and would shape the work of the entire office, including the enforcement agencies of the Treasury.

News of the first and second planes hitting the World Trade Center as well as the attack on the Pentagon traveled throughout the Treasury building very quickly. As I watched the thick black smoke from from across the Potomac, it was clear to me that the world had changed and that we were at war. Soon thereafter, the evacuation sirens blared, and everyone in the historic Treasury building poured out into the streets. A handful of us would retreat to Secret Service headquarters to watch the skies and radar for more planes, wondering what was next.

On September 12, the White House asked the Treasury what the department could contribute to the response. President Bush had directed that all elements of national power be leveraged to respond to the attacks on New York and Washington—and to prevent another attack from hitting our shores. He called for an unconventional response, and he wanted to go after all elements of the network—including Al Qaeda's support networks and lifelines. In this task, Treasury's role became clear when, on September 24, 2001, President Bush announced, "We will direct every resource at our command to win the war against terrorists: every means of diplomacy, every tool of intelligence, every instrument of law enforcement, every financial influence. We will starve the terrorists of funding, turn them against each other, rout them out of their safe hiding places, and bring them to justice."[1]

This meant going after Al Qaeda's money.

The 9/11 attacks themselves demonstrated the nimble and global nature of the Al Qaeda financial infrastructure. For years, it had used the funding coming from charitable donations, deep-pocket donors, and supportive allied groups to build up its capabilities. It paid for and trained thousands of recruits in its camps devoted to

Arab foreign fighters; it managed a hub of financial activity in Peshawar, Pakistan, to receive and disburse funds; and it paid for operations and pensions as needed. It had a budget for all its operations, and moneymen with the ability to raise and move money around the world.

In the 9/11 attacks, Al Qaeda relied on its tried and true financing networks, with Mustafa Ahmad al-Hawsawi serving as the money manager for that operation. The hijackers were wired money from accounts in Dubai. In Germany, they used Dresdner Bank,[2] and once in the United States, they used bank accounts in their true names at Sun Trust Bank in Florida and Bank of America as well as multiple regional banks. In San Diego, Nawaf al-Hazmi and Khalid al-Mihdhar used an administrator's bank account at the Islamic Center of San Diego to receive wire transfers from Ali Abdul Aziz Ali, Khalid Sheikh Mohammed's nephew in Dubai.[3] All nineteen of the hijackers used legitimate bank accounts in their own names, frequently making cash deposits and withdrawals as well as sending and receiving wire transfers from Dubai. None of the hijackers triggered Suspicious Activity Reports in any of their banking transactions, owing to the small amounts and the regular nature of their activity.

In total, the amounts used specifically for the attacks reached only half a million dollars—a modest investment for the mass destruction that was to follow. Al Qaeda had devoted millions since the mid-1990s to building the capabilities to launch 9/11, as well as the other operations known and unknown around the world that targeted the United States. Al Qaeda's investments would result in the most devastating terrorist attack on US soil in history. The resulting destruction, economic aftermath, and response would cost the United States billions of dollars.

The next attacks needed to be crippled and stopped. Following and disrupting the money flows within the Al Qaeda system became an imperative. The Al Qaeda financial support networks—charities, deep-pocket donors, and front companies—and the means by which Al Qaeda moved money around the world—banks, couriers, wire transfers, hawaladars—would become our targets.

In a subsequent meeting at the White House, Deputy National Security Adviser Gary Edson asked Treasury representatives to come up with steps it could take to squeeze Al Qaeda's finances. Edson was an economist responsible for international economic policy matters, and he was known for not suffering fools lightly. He and many others around the table were new to this world—the nexus between financial power and national security—but there were financial tools, already developed over the years, that were ready to be deployed, and a small group of actors within the government who knew about them. The challenge would be to shape the classic financial weaponry of anti-money-laundering strategies and sanctions into a robust set of tools that could disrupt Al Qaeda's operations and to then dismantle its networks. Though we didn't know it at the time, these first tasks would set the stage for a far broader campaign of financial warfare—with Treasury at the helm. But it all began with the campaign to combat terrorist financing.

Terrorist financing—the raising and movement of funds intended for terrorist causes—presents a unique problem for governments. In simple terms, the financing of terrorism has often been described as "reverse money laundering." Generally, money laundering consists of a financial scheme or transaction used to make illegitimate funds appear legitimate.[4] This allows criminal groups to cleanse the proceeds of crime so that the funds can be used more freely in the banking and commercial systems and appear legitimate.

Terrorist-related funds, however, are often derived from legitimate sources that are then diverted or used to support terrorist causes. Terrorist funds—often transferred in very small amounts and destined for operatives or sympathetic groups—are often commingled with money raised for legitimate causes. The transactions are veiled behind the uncertainties of determining the motivations and intent of those involved. The task of determining motivations is further complicated by the fact that although the funds may be used for nefarious purposes (e.g., paying a terrorist sleeper cell), they may also be used for legitimate purposes (e.g., feeding orphans).[5]

Tracking such money is also difficult, since those who handle it resort to a variety of different methods of hiding the origin, transfer, and ultimate destination of these funds. They use false identities to open bank accounts and to make wire transfers; layer their transactions with the use of pass-through and joint accounts, front companies, or charities; and use alternative remittance systems that may not be subject to the same oversight as the formal financial system.[6]

The commingling of legitimate and illegitimate funds is only one characteristic of terrorist financing. A terrorist financier's motivation or intent is a unique and defining component of the financing of terrorism. As a US government report explained, terrorist groups, unlike criminal organizations, are not necessarily motivated by greed in the first instance, but by "non-financial goals such as seeking publicity, political legitimacy, political influence, and dissemination of an ideology." As the report noted, "terrorist fundraising is a means to these ends."[7] Thus, when one is attempting to identify terrorist financing, for whatever purposes, the intent of those involved becomes a critical part of the calculus.

Since the political, social, or religious causes espoused by terrorist groups may coincide with the goals and beliefs of certain nation-states and individuals, terrorist groups also receive financial and other forms of support from countries and willing donors.[8] These sources of funding provide a font of resources to terrorist groups, and it is this type of support that differentiates these groups from traditional international criminal conglomerates.

Terrorist financing has historically taken several different forms, depending, in part, on the terrorist group involved and the region in which the group or its members operate. Terrorist groups are opportunists and do not shy away from the use of classic criminal activity to raise funds for their criminal goals. Like international criminal organizations, terrorist groups around the world have been known to use all forms of criminal activity to raise money, including drug trafficking, extortion, kidnapping, human trafficking, all forms of fraudulent schemes, and counterfeiting.[9] The Revolutionary Armed Forces of Colombia (Fuerzas Armadas Revolucionarias de Colombia, or FARC) developed from being a terrorist insurgency into a sophisticated cocaine-trafficking cartel. The Taliban has used the poppy and heroin trades to increase its influence and fuel its operations against North Atlantic Treaty Organization (NATO) and Afghan forces. Groups such as the Basque terrorists in Spain and France and the Tamil Tigers in Sri Lanka have used extortion against local populations and diaspora communities to raise funds for arms and political initiatives. Other groups, such as Aum Shinrikyo in Japan, have relied on financial criminal activity or the payroll of its membership to fuel their deranged agendas. Such financial schemes—taking advantage of whatever financial opportunities may be available—are seen throughout the world today as a means of sustaining terrorist operations and cells as well as a means of terrorizing those with whom the terrorist group comes in contact. We now needed to launch a campaign against terrorist financing.

Rick Newcomb, the director of the Office of Foreign Assets Control (OFAC), a veteran Treasury official and well known to a select few in the national security community, knew immediately what needed to be done with Treasury's powers to go after Osama bin Laden and his assets. Newcomb, a man with thinning hair and large circular glasses, was a savvy lawyer who had quietly built OFAC into one of the government's most powerful yet least understood offices. OFAC, which was small in government terms, with just over one hundred employees after 9/11, was responsible for the administration of all US sanctions programs and had the delegated ability to target and sanction violators with asset freezes and fines.

In World War II, the US government tried to control the assets of German, Italian, and Japanese companies and agents. It managed this with a little office at the Treasury Department known at the time as "The Control." The Control became the US government's primary tool for going after the assets of enemy regimes. In the 1950s, with the Korean War raging, The Control was renamed the Office of Foreign Assets Control, and it was used to target Chinese assets.[10]

After the Cuban missile crisis of 1962, OFAC became the hub for administering sanctions on Cuba. Restrictions were placed on what and who could enter Cuba in an attempt to strangle the Castro regime economically. A turning point for OFAC came during the Iran hostage crisis of 1979, after which Iranian assets—liquid assets as well as real property such as the embassy and consulates—became the subject of freeze orders. On November 14, 1979, President Jimmy Carter signed Executive Order 12170, which blocked all property of the government of Iran under US jurisdiction, totaling $12 billion.[11] The work of freezing and managing Iranian assets amid the hostage crisis—and subsequently, in resolution with the Iranian government via the Algiers Accords—made it clear that OFAC needed to become more than just a licensing office. It had to be expanded to manage this case and those to come.

In many ways, OFAC thrived on being seen as a technical office. A distinct mystery surrounded the office and its operations. OFAC, housed in the Treasury Annex next to leafy Lafayette Park, across Pennsylvania Avenue from the main Treasury building, was perhaps the most powerful yet unknown agency in the US government.

What made OFAC so powerful was not so much its ability to freeze assets or transactions as its power to bar designated parties and those associated with them from the US financial system. In the mid-1980s, Newcomb and one of his key deputies, Bob McBrien, decided to change the way they notified banks of OFAC's decisions. McBrien, a wiry, blue-eyed technocrat, had been part of the inner core of the US counterterrorism officials assembled by the White House after the 1972 Munich Olympics massacre to devise a strategy to address the new forms of terrorism then emerging. He was a rare breed at the time for Treasury and would spend most of his career working with Newcomb. In 1986, OFAC issued its first public list of Specially Designated Nationals, sending letters of explanation to the Federal Reserve banks. Of the thirteen banks in the Federal Reserve system, only the New York Fed paid much attention to the letters, in part because most of the transactions and assets subject to OFAC attention flowed through New York banks. But it was a start to isolating those designated from the banking system.

Those labeled as Specially Designated Nationals by the US government and subject to OFAC's jurisdiction and US sanctions laws would find it difficult to do business in the United States, because American citizens, businesses, and other entities were prohibited from interacting commercially or financially with them.

Though the government's authority was domestic in these cases and technically relevant only to those institutions and individuals subject to US jurisdiction, the nature of the list and the desire of citizens and businesses to maintain their access to the US financial system made this power a multilateral tool by effect. Banks around the world, especially those wanting to maintain a presence in the United States, had to monitor, if not honor, the lists. For years, banks in Latin America had implemented the OFAC list tied to the drug-trafficking cartels, often referred to in Spanish as "la lista Clinton" because of its use during the Clinton administration. The OFAC power was an inherently international power because of the importance of the American banking system and capital markets.

This power extended beyond US shores thanks to the United States' status as the principal capital and banking market worldwide. If you want to be a serious international institution with the ability to work globally, you have to access New York and the American banking system.

The reach of this kind of US financial power derives as well from the predominance of the US dollar as the principal reserve and trading currency around the world. Companies and traders use the dollar as a benchmark for international trade. Countries, companies, and individuals keep dollars or accounts in dollars as security against the uncertainties of other currencies. Dollar-denominated transactions of any sort—from oil deals to settlement of commercial contracts—have to pass through dollar-clearing accounts. For most dollar-clearing transactions—including oil deals—the transactions pass through a bank account in New York. Defying OFAC is therefore not an option for most banks or businesses. Compliance offices and law practices have been built around compliance with OFAC regulations.

OFAC would take full advantage of these kinds of targeted, public sanctions to go after Al Qaeda's finances. Newcomb knew how to freeze assets in the international financial system and stop any transactions suspected of being tied to Al Qaeda. All he needed was a new executive order expanding the Treasury's powers to go after the Al Qaeda financial and support network. At the same time, the Treasury general counsel, David Aufhauser, and his deputy, George Wolfe, saw such an executive order as a way of offering the White House powerful new armaments in the unconventional war on terror.

Aufhauser was a quintessential Washington lawyer. A partner at the famed, cutthroat law firm of Williams & Connolly, he had helped the Bush campaign manage its Florida electoral legal strategy. Aufhauser was sharp and relished the ability to make convincing arguments with the flair of a master litigator. Wolfe, his deputy, was a South Carolina lawyer. His southern drawl was disarming and endearing, but his words belied a cutting and deep intellect. Wolfe would become a key figure for the Treasury's legal work at home and in war zones. One of their chief lawyers, Bill Fox, a master problem solver and a big, jovial man who had been an attorney for the Bureau of Alcohol, Tobacco, and Firearms, would serve as Aufhauser's chief adviser and would begin to take a central role in the post-9/11 work of the Treasury Department.

The lawyers saw the executive order as a means of driving the financial war in a new direction. It could punish the bankers of terror and dissuade others from crossing the line to support Al Qaeda or other terrorist groups.

The drafting began, with Aufhauser's lawyers and the OFAC experts joining forces to lay out the contours of the executive order. In its scope and impact this order would be different from earlier ones. This was an emergency executive power to be wielded not just against Al Qaeda and its direct supporters but against terrorism support writ large. Prior attempts to use this power against terrorists had been limited to very specific terrorist targets and were not used to go after the financial infrastructure of the networks. This broader model had been used by OFAC against drug-trafficking organizations, but not against Al Qaeda.

The executive order itself laid out a new principle to attack terrorist financing: that financial supporters of terrorism, the companies or businesses owned or controlled by them, and those "associated" with them were potentially subject to designation. The bankers and passive investors in terror who may have played the game of willful blindness in the past were now on notice. The US government was making clear that straddling the fence, with one foot in the legitimate financial and commercial world and the other in the arena of support for violent extremism, was no longer acceptable. This approach opened up the spigot for potential targeting and sent a clear message to the private sector that banks tarred with the label of "terrorist support" risked having their assets frozen and reputations soiled. This would prove a powerful tool in the post-9/11 period.

Importantly, under the criteria of the executive order, the government did not have to demonstrate that designated individuals and entities actually intended to support terrorism or even knew that their money or activities were being used to support terrorism. This was not a criminal indictment or a civil forfeiture action. Instead, it was an emergency administrative power intended to arrest the assets of suspected support networks preventively. In this regard, this line of executive orders did not require prior notice or due process before someone was designated—nor did it provide for the usual rules attached to criminal processes, such as the right to confront witnesses. To do so would defeat the purpose of preventively freezing assets. If someone were notified that the government was considering freezing his or her assets, the funds would be transferred out of banks subject to US jurisdiction within minutes.

This was a powerful administrative weapon that had to be wielded carefully, because the impact on individuals and businesses designated under this power—especially the label of "terrorist supporter"—could be devastating. There needed to be evidence and an administrative record attached to listing someone under these powers—the secretary of the treasury had to have a reasonable basis upon which to believe that the designee fit the criteria of the executive order. Whole tribes of lawyers from the Treasury, State, and Justice departments would review any designation proposal for sufficiency of evidence.

On September 24, 2001, less than two weeks after the attacks in New York and Washington, President Bush announced the executive order—soon to be known by its number, "EO 13224." He said, "At 12:01 this morning a major thrust of our war on terrorism began with the stroke of a pen. Today, we have launched a strike on the financial foundation of the global terror network. . . . We will starve the terrorists of funding, turn them against each other, root them out of their safe hiding places and bring them to justice."[12] The president continued, "We're putting banks and financial institutions around the world on notice—we will work with their governments, ask them to freeze or block terrorists' ability to access funds in foreign accounts. . . . If you do business with terrorists, if you support or sponsor them, you will not do business with the United States of America."[13]

President Bush had signed the order freezing financial assets and prohibiting transactions with twenty-seven entities suspected of ties to terrorism. This act also ushered in a new operational role for the Treasury Department in fighting terrorism. In the same speech,

Bush announced, "We have established a foreign terrorist asset tracking center at the Department of the Treasury to identify and investigate the financial infrastructure of the international terrorist networks. . . . We will lead by example. We will work with the world against terrorism. Money is the life-blood of terrorist operations. Today, we're asking the world to stop payment."

There had been scrambling right after 9/11 to determine what steps could be taken to attack terrorist financing, but now a strategy had emerged. The tools, legal structures, and ideas that had animated past efforts to undermine drug cartels and organized crime would be used in new, more aggressive ways. We would wage an all-out offensive to meld financial power with national security. This was a new form of financial warfare.

Ferreting out terrorist support networks that are veiled as or commingled with apparently legitimate activities is a complicated thing to do, and it is not a panacea to the problem of terrorism. But stemming terrorist financing by all available means plays an important role in stemming terrorism itself for three fundamental reasons: it makes it harder, costlier, and riskier for terrorists to raise and move money; it forces terrorist leaders to make tough budget decisions; and it constricts the global reach of their organizations. Their most threatening ambitions, such as funding a program involving weapons of mass destruction (WMD), must be put on hold if there is no money to pursue them. When a counter-terror-finance effort is successful, it ostracizes known financiers from the formal financial and commercial worlds and deters fundraisers, donors, and sympathizers from giving support and money to terrorist groups. Finally, tracking terrorist financing can uncover the financial footprints and relationships of the terrorist network—trails that can lead to sleeper cells, support elements, and terrorist leaders.[14] If done well, a campaign to disrupt terrorist financing not only stops attacks, but can change the strategic reach and trajectory of the enemy's network.

The targeted sanctions and designations would be used to "name and shame" and freeze the assets and transactions of terrorists and their supporters. Those supporting terrorism would be isolated from the formal financial system. Intelligence and law enforcement would track money trails and identify and break up support networks. Regulators would put pressure on financial institutions to apply anti-money-laundering and financial regulatory mechanisms to ensure that their institutions were not being used by terrorists to hide or move money. There would be an effort internationally to leverage all the tools of the international financial system—including among the central banks and finance ministries—to amplify attempts to purge the financial system of tainted terrorist capital. There would also be alliance and capacity building with our partners around the world. And all of this would be expanded with new laws, regulations, and tools.

On Capitol Hill, Congress formulated the USA PATRIOT Act, with Title III of that law focused on addressing money laundering and terrorist financing concerns. The act provided the legislative mandate that Treasury needed to extend anti-money-laundering requirements to a range of commercial and financial actors; to expand financial information sharing between the government and the private sector, as well as between financial institutions; and to develop more powerful tools to enforce the expanded policies and regulations.

When President Bush signed the USA PATRIOT Act into law, it ushered in the most sweeping expansion of the US anti-money-laundering regime since the inception of the 1970 Bank Secrecy Act. Core anti-money-laundering requirements now encompassed not just banks but also nonbank financial and commercial industries, including money-service businesses such as Western Union, insurance companies, and brokers and dealers in precious metals and stones. Title III provided law-enforcement agencies and financial regulators with significant new tools to detect, investigate, and prosecute money laundering. With the adoption of the act, Treasury issued scores of implementing regulations to enhance the transparency and accountability of the US financial system, largely through improved customer identification, reporting, recordkeeping, and information-sharing requirements for an expanded range of US government and financial institutions.

Internationally, we leveraged relevant multilateral forums to address the issue of terrorist financing and to reiterate or define international obligations. Just days after 9/11 at the Treasury, Jimmy Gurulé took the international components of the National Money Laundering Strategy and directed his team to leverage key international organizations to focus the world's attention on terrorist financing. He asked Danny Glaser, a young staffer who had just been given the job of leading the US delegation to the Financial Action Task Force (FATF), to steer this international anti-money-laundering body to focus on combating terrorist financing. The FATF had been established by the G7 at a Paris summit in 1989 because of growing concerns over the threat of money laundering to the international banking and financial system. By 2012 it would have thirty-six members.

In October 2001, the FATF assembled for a Special Plenary at the Omni Shoreham Hotel in Washington, DC. Hong Kong held the chair from 2001 to 2002, and the special session was chaired by Clarie Lo, then Hong Kong's commissioner for narcotics. On hand were leading anti-money-laundering and law-enforcement experts from around the world. Secretary of the Treasury O'Neill spoke, along with Attorney General John Ashcroft and Interpol Secretary General Ron Noble, who had been Treasury's assistant secretary for enforcement in the mid-1990s. The main ballroom was packed with the attendees, who understood the historic importance of the gathering. At the end of the plenary, the FATF agreed on "Eight Special Recommendations" for countering terrorist financing (a ninth was added in 2005). The recommendations would require countries to put new laws and regulations into place to monitor the movement of terrorist funds. They focused on elements of the international financial system that were specific to terrorist financing and had previously been ignored or underaddressed in the anti-money-laundering system. Small amounts of suspicious transactions now had to be reported by banks to financial intelligence units, wire transfers had to contain more data, jurisdictions had to be able to freeze assets preventively and criminalize terrorist financing, and informal money-service businesses (often seen in the form of traditional hawaladar brokers) had to be regulated like other financial industries.

The effect of this decision was a greater focus on financial transparency, accounting, and regulatory oversight around the world. New laws, regulations, and processes would follow, with new sectors, such as money-exchange houses everywhere from Dubai to Detroit, now falling under anti-money-laundering scrutiny. These standards were later adopted by the World Bank, the International Monetary Fund (IMF), and the United Nations, creating a web of obligations around the world.

Within the Treasury Department, the Office of International Affairs, led by famed Stanford economist John Taylor, began an effort to leverage G7, IMF, and World Bank processes to focus attention on the need to combat terrorist financing. Taylor was well suited to usher the world of central banks and finance ministries into a world of security to which they were not accustomed. He was well respected among international economists and was famous for the "Taylor rule," a guiding principle for monetary policies stipulating that a central bank should raise its interest rate more than one percentage point for every percentage point of increase in inflation or output. Not only did most international finance officials know the Taylor rule, but many had been taught by Taylor or had read his work. In capital after capital, officials would reminisce about their first encounter with John Taylor.

Taylor assigned a seasoned veteran of the Treasury Department, Bill Murden, a mustached and masterful civil servant, to establish a war room to track what different countries were doing to cooperate in the war on terror—from commitments to G7 action plans to the tabulation of frozen assets. Murden knew how to get things done—

both within the US government and in the international financial institutions that the United States had long dominated.

At the State Department, Assistant Secretary for Economic Affairs Tony Wayne took over the process of coordinating the State Department work with the Treasury. Wayne was an effective State Department operator who would later serve as US ambassador to Argentina and Mexico and as special ambassador in Afghanistan. His job was to ensure that Treasury's drive to designate matched—or at least did not conflict with—America's other diplomatic goals.

US ambassador to the United Nations John Negroponte led an effort to expand the use of United Nations Security Council Resolution (UNSCR) 1267, which had been adopted in 1999 and established sanctions against Al Qaeda, the Taliban, and Osama bin Laden. UNSCR 1267 was an important international tool because it allowed the United States to internationalize the listing process—requiring the freezing of assets—of those designated as Al Qaeda or Taliban supporters. Negroponte, a tall, imposing man, was a well-respected career diplomat who would later become deputy secretary of state, ambassador to Iraq, and the first director of national intelligence. On September 28, 2001, the UN Security Council adopted Resolution 1373, which made it mandatory for all states to prevent and suppress the financing of terrorism and the provision of safe haven to terrorists, to criminalize the direct or indirect provision of funds for terrorist acts, and to freeze, "without delay," the assets of entities involved in terrorist networks.[15] This resolution was significant because it was not limited to Al Qaeda or the Taliban. Its scope was intentionally broad to ensure that the international community was putting broad measures into place to go after terrorist financing.

All of this work would help to shape the financial regulatory and diplomatic environment. Banks and jurisdictions knew that the world was watching and that there was a steep reputational price to pay for falling outside the lines of legitimacy as they were being redrawn. In Treasury and in these other entities we were reshaping and deepening the rules of the game to emphasize legitimate financial activity and standards, while excluding or punishing those who dared to flirt with tainted capital.

The tools were now in place—it was time to use them.

The whole US government—in particular, the FBI and the CIA, which had been responsible for tracking and stopping Al Qaeda—felt under the gun to uncover the networks tied to 9/11 and those who might be poised to strike again. The FBI established the Financial Review Group (FRG), led by a veteran financial investigator, Dennis Lormel, to direct terrorist financing investigations stemming from the 9/11 attacks. The FRG, which attempted to bring together the best financial investigators in the US government to trace the credit cards and bank accounts of the 9/11 hijackers, would later be converted into the Terrorist Financing Operations Section (TFOS). Lormel would lead the effort within the FBI to integrate financial analysis and investigation into counterterror investigations, something that was not embedded in Bureau culture.

For Jimmy Gurulé, the former federal prosecutor and new Treasury Department undersecretary for enforcement, this meant leveraging Treasury's historical law-enforcement agencies to discover and disrupt suspect money trails. These Treasury agencies had deep expertise in a variety of financial, criminal, tax, and money-laundering investigations and worked closely with the FBI in the field. The Secret Service's early work right after 9/11 uncovered the hijackers' credit-card transactions, leading to the initial confirmation of some of the hijackers' identities. Customs had some of the best anti-money-laundering investigators, with its history of going after corrupt bankers and banks globally. The history of the Treasury agent, with Eliot Ness, who took down Al Capone with tax evasion charges, as a model, was to use financial criminal investigations to take down big targets.

Gurulé and his onetime boss as US attorney in Los Angeles, Rob Bonner, the commissioner of customs and former administrator of the Drug Enforcement Administration (DEA), saw the need to set a new direction for Treasury law enforcement in the post-9/11 era. On October 25, 2001, Treasury announced, along with Assistant US Attorney General Michael Chertoff, the establishment of Operation Green Quest, a Customs-led Treasury investigative effort that would focus on illicit and suspect money flows. Green Quest was led by a tough-as-nails Customs veteran, Marcy Foreman, and began to pursue wide-ranging financial criminal cases with possible terrorism connections. Gurulé wanted a notable terrorist financier brought to justice, and he wanted Treasury to get that done. Green Quest sought to "augment existing counter-terrorist efforts by bringing the full scope of the government's financial expertise to bear against systems, individuals, and organizations that serve as sources of terrorist funding."[16] The two task forces, one established under the FBI and the other under Treasury's authority, along with their leaders, would clash repeatedly as law enforcement focused on terrorist financing investigations.

Early on in the process, Secretary O'Neill made clear how aggressive he wanted the Treasury to be in using its new authorities. Treasury had been granted emergency powers to be used to help thwart the next attack and to dry up Al Qaeda's funding. These tools were intended to arrest assets, not people, and to paralyze entire networks that were being used to funnel money into terrorist coffers. It was a preventive tool—not a prosecution—and we were targeting networks, not just criminals. In one meeting shortly after Executive Order 13224 was signed, O'Neill looked at the small group of us who were assembled and said, "We're applying the 80/20 rule."

In decisionmaking and business circles, the 80/20 rule popularizes the law of diminishing returns by encouraging workers to make decisions with 80 percent of the information rather than spending increasing time and energy to get the additional 20 percent (which may or may not be helpful). This meant that we needed to have 80 percent surety that our targets were legitimate. O'Neill was willing to live with some uncertainty and imperfection in the early days after 9/11 to ensure the effective and aggressive use of the powers the president had delegated to him. He did not want to engender a "paralysis by analysis" process. There was nothing legally problematic with this standard, as the secretary was authorized to take action when he had a reasonable basis upon which to believe that the evidence fulfilled the criteria contained in the executive order.

With focused intelligence and law-enforcement collection and analysis, there quickly emerged a set of targets and networks tied to Al Qaeda. Some of this work had been done prior to 9/11, but there had been little focus and no clear strategy for taking action against these Al Qaeda supporters. This analysis led to a picture of an Al Qaeda that relied on a steady flow of cash to generate the money needed for recruitment, training, sustainment and pensions; alliance formation and support with other groups; and influence operations and propaganda. Bin Laden leveraged the old Sunni extremist mujahideen support network and sympathetic donors for his recruitment and training efforts, promising fulfillment for pledges to support Al Qaeda's jihad against the United States, Israel, and the apostate regimes. Al Qaeda took full advantage of deep-pocket donors from the Arabian Gulf and the Islamic charitable sector to raise and move money. Its leaders sold their cause as holy, just, and obligatory under Islamic law.

They also relied on front companies—much like the Mafia—to generate and move funding. Speculation ran rampant that Al Qaeda had invested money in blood diamonds from West Africa prior to 9/11 in anticipation of a global crackdown on bank accounts.[17] This allegation turned out to be unprovable, as did speculation that Al Qaeda had shorted investments in US airline stocks in anticipation of the economic effects of 9/11. Even so, the terrorists did use every possible means to move money—and these means often involved banks and money-service businesses, cash couriers, or traditional hawaladar brokers and traders.

The aggressive use of designations as a preventive tool could expose these means and methods of funding, but could also cause tension with our international partners. The challenge inherent in this financial tool was that we were applying an emergency administrative power against terrorist financing like a net. This net was being placed over targets to stop flows of funds, but proving that every node or member of these targeted groups was criminally culpable would be impossible. As Secretary O'Neill had dictated, we were operating under the 80/20 rule. Our European partners and conventional law-enforcement agencies relied on a standard of proof beyond a reasonable doubt, whereas we were relying on a "reasonable basis to believe" standard. To freeze assets, we had to have a reasonable basis upon which to believe the funding could be headed into terrorists' hands or for their support.

The tension between these two standards of proof emerged vividly in our shutdown of the Al Barakaat network. Al Barakaat was an international remittance system founded in Somalia in 1986 to allow Somali expatriates to send remittances to their homeland, a nation with no formal banking system and a nonexistent governance structure. Al Barakaat eventually grew into a large international network of remitters, money-service businesses, and traditional hawaladars in more than forty countries, including the United States and several European countries.

Millions of dollars were coursing through Al Barakaat's network every year—mostly from innocent Somali expatriates remitting money to their relatives in Somalia. Intelligence analysis uncovered that the network was being controlled in Somalia by a savvy extremist businessman named Ahmed Jumale. Jumale and those close to him not only profited from the system but sent some of the proceeds to Osama bin Laden and Al Qaeda. Most of those remitting money had no idea this was happening, and elements of the money remittance operation around the world were certainly innocent of connections to Al Qaeda and would not be subjects of criminal prosecutions. But this did not mitigate the need to shut down the network.

In Treasury we made the decision to take the whole system down. On November 7, 2001, the Office of Foreign Asset Control designated the entire network, along with Jumale, and seized $1.1 million in the United States. The Treasury Department argued that Jumale had siphoned millions of dollars from Al Barakaat, with some 10 percent of global revenues going to Osama bin Laden and Al Qaeda.[18]

In January 2002, three Somali Swedes who were involved in the Swedish branch of Al Barakaat petitioned their government and the UN Security Council to be removed from the list. This triggered a Swedish government action to the UN Security Council to create a standard of evidence for future terrorist financial designations. Anna Lindt, the popular Swedish prime minister who was later killed by an assailant while shopping, paid the Treasury Department a personal visit in early 2002 to discuss this issue directly with Secretary O'Neill. The Swedish—and other Europeans—were very uncomfortable with a noncriminal standard when people's reputations and livelihoods were on the line. This was a legitimate concern, but we did not want to hamper our ability to freeze assets quickly. The administrative power to use targeted sanctions would have been significantly weakened by requiring a criminal process for each designation.

However, we also knew that there would have to be a credible delisting process attached to the UN's Resolution 1267 designation process for Al Qaeda and Taliban sanctions if we were to maintain the ability to use these sanctions for the long term. Under US law, individuals have the right of administrative appeal as well as the right to challenge the designations in federal court. Indeed, the onus was on the individual to challenge the government's assertions and actions, and there was a recognized set of procedures for doing precisely this.

Eight individuals tied to the Barakaat network availed themselves of that right, successfully demonstrating that they were not tied to the terrorist financing that concerned US officials, and they agreed to dissociate themselves from the money remittance network. In August 2002, the United States removed US-based remitters in Minneapolis and Columbus, Ohio, as well as two of the three Somali Swedes. Many saw the delistings as an admission by the government that we had made a mistake in casting the Al Barakaat designation net too broadly. This was not the case. It was a misreading of what happened built on the expectation of criminal legal standards. There had never been a claim that these individuals were criminally culpable or even knowledgeable of the terrorist financing and support to Al Qaeda that had taken place through the money-transfer services. The designation and delisting process had worked and achieved its purpose.

Secretary O'Neill's 80/20 rule had been our guiding principle. O'Neill had wanted us to push hard in using the designations publicly to attack the networks and individuals supporting Al Qaeda and other terrorist groups. This was a standard he would repeat to me, to his lawyers, and to others involved in the designation process. And for a time we followed that rule. Nevertheless, it would become an impossible standard to keep, given the concerns over litigation and diplomatic blowback, and within a year the 80/20 rule was no longer in effect. The need for 100 percent surety soon became apparent.

Shortly after 9/11, the White House established a National Security Council policy coordination committee (PCC) specific to terrorist financing to ensure coordination among the various actors in the US government. PCCs—now called "Interagency Policy Committees"—are policy groups of senior representatives from around the government charged with helping to shape and guide US policy. They feed their decisions and key questions to the deputies and principals of the US government who deal with the specific area of policy under the PCC's consideration. Aufhauser ran the PCC with a recognition that the designations by Treasury were drivers of the anti-terrorist-financing campaign—in part because they were public actions by the US government and drivers of UN action—but also that other actions could be taken to stop or deter terrorist financing. Over time, the number of designations and amount of assets frozen became markers for the success of the war on terror. They were concrete figures that spoke for themselves. Unlike other aspects of the war on terror— which were often kept secret—Treasury actions could be discussed publicly.[19]

In early 2002, Cofer Black, director of the CIA's Counterterrorist Center (CTC), paid Treasury a visit. It was the first time Black had set foot in the building, and he had expected to see "green-eye-shaded accountants walking the halls" when he entered the main gates. He was coming there to meet with Gurulé, Newcomb, and me to discuss a set of proposed designations that would encompass targets of interest to the CIA. He was there on a mission—to protect intelligence sources and operations that could be revealed with a planned Treasury designation.

We met in Gurulé's office on the fourth floor of the Treasury building on a corner facing south and west. There was a wonderful view of the White House and the South Lawn, especially in the winter when the leaves had fallen off the elms and oaks. In front of us was a large analyst's map that laid out the network we planned to designate. There were dozens of individuals, companies, and institutions that formed the web of the Al Taqwa network, based in the Bahamas, Switzerland, and Liechtenstein. Al Taqwa had ties to Yousef Nada and Ahmed Idris Nasreddin, alleged terrorist financiers, and other suspect individuals. The designation plan was ambitious, but it reached too far into the CIA's operational equities.

Black started simply and respectfully. He appreciated the work that Treasury was doing, but explained that there were operations underway in Europe to uncover Al Qaeda cells and support. Some of these operations were in Milan and had ties to some of the designation targets on the map. Black motioned to a large swath of targets and pointed to a number of entities that were under CIA watch and the subject of CIA action. Black was asking us to stay away from naming those targets. There was no reason to challenge Black. His presence and his explanation in Gurulé's office gave great weight to the CIA's objections. We talked about the possible timing of the CIA's actions and the possibility of future designations, but the conclusion was clear. The meeting ended cordially with the decision to scrap the designations that would complicate the CIA's operations in Europe.

Indeed, the growing complexity of US counterterrorism efforts worldwide made such meetings inevitable. A small group of CIA, FBI, State, Defense, Treasury, and White House actors began to meet separately in late 2002 in the back of the old White House Situation Room to coordinate operational activities. The Treasury actions—which were outing known terrorist supporters and networks—needed to be coordinated with the clandestine and covert operations underway around the world.

Treasury's strategy for designations aimed at targeting networks of key financial actors and nodes in the terrorist support system. The point was not necessarily to freeze assets in US banks—though this was a benefit—but instead to use the designations by the United States and the United Nations to make it harder for individuals who were financing terrorists to access the formal financial system. Our analyses therefore focused on the networks of actors and institutions providing the financial backbone to terrorist enterprises. Interestingly, we found that there were all-purpose financiers who would give to multiple causes—"polyterror" supporters.

These meetings also provided a way for the CIA and the FBI— along with the Department of Defense—to be more open about their operations. It was a space where the wisdom of public designations could be debated without reservation and the tradeoffs for delayed exposure could be discussed. Often, the operators asked me to back off from pushing designations; in return, we pushed for deadlines and assurances that disruptions and operations would actually occur.

Even with these tensions, the CIA and the Treasury Department

often made common cause. Soon after we began our outreach to
banks and countries, we were hoping to find evidence of Osama bin
Laden's riches in bank accounts or shell companies he controlled.
But bin Laden was less connected to the international financial system than most people assumed. Once he declared war on the Saudi
monarchy, he was cut off from his family's wealth, and after he left
Sudan, his businesses and operations were expropriated by the
Sudanese government. He would encounter difficulty running businesses from the hinterlands of Afghanistan.

We did find one bin Laden account in a Pakistani bank. Bin
Laden's name was on the account, and there was a modest amount
of money in it. The Pakistani government froze the account and
passed information about it to us. We tried for months to get a
financial forensics team into Pakistan to look at the account in
depth—we wanted to see the history of transactions, the contact
information, and anything else that might prove helpful. It became
an issue of great sensitivity, including with our embassy in Islamabad. Ultimately, we did not send in a team, but tried to acquire the
information through other sources.

We also started to learn more about Al Qaeda's money man,
Sheikh Said, the nom de guerre of the Egyptian accountant who
was responsible for the organization's books. He was Al Qaeda's
chief financial officer. Sheikh Said was a trusted confidant of both
bin Laden and Ayman al-Zawahiri, and he managed the organization's finances like a hawk. He was stingy with Al Qaeda's budget—
requiring expense reports and receipts from key lieutenants—and
would often be angered by sloppy recordkeeping and cost discipline.
He set out rules for the operational budget, with requirements for
approval from him and Al Qaeda headquarters before major expenditures could be made.

Sheikh Said was the man Al Qaeda relied upon to help make
hard budget decisions. The organization was now under pressure,
with diminishing resources and dwindling flexibility to move
money around the world. Said would make sure that the family

members of Al Qaeda fighters would be paid—with insurance-like benefits for senior members killed in the fight against the United States and its apostate allies. The price of this line item was rising quickly, and the sources of funding were beginning to dry up.

We saw him as our arch-nemesis—the chief enemy moneyman to be countered. He was an important pivot point around which we could build pressure on the network. His job had to be getting harder and harder month by month. The intelligence community also saw him as a prime target.

The intelligence community found and confirmed his true name by 2004—Mustafa al-Yazid—and then began the debate about what to do with it. I argued vigorously for making it public in order to further highlight his role and to isolate those willing to do business with or support him. The intelligence community wanted to keep his name quiet—in part to protect the methods by which we had acquired the name. This was a method that was worthy of protection, because it revealed other things about Sheikh Said and what he was doing to invest and diversify Al Qaeda's assets. The financial trackers soon learned that he was investing in gold and beginning to hold euros instead of dollars.

Said would grow in importance, especially as other senior Al Qaeda leaders were killed. He would serve as a gatekeeper as well as an operational manager—all the while using the trust put in him by Zawahiri and bin Laden in managing the organization's financial operations to pull the levers of the global organization. We continued to track him and to watch the directions he took and the measures he put into place with the organization. Ultimately, Treasury designated him in August 2010.[20] The US government wanted to make clear that we knew who he was and that anyone doing business with him would be targeted by intelligence and perhaps other US assets.

In many ways, our ability to squeeze and distort Said's budgetary decisions was the ultimate measure of whether we were succeeding. Were we able to affect Al Qaeda's investment in strategic attacks?

Could we ensure that Al Qaeda didn't have money to pay Pakistani scientists or Russian smugglers, to acquire the knowledge or materiel for a nuclear device or dirty bomb? Could we harm morale by delaying pension payments to relatives of deceased terrorists and payments to new recruits? Was it possible to squeeze Al Qaeda, as it adapted to our pressure, to ensure that we altered its global reach and influence? At the end of the day, could we use financial pressure to constrict Al Qaeda's threat to the United States and its allies? These were the strategic questions of import that would animate our discussions and our financial campaign against terror.[21]

Our hopes for success put a premium on finding financial trails so that we could understand Al Qaeda's network, disrupt its operations, and constrict its global reach and most strategic and threatening ambitions. Following Al Qaeda's financial footprints became a new discipline and formed the backbone of our efforts to crush the organization and its operations. And to follow these tracks, the United States needed to build a new enterprise that would leverage access to massive amounts of financial data.

The various tools and the community we began to forge after 9/11 to address terrorist financing would become the cornerstone of our ability to wage financial warfare more broadly. At the same time, we had begun to condition the financial system to the rejection of tainted capital, and our ability to tap and shape that environment would become a crucial element of Treasury's power.

2

FINANCIAL FOOTPRINTS

Within days after 9/11, Secretary O'Neill hosted a meeting in the Treasury Secretary's small conference room located on the third floor of the Treasury building. This room traditionally has been used for senior-level briefings and meetings with foreign finance ministers and heads of state. Pictures of the Treasury Department from the eighteenth century and examples of pre–Civil War currency hang on the walls, and historical artifacts—such as silverware that used to belong to the first treasury secretary, Alexander Hamilton—adorn the room. Its view onto the East Wing of the White House leaves no doubt of one's proximity to power. The intimate setting has a sense of deep historical import, and the room would be used to host some of the most sensitive and important meetings in the Treasury Department after 9/11. This was one of them.

It was to be a small interagency meeting to develop new means of accessing financial information around the world. It was not enough merely to expand designation powers, investigate cases, or deepen Treasury's global regulatory reach. The US government needed as much information as possible about the Al Qaeda network's financial backers and conduits to be able to direct more intelligence collection and law-enforcement focus to this endeavor, and ultimately, to disrupt the financing of terrorist operations and infrastructure.

Secretary O'Neill and Treasury had been given the job of launching an aggressive counter-terrorist-financing campaign. This was a new and unprecedented mission for the Treasury Department. The reality was that Treasury had been a minor institutional player in the world of terrorism until 9/11. Al Qaeda and terrorism in the 1990s had been the province of the big boys of national security: the CIA, the National Security Agency (NSA), the FBI, and the Defense and State departments.

That was about to change. This meeting would spur the development of a new discipline for acquiring and analyzing financial intelligence—what would later be called "FININT."

Though technically part of the intelligence community, the Treasury Department had historically been little more than a passive consumer of intelligence products. In the wake of 9/11, what became clear to the department's general counsel, David Aufhauser, to me, and to others in Treasury was that we needed to develop a more active financial intelligence capability, both at the Treasury Department and on behalf of the government as a whole. If the US government hoped to attack the financial underpinnings of terrorism, Treasury's relationships and insights would be essential to developing the necessary financial intelligence to identify them.

Financial intelligence can be defined in many ways. In its broadest sense, financial intelligence is any bit of information—however acquired—that reveals commercial or financial transactions and money flows, asset and capital data, and the financial and commercial relationships and interests of individuals, networks, and organizations. Such information can come in a variety of forms—crumpled receipts found in terrorist safe houses, the detailed ledgers of hawaladars, suspicious transaction reports from banks, and transnational wire-transfer records. Ranging from the incredibly vague to the blindingly detailed, such data can give focus and context to a mosaic of intelligence information. The most secret or closely held types of financial intelligence are those bits of data purposely hidden from view and considered inherently revealing and valuable by others. Tax cheats, money launderers, and terrorist financiers alike seek to cloak this kind of information from detection.

Some crucial forms of financial intelligence have long been available to Treasury officials. The quintessential form is the information used and kept by banks and other financial institutions on its clients, customers' accounts, and transactions. For this reason, the national and international anti-money-laundering frameworks built in the 1980s and 1990s focused on setting reporting requirements for banks and other bank-like financial institutions. These requirements were expanded well beyond the classic banking sector with the passage of Title III of the USA PATRIOT Act, which further expanded the reporting requirements to nonbank financial institutions such as insurance companies, money-service businesses, and brokers and dealers in precious stones and metals.

Thanks to these requirements, it is an expected and standard requirement around the world today for banks and regulated institutions to submit suspicious transaction reports and currency transaction reports above a certain amount ($10,000 in the United States) to their host governments. Banks that make cross-border wire transfers are required to report specific information about the originator and ultimate beneficiary of any transaction. The governmental bodies throughout the world charged with interacting with financial institutions and collecting suspicious activity and currency transaction reports are known as financial intelligence units (FIUs). The US FIU (Financial Crimes Enforcement Network or FinCEN), sits within the Treasury Department.

Perhaps just as important, the Treasury Department also has economic expertise and insights thanks to its cadre of economists and tax experts and their daily contacts with foreign counterparts in finance ministries, central banks, the international and regional financial institutions such as the IMF and World Bank, the financial regulatory communities, and the private sector. Their insights and information constitute an underutilized and underappreciated form of financial intelligence necessary to understand the international financial ecosystem.

Although there had been financial intelligence available prior to 9/11, with significant use by law enforcement to prosecute cases, its collection, analysis, and use were not given pride of place to address national security threats and issues. What makes financial intelligence so valuable is that it can reveal clear contours of relationships. Unlike the vagaries and complications of human intelligence (HUMINT) or misinterpreted and incomplete captured communications (SIGINT), financial footprints don't lie. The passing of cash between operatives confirms a connection; the wiring of money between banks unveils a relationship between the account holders; the transfer of money or goods between brokers identifies historical business ties. The records of those transactions—addresses, phone numbers, real names, banks utilized—can be a gold mine of information. Money trails as well can reveal unanticipated and unorthodox ties and connections, since the thirst for profit or the need for material support can spawn unlikely marriages of convenience. Money is the great facilitator and connector—even among enemies. And money or value changes hands only where a relationship actually exists.

The right information about the sender or recipient of funds can open a window on broader networks or identify unseen ties. If it is timely and specific enough, such intelligence can help disrupt terrorist acts. If intelligence services know that a terrorist operative will be receiving a financial infusion from an overseas donor or supporter, then the trail can be followed and the operative can be physically tracked and caught.

Still, more often than not financial information alone doesn't trigger counterterrorism operations, and it may not be the sole piece of data that stops a terrorist attack. The real value comes well in advance. The receipts found in an operative's pocket, or the budget spreadsheet on a terrorist fundraiser's computer hard drive, give context and meaning to existing understandings of the enemy's operations. Relationships between terrorist leaders, operatives, couriers, and funders can be explained, and the ways that funds flow within a terrorist network crystallized, with financial intelligence. Such information can help complete the mosaic of intelligence being gathered by other means. The enemy networks can then be targeted, watched, and disrupted.

Improving the collection and coordination of financial intelligence was the primary focus of the meeting in the secretary of the treasury's conference room that day. Treasury would need to execute the most aggressive financial intelligence collection campaign it ever attempted. O'Neill and others had asked the question whether the U.S. government had access to the bank-to-bank transfer information contained in the databases of the Society for Worldwide Interbank Financial Telecommunication (SWIFT), which operates a financial messaging service for financial transactions communicated between member banks. The SWIFT system, known well to the world's bankers, is used daily by thousands of institutions around the world. The Treasury never had access to this information, but it would need to find a way of gaining access to this treasure trove of financial data.

SWIFT, based in a well-manicured chateau in Brussels, is a member-owned cooperative that was founded in 1973 to standardize the communication of global financial transactions, and it forms the communication backbone of the formal financial system.

Central banks from the Group of Ten (G10) countries oversee SWIFT. These include the Bank of Canada, Deutsche Bundesbank, the European Central Bank, Banque de France, Banca d'Italia, the Bank of Japan, De Nederlandsche Bank, Sveriges Riksbank, the Swiss National Bank, the Bank of England, and the Federal Reserve System, represented by the Federal Reserve Bank of New York and the Board of Governors of the Federal Reserve System. The National

Bank of Belgium serves as the lead overseer, while SWIFT's board is made up of top executives from the world's major banks, including Citibank and Chase Manhattan in the United States.

SWIFT exists to enable coordination between banks. When assets are moved across borders from one bank to another, banks need a harmonized, secure system by which to communicate and transfer those assets—detailing where the transfer is coming from, what amounts are being transferred, and what institutions and clients are the recipients and beneficiaries. SWIFT is that clearinghouse messaging system and has a virtual monopoly as the switchboard of the international financial system, ensuring the rapid and secure communication of these messages between its members worldwide.

The SWIFT data is quintessential financial intelligence. Its messaging traffic is broken into data fields with specific information about the banks involved, accountholders, amounts transferred, dates and times of transactions and transfers, and contact information. SWIFT provides deep financial footprints for international transfers of assets. Access to SWIFT data would give the US government a method of uncovering never-before-seen financial links, information that could unlock important clues to the next plot or allow an entire support network to be exposed and disrupted. Blended with other intelligence, the potential of SWIFT data to reveal links and ties between unknown actors was enormous.

This wasn't the first time the US government had focused on SWIFT data. In the late 1980s, the Justice Department had approached SWIFT to ask the organization to change its messaging system. The American officials, led by Bob Mueller, who was then assistant attorney general but would become the director of the FBI in September 2001, wanted to be able to subpoena these messages and peer behind the veil of financial transactions to find out where money was coming from and who was receiving it. They made little progress. The American officials had no real authority to mandate this change, and the SWIFT officials and their lawyers knew it. At the end of a series of cordial meetings, the Justice Department officials were thanked for their interest and ushered to the door—without any concessions by SWIFT.

Though past efforts had failed, Treasury officials and others knew that the SWIFT information could be incredibly valuable—providing direct access to the financial trails between banks. They also knew this had to be done quickly and quietly to ensure we understood Al Qaeda's financial networks and to use that information to disrupt follow-on attacks. In theory, the information could have been used as part of an expansive, real-time capability that would allow the Treasury to access SWIFT data the moment a transfer occurred—allowing the government and its partners not only to see transactions but to act on the information if necessary.

O'Neill and Aufhauser wanted the Treasury to control access to this information and relationship. They were instinctually wary, as their predecessors had been, of the intelligence and law-enforcement communities getting too close to the inner workings of the international financial system. They didn't know the leadership of SWIFT personally, and didn't know whether procuring data would even be feasible, let alone desirable.

Nevertheless, the idea of leveraging SWIFT data intrigued Aufhauser. He and O'Neill recognized that Treasury needed to do anything it could to disrupt terrorist financing. As Aufhauser's lawyer's mind churned, he thought of a simple and direct way to acquire SWIFT's data—perhaps right through the front door. Aufhauser had made his legal career finding solutions to hard problems by convincing litigants and adversaries, with careful confrontation, that it was in their interest to concede legal points and to cooperate. Risky as it might be for SWIFT to give up its data willingly, this was a rare moment in which they might be convinced. This would be done Treasury's way.

Within days, the deputy secretary of the Treasury Department, Kenneth Dam, had invited the CEO of SWIFT to visit the Treasury building.

The CEO was a Massachusetts Institute of Technology–trained American, Leonard "Lenny" Schrank, who had risen to the heights of the financial world with business acumen and a New Yorker's classic cutting wit. Schrank and SWIFT had been approached before to cooperate with authorities—including a 1992 visit from the chairman of the FATF arguing for more information to be shared with international law enforcement. Out of these discussions and requests for information, SWIFT developed policies and procedures for refusing subpoena requests for SWIFT messaging data.

Aufhauser brazenly opened the meeting with a declaration: "I want your data." Without a pause, Schrank responded, "What took you so long?" Aufhauser knew he had to convince Schrank to cooperate—to allow access to SWIFT data and to comply with broader administrative subpoenas without a legal fight. Aufhauser understood he was making the opening argument for a new relationship that would put SWIFT at some risk and would stretch the bounds of what the US government had done in the past with financial data. He had already determined that the legal authority to request and search the data was on the government's side. Even so, he wanted to avoid a costly court battle that could delay access to the data and reveal publicly what the US government was seeking.

As soon as Aufhauser and Schrank met, Aufhauser was convinced that they could make a deal. Schrank was there to cooperate—seeing himself first and foremost as an American—but he did not want SWIFT to be harmed in the process.

Schrank, who had lived in Europe since 1981, also wanted to explain what SWIFT was and the sensitivities and limitations of what it could offer. Schrank did just this, staking out SWIFT's need for legal clarity. SWIFT needed to remain apolitical to preserve its role in the financial world. Aufhauser spoke with the directness and rhythmic cadence of a seasoned litigator. "I know you could go into court to challenge our subpoenas. It would be destructive for both of us to go into court, and I don't think this is a fight you can win. More importantly, it's a fight you don't want to win."

Sensitive to the tough position he was putting Schrank in, Aufhauser offered to help address any of SWIFT's concerns about the privacy of its data and any agreement. Aufhauser knew SWIFT might be unwilling to allow the US government direct access to its databases, or even be technically unable to do the kind of targeted searches in their system that the US officials desired. Aufhauser tried to reassure Schrank, saying, "We can build a model that protects our interests—one that allows us both to search for the bad actors misusing the system."

Schrank and the SWIFT lawyers listened intently. They understood that the US government would not wait long for their answer. Soon after the meeting, the SWIFT officials delivered the verdict: they would cooperate. Schrank knew that 9/11 had changed everything, later noting, "Given the magnitude of what was now at stake, SWIFT would cooperate—although they would extract the most rigorous protections for their members' data."

Aufhauser would later recall that the entire arrangement between Treasury and SWIFT could not have worked without Schrank's commitment, trust, and willingness to take a risk. "Lenny was everything," he said. Schrank has said that the key to working with the US Treasury was officials' willingness to "problem solve" complex issues rather than "just negotiate with a legal club."

Although the program was legal, SWIFT was still taking a giant leap of faith by allowing US government access. Even if Schrank could persuade his board, the banking community and the court of public opinion might not be so forgiving. SWIFT was supposed to be apolitical and neutral, but with this move, it seemed to be cooperating with the United States in its war on terror. The SWIFT officials had made a hard and risky decision to comply. They knew they could be opening themselves up to criticism from their member banks, European politicians, and a European public wary of invasions of privacy.

By the end of October 2001, the Treasury Department was getting the information from SWIFT that it requested and beginning to build the program that would later become known as the Treasury Terrorist Financing Tracking Program. Within Treasury, we affectionately gave it the code name "Turtle"—the opposite of SWIFT—so we could speak about it outside of classified arenas. The program took on a great deal of secrecy and more code names, with limited access given to a select group of officials and analysts.

Aufhauser would later set off for Brussels to meet with the SWIFT officials, including their general counsel and their private lawyers, to nail down the mechanics of the process. In the early days of the program, requests for SWIFT data were urgent, tied to suspected terrorist plots. The entire US government was bracing for another Al Qaeda attack, and the intelligence community was under intense pressure to find any shreds of data to uncover and disrupt plots. Aufhauser was the middleman for these early requests from the US government. Having pledged not to abuse the arrangement, but to back up requests with subpoenas, first he would cross-examine the requests for SWIFT information. Then he would call Schrank directly to ask for particular streams of data. He was careful to keep the requests to a minimum, so that SWIFT and their lawyers would not be tempted to conclude that he was crying wolf. Starting in October 2001, the Treasury Department typically served one subpoena per month to SWIFT, with each subpoena incorporating multiple requests for data.[1] Treasury was required to have reason to believe that an individual was involved in terrorism to access his or her records.

Initially, Treasury got access to a subset of the SWIFT financial database. Technically, SWIFT did not have the forensic capability on its own to do the targeted searches for specific names, addresses, dates of transactions, and bank accounts that the Treasury was requesting. At the same time, the Treasury Department did not want to create a system where it had to spoon-feed every classified query to SWIFT, in part because this would require revealing key bits of terrorism-related intelligence necessary to target the searches. The subpoenas therefore were crafted to request data in bunches for select periods of time. The data would be handled in a separate, quarantined database. The restrictions on the program and the inability to blend it with other intelligence community databases chafed at those who wanted to use the data more expansively.

From the start, some within the US government argued that the procedure should allow for real-time access to permit the possibility of real-time disruptions. Others also argued that the data should be searched more aggressively and widely to look at the intersection of terrorist and proliferation, criminal, and state-sponsored networks. Experts and analysts knew that apparently unrelated criminal or suspicious financial tracks could lead to terrorist actors. Such experts were worried that the United States was needlessly blinding itself to possible financial leads and tracks by only querying limited parts of the SWIFT data fields with specific terrorist suspect names. The information and program were very good, but for some in the US government, the SWIFT data was not being used to full effect.

This was not an all-out fishing expedition in a sea of financial data. There were clear—and in some ways artificially constrained— limits to what could be done with the SWIFT information. The Treasury remained cautious about access and use of the data. For those in the intelligence community, this was an odd program. The information was being subpoenaed by the US Treasury, and the relationship with the source was being handled by a small team of lawyers and policy officials. SWIFT was actively involved in managing the contours of the program and the limits of the data's use. And there was a relatively wide array of banking and government officials in Europe and the United States who were made aware of the agreement.

Many eyes were on this program. Treasury's deputy general counsel, George Wolfe, had recognized from the start that the program needed to be legal, constrained, managed, and monitored closely. All of us knew that if this program were not handled carefully it might bring down SWIFT and create a public firestorm that would call the integrity of the US Treasury and the entire financial system into question. This preoccupation drove Treasury officials to constrain the program, ensuring that it was limited to only that information that was useful and that could be scrutinized and audited to head off concern from the SWIFT board—which only increased as the program went on.

As SWIFT grew increasingly antsy, it was Aufhauser's job to maintain the trust of the board. The litigator in Aufhauser knew he had to make a convincing case that the information being shared was actually needed to disrupt terrorism. The problem was that analysts in the intelligence community did not want to reveal secrets tied to ongoing operations.

Aufhauser pressed his case: he needed examples to share with the SWIFT board that were authentic, understandable, and demonstrated real value. Aufhauser and the team settled on five examples, all of which remain classified.

Aufhauser and Bill Fox flew from Washington to Brussels ready to make the "value" presentation. There was so much concern over the sensitivity of the information being conveyed that an agent was sent on the trip to hand-carry the briefing material in a classified, locked bag, which remained handcuffed to the agent's hand until they arrived at the US embassy in Brussels. The agent and the material handcuffed to his hand flew in first class. Aufhauser and Fox flew in back, in coach.

Aufhauser again treated this meeting like an opening argument, trying to win over the jury that would judge whether the program was valuable and SWIFT's risk was worth it. He underscored the value of the program and the gratitude of the US government and then launched into the five case examples—one by one—telling the committee members exactly how the SWIFT data had helped in each. Terrorists had been arrested, networks disrupted, and lives saved around the world. Each example was impressive on its own—and SWIFT data had provided the critical link in every case. Strung together—moving from plot to plot and country to country—the examples were remarkable. When he finished—with the flourish of a closing argument about the immense and growing value of the program—the committee members sat there stunned and silent. Some of the silence probably resulted from the shock of being allowed to see some of the fresh information about arrests and disruptions just made. Schrank, along with a representative from the Swiss banking giant UBS and the SWIFT lawyers, were clearly convinced—and relieved that their earlier decision to cooperate was justified.

When he left the committee room, Aufhauser knew that he left no doubt about the significance of SWIFT's data in fighting terrorism. The integrity of Treasury's assurances about the value of the program was now clear. This did not mean that SWIFT would simply acquiesce to providing the data forever. Aufhauser knew that the trust established needed to be maintained and measures taken to limit the use of the data as much as possible. SWIFT would continue to demand that access be limited and the scope of the queries reduced, regardless of the value of the data to security services.

Treasury lawyers and officials traveled to Europe in the summer and fall of 2002 to reassure the key overseer banks and stakeholders in SWIFT. Federal Reserve Chairman Alan Greenspan reassured his fellow central bankers at meetings and in phone calls. Greenspan's voice and assurances throughout the duration of the program proved invaluable for the treasury secretary and his foreign counterparts. Aufhauser, Fox, and their small team would meet with the Technical Oversight Board for SWIFT seven times during Aufhauser's tenure as general counsel. This proved to be a critical series of meetings and relationships that kept the program alive and well.

Some meetings and briefings regarding the program did not go well, especially as more individuals were briefed about the details of the program. Deputy Secretary of the Treasury Dam had met with the head of one of the foreign overseer banks to brief him on the program. The central bank governor told Dam to "stop it," which then required an entire effort to ensure that this bank and host government were comfortable with the contours of the program at every turn—to include frequent meetings between Paul O'Neill and the head of that country's finance ministry.

On one occasion, Aufhauser met with the central bank governor of another country over coffee and briefed him on the program. As soon as Aufhauser finished his initial, informal presentation, the governor of this bank looked straight at him and said, "What you have just told me, I want to know nothing about. Our meeting is over." The governor stood up and left.

SWIFT periodically became nervous about the program in spite of Aufhauser's work and its commitment to keeping the cooperation going. SWIFT soon grew impatient and worried about the direction of the program and the use of the data. With each day that passed and every subpoena received, SWIFT wondered when the program would end. Some of the SWIFT board members had assumed there would be a short shelf-life for the project.

On two occasions—once in 2002 and again in 2003—SWIFT leadership visited Washington to discuss the program with US leaders. Each time, the US government rolled out the red carpet. In addition to the secretary of the treasury and Chairman Greenspan, core leaders of American national security, including FBI Director Bob Mueller, CIA Director Porter Goss, and National Security Adviser Condoleezza Rice, met with them—including in the White House Situation Room—to reassure them of the value of the program and US fidelity to the constraints placed on the use of the data. Vice President Cheney hosted Schrank several times at his residence. All of this was intended to demonstrate the importance of the data and the seriousness with which the US government took the program and SWIFT's cooperation.

Even with all this, Schrank drove a hard bargain, and SWIFT demanded that more processes be put into place to ensure the integrity of the data. SWIFT insisted on outside, independent auditors to ensure that the data was being handled properly and that access and probes were limited to terrorism queries. The auditors submitted reports to the SWIFT board. If there were any problems, they were immediately fixed or addressed. SWIFT also demanded that "scrutineers," appointed by SWIFT, have real-time access to each search made by US government analysts to verify the terrorism nexus. SWIFT called for a "red button" function to be created, so that the scrutineers could block access to the database immediately if they were concerned about a request. All financial searches of the SWIFT data would eventually be reviewed by at least two SWIFT scrutineers, and internal audits were done to verify that the monitoring was effective. Over time, SWIFT and Treasury officials also agreed to reduce the range of data fields required to fulfill subpoenas—as a fair bit of the messaging information had not proved useful to analysts. This was a remarkable program, with the concerns of civil liberties, privacy, and perceived intrusion inform-ing its very architecture. It was unprecedented for a highly classified and critical information-gathering program to be managed so directly by both Treasury officials and outside actors.

Although the program was to remain secret and compartmental-ized, it was also clear that the Treasury Department should be open about its intentions and desires to track terrorist funds and use all means available to disrupt Al Qaeda's finances. We injected this theme into any testimony that Treasury senior officials gave. This was part of an explicit communications strategy to explain what we were doing without revealing the details of the methods we were using. I was explicit on more than one occasion in testimony about the tracking of terrorist funding as a core component of the US gov-ernment strategy in the war on terror. Everyone who was involved in this issue did so—because it was what we were doing. Our ene-mies and the public just did not know exactly how we were doing it.

At the same time, we attempted to make it clear that getting access to more usable cross-border wire-transfer data was a com-mon international goal, based on FATF standards and best practices.

The anti-money-laundering community required law enforcement, financial intelligence units, and regulators to use such information to detect suspect transactions and to take action to freeze assets. These were accepted principles, but the world did not yet know how the United States was tracking terrorist financing bank transfers so effectively. That story was yet to be printed.

The Treasury was not the only element of the US government focusing on leveraging financial intelligence. The intelligence and law enforcement communities were developing offices and analytic teams to focus on financial leads and information that could uncover leads to terrorist networks, pinpoint operatives, and help disrupt attacks. At the FBI, long-standing financial crimes experts and agents were assigned to the terrorist financing task force, eventually called the Terrorist Financing Operations Section (TFOS). In the intelligence community, new offices and resources were applied to collect and analyze financial information.

In the late 1990s, Cofer Black and his team tracking Osama bin Laden in Sudan had offered suggestions for disrupting the bank accounts and financial mechanisms that bin Laden was relying on to store and move money as part of his business enterprise in the Sudan. The intelligence community had proposed aggressive methods to monitor and disrupt Al Qaeda's financing. Such suggestions were anathema to the Treasury at the time. Revelation of such operations—which was considered inevitable—could crumble US credibility and shake international confidence in the US and global financial system. The Treasury Department had always been reticent to let the intelligence community near the financial system. The government thus resorted to self-censorship to avoid any actions that might be perceived to upset the balance of the international financial system.

This was a common Treasury view in all the administrations before 9/11. The intelligence community felt burned by this experience. Congressional overseers and the White House had demanded that intelligence agents "follow the money" prior to 9/11, yet from the intelligence community's perspective, thanks to Treasury, it had been hamstrung in its efforts to disrupt Al Qaeda's finances. Now, with the smoldering remnants of the 9/11 attacks still filling the air in New York City and Washington, intelligence and law enforcement leaders were not only being asked why they had failed to do more to prevent the attacks, but being asked to disrupt the next one. To create capabilities to prevent the next attack and follow the terrorist financial trails, the intelligence community turned to some of its veterans in this field.

The intelligence community had gotten into the illicit financing game as early as 1972 in the hopes of better understanding the growing ties between the narcotics trade and organized crime. Analysts and operatives at the time studied both the networks and the money that bound the people and organizations in the narcotics trade—a business worth billions of dollars coursing through US and other banks.

Financial investigations and intelligence uncovered the intricate financial networks of the Bank of Credit and Commerce International (BCCI) in the late 1980s. BCCI, which became known as the "Bank of Crooks and Criminals International," was an all-purpose illicit financial hub, providing banking services for drug trafficking, arms trafficking, and money laundering from the Middle East, Europe, and South America. It was the quintessential bad bank.

The small group of financial intelligence analysts, operatives, and agents saw in the BCCI case and the illicit financial cases and operations a pattern that proved fundamental to the world of illicit financing: "There was always a bank controlled by the enemy." Banks were essential components of any global network and the enabler of global commercial and financial activity. If you needed to ship something, you needed a bank for lines of credit. If you needed to shift assets from one country or account to another, you often needed correspondent accounts in banks to do it. (A correspondent account is one held for another financial institution to allow access to banking facilities.) And if you wanted to store money and use it to leverage trading relationships or conceal the origins of the proceeds, you needed a bank willing to take, hide, and/or move the money for you—or at least one that would accept its fees while turning a blind eye. Illicit financial networks of any scope or reach need banks to do business.

In the late 1990s, the intelligence community focused on financial operations tied to nuclear proliferation. The financial trackers knew that it was money that allowed rogue regimes to slip nuclear equipment and materiel past international sanctions and controls. In 1996, financial operatives began counterfinancial operations against Iran's incipient weapons program,[2] fully aware that it was financial networks that allowed the proliferation trade to metastasize and attract global players. Financial intelligence could make the crucial difference in uncovering and disrupting proliferation networks.

They were right. Money motivated key actors, such as Abdul Qadeer (AQ) Khan, the father of the Pakistani nuclear program, to develop a worldwide proliferation network. AQ Khan sold nuclear secrets, expertise, and specialized equipment to anyone willing to pay. Rogue regimes, including Libya, North Korea, Iran, and Syria, were willing, lined up, and ready to pay his price.

In 2001, Alec Station, the part of the CIA that was charged with hunting Osama bin Laden and the Al Qaeda network, was not yet focused on tracking the global financial footprints for the network. Cofer Black, the head of the Counterterrorism Center and by then a veteran of tracking bin Laden—having watched him directly as the station chief in Khartoum—was ready to act. Bin Laden had watched Black, too, with direct threats to Black's life coming from the Al Qaeda network. In Black's experience, although bin Laden sometimes used banks to move his money, he would more frequently rely on trusted couriers to move money to agents and operatives outside of Sudan. Bags of cash were being walked across border checkpoints and into airports. Black would approve a plan to help pierce the shroud of Al Qaeda's financial networks.

The crux of the plan amounted to an aggressive effort to uncover money trails to terrorist networks—with the ultimate goal of finding terrorist targets and disrupting attacks. Existing sources of financial information would not be enough. They would need to procure more intelligence from the banking and nonbanking worlds, while also finding new ways to track financial transactions—and quickly.

This strategy became the intelligence community's roadmap in the financial war on terrorism. The plan would be presented to the intelligence community. Those briefings would be followed later by a meeting with Vice President Dick Cheney and National Security Adviser Condoleezza Rice.

Along with others in the intelligence and law enforcement communities, this plan and the financial operatives who would execute it would build the financial capabilities to track terrorist financial trails—using the financial debris of networks to piece together maps of terrorist relationships. That information and the work of intelligence analysts throughout the government uncovered never-before seen links and led to disruptions of terrorist plots around the world.

Later, Treasury would make two cases of value from the SWIFT program public. These were the cases that we briefed to the 9/11 Commission. In one of them, the SWIFT data helped catch one of the most wanted Al Qaeda terrorists in the world, Hambali.

Hambali was the nom de guerre of Riduan Isamuddin, a leader of the militant Indonesian Islamist group Jemaah Islamiyah (JI, Islamic Congregation), which had long-standing ties to Al Qaeda. JI was one of the most dangerous groups operating in Southeast Asia, with cells in Indonesia, Malaysia, Singapore, the Philippines, and Thailand. Hambali was critical because he served as the main link between JI and the core Al Qaeda leadership. Hambali was a true believer and was dangerous. Ever since 2000, Hambali had been operating underground, orchestrating a series of bombings in Indonesia from his place of hiding.

In October 2002, he helped organize the deadliest act of terrorism in the history of Indonesia in Bali, killing over 200 people, including 88 Australians, by detonating a suicide bomber, a large car bomb, and a smaller device outside nightclubs and a US consulate. JI would later claim responsibility for attacks on the JW Marriott Hotel in Jakarta and the Australian embassy. JI cells were being wrapped up in places such as Singapore, where they had been planning more attacks against transportation sites and civilian targets. Hambali was on the top tier of wanted Al Qaeda operatives around the world and was being hunted in the region. Authorities were worried that more attacks were coming, and were most concerned about a possible biological attack from Hambali and his henchmen.

The US government, in concert with allies around the world, was looking for any signs of Hambali, and a small team of analysts uncovered some financial tracks. The analysts looking for Hambali found SWIFT data to identify a previously unknown figure in Southeast Asia who had financial dealings with a suspected Al Qaeda member. The financial data helped identify a key operative who served as the connection between Al Qaeda's core and Hambali's operations in Southeast Asia. This was the missing link to track Hambali.

Hambali was in Thailand, planning attacks against Thai hotels to coincide with the 2003 Asia Pacific Economic Cooperation (APEC) summit. He and JI were looking for more spectacular and politically significant attacks to undertake, and the APEC summit provided a ripe and local opportunity. The attacks were thwarted. On August 11, 2003, Thai police took Hambali into custody, seizing explosives and firearms. He was transferred to CIA custody and ultimately moved to Guantanamo Bay.[3] According to US officials years later, the Terrorist Finance Tracking Program "played an important role in the investigation that eventually culminated in the capture of Hambali."[4] One of Al Qaeda's most important and dangerous terrorist lieutenants had been taken off the battlefield—with the help of the financial trackers.

The Treasury Department would later release even more examples of cases where financial information helped save lives—in the United States and abroad. From the plot to attack JFK airport in New York in 2007 to the plan to attack US bases in Germany that same year, financial information provided key investigative leads. Financial nuggets from the program would often serve as the missing puzzle piece to help authorities around the world disrupt terrorist activity.

This kind of financial intelligence would form the basis for our ability to track and stop terrorist funding, and the growing discipline of financial intelligence would animate efforts to isolate rogue financial behavior and the movement of money by America's enemies. We were now aggressively looking for terrorists' financial footprints and using a variety of tools at our command to freeze assets and arrest suspects. This work, however, had to involve cooperation with our closest allies in the very places where Al Qaeda and other terrorist groups were getting their funding. We had to use aggressive financial diplomacy to ensure the international cooperation we needed to isolate terrorists and their rogue allies. This would take us to the heart of the Arabian Gulf.

3

Nose Under the Tent

When our Treasury delegation landed in Jeddah on Air Force Two in the spring of 2002, the first thing we saw was the special airport terminal that the Saudi monarchy had built especially for the Hajj, the annual Muslim pilgrimage to Mecca. The terminal was enormous—a bright white edifice that looked like a large tent in the desert. Lines of buses for as far as the eye could see take the pilgrims from the airport to hotels and holy sites. The Saudi government had built a logistical marvel of transport and accommodation to handle the inflow and outflow of humanity's largest annual migration.

Led by Secretary O'Neill, our small, senior-level Treasury delegation had come to the Kingdom of Saudi Arabia to engage the Saudi monarchy in an uncomfortable discussion about terrorist financing. Crown Prince Abdullah, the heir apparent to the ailing King Fahd, along with other senior members of the Saudi royal family and several Saudi officials, would receive us in this modern city, the country's second largest after its capital, Riyadh. This would be the first time the Saudis would host the secretary of the treasury since 9/11. Despite decades as close allies, the United States and Saudi Arabia found themselves at a critical juncture. The role of the fifteen Saudi hijackers in the attacks had cast a pall over the relationship between the two countries. These tensions only deepened as Treasury officials began to delve into the financing of Al Qaeda, as part of that funding had been coming from Saudi Arabia and the Arabian Gulf for years.

To be clear, there was no suggestion of state sponsorship of Al Qaeda. The Saudis had long ago disavowed bin Laden, who considered the Saudi monarchy to be an apostate, corrupt regime worth targeting and toppling. The problem was that the Saudis had built an infrastructure of donors, charities, and sponsors in the 1980s to help the Afghan mujahideen and foreign Islamic fighters in their opposition to the Soviet invasion of Afghanistan. That infrastructure still existed, and violent jihadist causes took full advantage of it. Fighters battling the Russians in Chechnya, the Israelis in the Palestinian territories, the Americans in Afghanistan, and apostate or infidel regimes in Asia reaped the rewards of this system.

We were there to provide a much-needed reality check to the highest levels of the Saudi monarchy about the need to shut these kinds of charities down. It would not be easy.

Saudi society was not predisposed to look favorably on such an initiative. Within the Saudi populace, there still remained some denial as to the perpetrators and motivations behind 9/11. There was some agreement that, like the 1979 seizing of the sacred mosque in Mecca by violent radical Muslims, the attacks had been an anomalous act by religious fanatics, to be condemned and prevented from happening again. Yet for the Saudis, the sins of these actors were not a reason to implicate an entire society or the monarchy. Some saw 9/11 as an isolated act of terror, not symptomatic of something more dangerous emerging from within their society or even from the broader Sunni extremist movement.

But there was more at play than most were willing to admit. The issue of financial support for Al Qaeda pointed to a deeper question about how money from Saudi Arabia was being used around the world. The Saudis had been committed for decades to the export of an extreme form of Sunni Wahhabi Islam. When the House of Saud established its rule over the Arabian Peninsula in 1932, the royal family made a pact with the ultraconservative clerical establishment to allow the Saudi regime to maintain power and legitimacy. The kingdom's leadership and royal family derived their ultimate legitimacy from their role as the "Keeper of the Two Holy Mosques." This meant that the king was not only the head of state but also the religious guardian of the first and second holiest sites in Islam, the cities of Mecca and Medina. They required consistent validation from the Sunni clerical establishment in Saudi Arabia, which espoused the Wahhabi, Salafi ideology and embedded its strictures into Saudi culture. The Saudi government was thus wedded to the promotion of this theology and used its money around the world to establish Islamic centers and mosques and to export Islamic scholars who reinforced this extreme interpretation of Islam.

The Saudis had built an extensive global network for spreading a certain brand of religious thought, but in so doing they had provided a platform for Al Qaeda and its like-minded adherents, who benefited greatly from this network both financially and in terms of growth. The Wahhabi theology and Saudi proselytization around the world provided an ideological baseline for Al Qaeda and the recruitment of like-minded believers. Al Qaeda's leaders advocated the practice of declaring others as apostates (*takfir*) and the right to use violence against them and to defend Muslims against perceived assaults. Many of the Wahhabi institutions funded out of Saudi Arabia served as way stations for Al Qaeda operatives and fundraising. Distinguishing between some of the international Wahhabi organizations and terrorist support networks was nearly impossible, especially when support for Al Qaeda and support for spreading Wahhabi beliefs seemed to blend together so seamlessly. This was true in the work of some of the branches of Saudi-based institutions, such as the International Islamic Relief Organization (IIRO). For us, cutting off flows of funds to Al Qaeda thus meant much more than just targeting a few select individuals or institutions. It was ultimately about challenging a fundamental element of Saudi policy by constricting how the Saudis and their institutions funded activities abroad.

This was a critical aspect of our work. Al Qaeda's financial and logistical base consisted of a network of radicalized Islamic fundamentalists and institutions around the world whose roots could be traced to the days of the Afghan mujahideen. This meant that Al Qaeda could take advantage of certain madrassas (educational institutions), Islamic cultural centers, and Islamic charities around the world both to promote its militant ideology and to raise, hide, and move funds. Such funds were intended, at least partially, for the maintenance of the terrorist network and allegiances as well as for operations.[1] The money chain traveled from sympathizers in the Arabian Gulf and around the world to hot spots such as Afghanistan and Pakistan where Al Qaeda was recruiting and operating.

The flow of money was constant. Al Qaeda and other violent extremists used the Islamic obligation of *zakhat* (charitable giving) and their interpretation of obligatory jihad to generate financing through charity. They used the logistics, networks, and funding of charities to support their operations and build allegiances. This was a well-established strategy and structure. For certain groups, such as Hamas and Hezbollah, charitable operations—and their Dawa (fundraising) committees—were a key function that allowed them to provide services to people in need while building allegiances necessary for recruitment outside the confines of the state or official channels. They fiendishly used the infrastructure and nature of charity to enlist devotees and move operatives around the world under a benevolent cloak. It was a devious and ingenious way of raising and moving money—especially with chapters of charities located around the world. Charities might be providing services to widows and orphans, but their funding and recruitment would often send suicide bombers into buses and cafés.

Despite our attempts to be surgical in our financial strikes, sometimes our actions and tools proved blunt and imprecise against charities. There was a legitimate concern that the effects of US designations, raids, and asset freezes on charities were creating unintended consequences and an impression that US policy was intentionally trying to extinguish Islamic charity. Many worried that the aggressive actions we had taken were chilling good-faith giving and philanthropy, a hallmark of American culture.[2] Al Qaeda leaders latched onto this theme, with Ayman al-Zawahiri—then bin Laden's deputy—highlighting the "American war on Islamic charity" in the wake of the devastating Pakistani earthquake in 2005.[3]

There was no doubt that charity now required new layers of fact finding and diligence—especially if organizations were doing business or sponsoring projects in places where terrorist organizations were known to run charitable services. They intermingled their activities and funds, and we had no easy way to carve their organizations or activities neatly between the legitimate and the illegitimate, or to distinguish consistently between funds going to Al Qaeda or other terrorist groups and funds going to charitable causes. We were careful with our designations and began trying to encourage "charitable backfill" in communities around the world where our targeted sanctions and enforcement efforts were shutting down critical services and legitimate funding flows.

Al Qaeda and groups like the Taliban were also clever to leverage the Hajj as cover to gather donations and move cash donations out of Saudi Arabia back to Afghanistan, Pakistan, and the rest of the world. Though the Saudi authorities would do what they could to monitor the movement of people in and out of the country for the world's largest annual migration, groups like the Taliban and Hamas would send special representatives to meet with donors and collect money, jewelry, and other financial commitments from fellow Muslims from around the world—including wealthy donors. Despite our protestations, the Saudis had been unwilling to deny access to Mecca to pilgrims who were also potential fundraisers. Instead, they opted for monitoring, but even that proved difficult as a flood of pilgrims flowed in and out of the airport at Jeddah.

The American approach was far more visible. We were using an aggressive notification method to stop and deter terrorist financing, publicly designating individuals and entities as terrorist financiers as our cudgel. Not only did this freeze millions of dollars around the world, it made the organizations we designated radioactive to others doing business. Our flurry of designations was intended to clog Al Qaeda's financial system and to send a clear deterrent message to those who would support or finance terrorism that they could be next.

When it came to companies, organizations, and individuals abroad, our work would have more impact if the host government took actions along with us to freeze assets and shut down suspect operations. This is why we still needed Saudi help. What we were asking the Saudis to do would be difficult, considering the internal dynamics of their country. The House of Saud ruled because the leadership was able to balance the power centers within the king-dom and to reassert legitimacy with each decision made. To avoid upsetting harmony among tribes and power brokers, the Saudis preferred to isolate rogue individuals quietly or to co-opt or force them to submit to the monarchy's wishes. The Saudi approach was less about punishment and more about channeling internal support for extremist causes into support for the government's actions. Part of this strategy entailed building opposition to Al Qaeda slowly but surely. This approach took time—and it was not what Washington was looking for from the Saudis in the aftermath of 9/11. We wanted quick, visible action.

Our specific goal in this meeting was to gain Saudi approval to shut down its largest Islamic charity, the Al Haramain Foundation. Al Haramain had established branches around the world, including in the United States, to raise money for Muslim causes. Despite sup-porting some legitimate charitable causes, however, Al Haramain was also a platform for Al Qaeda to raise and move money into places like Bosnia and Indonesia. It seemed that the organization's head, Sheikh Aqeel Abdulaziz al-Aqil, was well aware that this was going on, and quite willing to let it happen.

We wanted to close down all of Al Haramain—its headquarters and all its branches (including in Oregon)—but knew that we would need to take this one step at a time. This was not about targeting Islamic charity. It was about shutting down conduits that had been used by terrorists and could be used in the future by Al Qaeda. We needed to be sensitive to the perception that we were simply trying to attack Islamic charities as we targeted groups that were funding terrorist groups.

To get this done, we hoped to build a case against the entire Al Haramain organization. We would focus on the most problematic branches and work toward closing down the entire network. This would not happen overnight, but we needed to take a first step. It was imperative for us to get the Saudis on board with us to make a public announcement, and we hoped they would commit to shutting down all suspected conduits and donors for Al Qaeda. From Washington and with the help of our embassy in Riyadh, we had prescripted what could be done, but the Saudi decision ultimately had to come from the top.

The Saudis received us warmly. Red carpets led into the main VIP terminal. We raced after Secretary O'Neill, who was always quick off the plane and first to the motorcade or meeting. In the terminal, we met our ambassador, Robert Jordan, and the deputy chief of mission, Margaret Scobey, and discussed where things stood with the Saudis before heading in a long motorcade to the Conference Palace Hotel. We would prepare for our planned site visits and await word of our meetings with Crown Prince Abdullah.

Once we received word that he was ready for us, we got into the motorcade and were escorted into the royal palace in Jeddah. I did not know what to expect, but I was eager to see whether there would be agreement on a joint designation of Saudi Arabia's biggest charity. More importantly, I wanted to see whether the Saudi leadership was taking the problem of terrorist financing seriously.

We entered the grounds and were escorted by the crown prince's royal guard into a waiting room in the palace near his office. We waited briefly amid lush couches as the protocol officers made sure they knew who would be attending the meeting and how we would introduce ourselves. John Taylor, Michele Davis (the assistant secretary for public affairs), Bill Murden, and I shuffled to stay close to the secretary for fear of being left outside the bubble and missing the meeting altogether, which had been known to happen in the past.

Secretary O'Neill led the way along with our ambassador into the large, opulent office, introducing all of us as we greeted Crown Prince Abdullah. The crown prince appeared like a figure out of biblical times who had walked into the ornate and relatively modern office straight out of the desert. His stark black goatee and flowing royal thobe and cloak, accented in gold and black lining, gave shape to his large frame. His sandals reminded me of the desert origins of the Saudi monarchy. The green Saudi flag framed his desk, with couches on each side of the office for the guests and Saudi officials who would join the meeting. His deep, baritone voice welcomed us and filled the large office with his authority. King Fahd was very ill, and it was no secret that the crown prince was running the kingdom. Crown Prince Abdullah would become the king of Saudi Arabia in 2005.

Directly next to the crown prince was his adviser and translator, Adel al-Jubeir, who would later become Saudi Arabia's ambassador to the United States. Al-Jubeir, a thin, cerebral man who spoke perfect English, would prove critical in this period as a trusted figure on all sides on these issues, acting as a shadow ambassador in the United States even though he was not a royal. Educated in the United States, he also handled Saudi Arabia's public relations campaign in the West, while long-standing Saudi ambassador Prince Bandar weathered criticisms.

The office was covered with beautiful oriental rugs. Sitting on the other side of the room were key Saudi government ministers, including the interior minister, Prince Nayef bin Abdulaziz al-Saud; the Saudi finance minister; and the central bank governor. This was the first time an American treasury secretary had met with the Saudi leadership to talk almost exclusively about terrorist financing.

Crown Prince Abdullah and Secretary O'Neill sat next to each other, and we sat along the couch and seats next to Secretary O'Neill. Saudi hospitality, with multiple rounds of coffee, tea, and juice, would follow in due course.

After some basic pleasantries and a discussion about the world economy, the real discussion began. O'Neill and the crown prince talked about the importance of attacking the financial support for Al Qaeda and terrorism—with O'Neill emphasizing the need to take aggressive action against those we suspected of assisting Al Qaeda. The deep sting of 9/11 was still with us, and there was a desire to do everything possible to prevent another attack and to send signals throughout the world that financial support for Al Qaeda would be met with economic isolation and ruin. Having clarity on Saudi Arabia's position was critical. The crown prince agreed but underscored the need for any steps taken to be in the right sequence. O'Neill and Crown Prince Abdullah then began to discuss the problems with Al Haramain, with O'Neill suggesting that we take action together against some of its branches and investigate its leadership—all with the aim of shutting down its worldwide operations.

The proposal itself had been prescripted behind the scenes with the Saudi government. We already knew that the Saudis were amenable to taking the step we were proposing, with the prospect that this could lead to tougher and tougher actions on their part over time. Still, the Saudis also wanted to modulate their actions, being careful about how aggressively and how quickly they confronted influential elements within Saudi society. We would not be shutting down the entire charity right away, but would take the first step in this direction. Furthermore, it behooved both countries to demonstrate cooperation on this matter. We wanted to send a clear signal that the United States and Saudi Arabia were cooperating closely on countering terrorist financing.

The presentation proved persuasive. Crown Prince Abdullah agreed to take the action we were requesting—as the first of many to follow. He seemed committed to cutting off funding for Al Qaeda.

Furthermore, the Saudis understood that the perception that they allowed funding to occur was not good for their reputation globally and in the United States—and was in fact dangerous to the survival of their regime. The resulting joint designation of the Al Haramain branches would be the first joint designation with any country. This was a way of signaling cooperation publicly and diplomatically, undercutting any attempt by Al Qaeda to drive a wedge between two of its enemies and catalyzing more action against Al Qaeda's support network in Saudi Arabia.

On March 11, 2002, the United States and Saudi Arabia made their first joint submission to the United Nations and designated the Bosnian and Somalia branches of the Al Haramain Foundation.[4] The United States and Saudi Arabia would later designate other branches of the charity and launch an investigation of Sheikh Aqeel Abdulaziz al-Aqil, the head of the organization. As it turned out, thanks to a strategic mistake by Al Qaeda, Saudi Arabia would soon be aiding our campaign even more aggressively than we could have hoped.

The catalyst was a new act of terror on Saudi soil. In May 2003, Al Qaeda cells in the kingdom executed deadly attacks on housing compounds in Riyadh, killing dozens. The attackers used suicide car bombs to target housing and apartment complexes of foreign workers, including Americans.

The Saudis responded ferociously. Counterterrorism units in the Mubahith—the internal security and intelligence service—published most-wanted lists for Al Qaeda operatives and supporters in the kingdom and proceeded to painstakingly track them down and kill them. New wanted lists emerged every few weeks. At times, it was difficult to keep up with the Saudis' extermination of the Al Qaeda operatives. By picking a fight with the Saudis, Al Qaeda had inadvertently given the Saudi monarchy the leeway it needed to crack down—not only militarily, but also financially. By 2004, our ultimate request had been granted, and the Saudis would shut down all of Al Haramain, ultimately prosecuting its director for financial irregularities.

The leader of the Saudi effort to break Al Qaeda's back in the kingdom was the ruthless but mild-mannered Prince Muhammad bin Nayef, the deputy interior minister and son of the Saudi interior minister, Prince Nayef bin Abdulaziz al-Saud. "MbN," as the deputy minister was called within the US government, managed the kingdom's counterterrorism efforts, and he was trusted by both the crown prince and the United States to protect the kingdom and pursue its counterterrorism policies. He led the Mubahith's investigations, raids, and crackdowns on Al Qaeda operatives—whom we called the "Vampires" because of their middle-of-the-night work hours and their ability to strike after dark.

MbN developed a smart and stealthy strategy that was lethal in its execution. His approach was to make cases and examples of those supporting Al Qaeda within the Saudi court system—with the clerical establishment and judiciary condemning the acts—while leveraging the shame and constrictions embedded in Saudi society to punish those willing to support the terrorist group. He would argue for taking the long view, where the bad guys would be killed, deterred, or reconciled. MbN would establish the now famous and well-studied Saudi rehabilitation program for recruits into Al Qaeda, creating a system of theological and social deprogramming and reintegration. Such reintegration would include incentives such as homes and wives, creating a collective familial and tribal responsibility for the extremists who were allowed to return to Saudi society. Some of those released from the program would go on to kill again, but the program has nevertheless been seen as one model for addressing the ideological underpinnings and allure of Al Qaeda's message.

The importance of MbN's role in breaking the back of Al Qaeda was not well known. MbN kept a low profile, and he preferred not to receive public recognition, though he was named minister of the interior in 2012. He was focused on his mission and on protecting his men and the Saudi people. But Al Qaeda knew how important he was. On August 8, 2009, an Al Qaeda operative who claimed to be willing to reconcile and meet with MbN instead attempted to assassinate him. Though the man was searched by Saudi security, they missed the explosive that was contained in his rear end. The operative exploded the bomb, and MbN was wounded but not killed. Al Qaeda in the Arabian Peninsula (AQAP)—the Al Qaeda affiliate in Yemen made up largely of Saudi and Yemeni operatives—claimed responsibility for the attempt. Just a few months later, AQAP would send an underwear bomber on an airliner to Detroit to try to hit the United States.

This personal attack only strengthened the kingdom's resolve. In meeting after meeting thereafter, there was never any wavering on Crown Prince Abdullah's part about tackling terrorist financing, even after 2005 when he became king. In time, he came to challenge us to do more to go after the nexus between drug trafficking and terrorism. In September 2003, when Secretary O'Neill's successor, Secretary John Snow, visited with Crown Prince Abdullah, they talked about the need to take additional steps together against terrorist financing. When Secretary Snow told the crown prince that our Treasury delegation was traveling to Afghanistan, the Saudi leader stopped Snow and told him he had to be especially careful. He leaned into the secretary and said, "The terrorists are most afraid of you because you go after their money."

Despite this high-level commitment, countering terrorist financing would remain a constant irritant for both countries. The fundamental tension and issues persisted. This was not just about institutions and an infrastructure of financing for extremist causes. There were individuals in the Arabian Gulf who were committed to supporting Al Qaeda. We sought to find the "deep-pocket donors" who were supplying Al Qaeda and its allies with necessary and consistent funding, but Al Qaeda treated the identities of its most important financial supporters as prized possessions, secrets held within the inner sanctum where its other sacred secrets were contained. This was information not widely known even within the Al Qaeda network itself, and it was not easily uncovered. As with the possible location of Osama bin Laden and Ayman al-Zawahiri (known within the US government as "high value targets," specifically, "HVTs 1 and 2"), high-level detainees were not providing names. Meanwhile, intelligence and arrests were not revealing the core investors in terror, either.

In Sarajevo in 2002, security services came across an interesting and potentially explosive find that seemed to be the "Golden Fleece" of Al Qaeda financing we had long sought. Bosnia had been the site of Islamic extremist militant activity in the 1990s, at the height of the war in the Balkans—with groups like Al Qaeda issuing a clarion call for Muslim men to join the fight to defend fellow Muslims. The Balkans campaign became another jihadi battlefield—like Chechnya, Kashmir, and Somalia—animating the movement after the Soviet withdrawal from Afghanistan and the initiation of Taliban control over much of the country.

While raiding a terrorist safe house, Bosnian services collected incriminating documents and computer files about the Balkan-based fighters and their support network. Using this information, the Treasury designated the Saudi-based Benevolence International Foundation (BIF) as a terrorist financier, citing the handwritten correspondence between Osama bin Laden and the BIF director, authorizing the latter to act on behalf of the terrorist mastermind, as evidence.[5] The FBI would later raid BIF offices in Chicago, and its leader would be prosecuted for financial crimes. In the trove discovered in Bosnia, authorities found a list of twenty-three names— some of them prominent Arab businessmen—described as primary donors to Al Qaeda.

Heretofore, there had been little intelligence about the big names and deep pockets behind the Al Qaeda movement. There were certainly suspicions about the families and wealthy businessmen in the Middle East—especially in the Persian Gulf countries—who might be behind the day-to-day budget that Al Qaeda needed to pay for its members, their families, and recruitment and training. This list was the first concrete set of subjects. Prominent and wealthy names long familiar to law enforcement appeared on the list. Not surprisingly, many of these men were prominent Saudis—such as Suleiman al-Rajhi and Khalid bin Mahfouz. Most of those named were involved in charity organizations as founders or board members in addition to their formal employment. The list, which became known as the "Golden Chain," was later reported to be verified as authentic by former Al Qaeda member Jamal al-Fadl.[6]

As promising as the list seemed, though, it raised several crucial questions. Were those on the Golden Chain list really the select group of long-standing deep-pocket donors we were looking for? Had these investors been the main support for the global extremist movement? Was it current, post-9/11, Al Qaeda support, or was this just a historical list of those who had been supportive in the past? Or perhaps, even more vaguely, was this merely a wish list for jihadis holed up in Bosnia who were looking for funding from a supposed group of sympathetic wealthy actors? Importantly, could those on the list provide insights into the terrorist support, or even tracks to find HVTs 1 and 2? Although we did not yet know the answers to all the questions, the list did provide concrete leads. And it sparked an important debate over past and potential current support from wealthy Saudis to Al Qaeda and like-minded terrorist groups.

The list underscored the nature of terrorist financing for the broader Sunni violent extremist movement, which was reliant over time on key donors and donations. The donors to Al Qaeda were often not just passive contributors, but demanding investors in a cause. Over time, the donor class would grow increasingly demanding of Al Qaeda, asking to hear directly from bin Laden and requiring that their funds be leveraged specifically to launch significant attacks.

Al Qaeda obliged with recorded messages from Osama bin Laden reassuring supporters of the centrality and vitality of Al Qaeda's cause. Radical ideologues reminded followers of their obligation to provide financial support to their jihadi brethren. Their plots would continue to materialize, but Al Qaeda would find it increasingly difficult to mount successful attacks against the West—in large part because it became difficult to raise, control, and move money.

The question of whether deep-pocket donors as a class or segment of the terrorist network actually existed would persist for years. We had designated a few well-known, suspected financiers of Al Qaeda and its causes, such as Yasin al-Qadi on October 12, 2001. Qadi was a Saudi businessman who was considered a key financier for Al Qaeda as well as Hamas. He ran the Muwafaq Foundation, which the Treasury exposed as a conduit for Al Qaeda funding. Qadi was also a principal funder for the Al Barakaat Foundation, an Islamic charity believed to support Al Qaeda operations around the world prior to 9/11, and had served as a conduit for Al Qaeda banking in the Sudan, Saudi Arabia, and Afghanistan. Qadi's business enterprises and investments extended from the Middle East into Turkey and Europe, including Albania.[7]

Once Qadi was designated, his assets were frozen throughout Europe, and this complicated his business transactions around the world. It became difficult for Qadi to move money through banks, and investors and partners became wary about doing business with him. The spotlight had been put on him, and he was required to demonstrate that he was not funding bin Laden. Qadi quickly instructed his lawyers to challenge the designations in courts in London and in the European Court of Justice.[8]

He enlisted the support of friends and supporters, including Turkish Prime Minister Recep Tayyip Erdogan, who proclaimed in 2007 that he would not abide by the UN mandate to freeze Qadi's assets. His efforts to delist himself from the UN sanctions list and from the European list succeeded, with his delisting taking effect on October 21, 2012. The United Kingdom and the European Union proceeded to delist him as well. Qadi had succeeded in pleading his case. Nevertheless, the designation and the resulting international scrutiny had put a spotlight on those who had supported bin Laden prior to 9/11 and forced those designated to end any such support.

We designated others as key financiers, such as bin Laden's brother-in-law Mohammed Jamal Khalifa. He would later be killed in Mauritania under suspicious circumstances. Even so, skeptics remained, especially in the intelligence community, because we had found little hard evidence of a terrorist donor class. Detainees were not revealing names, and our intelligence collection efforts and work with liaison and law-enforcement partners had not revealed such information. The Golden Chain list was a helpful marker, but it was not seen as an authentic list of current Al Qaeda financiers. One's appearance on the list could not alone justify severe actions against someone. In truth, we had little actionable information about those continuing to bankroll the movement. This was enormously frustrating and problematic.

Still, we would learn more about the financial networks and donors over time. With the growing success of the Saudi crackdowns on terrorist networks—including arrests of terrorist financiers—and mounting efforts to stop terrorist financing, funding coming from Qatar and Kuwait soon became the greater issue.

In 2006, we would designate three deep-pocket donors from Kuwait for their role in supporting terrorism. In 2007, the Saudis would wrap up a network of financiers who were passing along mobile messages from Ayman al-Zawahiri exhorting supporters to donate to the cause. In June 2008, we named additional Kuwaiti financiers tied to groups supporting Al Qaeda, including a charity called the Revival of the Islamic Heritage Society (RIHS). RIHS's Peshawar office in Pakistan was a charity, but it was also a front for moving funding directly from Kuwait to Al Qaeda in western Pakistan. In 2011, the Treasury Department would publicly designate the most significant Al Qaeda terrorist financing network that had been revealed in the past five years. The network relied on several donors in Kuwait and Qatar—Ezedin Abdel Aziz Khalil, Atiyah Abd al-Rahman, Umid Muhammadi, Salim Hasan Khalifa Rashid al-Kuwari, Abdallah Ghanim Mafuz Muslim al-Khawar, and 'Ali

Hasan 'Ali al-'Ajmi. These donors were providing funding directly to the Al Qaeda core via a financial facilitation network in Iran. In designating this Al Qaeda financial network, the Treasury announced, "This network serves as the core pipeline through which al-Qa'ida moves money, facilitators and operatives from across the Middle East and South Asia."[9] In October 2012, the Treasury would add another name to the list of those who formed part of this Iran-based financial network.

We knew we were going to have a generational struggle and a problem on our hands for years with supporters of terrorist causes in the Arabian Gulf. The dialogue with the Saudis, Kuwaitis, and Qataris would remain tense, with the Treasury Department serving as the gadfly. A series of Treasury officials would publicly articulate our frustration with slow progress in shutting down and regulating suspect charities, holding terrorist financiers accountable, and addressing the underlying problem of Wahhabi proselytization. In 2003, David Aufhauser, Treasury's general counsel, testified before the Senate, calling Saudi Arabia the "epicenter of terrorist financing." These episodes were deeply embarrassing to the Saudis and did not match up with their sense of friendship with the United States and their broader cooperation with the United States' counterterrorism efforts.

The Saudis would often push back, asking for the evidence to justify our charges. Sometimes we could not provide the information they requested because of the sources and methods we had used. Other times, we just did not have enough information to satisfy the Saudis—especially when taking controversial actions such as freezing assets or arresting a prominent individual. The Saudis frequently complained that they were providing information to the United States and could not understand why the Treasury Department was complaining—but the problem in some cases was that they were giving the information to the CIA, and the CIA was not sharing the information with the Treasury Department.

To manage this important counterterrorism relationship across the board, the White House assigned Frances M. Fragos Townsend, who was then the deputy national security adviser for combating terrorism, to the job of referee. Townsend later served as homeland security adviser to President Bush from 2004 to 2007. It would be left to her to smooth ruffled feathers when Treasury officials criticized the Saudis, and it would be her job to ensure that there was information sharing within the US government—especially between Treasury and CIA. Townsend would take interagency delegations with her to Saudi Arabia to present a united front. On several occasions, I was a part of these delegations. By 2007, Treasury had assigned a full-time attaché to sit in Riyadh to interact with the Saudi government. All of these measures helped to improve the level of communication between Treasury and both the Saudis and the CIA.

The pressure on the Saudis was real—and not just from the Treasury Department. There was public and congressional scrutiny over their actions, public heat from Treasury designations and statements, and FBI investigations over Saudi embassy funding that found its way to some of the 9/11 hijackers.

In late 2003, Prince Bandar, the longtime Saudi ambassador to the United States and dean of the diplomatic corps, paid a visit to the Treasury Department to meet with Secretary Snow about the state of US-Saudi relations. Bandar could get a meeting with the president whenever he needed, and he was always considered a critical figure in the relationship between the United States and Saudi Arabia, though he took a less and less public role in the United States after 9/11. Bandar considered himself a real friend to the United States, having trained to fly military jets with American pilots. He had served as the key interlocutor in the early 1980s to ensure funding to equip the Afghan mujahideen against the Soviets.

Secretary Snow received Prince Bandar in his small conference room. It was not clear exactly what Bandar wanted to discuss, so Snow included a small group of us to listen and assist if necessary. From the moment Bandar entered the small conference room, he filled the space with his larger-than-life presence and big personality. As always, Bandar was friendly and garrulous, but he had come with a specific problem in mind. Bandar was disturbed by the investigations into the embassy banking practices led by the FBI—they were proving embarrassing to him and the Saudis. Much public attention had been given to the cash payments from the embassy to Saudi citizens out of its account at Riggs Bank. These had included some payments to Khalid al-Mihdhar and Nawaf al-Hazmi, two of the 9/11 hijackers. Although there was no evidence that the Saudi government had tried to assist the 9/11 hijackers, the payments looked very bad. The FBI was investigating to get to the bottom of suspicions that the embassy had been subsidizing the hijackers' stay in the United States.

Bandar sat down and spoke passionately for over an hour. He laid out the history of his relationship with the United States and the role he had played as a trusted interlocutor from president to president. He spoke of the 1980s and how he had brokered payments to the Pakistani government and ensured that weapons and supplies were delivered to Afghan mujahideen who were fighting the Soviets. He talked of the checks that were written and cut to fund weapons and allegiance using the very same embassy bank accounts. Bandar saw himself as America's closest friend and most critical Cold Warrior. Why was he now under scrutiny?

This was a new period, where the old rules no longer applied. What was clear was that Bandar was making a plea for a return to a time when the allies trusted each other implicitly, and when money could flow easily without questions to allied causes and people. The conversation he had with us was more about a longing for a different period than a realistic argument for any change in policy. September 11 had changed this relationship and the nature of the world forever.

There was now suspicion between the longtime allies. Those whom we had supported in Afghanistan had now turned their guns on us, and money had to be monitored. Suspicious and blind transactions now had to be questioned. We listened respectfully, and the conversation ended without any conclusion or course to follow. The conversation left a deep impression on me as well as on the others who were present that day. Secretary Snow recalls this meeting as one of the most interesting of his tenure. Prince Bandar was a good friend to the United States, and he would continue to play an important role in the relationship between our two countries. Importantly, Bandar has reemerged in 2012 as the Saudi external intelligence chief—helping to orchestrate Saudi Arabia's efforts to counter Iran in the region and to support Syrian rebels in their fight against President Bashar al-Assad. Saudi funding and Prince Bandar are again in the middle of a critical international security crisis—one vital to the United States.

The private sector did not know how to address the changing environment in Saudi Arabia. There were suspect individuals with historical ties to bin Laden or groups associated with Al Qaeda in the Saudi kingdom. There seemed to be tainted money flows coming out of Saudi Arabia. And there were actions by the state that could not be fully reconciled with the requirements that states now had after 9/11 to ensure that their banks were not being misused by terrorist groups and financiers.

In early 2002, the CEO and representatives from Citibank paid a visit to the Treasury Department to talk about Saudi Arabia. Secretary O'Neill hosted the large group, to include Citi's chief lawyers, in the main conference room. The Citibank officials wanted to know whether they should stop doing business in Saudi Arabia altogether due to the risk of terrorist financing.

At issue was what they referred to as "Account 98." This was a series of unified charitable bank accounts at major financial institutions in Saudi Arabia. Created in October 2000 by order of the Saudi royal family, Account 98 held funds dedicated to "humanitarian" efforts in Palestine—including both financial and material aid—during the Al Quds Intifada. The initiative was managed by the Saudi Committee for the Support of the Intifada Al Quds (later renamed the Saudi Committee for the Relief of the Palestinian People), run by Interior Minister Prince Nayef bin Abdulaziz al-Saud. It also received support from Prince Salman bin Abdulaziz, governor of Riyadh.[10] The account was similar to others dedicated to needy Muslims in areas such as Bosnia and Chechnya.[11]

According to a 2001 official Saudi report published in the United States by the Middle East Media Research Institute, funds were directed through the Palestinian Authority under the close supervision of several top-ranking Saudi officials and the Arab League.[12] The report also shows that in its first year alone, Account 98 was used to funnel 10,000 to 20,000 rials to 986 families of Palestinian "martyrs," many of them suicide bombers and members of Hamas.[13] Increased scrutiny of the funds' use showed a pattern of terrorist financing. In one case, Israeli authorities searching the possessions of a Hamas operative who was involved in a deadly bombing discovered a spreadsheet bearing the official mark of the "Kingdom of Saudi Arabia, the Saudi Committee for Support of the Intifada Al Quds," and detailing funds received by the operative, his family, and eight other suicide bombers through Account 98.[14]

Despite criticism from the US Treasury Department, Saudis renewed calls for donations to Account 98 in a December 2001 announcement on a government website.[15] In April 2002, King Fahd sponsored a telethon that raised over $110 million.[16] When outright allegations of terrorist financing arose, Saudi officials insisted the funds were being channeled through international organizations such as the Red Cross and the United Nations and used for legitimate humanitarian purposes.[17]

The growing public discussions and questions about Account 98 were disconcerting to American financial institutions doing business in Saudi Arabia. It wasn't just their reputation that was on the line— Citigroup had held a 20 percent stake in the Saudi American Bank (Samba) since 1955.[18] The activities of Samba and the role of Account 98 in funding families of suicide bombers became a central issue for Citibank. Citigroup had run the bank under a management contract since 1980 and had 62 offices in Saudi Arabia to maximize the bank's ties to the Saudi elite. In 2002, Samba was named as a defendant in a lawsuit filed by 9/11 victims for allegedly collecting Saudi funds to support the Palestinian uprising. Samba filed a motion to dismiss the case, but Citigroup attempted to investigate the allegations.

Citi's leadership wanted answers from the US Treasury. In the meeting in the secretary's conference room, the mood was dark and serious. The Citi executives had a major problem on their hands and had little information to help them make a hard choice. Would they stop doing business in Saudi Arabia because of concerns about potential terrorist financing? Was there enough information to make that risk assessment? This was a major decision for a quintessential American financial institution that had done business in Saudi Arabia for decades.

As we sat across the large conference table, the Citi officials explained their predicament and asked for as much information as possible regarding Account 98 and our suspicions about terrorist funding out of Saudi Arabia. Citigroup claimed not to have taken note of the special account earlier because Saudi secrecy laws limited access to information about it.[19] We did not know much more than they did about Account 98. We knew it had been mandatory for banks operating in Saudi Arabia to establish these accounts and to transfer the monies deposited to the Palestinian territories. It appeared that some of the funding did go to help those in need, but it was also clear that there were problematic transactions and uses, including the payments to families of suicide bombers. We were pressuring the Saudi government to shut down the accounts or stop problematic payments and to lift the requirement that the account be maintained in all the relevant institutions. There was little that we could say that would satisfy the Citi leadership. They wanted more information and clarity to be able to make a decision. They didn't get much of either. In early 2003, Citi requested information officially from the Saudi government, Treasury, and the State Department, but with little success.[20]

The Citigroup executives made a decision to limit their exposure and potential liability. They could not operate in an environment in which their institution might be used to support terrorist causes and could not bear the reputational risks and liabilities that came with this. Account 98 has now been phased out and the funds directed to other accounts.[21]

This would not be an isolated action or consideration for the private sector. The new international environment had shifted the paradigm of risk and reputation for the banks. Governments—driven by the United States—were now requiring financial institutions to apply strict compliance standards and programs to their business. The color of money had changed, and reputational risk was now a key element of a bank's bottom line. Large, multinational banks needed to make sure that their institutions were not being misused by terrorists, and they were being forced by government regulations and policies to prevent the infiltration of the financial system. The banks were now viewed and treated as the guardians of the integrity of the financial system.

Many of the biggest financial institutions—including American, European, and Asian banks—were increasing exponentially the amount of reporting they submitted to government entities about suspicious financial activities. Banking officials were now spending hundreds of millions of dollars to ensure that they were scouring their systems to check for those designated or those suspected of illicit financing. These searches were not limited to Saudi Arabia. The concerns lay around the world—especially anywhere there was lack of transparency or accountability for financial transactions. The risk calculus had changed, and banks did not want to find themselves in the middle of a terrorist financing scheme.

Switzerland, Luxembourg, and Liechtenstein in particular were confronting an uncomfortable reality. The tradition of bank secrecy they had long followed was being pierced by the intensity of the international community's focus on transparent and accountable financial transactions. It was no longer acceptable for a banking center or country to say simply that they did not know or could not find out whether tainted money was nested in their banks. Banking centers in places such as Dubai and Beirut would have to confront the financial activity in their midst, where commercial actors and players from around the world converged. These countries would need to adjust their systems and find a balance that ensured they were being cooperative with the international community while still allowing their banking system to survive and take on customers from around the world. They all had to adjust to the new risk calculus for financial institutions.

Quiet cooperation often followed, with bank accounts frozen and financial intelligence shared. Countries such as the United Arab Emirates and Bahrain wanted to demonstrate the vitality and integrity of their financial centers—sponsoring conferences and expanding their role in international bodies like the Egmont Group of Financial Intelligence Units and the regional bodies of the Financial Action Task Force. In the classic banking centers of Europe, there was a hard shift to greater transparency and accountability, with the Swiss and Liechtenstein governments leading the way to reconsider their bank-secrecy foundations. The evolution occurred quickly, with the Swiss ultimately launching a "white money" campaign in 2010 to ensure that all its banking practices maintained the integrity of the system. Money, indeed, had a color after 9/11, and the banks and financial centers wanted to paint it white. It would be up to us at Treasury to leverage these changing dynamics of the financial industry explicitly in the financial campaigns to come.

By the time Osama bin Laden was killed, Treasury's work had paid off. Al Qaeda's old financial networks had been decimated, and the Al Qaeda core was pleading for money from its affiliates and donors and trying to find new ways to raise money. The Saudis and others had taken the concerns about terrorist funding seriously. Even Israeli counterterrorism officials marveled that by 2007, the flow of funds from Saudi Arabia to Al Qaeda had been greatly diminished. Regardless of diplomatic or geopolitical disputes, the fight against terrorist financing remained a consistent arena of cooperation. The art of financial diplomacy—with governments and banks—would play a prominent role in the financial battles ahead.

The Treasury had learned to flex its muscles and use most of the new tools and networks at its command aggressively along with new forms of financial intelligence. At times, the tools could be blunt financial instruments, but they were proving effective in isolating suspect people, institutions, and money. Now it was time to refine and sharpen our approach to address the financial chokepoints and vulnerabilities that remained.

4

FINANCIAL CHOKEPOINTS

Money finds a way to move efficiently—even in the most remote parts of the world. The US Treasury Department had to find a way to deal with the movement of money outside of the formal financial system and the neatly regulated hallways of banks. We had to find a way to address the movement of illicit funds through traditional hawaladars and cash couriers. And we needed to find ways to target and incapacitate the financial chokepoints that allowed transnational terrorist and criminal groups to operate globally.

Hawala is a traditional way of exchanging and moving money in Central and South Asia, the Middle East, and Africa. Like Western Union's wire services, hawala is a system built to move money across borders and around the world. Instead of wire transfers, however, it relies on trusted relationships and networks of brokers connected by phone calls, faxes, and cash to exchange and deliver money in places where there are no ATM machines or bank branches. For a percentage fee, a customer can send money to someone across the world with an expectation that it will be delivered, often to their door, within hours—simply based on the trust between networked brokers. At a certain point—often monthly or quarterly—the brokers reconcile their accounts and exchange-rate differences, usually using bank accounts, exchange of commodities, or credit.

The system is widespread and embedded in the commercial cultures of places such as Afghanistan, Pakistan, and Somalia, where formal banking or wire companies are often remote, expensive, and inaccessible. Like all financial systems, at its core the hawala system relies on trust—in this case between the brokers (or hawaladars) and with their customers. For farmers, merchants, and anyone who relies on relatives who work abroad, hawala is a principal financial system that undergirds economic life. In many cases, trusted hawaladars are considered more reliable and accountable than antiseptic bankers sitting behind teller windows.

As the term *hawala* began to hit the headlines in the West, hawalas quickly acquired a shady reputation. They were viewed as secretive and inherently suspicious, having no official recordkeeping, no connection to the formal financial system, and no oversight by modern regulatory bodies. Furthermore, there was no doubt that hawalas had been leveraged by Al Qaeda and the Taliban to move money in and out of Afghanistan and Pakistan. The hawala system's reach into hinterlands untouched by banks provided financial access where Al Qaeda had established safe havens and a physical presence. This made hawalas the preferred vehicles for moving money quietly and in smaller batches in and out of the places where terrorists were operating.

But the developing attitudes about hawalas in the West were plagued by ignorance. Though there was some academic attention paid to the importance of hawalas in the remittances of foreign workers and the economies of certain regions and communities before 9/11,[1] there were only a handful of people in the US government who actually understood how the hawala system worked and what it meant to those who practiced it.[2]

Though they may have seemed alien to Americans, hawalas were actually well-functioning, necessary financial networks providing access to cross-border transfers of money to those who would otherwise have had none. The system tended to be cheap, accessible, and reliable, as the brokers knew their customers better than most bank tellers do in New York or London. Contrary to Western misperceptions, the hawaladars also kept meticulous records—in detailed ledgers and computers—because their business depended on it. Since their money transfers were also tied to ongoing trade and exchange rates, and mercantile deals, this put a premium on tracking the transfer of money and goods.

In the months after 9/11, the Treasury Department targeted and shut down suspected hawaladar networks that were being used to siphon money for Al Qaeda, but we understood that the hawala system as a whole was not going to be eradicated. We knew, in fact, that it could serve important purposes, but early on we determined that it needed to be regulated and brought into a framework wherein its transactions could be monitored. Financial Action Task Force (FATF) Special Recommendation VI, adopted in October 2001, provided for the regulation of alternative remittance and informal value transfer systems, including hawala.[3]

At the first global hawala conference in Abu Dhabi in 2002, various presenters attempted to build awareness of how hawala worked and how different countries were addressing the challenges of informal money flows. The real work of the conference, however, happened on the margins of the meeting. I led the US delegation in discussions with the central bank governor of the United Arab Emirates, Sultan al-Suweidi, as we began to hammer out the language for an international understanding of how to treat hawala in the post-9/11 world. The result would be a roadmap that the UAE and other countries would use to frame their next steps to regulate the hawala market.

Having to deal with hawala was a burden for developing countries that wanted to be seen as modern financial centers. The Indian government did not want to see any treatment of the issue in an international forum. Frustrated, its representatives flatly argued that hawala should be made illegal categorically and that the Indian government could not acknowledge its existence. Even so, simply ignoring hawala was not a realistic approach to the problem.

Instead, we pushed forward with a declaration that allowed countries to regulate hawala as they deemed appropriate but highlighting the need for greater transparency, regulation, and accountability in the sector.

This was one of the sea changes in the financial world after 9/11. Hawala was recognized. Now, it had to be regulated. However, it was important for such a declaration to come from the Middle East itself. The UAE had much to gain—or lose—by ensuring that its financial centers were seen as being open, transparent, and cooperative. This was why the UAE government had taken the initiative to host the conference.

Governor Suweidi and I hammered out the final wording of the statement, along with experts such as Dr. Nikos Passos, and the conference delegates agreed to the publication of what became known as the Abu Dhabi Declaration on Hawala. The declaration acknowledged the important role hawala plays in legitimate business practices around the world, but stated that "the participants also raised concerns about hawala and other informal remittance systems, noting that a lack of transparency and accountability, as well as the absence of governmental supervisions, presents the potential for abuse by criminal elements."[4]

We continued to push for the regulation of hawala and the development of alternative, cheap banking services for large swaths of the developing world that did not have access to formal banks. This was not just about enforcing US security interests. It was also a development issue: improved access to banking and capital would provide more economic opportunity even as it offered more visibility to regulators and security officials.

In November 2002, at Secretary O'Neill's last G20 Finance Ministry meeting in New Delhi, he led a discussion on hawala with the finance ministers of the twenty leading economies in the world. In a huge conference room at the Sheraton Hotel, he spoke with expert fluency, laying out the framework for regulation and the creation of alternatives. Over time, perhaps hawalas could be rendered obsolete.

Eventually, access to wire services like Western Union and to cheap banking and wire alternatives would be through separate, dedicated bank "windows." Perhaps even mobile banking technologies and smartphone applications would one day supplant hawalas—or even banks—but that was not going to happen in 2002.

As O'Neill made his presentation in New Delhi, the Indian finance minister who was hosting the meeting kept a serious and skeptical eye on the proceedings. Other ministers, who were seated behind their countries' flags around an enormous square conference table, weighed in with comments. Many explained what their countries were doing to regulate hawalas; others asked questions intended to probe whether regulation of the informal financial sector was even possible. O'Neill responded to the points, arguing that there needed to be a realistic attempt to network the regulation of hawalas among nations with an eye toward extending formal banking services and conveniences to the unbanked. He finished the session with great command of the issues. As he did, he looked around the room with some satisfaction, then turned to look at me, asking, "How'd I do?" "That was great, Mr. Secretary," I said as I leaned forward—proud that the US treasury secretary had recognized the importance of these complex issues to the international financial community.

Two years later, after O'Neill's departure, we were still seeking ways of converting that global focus into fresh strategies for dealing with hawalas. One of the keys would be finding someone with the right mix of unbridled energy and a quest for impact and innovation to take on the task.

The walk from the Afghan Finance Ministry to the central hawala market in Kabul took only about fifteen minutes. Making that trek in November 2004 was Amit Sharma, a friendly, confident twenty-seven-year-old Indian American with thick black curly hair. Originally recruited to join the CIA, Sharma was barred from doing

so by a restriction that prevented Peace Corps volunteers from joining the CIA within five years of their service. When the CIA sent
Sharma my way, I couldn't hire him fast enough. He was among my
first hires into the Treasury's Executive Office of Terrorist Financing
and Financial Crimes in the fall of 2003. A year later, he was my
emissary to the world of Afghan finance, helping us get a better
handle on the evolution of hawala—the backbone of Afghanistan's
informal financial system.

When he arrived in Kabul, he was determined to see the hawala
market firsthand. Brimming with youthful confidence born from his
time on the Mongolian plains and Argentine polo pitch, Sharma
didn't think much about defying US embassy lockdown orders after
the Taliban's abduction of UN aid workers. He just took a walk.

Dressed in a beige suit, Sharma walked through downtown
Kabul, across a dry riverbed and over a bridge, with the detritus of
plastic bags and bottles strewn about the streets. The streets were
crowded with Afghans, and the buildings were almost all one-story
structures. The hawala market was one of the largest buildings in
the neighborhood, at four stories. Its entrance was lined by a string
of small roadside stalls selling sundry goods, food, rugs, and ani-
mals. The market building itself had a narrow double door guarded
by a uniformed man with a rifle nestled against his shoulder. The
guard was fast asleep when Sharma and a Finance Ministry official
walked through the doorway.

A Western Union office, with brightly lighted signage, occupied
the first office in the building on the ground floor. There were other
offices on this floor, some with business names painted on wooden
boards or written with marker on paper taped to the inside of glass
doors. The building opened into a center courtyard, with balconies
ringing above the inner courtyard. There were about 240 money-
service businesses and another 40 or so money-exchange dealers
here, and each had a small office.

In the central courtyard, hawaladars and money-exchange dealers sat on rugs with stacks of cash in different currencies—the

afghani, US dollars, Pakistani rupees, euros, Japanese yen, British pounds, Chinese yuan—organized neatly on tables and on the floor. Almost all the hawaladars were bearded and wore sandals and traditional white or gray *kurtas* with beige and black vests. They moved about the courtyard trading with each other, communicating with a sense of purpose, and sometimes carrying handfuls of cash from one pile to another. The exchange dealers in the courtyard were constantly moving and yelling various currency and exchange rates up to the balcony as customers walked in and out from the street.

The customers—often businessmen and those with relatives abroad—wanted to exchange currency—afghanis for dollars, euros for rupees—or send money to places like the United Arab Emirates or Pakistan. The brokers and customers handled money easily and in batches and bundles. In the courtyard, cash was the commodity, and the market was open for business.

As Sharma watched, the hawaladars nodded at him—curious as to who he was and what he wanted. Sharma and his Afghan companion moved out of the courtyard into the offices.

Several brokers sat on rugs in each of the offices, smoking and drinking tea while talking quietly among themselves. It was rare to see a woman. The brokers were polite to Sharma, shaking hands or nodding. Sharma spoke Hindi intentionally, but was candid with them. His friend had also been open—explaining that Sharma was from the United States and working in the government. It would have been hard to fool the brokers, who knew how to read their customers and could sniff out alien behavior. They could read Sharma and knew he was Indian born but raised in the United States. After introductions and much talk about families and home life, they sat comfortably with Sharma and the Afghan official and answered questions about their businesses.

Most of the offices had computers, and almost all of the hawaladars also kept ledgers—long, thin notebooks with hand-drawn lines where they listed their customers' names, debit and credit balances, and exchanges with other dealers. The entries were all numbered, and there were different ledgers for different dealers, for different geographic areas, and for particular regular customers. Like methodical accountants, these men did not do anything haphazardly. Keeping track of their money and their transactions was their business.

Sharma spent most of his time during this visit with the union boss for the Kandahar Exchange. He was treated to a full tutorial on the workings of the hawala system both inside and outside of Afghanistan, learning about the well-established, trusted network of brokers who formed part of the union; the connection between the money-service businesses, the money exchanges, and retail customers and businesses; and the codes of conduct used to self-police the system and expel rogue brokers. Almost all of the brokers were not only dealing with money but facilitating trade within Afghanistan and across borders. The union boss explained that there were numerous money-trading centers throughout the city, with multiple mobile units representing four or five dealers each. The mobile units used cars and vans carrying cash in multiple currencies, allowing the brokers to meet demand and delivery needs. They were like traveling ATMs.

After his day at the market, Sharma walked back to the Afghan Finance Ministry and then to the US embassy compound. After just one lesson, he had a deeper appreciation for how the hawaladars worked and for the importance of the hawala system to the Afghan economy. In an out-briefing with US Ambassador Zal Khalizaid, US Agency for International Development (AID) representatives, and others from the embassy, Sharma suggested that the US government find a way of using the hawaladar network more directly and aggressively—not only to leverage its reach, but also to gain greater insights into how the system worked and to build trust with the brokers and the hawaladar union. The AID officials were instantly dismissive of the idea, citing US policy to build up and rely on the formal financial system in Afghanistan. Though they were correct that it was important to build up the formal banking system and to institutionalize practices such as direct deposit of salaries, which would curb corruption, it was equally crucial to take the realities of financial relations in Afghanistan into account. This was something that nongovernmental organizations (NGOs) and security companies doing work in Afghanistan already realized—they were utilizing hawalas every day.

After Sharma returned to Washington and we discussed his impressions, we decided that we needed to leverage the hawaladar unions more directly to self-regulate the system and isolate rogue actors. Official regulation and enforcement pressure could help shape the environment, but it would be the hawaladars themselves who would know their customers, sniff out suspicious transactions, and become the gatekeepers to the hawala system. Meanwhile, we would also benefit from putting more eyes and ears on the hawala system.

The solution did not lie in attempting to destroy the hawala system, but in using the system itself to monitor and isolate rogue behavior. Overt regulation would not solve the front-end problem of the use of the hawala system by terrorists and drug traffickers to evade scrutiny. There was just too much profit and tainted money in the system to stop these money flows cold. We needed to find ways of co-opting the hawaladars so that they would do the work themselves of policing their own system. This would become our strategic approach.

We had to refine our approach in more ways than one. The campaign against terrorist financing had continued throughout 2003, with the strategy and processes we had put in place in the early days after 9/11 continuing to yield results. But we had learned some important lessons in the first two years. It was time to refine and sharpen the use of Treasury's tools.

In the first instance, we were beginning to recognize that some of our initiatives were having unintended consequences. We knew that our efforts to secure the formal financial system in fact not only made hawalas more vulnerable for abuse but underscored terrorist groups' use of cash couriers to move money across borders. Terrorists, not surprisingly, turned out to be much like drug traffickers and organized crime figures, at least in one respect: in response to greater scrutiny from banks and formal financial institutions, they resorted to the most basic forms of money movement, including men and women carrying satchels and briefcases full of cash as they traveled. We had seen evidence that Al Qaeda was relying more and more on trusted couriers to move money, understanding that the organization was now more exposed by using banks and charities to get money from the Arabian Gulf and Europe to South Asia. We also knew that customs officials at borders and ports of entry and exit were susceptible to bribes, which made it even more difficult for us to detect and stop this type of money flow. While Sharma continued traveling to Afghanistan in an attempt to make inroads with the hawaladars, we needed to find a new strategy to head off the system of couriers.

We turned our focus to finding chokepoints. If we could check those carrying cash for Al Qaeda, we could disrupt their ability to move money from donors to operatives. Not only that, but stopping suspect cash couriers could provide us with a window into the evolving terrorist network and their dependencies and locations. At a minimum, putting pressure on the courier system would inject some valuable risk and uncertainty into Al Qaeda's use of couriers around the world. We applied a three-pronged strategy.

First, we needed to establish the importance of monitoring and checking the inflow and outflow of cash globally. We did not want to stop the flow of this kind of capital around the world, but we needed the international community to focus on the use of reporting requirements and enforcement operations to catch illegal cash smuggling. For instance, in the United States, it is not illegal to move cash or other monetary instruments in and out of the country. It is, however, mandatory to declare amounts larger than $10,000 when moving these sums across borders. For these amounts, travelers coming into or going out of the country are required to fill out a Customs form called a Report of International Transportation of Currency or Monetary Instruments. The United States has demonstrated over the years that you can target narcotics-related cash couriers at major airports that are hubs for international travelers without stifling the legitimate flow of money in whatever form.

In theory, targeting suspect cash couriers should not have been difficult. Cash couriers are not new or unique to terrorism, and the lost tax and customs revenue for undeclared movements of cash should incentivize governments to be vigilant. Even so, the prospect of adding another layer of regulation onto the anti-money-laundering system was not welcome, especially as countries were still grappling with the new requirements for banking and nonbanking financial institutions that had been put into place after 9/11.

Nevertheless, something needed to be done. I tasked Paul Der-Garabedian, a veteran anti-money-laundering expert who understood how to pull the levers of the international system, with developing the framework for an international standard. He worked methodically with law enforcement, customs and border agencies, and regulators around the world to develop "typologies" of how terrorists had used cash couriers in the past as well as "methodologies" for stopping them in the future.[5] With these typologies and methodologies as a starting point, we could move toward a new FATF Special Recommendation that would obligate members of the FATF and FATF regional-style bodies and the rest of the world to put detection and enforcement structures into place to stop the illicit movement of cash across borders. And once this requirement was in place, jurisdictions like Hong Kong began to pass laws, implement reporting requirements, and put systems in place to track the physical movement of cash in and through their ports of entry and exit.

Second, while we moved on developing these requirements, we needed to help train and impel foreign law-enforcement and customs officials. They would need to enforce their own laws and international requirements. In many cases, laws to catch illegal movements of cash already existed, but were not being enforced. In other cases, customs officials had poor training or lacked any political backing to begin checking the luggage of travelers who appeared suspicious or failed to declare their possession of cash or monetary instruments. Over time, US Customs officers were dispatched to train their counterparts in other countries at conferences and in key jurisdictions. They focused on operational techniques and practices designed to target high-risk passengers and flights.

Finally, we needed to make sure nothing would hinder our efforts to have a material impact on the movement of illicit capital. It was fine to have the standards in place, laws and procedures adopted, and customs officials trained, but they needed to be directed to have a real-world impact on illicit financial flows. This would become the most frustrating aspect of our cash-courier endeavors. The idea from the start was that customs and border agents would be coordinating and implementing risk assessments for key transit points and at critical travel chokepoints globally. If we could be certain that the major ports of entry and exit in the international travel system were being methodically covered, particularly when it came to high-risk flights and passengers, then we might have a disruptive impact on the flows of cash to Al Qaeda and other terrorist organizations. Looking carefully at potential suspect cash flows on flights from Dubai to Karachi, or London to Islamabad, would be important. At a minimum, as money was seized and names identified, we would gain insights into the flows of cash around the world. We would also, perhaps, disrupt some illicit financial flows and deter others by adding greater risk into the system. In the best-case scenario, we would have found another way to squeeze an Al Qaeda money channel—and might even nab some Al Qaeda couriers.

To do this, we had to enlist transit points where illicit and terrorist financing was likely to flow. This meant including not only important chokepoints such as Dubai, Doha, and Istanbul, through which terrorist operatives would travel, but also important crossroads such as London, Frankfurt, and Hong Kong, through which terrorist funding might flow. Getting American security officials—Customs or otherwise—into the relevant countries to help train and then coordinate operations was a sensitive and difficult project. Many countries did not want to create new security requirements that would slow the movement of passengers and tourists through busy airports. The United Arab Emirates and numerous other countries were sensitive—with good reason—to having any American presence at the point of interaction with passengers. Others, such as Qatar, were just not interested at all. The key, however, to giving greater strategic effect to targeted inspections and the new cash-courier requirements was to create a global net focused on important chokepoints and coordinated operations based on the experts' best estimates of suspect movements of cash.

Through persistent efforts, such operations were put into place over the years, but never to the full extent that we had envisioned. In several locations, the program had an impact, and some seizures did occur. For example, Egyptian authorities would catch Hamas officials and couriers moving suitcases of cash across the Rafah border crossing because Hamas bank accounts had been shuttered.

In August 2003, British authorities at Heathrow Airport noticed a suspicious individual who was flying from London to Damascus. His name was Abdurahman Muhammad Alamoudi, a naturalized American citizen. Born in Eritrea in 1952, and a graduate of Cairo University in 1975, Alamoudi had already attracted law-enforcement attention in the United States after September 11. He had long been a prominent member of the Muslim community in the United States and abroad. He was the founder of the American Muslim Council (AMC), where he served as executive director and was on the board of directors. He was also the founder of the American Muslim Foundation (AMF), where he served as president.[6] Moreover, Alamoudi was involved with the SAAR Foundation and the Success Foundation,[7] which had been the subject of intense investigation under Treasury's Operation Green Quest and from the US Attorney's Office in the Eastern District of Virginia.

When British officials opened Alamoudi's suitcase, they found $340,000 in cash. When asked about the money, Alamoudi claimed it was the proceeds of a fundraising venture for AMF and had come from the Islamic Call Society, a Libyan group. British authorities also found Alamoudi in possession of two passports from the United States and one from Yemen. Examination of these passports exposed Alamoudi's frequent travel to Libya in 2002 and 2003, with stays as long as five days, in violation of US travel restrictions to states sponsoring terrorism.[8] Alamoudi had deliberately attempted to conceal his travel to Libya, Lebanon, Syria, Yemen, and Egypt in earlier conversations with customs officers.[9] When questioned further, he admitted that he had traveled to Tripoli multiple times to arrange the donation for AMF. All of this was extremely fishy. As investigators began to dig, they began to uncover a major geopolitical plot, with Alamoudi sitting in the middle as the moneyman and choreographer.

The intelligence community believed the Islamic Call Society to be an agency of the Libyan government, founded by Muammar el-Qaddafi in part to serve as a terrorist fundraising and support front.[10] The investigation of Alamoudi's accounts disclosed wire transfers ($5,000 in December 1999) and checks ($2,000 in November 2000) from the Libyan Mission to the United Nations to Alamoudi, ostensibly sent as donations to the AMF. Alamoudi also sought reimbursement for travel expenses of $7,000 from the same source in August 2001.[11] He used four US bank accounts to launder Libyan money back to the United States, and he had other bank accounts in Riyadh and Zurich. Additional funding came from Alamoudi's five wealthy brothers in Saudi Arabia, who had sent him more than $550,000 to assist with his overall activities.[12] None of this money was disclosed on tax returns—nor did his tax returns disclose his bank accounts in Riyadh and Zurich.[13]

Alamoudi's funding ties exposed his involvement in an elaborate Libyan plot to assassinate Saudi Crown Prince Abdullah. Between Qaddafi and the Saudi monarchy there was a long-standing animosity, which periodically revealed itself in harsh comments at Arab League summit meetings. However, attempting to kill the Saudi leader was a far cry from anything that had been seen in the past between the two nations. Paid by the Libyan regime to coordinate the plot, Alamoudi had recruited assassins for the plot by introducing Libyans and Saudis in London, and he had facilitated the transfer of Libyan funds to dissidents who were to carry out the plan.[14] Being caught red-handed with a briefcase full of cash at Heathrow put a stop to the scheme.

British and American security and customs officials coordinated the investigation and the next steps. On September 28, 2003, Alamoudi was allowed to return to the United States and was detained upon reentry at Dulles International Airport in Northern Virginia. He was charged with violation of the International Economic Emergency Powers Act (IEEPA), executive orders, and Libyan Sanctions Regulations, as well as with the misuse of a passport and interactions with state sponsors of terrorism.[15] The affidavit submitted by the United States for the case outlined Alamoudi's connections to an extensive terrorist financing network that was part of a broader scheme to conceal wire transfers and transactions abroad from immigration, customs, and law-enforcement officials.[16]

Alamoudi had been an influential figure in the American Muslim community and had interacted officially with both the Clinton and Bush administrations.[17] He had engaged in spreading goodwill for the US State Department, traveling frequently to Muslim countries on America's behalf (and on taxpayer expense) during the 1990s. He had also founded the Muslim chaplaincy program for the US military.[18]

Yet Alamoudi's views and connections had been suspect all along. In a 2000 speech given at Lafayette Park in Washington, DC, Alamoudi cried, "We are all supporters of Hamas. . . . I am also a supporter of Hezbollah." He expressed similar opinions in newspaper interviews.[19] Other allegations against Alamoudi included significant funding ties to Al Qaeda operatives and business relations with men and organizations later designated as terrorists and fronts.[20] The money trail had exposed Alamoudi as more than just a suspect individual with terrorist sympathies. It had put him at the heart of a major international assassination plot that could have had major geopolitical impact.

Alamoudi pled guilty to charges of violating IEEPA, making false statements in his application for naturalization, and concealing his transactions with Libya and his foreign bank accounts from the Internal Revenue Service. He forfeited the $910,000 he had gained from his involvement in the Libyan scheme and was sentenced to twenty-three years in jail, but, as part of the plea agreement, was not charged directly in the failed assassination plot.[21]

Even with these successes, we never had a magic, demonstrable moment when a key Al Qaeda courier was caught with cash in an airport terminal. We had to hope that the random checks at airports would at a minimum make it riskier for Al Qaeda to try to move money across borders in suitcases and satchels.

The halawa and courier systems weren't our only targets by 2003. Our department continued to employ terrorist financing designations as a potent weapon. The trouble was that, almost two years after 9/11, targets were becoming harder to find. The low-hanging fruit had already been picked, and our enemies were beginning to adapt to the global pressure on their financial networks. Within the US government, the sense of urgency that characterized the post-9/11 period was beginning to wane. O'Neill's 80/20 rule had given way to a cautious demand for 100 percent surety of any action, given the perceived legal, diplomatic, and intelligence costs of public designations. Adding to this was a growing concern in the international community about the aggressive use of asset freezes to disrupt fundraising networks—especially when those affected had no direct link to acts of terror and there was no clear path to get out from under the sanctions.

We needed to leverage our authority—and the designation process—more precisely for long-term strategic impact against the terrorist movement, and we needed to expand the international efforts to account for how Al Qaeda and related groups were adapting to the pressure we had put on them. We needed to find and go after terrorism's most deep-pocketed donors.

At the Treasury Department, we realized early on that while actual suicide bombers might not be deterrable at the point of detonating an explosive, the financiers could be. For many of the financial backers of terrorist organizations, fighting a holy war was not their day job. They were often successful businesspeople with one foot in the legitimate financial and commercial world and another in the world of violent global jihad. Supporting terrorist causes was in line with their sense of religious obligation—and often seen as a form of *zakhat* (charity). Al Qaeda and those who stoked support for the terrorist movement with religious rulings (*fatwas*) and exhortation would often make the point that if a person could not join the physical jihad himself, then he had an obligation to support it financially.

We thought then that our strategies and tools should be directed at both stopping those who were currently investing in Osama bin Laden's movement and deterring future donors for Al Qaeda's cause. Deterrence of the financial supporters would be a driving principle for Treasury's efforts. Part of this strategy was demonstrating that any money spent to support Al Qaeda would be pouring money down a rat hole for a losing cause. No one wants to back a losing horse—especially if it also meant putting their livelihoods at risk. Much of this strategy required ensuring that such financiers understood there would be a dangerous, direct cost to them and their financial futures if they continued to finance these activities. And this threat to their commercial and financial legitimacy could

impact their decision making—making it easier for them to slow or
end their wire transfers and donations to Al Qaeda.

We proceeded by targeting key financiers with our financial
tools—freezing the assets of those designated as well as of the entities and companies they owned or controlled. We fence-ringed
those identified so that others—banks, business partners, and
investors—would quarantine these individuals from the legitimate
commercial and financial worlds. The effect would be a form of
forced divestment conducted by the private actors themselves for
fear of being tainted by the association with a designated terrorist
supporter and affected by the consequences to their reputations and
business interests. We wanted to demonstrate that those who were
willing to cast their lot with Al Qaeda were going to have to forfeit
their wealth and access to a legitimate financial future. We wanted
to make Al Qaeda radioactive to the financiers.

The Al Qaeda operatives did not exist in a vacuum. They relied
on an entire system and support structure. The financial networks
and the money were essential to their ability to operate and for the
movement to survive in the long term. That support structure was
made up of different types of actors, with varying motivations and
vulnerabilities. For the financiers—who often were not as ideologi-
cally committed to the cause as the terrorists themselves—money
was a factor, and they valued their bank accounts and businesses.
They wanted and needed to continue to do business across borders.
Thus, we could find ways of altering the decision making of those
donors, suppliers, and supporters who would value their ability to
continue to do business. If their access to the legitimate commercial
and financial systems were blocked, we reasoned, then they might
reduce their support, desist for a time, or never provide support
again. Any of these would be good outcomes.

This theory became an important driver of our strategy. We
wanted to impact the variety of networks necessary for Al Qaeda to
survive and succeed—from deep-pocket donors to smuggling networks and counterfeiters who were willing to assist Al Qaeda for

profit. This approach would also inform how we thought about engaging the clerical establishment—we had to "delegitimate" terrorists and show that there was no moral or theological justification for terror or the use of weapons of mass destruction. There were some, such as Samantha Ravich, a senior staffer for Vice President Cheney, who were thinking creatively about how to deter communities that might support terrorist causes—for example, by building awareness of the global and local economic impacts of a nuclear attack on the United States.

In 2006, well after I arrived at the White House, we took this a step further and began to look at designating terrorist ideologues—those who attempt to provide ideological and theological justification for terrorism but often sit comfortably beyond the reach of legal strictures in legitimate societies, where freedom of speech often allows the advocacy of murder. For this work I relied on Todd Hinnen, a brilliant lawyer and former computer crimes prosecutor who was sensitive to the balance between First Amendment rights and the need to clamp down on material support to terrorism. I had recruited Hinnen, a close friend of mine and a former Harvard Law School classmate, who looked like he belonged on the cover of *GQ* magazine, into the National Security Council with me to ensure that our counter-terrorist-financing efforts were tied directly to our broader strategies and policies—both globally and in the war theaters. Hinnen would later become a chief legal adviser to Senator Joe Biden and acting assistant attorney general in the national security division for the Obama Justice Department.

This project took on additional importance, with our counterterrorism strategy beginning to focus more heavily and directly on the ideological undercurrents and threats from Al Qaeda and its adherents. After the international community adopted a UN resolution in September 2006, driven by British Prime Minister Tony Blair, to highlight the dangers of radical ideology to the incitement to violence, we launched the effort in earnest to designate known terrorist ideologues who were also providing material support to Al Qaeda and related terrorist movements.

At the top of this target list were two Scandinavian ideologues: Mohammed Moumou and Mullah Krekar. Moumou and Krekar had long lived in the safety and comfort of Sweden and Norway, respectively, and were known to advocate the violent causes of Muslims around the world. But they were more than just cheerleaders for Islamist terrorism. They had deep operational connections with Kurdish and Iraqi terrorist organizations and supported Al Qaeda's cause directly, sending money, materiel, and new recruits to fight in Iraq.

Krekar, also known as Najmuddin Faraj Ahmad, was a well-known extremist who, in December 2001, founded the Kurdish terrorist group Ansar al-Islam (AI), now known as Ansar al-Sunnah (AS), and served as AI's first leader. From the comfort of Norway, he managed a full range of terrorist activities and exhorted others to violence, supplying religious justifications for murder. In a 2004 interview, Krekar supported holy war in Iraq and identified targets, stating, "Not just the officers, but also the civilians who help the Americans. If anyone so much as fetches them a glass of water, he can be killed. . . . Everyone is a target. If an aid organization gives the Americans as much as a glass of water, they will become a target." By the spring of 2005, Krekar had founded a nongovernmental organization with branches throughout Europe that he used to send money into Iraq and to recruit operatives into AS. He would leave Scandinavia for fundraising trips to Germany and route funds through contacts in Bulgaria.[22]

Krekar was doing more than orchestrating financing from Europe into Iraq. He would also travel to Iraqi Kurdish areas to organize militant activities, establishing two terrorist sniper teams in 2005 and recruiting numerous combatants.

Moumou, a Moroccan national who had gained Swedish citizenship, was a long-standing extremist with ties to terrorism going back to the mid-1990s, when he traveled to Afghanistan to participate in the Al Qaeda–run Khalden terrorist training camp. Moumou kept his Al Qaeda ties to the global network and became the leader of an extremist group in Stockholm centered on the Brandbergen Mosque, known as an extremist hotbed by security services around the world. Moumou would become Abu Mus'ab al-Zarqawi's representative in Europe, with some reports indicating that he was responsible for helping Zarqawi with his chemical and biological weapons ambitions. Zarqawi, a Jordanian, was the leader of Al Qaeda in Iraq.

Krekar and Moumou were well-known characters in the world of violent extremism, but they had been allowed to operate under the veil of legitimate political advocacy because they had not violated any domestic laws in Norway and Sweden. They had avoided extradition elsewhere based on human rights grounds. They were also opposing America's invasion in Iraq, which was a position that matched the opinion of many. The designations were a way of highlighting their misdeeds—not their words—and stopping their activity. It was also a way of making the Blair-led Security Council resolution tangible.

Hinnen ran the interagency terrorist financing work and drove the back-and-forth of the internal debates of the designation process. Justice lawyers were worried that we were overstepping the First Amendment, while State and Treasury lawyers were concerned that we were expanding the use of targeted sanctions beyond what was intended or wise. These were important debates, but they delayed the action for weeks despite our pushing—with lawyers wrangling over the scope of the designations and how we expressed the reasons we were targeting these individuals. There was no question that Krekar and Moumou should be subject to our designation authorities, but there was angst about highlighting their speech as part of our targeting rationale.

We eventually worked out the right language, and the 100 percent surety rule remained intact—with some other targets falling by the wayside. By the time we announced the designations on December 7, 2006, Moumou had left Sweden and traveled to Iraq;

he later became the number-two leader of Al Qaeda in Iraq when Abu Mus'ab al-Zarqawi was killed by US forces. Moumou relied on his historical ties and specialized in recruiting foreign fighters, especially from Europe. Eventually, he, too, was tracked down by US counterterrorism forces and killed, as Al Qaeda in Iraq was pressured and its leadership hunted in 2007 and 2008. Krekar remained in Norway under constant scrutiny from security services and the media—falling prey to the increased attention to temper his activities. He had also become the target of a comedienne, who approached Krekar on stage in 2005 while he was preaching and proceeded to pick him up and put him down—a mocking and belittling gesture. Krekar had lost his standing and was in the public's crosshairs. In March 2012, Krekar was convicted by an Oslo court of threatening public officials and other Muslims—who he felt had lost their faith—and sentenced to five years in prison.[23]

Money has a way of creating connections and relationships of convenience. Beyond the designation process, by 2003 our Treasury team recognized that we needed to expand our use of targeted sanctions and financial pressure to impact the growing nexus between international criminal activity and terrorism. In many ways, Treasury's powers and influence were most effective when they were focused on illicit financial activity and individuals who relied on the global commercial system.

I knew that we could have a dramatic impact by isolating transnational criminals and financial facilitators of concern. Global criminals doing business needed banks and access to accounts and money—and wanted to preserve their ability to do business. They played the game for profit. We could affect that dynamic directly with designations that would both isolate them from the financial system and deter others from following the example of global businessmen who were willing to dabble in gray markets and illicit financing. So we directed our analysts and authorities at key criminal underworld figures who could give global reach and capacities—funding, logistics, or arms—to rogue regimes, criminals, and terrorist organizations. These would become our next fixed targets for financial isolation.

The first on our financial hit list was Dawood Ibrahim. Ibrahim, a notorious Indian crime lord, represented the nightmare scenario of the allegiance between powerful international organized crime and terror. We needed to put an international spotlight on him.

Ibrahim, standing at five foot six inches, was born December 26, 1955, the son of a police constable. He launched his criminal career as a gangster in the South Asian criminal underworld on the streets of Mumbai, India. He made money initially by controlling and selling pirated Bollywood films. He built his strength on the legend of his ruthlessness and on the back of his smuggling operations in India, Pakistan, and the United Arab Emirates.

By the 1980s, he had built a smuggling empire—known as "Company D"—that reached from South Asia and the Middle East to Europe and Asia. Company D expanded to include a wide network of narcotics traffickers, money launderers, and smugglers. He became known as one of the major international crime bosses—wielding power across continents. Ibrahim could get anyone or anything in and out of most countries illegally and with ease. He would do it for a price and for profit.

Dawood Ibrahim—sometimes known as Sheikh Dawood Hassan—was not just a notorious international crime boss. He demonstrated a willingness to help Al Qaeda and financed and supported Lashkar-e-Taiba (LT)—the Pakistan-based terrorist organization focused on the liberation of Kashmir—against his home country. His help to LT became manifest in the 1993 Mumbai serial bombings facilitated by Company D's illicit network.

On March 12, 1993, a powerful bomb exploded in the basement of the Bombay Stock Exchange, killing 50 people in the high-rise above. The blast was followed thirty minutes later by a series of blasts throughout the city. Over more than three hours, thirteen additional bombs detonated, killing 257 people and injuring more than 700. The attacks followed the 1992–1993 anti-Muslim pogroms in India and were regarded as retaliation by violent Islamic extremists.

Ibrahim's network, which had helped to launch these devastating attacks, had direct ties to Pakistani militants and the Pakistani intelligence services, notably the Inter-Services Intelligence Directorate (ISI). Ibrahim fled to Pakistan following mounting international pressure amid investigations and accusations from the Indian government about his complicity in these and other attacks—along with attempts to destabilize the Indian government.

He has remained in his villa in Karachi ever since—protected from international reach. He has also remained active and dangerous. Ibrahim has been a primary financier of the narcotics trade in Afghanistan and maintained close ties to Al Qaeda's senior ranks. In the 1990s, he was sponsored and protected by the Taliban when he traveled to Afghanistan. Most disturbingly, Osama bin Laden and Al Qaeda relied on Ibrahim's smuggling routes, with reports that a financial arrangement had been made for bin Laden to be able to use the routes and elements of the network to move men and materiel for Al Qaeda safely through the Middle East and South Asia.

Ibrahim may not have been a classic Al Qaeda jihadist, but he was a most dangerous facilitator. And he was the kind of target we needed to isolate financially. On October 16, 2003, we designated Ibrahim, sending messages out to banks and our foreign counterparts around the world to do whatever was possible to identify and freeze Ibrahim's assets. When we designated him, I laid out what the action meant to our strategy: "This designation signals our commitment to identifying and attacking the financial ties between the criminal underworld and terrorism. We are calling on the international community to stop the flow of dirty money that kills. For the Ibrahim syndicate, the business of terrorism forms part of their larger criminal enterprise, which must be dismantled."

Our actions helped to isolate Ibrahim, but he remained protected by the Pakistani government, and the Indian extradition request lay unanswered. When the attacks on Mumbai were launched in November 2008, and we were managing the fallout from the White House, my thoughts fell directly on Ibrahim and Company D. I knew he may have been involved—and would certainly be implicated by the Indian government. When the Indians laid out their list of most-wanted figures—the men they wanted to be handed over by the Pakistanis—Ibrahim topped the list. He remains in Karachi—isolated, but active still.

We next turned our sights on the Tri-Border Area of South America (TBA), where Brazil, Argentina, and Paraguay meet near the beautiful Iguazu Falls. This major trading zone is also where Hezbollah had found a permissive and lucrative environment for trading and smuggling to raise and move money. Assad Ahmad Barakat was Hezbollah's treasurer for the region as well as deputy to Hezbollah financial director Ali Kazan and the primary liaison in the TBA for Hezbollah's secretary general, Sheikh Hassan Nasrallah.

Barakat ran a string of import-export businesses in the TBA that relied on counterfeit goods and over and under-invoicing to make profits. These activities also acted as cover for the movement of people, money, and information tied to Hezbollah. We identified Casa Apollo and Barakat Import Export Ltd., specifically, because we had information that Barakat used each for Hezbollah's purposes. Casa Apollo was an electronics wholesale store that served as a cover for Hezbollah fundraising and intelligence operations. Barakat Import Export was used as a front as well—it had been used, for example, in a bank fraud scheme to raise money for Hezbollah in Lebanon. Barakat ran a counterfeit currency ring and was also known to extort Lebanese businessmen in the Tri-Border Area for funding for Hezbollah, often threatening to put their relatives in Lebanon on a "Hezbollah blacklist" if quotas were not paid.

Funds were then bundled and wired or carried back to Lebanon for use by the Hezbollah leadership. Barakat would also collect information for Hezbollah—for example, he tracked the activities and travel of Arabs in the TBA. He would return at least once a year to meet with Nasrallah and other Hezbollah brass. There were also reports from the Paraguayan press that Barakat had provided funding to Osama bin Laden through real-estate deals and fraud.

Our intelligence and law-enforcement services had been working since 2001, with their counterparts in the region, to monitor and shut down Barakat's operation—with some effect. Part of this was helping the countries in the region think about using financial criminal activity and tax evasion as the basis for action. Much like the arrest and prosecution of Al Capone in the United States, Barakat would be arrested in June 2002 by Brazil on the basis of a Paraguayan charge of tax evasion and criminal association. He served six years in prison and was released in 2009.

Even though Barakat was in prison, we wanted to isolate his financial dealings and make clear what we knew about him and his network. We used the designation to spell out the US government's bill of particulars—in public for the world to see. When we designated Barakat on June 10, 2004, I noted the following in the Treasury press release: "Today, we are designating a key terrorist financier in South America who has used every financial crime in the book, including his businesses, to generate funding for Hizballah. From counterfeiting to extortion, this Hizballah sympathizer committed financial crimes and utilized front companies to underwrite terror."

The designation not only isolated Barakat's businesses, but laid bare how Hezbollah was using its presence in the TBA to raise and move money and operatives. It also forced the governments in the region to take note—undercutting the argument often heard by the Brazilian government that there was no terrorist financing happening in the TBA. The designation brought the debate into the open and put financial institutions—especially in Latin America—on notice that the United States was watching the financial flows in the region that were tied to terrorism. This focus was not just on Al Qaeda but also on groups like Hezbollah whose activities were threatening the integrity of the financial system. Finally, this action was part of a concerted public diplomacy campaign to demonstrate that Hezbollah ("Party of God") was not a pious resistance movement in southern Lebanon but a global criminal enterprise whose leaders had no qualms about committing financial crimes to line their pockets.

That focus would continue for years, with the revelation of a major Hezbollah money-laundering and drug-trafficking operation in 2011. In that operation, Hezbollah relied on the Lebanese Canadian Bank (LCB) to launder millions of dollars of drug proceeds from South America through the United States and then on to Lebanon. Hezbollah also used the trade in used cars—relying on a network of used-car dealers in the United States—to raise millions that were then sent onward to Hezbollah in Beirut.

We then turned our financial targeting attention to Viktor Bout, the "Merchant of Death." Viktor Bout reigned as the world's most notorious arms merchant for nearly two decades. Following the end of the Cold War, Bout built a global network of arms dealers, air transport and logistics experts, and customers in conflict zones worldwide. Born January 13, 1967, in the Soviet Union, Bout served in the Russian military and attended the esteemed Russian Military Institute of Foreign Languages. He is rumored to have received intelligence training while serving in the Russian Air Force.[24]

As centrifugal forces tore the Soviet empire apart, the vast arsenals of the Red Army went to the highest bidder. At the age of twenty-five, Bout—recognizing a business opportunity—purchased three Soviet Antonov cargo jets to fly loads of illicit arms and other goods to conflict zones. Bout's business quickly spread to include a large fleet of aircraft that serviced clients in conflicts ranging from Afghanistan, Pakistan, and North Korea to Liberia, Colombia, the Democratic Republic of the Congo, Angola, Iraq, and elsewhere.

Bout's network was unique in that it took care of all aspects of the illicit arms process for the customer: the weapons themselves;

transportation of the cargo, regardless of location or international restrictions on arms transfers; and money-laundering mechanisms to disguise the purchases. If a customer could pay, Bout would deliver arms of any sort—from AK-47s to attack helicopters—to anywhere in the world, without care for international restrictions or moral boundaries.

Bout became such a prominent fixture in the global airlift market to war zones that he was frequently contracted for services by both sides of a conflict. In the 1990s, he provided arms to the Taliban as well as to the Northern Alliance that was fighting Taliban rule in Afghanistan. He also supported UN peacekeeping missions, delivering food and other supplies, while selling arms to the forces involved in hostilities. His services were well known and profitable—but they were also evading sanctions and fueling horrendously violent conflicts in many places. Following the US invasion of Iraq, Bout's shell companies flew supplies to US contractors working to reconstruct the country despite the fact that Bout had been officially designated by the Treasury Department years earlier.

Bout began to draw the attention of Western intelligence and law-enforcement organizations in the mid-1990s as his network increasingly supplied forces in the primary conflict zones across the world. To ensure that his fleet of aircraft had access to airspace anywhere in the world, Bout had registered the aircraft within a broad series of shell companies. The first of these shell companies, and Bout's flagship entity, Air Cess, was founded in Belgium in 1996 and later registered in Monrovia, Liberia, with Bout at the head. Other firms included Centrafrican Airlines, San Air General Trading, Air Bas, CET Aviation, Irbis, Transavia Travel, and Santa Cruz Imperial. San Air and Centrafrican played key roles in supplying arms to Charles Taylor's regime in Liberia and the Sierra Leone rebel group, the Revolutionary United Front (RUF). The RUF became infamous for its brutality when its militant members began chopping off hands and limbs with machetes—some of their victims had done nothing more than vote in elections.[25]

The air-transport operation was based in Sharjah, a lesser known emirate of the United Arab Emirates. There, Bout operated a fleet of cargo aircraft able to fly weapons, ammunition, and other goods from Europe and the former Soviet bloc countries to conflict zones throughout the Middle East, South Asia, and Africa. In 2002, the Belgian government requested an Interpol "red notice" against Bout on charges of money laundering through his Belgian front company. Again, the pathway to one of the world's most notorious criminals was through his money.

At the Treasury Department, we knew we had the ability to impact Bout's global operations by drawing scrutiny to his business empire and financial operations—including his illicit financial operations. Andreas Morgener, an analyst at the Office of Foreign Assets Control, mapped out what was known about Bout's international businesses. OFAC hooked Treasury's jurisdiction into Bout because he had been a major supplier for Charles Taylor during the Liberian and Sierra Leone civil wars. Taylor was subject to US and European sanctions, and OFAC ran a Liberia program. That was the hook.

Morgener was methodical—detailing with evidentiary packages and a wall-map-sized chart where Bout had a web of bases and operations. In briefings with Morgener and his boss, Bob McBrien, we decided to move forward to expose Bout's air fleet and empire. We could do this under US law because of Bout's prior support to Charles Taylor in violation of UN sanctions. This would also give our action amplified international effect. On April 26, 2005, the US Treasury Department designated Viktor Bout and thirty companies associated with him. The designations froze Bout's assets and increased the pressure on his global network as it continued to operate throughout the world.

When I arrived at the White House and saw the Drug Enforcement Administration's growing capabilities and willingness to go after international criminals, it became apparent that Bout was a prime target. In 2006, DEA officials briefed me on a series of sensitive national security–related cases they were building. They were

attempting to lure and prosecute a full range of international criminals tied to the drug trade and terrorism. Congress had given the
agency greater license to develop these cases in 2006 with the passage of a law that made it a federal crime to engage in drug trafficking tied to terrorism. In that meeting, I asked DEA Chief of
Operations Mike Braun and the assembled DEA leadership whether
they had ever considered looking at Victor Bout, because of the
dangers he presented across the board to national security. They had
not, and they grew quite intrigued as I told them about Bout's history and what he represented in the world of international criminality. He was an all-purpose force multiplier for international
conflict—for states, rogues, and criminals alike—who was willing to
play with anyone willing to pay his price. Bout had also been
untouchable, protected in Russia despite arrest warrants from
Europe and the intelligence and law-enforcement agencies from
around the world that were trying to hunt him down.

Within seven months of that meeting, the DEA had its hooks
into Bout and was in the process of luring him to a lucrative deal
that would take him out of Russia. The DEA agents posed as representatives of the Revolutionary Armed Forces of Colombia (FARC),
a Colombian terrorist insurgency, and requested the purchase of
antiaircraft missiles and other weapons to attack US and Colombian
forces. Bout was fooled by the undercover operatives and traveled
to Thailand on March 6, 2008, to seal the multimillion-dollar deal
with the rebel representatives. I had received a message at the
White House noting that Bout had taken the bait and that the DEA
would be waiting for him. Bout arrived at Bangkok's Sofitel Silom
Hotel, and the undercover operatives taped him agreeing to the
arrangement. He expressed his desire to ally with the FARC to hit
the Americans. At the right moment, Thai police and US law-
enforcement officers swarmed the premises and took him into custody along with two of his bodyguards. At first, Bout seemed
stunned. Then he simply said, "The game is over."

The US sting finally gave teeth to what the US government had long wanted, the ability to prosecute Viktor Bout in a US court of law. By agreeing to sell weapons to FARC, Bout had committed a cardinal sin in the post-9/11 world: agreeing to provide weapons to a designated foreign terrorist organization. This violation allowed the United States to petition the government of Thailand to extradite Bout back to the United States for prosecution on his charges.

It did not happen right away, but on November 16, 2010, the Thai government finally extradited him after nearly two years of legal fighting between Bout, the Russian government, and US officials. The Russian government, Bout's longtime patron and protector, sought to prevent the extradition, and the Russian effort included bribing Thai officials and witnesses to scuttle the extradition hearing.

Bout was later found guilty in the Southern District of New York—where the highest-profile terrorism cases have been brought—of several federal charges, including providing material support for a designated terrorist organization, conspiring to kill Americans and American officers, and conspiring to acquire antiaircraft missiles. On April 5, 2012, he was sentenced to twenty-five years in US federal prison.

The DEA agents had spoken to Viktor Bout once he was in custody in New York. When asked about the effects of the US Treasury designations and pressure on his business, Bout reportedly told the agents that the actions had cost him $6 billion.[26] His business empire had been squeezed, and his quest for the next big deal had presented itself. Greed led Bout out of Moscow and into the DEA's trap.

In the post-9/11 world, we needed to train our sights on the transnational networks and lynchpins that could provide terrorist groups and organized crime with the resources and reach to threaten American security interests. We had started to find ways to do just this with the leading edge of Treasury and enforcement tools. The question remained whether we would survive to continue this work.

Part II

A New Paradigm

5

BLOWFISH

On June 6, 2002, Jimmy Gurulé and I, along with our Treasury spokesperson, Tasia Scolinos, landed in Rome. We had made significant progress in finding and choking off avenues of funding for Al Qaeda around the world. Even so, we had come to Europe to discuss new strategies we could take with our foreign government counterparts against the funding of terrorist groups. We were set to meet with Italian finance ministry and central bank officials along with prosecutors and investigators who had begun to apply their well-tested anti-Mafia tactics and techniques against Al Qaeda and its support networks running through Italy and Europe.

Italian investigators had learned a great deal from dealing with the Mafia's financial underworld throughout Europe, and we hoped to draw from their experience. Working in cooperation with the Italian authorities, we hoped to target the network of financial and material support for violent Islamist extremists that had long crisscrossed Italy through North African immigrant communities and cities like Milan. But news from Washington would interrupt our trip and call into question the future of our work.

My cellphone rang just as I was standing up and collecting my things to deplane. It was the Treasury front office, wanting to speak with Jimmy Gurulé. From the curt tone, I could already tell that this was likely not going to be good news.

There had been hints of what was coming. Since early 2002, there had been ongoing discussions in the White House about creating a Department of Homeland Security (DHS). In light of the perceived failures to prevent the 9/11 attacks, Congress was pushing for a consolidation of border agencies and intelligence functions to improve coordination. The idea was that it would be more natural for a single department to juggle everything from tracking of terrorist travel across borders and protection of ports and critical infrastructure to coordination of crisis and consequence management in response to terrorist attacks. There were approximately one hundred agencies scattered throughout different departments of government that touched on homeland security in some way, and Congress sought for them to be unified under a single umbrella.

The Bush administration had been resistant to this idea at first, not wanting to create a new and unnecessary bureaucracy. By early 2002, however, the White House was beginning to explore how such a department might be formed. The effort quickly met with fierce resistance across the government—with departments and agencies defending their existing structures and raising red flags—some legitimate and others purposefully imagined—about shifting entire agencies into a massive, hodgepodge department.

From such a reorganization, the Treasury Department stood to lose its Office of Enforcement. Treasury's enforcement role had been born in the early days of the republic as a way of ensuring the collection and payment of tax revenues—whether from tariffs at ports or the modern-day income tax. This is why the Customs Service; the Bureau of Alcohol, Tobacco, and Firearms (ATF); the Internal Revenue Service–Criminal Investigation Division (IRS-CID); and, eventually, the Federal Law Enforcement Training Center (FLETC) were Treasury enforcement bodies. The Secret Service was made part of the Treasury Department out of the need to preserve and regulate the integrity of US currency and the financial system.

Treasury represented about 40 percent of federal law enforcement. The Treasury agencies had jurisdiction over financial crimes

enforcement—from money laundering and trade-related violations to tax evasion and the counterfeiting of currency. Treasury
"1811s" (the technical term in federal law enforcement for gun-
toting special agents) were considered some of the best financial
investigators in the world. From the legendary Eliot Ness to the
Customs agents who exposed the most important international
bank fraud schemes in the modern era, such as the BCCI scandal,
Treasury agents were considered the best financial forensic investigators in the country.

Even so, the enforcement element of Treasury was traditionally
seen as the little brother to the 800-pound gorilla of federal law
enforcement, the FBI, and the Department of Justice, whose primary mission was to enforce the law. "Enforcement," as the office
and its "guns and badges" had been known for decades, always
seemed an odd fit at the Treasury Department. Treasury was better
known for setting fiscal policy, issuing debt, printing money, and
housing the government's best economists and tax experts. Secretaries of the treasury throughout history were titans of the financial,
economic, and commercial worlds and always struggled with the
enforcement dimensions of Treasury's mission. Most wondered
what the Treasury Department was doing mixed up in the law-
enforcement world. The department's guns and badges had a long,
storied history, but in the modern era, they seemed to play second
fiddle to the Department of Justice.

To design the new Department of Homeland Security, Homeland
Security Adviser Tom Ridge and White House Deputy Chief of Staff
Joe Hagin assigned a small, tight-knit group of advisers within the
White House. The effort would take on a clandestine quality to
avoid bureaucratic backlash, with Hagin controlling access to the
deliberations. One of the defining principles of this effort was to
carve deep and wide into the existing governmental structures to
pull whole agencies and departments into a new configuration. If an
agency or bureau had an essential function that would fit into the
new department's mission, then it would be moved wholesale. No

time or political capital would be spent on carving out or leaving behind missions within agencies or bureaus that had little or nothing to do with homeland security. An approach that attempted to surgically remove parts of agencies would prove too messy and difficult to manage, with every agency arguing for some aspect of their work or resources to be held back or split from the "homeland security" functions.

Though it was likely the easiest and most realistic way of executing such a massive shift in government—the largest change in the US bureaucracy since World War II—it would also create problems for the new department. The result was an assemblage of disparate agencies with multiple missions kluged together, some of which had little to do with the concepts of homeland security as originally envisioned.

As feared, Enforcement at Treasury was doomed. Secretary O'Neill, like many of his predecessors—but not, most notably, like the first secretary of the treasury, Alexander Hamilton—was extremely uncomfortable with the law-enforcement mission at the Treasury Department. It was not wholly clear to O'Neill why Customs, the Secret Service, and the Bureau of Alcohol, Tobacco, and Firearms were Treasury agencies. He felt that the Treasury itself had become a hodgepodge repository of law-enforcement agencies.

To O'Neill, the transfer of these Treasury enforcement arms to the new Homeland Security Department was a welcome rationalization of functions and did not present a bureaucratic threat. In meetings with President Bush, O'Neill argued for the wholesale transfer of Treasury enforcement assets, along with the transfer of the FBI to the new department. The former Alcoa executive took great pride in disrupting long-standing practices and structures to create new efficiencies. O'Neill had made a stir within the Treasury when he first arrived because he had wanted to tear down historic walls to make room for open offices full of cubicles. For him, the law-enforcement mission could be handed away without affecting much of what Treasury did at its core—and he could be rid of potential headaches that seemed to fit neither the Treasury Department nor his job description. If the president intended to create a new Department of Homeland Security, O'Neill wanted to help push it into existence.

In the spring of 2002, White House Chief of Staff Andrew Card called O'Neill to explain that most of Treasury's enforcement assets—including Customs, the Secret Service, and FLETC—were to be transferred to a new department. O'Neill could have objected strenuously or threatened to go up to Capitol Hill to mount resistance to the administration's plans, but he did not. Instead, he agreed wholeheartedly with the move, asked Card why the transfer did not also include ATF, and requested that ATF be transferred to the new department as well. Card obliged, and the ATF special agents would soon be on their way to the Department of Justice. Without much of a debate or discussion, the change was made, and Treasury Enforcement would be no more.

When we arrived at the baggage claim in Rome, I gave Gurulé the cellphone as we waited by the carousel to pick up our bags. Gurulé called back to Treasury, expecting bad news, and that's exactly what he got. With a deep sense of shock and resignation, he said in his deep voice, "Not the Secret Service, too!" For some time during the deliberations over the new department, there had been a question as to whether the Secret Service—whose mission of presidential protection and security seemed to fit into the new Homeland Security Department—would be ripped out of the Treasury. With its financial investigatory role focusing on counterfeiting and its increasing role in investigating cyber-crimes, however, the Service was not a neat fit in the new DHS. It also was not clear that the Secret Service leadership wanted to be disturbed with a bureaucratic move to an unknown, and likely chaotic, department. The Secret Service would have preferred to be left alone in its historical home, the Treasury.

For those of us in Treasury, it was as though we were losing the crown jewel of our enforcement agencies—the one with the most prestige and romantic appeal. Even for those unaffiliated with the enforcement mission at Treasury, the Secret Service was an enormous point of pride. It is a law-enforcement agency known traditionally for its meticulous professionalism and its refined expertise—qualities its agents bring to everything they do, from the president's protective detail to sharp shooting, behavioral analysis, cyber and financial forensics, and counterfeit currency detection. Without the Secret Service, the Treasury simply would no longer be in the law-enforcement business. If the Secret Service were moved along with Customs, ATF, and FLETC, the only "guns and badges" left at Treasury would be IRS criminal investigators, who focused almost exclusively on tax-related crimes.

Gurulé put down the phone and confirmed that a massive organization would rip away the Secret Service along with most of the other Treasury guns and badges. With the transfer of the vast majority of Treasury's enforcement agencies, the Treasury was denuded of some of its most important, historical, and identifiable assets. The raison d'être of the Office of Enforcement was gone. Gurulé felt as if he had been kicked in the stomach.

The Office of Enforcement would soon be dismantled, and Gurulé would be out of a job. Treasury's centuries-long enforcement identity was coming to an end. This decision forever changed the shape of government and the nature of the Treasury Department. There was nothing to do but deal with the consequences.

From my hotel room in Rome very late that night, I watched the president's speech announcing the creation of the new Department of Homeland Security. I understood the impetus behind the new department. Still, I had major reservations about whether the experiment would work and whether its mission could be defined distinctly from what other departments and agencies were doing.

My main concern was with what would happen to Treasury and to the mission we had begun to forge. We had launched an effort to attack terrorist and illicit finance in the most aggressive way the United States had ever seen. The Treasury tools we were using to protect the integrity of the international financial system had little to do with the guns and badges that were being transferred. The parts of Treasury that would remain—the Office of Foreign Assets Control (OFAC), the Financial Crimes Enforcement Network (Fin-CEN), the Treasury Executive Office for Asset Forfeiture (TEOAF), and IRS-CID—still had a leading role to play in implementing sanctions, working with banks to uncover suspicious activities, and ensuring that the international community remained focused on securing the financial system against abuse.

Yet I feared that the perception would be quite different. With the most visible and powerful of the Treasury agencies moving to a new department focused on preventing terrorism, the common assumption within the executive branch and on Capitol Hill would very likely be that the Treasury was no longer relevant on terrorism and other national security issues. Those agencies with the core resources and ability were now going to be located at the Department of Homeland Security and the Department of Justice.

The fact was that there was a deep and pervasive misunderstanding of what Treasury was actually doing to combat terrorist financing. Contributing to this misperception, Treasury officials had relied too much over the years on the prestige and weight of the Customs Service and the Secret Service to justify and define the Treasury Department's place at the US government's law-enforcement and national security table. With these agencies gone, there would appear to be little reason for Treasury to be involved or to have a seat at the table on such issues. The prevailing opinion would be that Treasury should restrict itself to taxes, financial regulation, fiscal policy, and issuing commemorative coins. I worried that our innovative campaign would be buried and lost in the massive reorganization.

After we returned from Italy, Secretary O'Neill held a meeting with the Enforcement leadership in the secretary of the treasury's ornate conference room. Gurulé, who had yet to speak to the secretary about this decision, was in attendance, along with the leadership of the Treasury enforcement agencies he oversaw. Sitting at the huge mahogany table were Judge Rob Bonner, customs commissioner; Brian Stafford, director of the Secret Service; Brad Buckles, ATF director; Ralph Basham, director of FLETC; Jim Sloan, head of Fin-CEN; Rick Newcomb, OFAC director; and Eric Hample, acting director of TEOAF. These were serious figures in the law-enforcement and regulatory community, and they had come to this meeting expecting to hear a plan of transition, an explanation of what was next, or at least a pep talk.

Instead, what they heard was a discussion of issues they felt were mundane and irrelevant. Secretary O'Neill, who had done much in the private sector to improve workplace safety, and had made it a priority to protect workers throughout the Treasury Department, started every meeting with a review of workplace safety. He focused his time with his Enforcement leadership that day on safety improvements at the Treasury. To the Enforcement leaders, he seemed oblivious to the enormous elephant in the room— the very existence of Treasury Enforcement and its centuries of history. Instead, he spent the time talking about the number of workplace hours lost to injuries and accidents on the job and the desire to reduce the number of such instances.

Gurulé and the others were incredulous. They looked at each other dumbfounded and deeply disappointed. Gurulé and the chief of staff, Tim Adams, locked eyes. Adams looked apologetic and in disbelief. After a short while, the secretary was pulled out of the meeting for a call from the White House. When he returned, O'Neill apologized, indicated that he had to leave for another meeting, and left the room for good. That was it. The Treasury Enforcement leadership sat together stunned at what had just transpired. Gurulé approached Adams to complain about the lack of sensitivity and leadership for the thousands of employees to be affected by this decision. Adams agreed and could only meekly apologize for his boss. Everyone walked away in shock.

This was the start of the oddest, most confusing, and difficult period of my professional life. The Office of Enforcement would melt away. Most of its leadership left government while the employees were being transferred to the new department. There was no certainty as to what would happen next, who would be transferred to DHS or Justice, and whether any functions would be left at Treasury to drive the policies and strategies tied to our promising counter-terrorist-financing and financial-crimes activities. We feared the worst—that bureaucratic reshuffling would inadvertently lead the United States to lose its most potent financial weapons.

Soon after the announcement, Tim Adams talked to me about staying on board. He asked me if I would remain to run and oversee Treasury's remaining offices and functions related to the counter-terrorist-financing and anti-money-laundering programs, asset forfeiture, the Bank Secrecy Act, and sanctions enforcement. Adams, and his deputy Jeff Kupfer, made clear to me that they needed and wanted me to stay on to run what was left of Treasury. David Aufhauser made a case to me for staying as well—saying he would not stay unless I did, too. I appreciated the flattery, but I remained confused. It was not clear to me what or who would be left to run. Frankly, they weren't sure either.

In meetings with Treasury management staff, we would assemble and listen to assurances that there was nothing to worry about, but we received few specific answers to our questions. In one such meeting, the remaining Enforcement staff members present felt so uncomfortable that they stood along the walls of the conference room, unwilling to sit at the table. The assistant secretary for management at the time who was leading the meeting ended the painful gathering by sliding small American flag pins wrapped in plastic across the conference table to those standing in the room. It felt to me like we were watching a carnival ringmaster callously rolling dice with the future of the people in the room. I could not bear to look my colleagues in the eye. It was awful.

Perhaps the worst indignities the staff suffered involved sitting through farewell ceremonies. These were mixtures of back-slapping award ceremonies for departing officials and veritable institutional wakes for the departments and agencies departing the Treasury Department. While officials left and new offices made their way into the Department of Homeland Security, the career staff, which was still working every day, had to listen to speech after speech. They felt adrift and alone, not knowing what was to come.

What made this period even worse was that Treasury continued to do the same indispensable counterterrorism work it had been doing since 9/11. The demands remained high. Via designations of terrorist financiers, meetings in major capitals around the world, and private-sector outreach, we were achieving a great deal. Yet this work seemed oddly and frustratingly divorced from any decisions being made and discussions had about the transfer of Treasury's assets to the new Department of Homeland Security.

By the end of the summer of 2002, the shock of the initial announcement and the crumbling of Treasury Enforcement around us gave way to my determination to stay and lead what would be left. I was angry that there had been so little thought as to how this transition would occur and how it might impact Treasury's current and future mission. But I was determined to keep a team alive that could manage and drive the core issues that mattered most to Treasury.

More importantly, I saw an opportunity. In conversation after conversation with my closest colleagues, I grew convinced that this was a moment of potential rebirth. Treasury had been stripped at last to its core strengths. With the transfer of almost all of Treasury's law-enforcement resources and the end of Treasury Enforcement, we would no longer be considered a lesser law-enforcement agency. We could instead focus on what made Treasury powerful, valuable, and unique.

Treasury was the only department in the US government that was responsible for the management and integrity of the domestic and international financial system. Because of this, Treasury has special powers within the US legal system—to regulate, sanction, and determine access to the financial system. It can require banks and nonbank financial institutions to do specific things—from freezing assets, closing accounts, and blocking wire transfers to enforcing regulations requiring reporting of information about certain types of clients, transactions, and correspondent bank accounts.

Treasury maintains and has access to unique financial data about flows of funds within the international financial and commercial system—from tax information to currency transaction reports. The USA PATRIOT Act expanded all of this, making due diligence and know-your-customer rules ubiquitous and increasing the amount of financial intelligence being produced by the private sector.

Treasury also operates in a unique community of key financial actors in the world. The Treasury is the primary interlocutor with finance ministries, central banks, financial regulators, the IMF, the World Bank, regional development banks, and the CEOs and compliance offices of the major banks in the United States and around the world. Those channels are not about classic government conversations or interactions between diplomats. This is the arena of the technocrats and managers of the international financial system, who see themselves as part of an exclusive club with control over the levers of money flows around the world.

Beyond legal and regulatory authorities, financial information, and unique channels, the United States Treasury has the power of suasion—the ability to convince and coerce behavior simply based on what it says and does. Banks, foreign finance ministries, and central banks well beyond our borders care about what the US Treasury declares. Financial advisories, communiqués, or the talking points of a Treasury official are scrutinized and credited in the decision making of financial actors around the world. Treasury's word can move markets.

Treasury sits uniquely at the epicenter of the flows of money around the world in the world's most powerful economy. With this comes real power and influence. Overshadowed by its law-enforcement mission, Treasury's real strength to protect the integrity of the financial system had long remained untapped and unrecognized. And our work pursuing terror financing was only scratching the surface of what the department was capable of doing.

Treasury had unique authorities, information, relationships, and influence. No other department or agency could claim these, and no other department or agency could isolate the flows of illicit financing around the world. As we rebuilt Treasury, this was our refrain—and we repeated it like a mantra in memos, briefings, hearings, and speeches. Though we had lost about 95 percent of our personnel and budget, we could start anew to prove Treasury's relevance to national security in a more fundamental and lasting way. This then became my mission—to redefine Treasury's role, demonstrate its unique powers, and prove its growing and essential relevance to national security.

In November 2002, on the plane returning from the G20 meetings in New Delhi with Secretary O'Neill and Tim Adams, I sketched out a vision for the office on a legal pad. With my notes in hand, I sat down with Secretary O'Neill while in flight and laid out for him what I had in mind—our priorities and what we would need to do to maintain momentum on our core responsibilities. For an hour we sat face to face eating tortilla chips as we flew over the Atlantic. He understood my vision, asked the right questions about what we would have to jettison, and was completely on board and supportive with the plans. It was the best I had felt in months, and I felt reassured that we could make this work. Later in the flight, Adams and I spoke about the office. Adams looked me in the eye and asked if I was ready to take on the role, knowing I would be given a skeleton crew at best. I said yes. I was excited and now on a mission.

And then the rug was pulled out from under my feet again. A few days after we landed, the president fired Paul O'Neill. I was in shock—not that he was fired, but that we had lost a secretary who had started to become an advocate. O'Neill had finally gotten it—

and understood why Treasury—in its stripped-down form—was important to national security. And now he was gone. Institutionally, Treasury was reeling.

But I couldn't look back. My first mission was to save what I could of our resources. The Office of Management and Budget (OMB) and the White House were demanding significant cuts, and I knew holding onto any personnel would be a struggle.

There could not be a sense that we had missed a beat or that our focus was distracted. Substantively, we had to stay ahead of our country's enemies as they raised and moved money around the world and evaded financial controls and sanctions. We would need to continue and build on what we had been doing since 9/11. We had to continue our work in capitals around the world and flex our muscles within the government. The number of people I could keep—and which people I could keep—would become the most critical questions for the survival of the office and our efforts. Treasury was blessed with some of the world's top experts on money laundering and illicit finance, and we needed to keep as many of them as possible.

I focused on keeping a core team at Treasury that would allow me to oversee the work of the remaining agencies while driving the initiatives that would allow us to demonstrate our value. This proved to be a painful process. I had negotiated to keep six employees, so we had to winnow the remaining staff to keep the essential members. We assembled a team that was willing and able to do everything from take out the trash to meet with prime ministers. More importantly, I needed true believers in our mission.

First and foremost, I had to keep Danny Glaser, the anti-money-laundering expert and lawyer who was the head of the US delegation to the Financial Action Task Force. Without Danny, the office could not function, and despite his initial doubts, he shared my vision of what the office could be. I also needed Chip Poncy, my best friend from college, who had just left his previous job at my urging and had already demonstrated that he had an intellect deep enough to disentangle arcane issues, the charisma to get along with anyone, and the seeming energy of five men. Chip, who would become the head of the US delegation to the FATF, quickly became my confidant and is now recognized as one of the world's great anti-money-laundering experts. I also needed to keep Jeff Ross, the seasoned southern anti-money-laundering prosecutor who had deep experience with the financial criminal world and whose inter-agency and law-enforcement credentials would buttress Treasury's seat at any table.

With three slots left, we had some very hard decisions to make. The deputy chief of staff, Jeff Kupfer, who would later become the deputy secretary of energy, and I began interviews for those who wanted to stay. We interviewed and kept Nan Donnells, who was a Caribbean money-laundering expert and the lynchpin to our international engagement with the FATF and all its regional bodies. We also kept Anne Wallwork, a Wellesley graduate and Yale-trained lawyer who could be frenetic and scattered but was capable of diving hard and deep on myriad issues.

In the final interview, Paul DerGarabedian, a long-standing Treasury expert and well-known figure in the Asian anti-money-laundering world, walked in, having just returned from leading an evaluation of the anti-money-laundering system in the Philippines. DerGarabedian, who often rode a motorcycle onto Treasury's Hamilton Place, was known for being a blunt, tough character. On this occasion, he was in rare form—confident and on cue. Der-Garabedian sat down for the interview wearing jeans and a wrinkled shirt, having just landed from a twenty-one-hour journey from Asia. He sat back and plopped the front page of a newspaper from the Philippines onto the coffee table. It had been published that day. On the front page, top fold, DerGarabedian was pictured amid a crowd of media representatives in Manila—as if he were a celebrity. The article reported on his verdict on the country's anti-money-laundering system. He proceeded to explain to us why he should be kept on board, especially given the growing importance of Asia to the financial system. It was illustrative of the situation we were in. Our work was front-page news around the world, but we were struggling to prove our relevance to our own government. Der-Garabedian would stay.

We lost some very important experts in this process, to the benefit of DHS. Most were people I considered friends. Unfortunately, I had no choice. Later we would add three important members to the team: Linda Johnson, Traci Sanders, and Charlie Ott. Johnson was a Treasury institution who knew everyone in the building and how to get what we needed. She wore her pepper gray hair closely cropped to her head, and she could convert someone instantly with a smile or chill them with a steely glare. There was no one better at filtering bluster from what was important. Johnson would serve as the administrative assistant for the office while I was at Treasury, and was an indispensable guardian angel both while I was at Treasury and later when I was at the White House. Sanders, a redheaded, no-nonsense lawyer, would prove to have a pragmatic, steady hand. She knew how budget games were played and would help to manage the office through the challenging times to come. Ott was a grizzled veteran who had a pulse on European anti-money-laundering circles. He would allow us to retain a presence and face in the Central European and Central Asian anti-money-laundering groups.

We had to fight an internal battle to explain our relevance. This was not just about bodies (known in budget parlance as "FTEs," or full-time equivalents), but also about office space. I would have to fight to ensure that our office remained in the main Treasury building and would not be confined to its basement forever. In meeting after meeting, we campaigned for the office to rise after renovations to its traditional fourth-floor perch just above the secretary's office.

The budget and management professionals, both in the White House and at the Treasury, had no clue what we did substantively. They would not be the only ones. As we would make good on our mission in the years to come, many members of the government misunderstood our work and the import of the tools we were using.

For now, we had to do whatever we could to overcome the increasingly common assumption that Treasury's role in national security and law-enforcement issues should fade away with the transfer of the guns and badges of the old Treasury Enforcement team to DHS.

At times, it felt as if sharks smelled blood in the water and were trying to pick at the remnants of Treasury Enforcement. Rumors were swirling that OFAC would soon find its way to the State Department, while the Justice Department was making a case for the transfer of FinCEN and TEOAF. Gurulé had advised me to leave, as he returned to teach at Notre Dame Law School, since Treasury was facing an uncertain and likely disastrous period. I knew we had to do a better job of defending our office outside of Treasury. In many ways, we had to become like a blowfish. We needed to demonstrate our continued relevance on the issues that mattered to us and the rest of the government. We needed to look bigger than we were to defend our remaining staff and the important work we had to do against the bureaucratic sharks circling us daily.

This problem was especially evident at one of the meetings that Ross and I attended around this time. Hosted by the National Security Council, the meeting was about drug trafficking abroad, and we wanted to offer some ideas about the strategy being discussed. We also wanted to be at the table because we knew the Treasury Department could offer important input on sanctions, financial intelligence, and financial investigatory work. I had anticipated some resistance to our attendance, and we got a frontal assault. The first hand up in the meeting was from the long-standing deputy assistant attorney general, Mary Lee Warren, who oversaw the Department of Justice's anti-money-laundering, narcotics, and asset-forfeiture operations. Warren, a seasoned veteran who had been Ross's boss at the Department of Justice, was a well-respected prosecutor and player in the interagency world of Washington. She politely asked the NSC chair of the meeting, without looking my way, why Treasury was in the meeting at all, since we had lost all our enforcement assets. I grinned—happy to accept an invitation to explain our relevance—and I did so with glee. Treasury had tools, authorities, and resources to bring to bear on this problem, as we had for decades and would continue to have in the future. We could isolate rogue actors—drug traffickers, terrorists, or proliferators—unlike any other entity in the government, and we could do it globally and systemically. The Treasury Department worried about the integrity of the financial system, and our tools allowed the US government to have reach beyond its shores to affect the bottom line of our enemies. We also had ideas and potential actions to put on the table. We weren't going anywhere.

By 2003, we had established who would be staying, where we would be sitting, and the chain of command. I would be reporting to the deputy secretary, but in the absence of someone in that role, I would report to David Aufhauser, the general counsel. Sam Bodman came on board as deputy secretary in early 2004. Jeff Ross insisted that we call the new office an "Executive Office" to connote its close connection to the secretary. He also hammered into me the need to inject the term "financial crime," in addition to "terrorist financing," to ensure that our broad mandate was clear on first blush. This produced the name "Executive Office of Terrorist Financing and Financial Crimes" (EOTF/FC). It was not an easy acronym to roll off the tongue, but it made it clear what we were about—and it wouldn't be long before it would change again. Sam Bodman would often make fun of the name. O'Neill's successor, Secretary John Snow, endorsed the office, and he announced its creation on March 3, 2003.

In my mind, the clock was already ticking. We had limited time to demonstrate why we were relevant—within the Treasury, to the White House and Capitol Hill, and to the rest of the world. As Deputy Secretary Bodman would later say, "the Treasury Department is easy to explain. It's all about money." That's what we were about, clearly and simply—except that we were all about stopping bad money from infecting the financial system and isolating those who would abuse the system to the detriment of the United States. This would become our guiding principle and our mission.

We had to demonstrate quickly why Treasury was uniquely positioned to impact illicit flows of funds and to isolate rogue financial
actors from the international financial system. My principal goal
was to resurrect Treasury—not as a chief law-enforcement body, but
as a pivotal national security player. I wanted to ensure that Treasury tools and powers were considered essential in any strategy of
national security import. We would need to use all our tools, contacts, and suasion in concert to make this happen. It was necessary
for the country, important for international security, and critical for
the Treasury Department. The problem was that no one realized this
except for a small group of us—those of us who had been left
behind to rebuild Treasury.

6

BAD BANKS

If our new office was going to survive, I knew that we had to push the envelope. We needed to amplify what the Treasury Department was already doing to isolate rogue financial behavior. We needed to demonstrate why Treasury was indispensable to US national security. And the clock was ticking for us to prove our relevance.

In early 2003, after the dust from the creation of the Department of Homeland Security settled, I gathered our small team in a conference room near my office on the second floor of the Treasury building to discuss a new project—one that would define a new form of financial pressure and eventually reshape the Treasury's role in US national security.

Bad banks would be our target. There are always banks engaged in fraudulent and criminal activity someplace in the world—some evading local laws and defrauding customers and investors. More interesting, for our purposes, were the banks serving rogue regimes and terrorist networks. They not only provide criminals access to banking services, but also allow for illicit financial activity to be hidden from the view of regulators, law enforcement, and intelligence services. BCCI, as an all-purpose bank for criminals and suspected terrorists of all stripes, was one such bank that we had seen in the past.

We knew there were banks around the world that were serving as nodes of illicit financing. At these banks, the dirty money of suspect actors mixed to access the international financial system. For any criminal or terrorist enterprise to have global and sustained reach, it must have a financial infrastructure to raise, hide, and move money to its operatives and operations. Banks are the most convenient and important of these nodes of the financial system and are critical to nefarious networks. Where there is a transnational network of concern, there is likely also a bank or family of banks serving as a facilitator of that activity. These bad banks would fall into our crosshairs, and the rest of the banking world would necessarily take notice.

If anything fell under Treasury's classic purview, it was the activities of banks like BCCI. If we could target and bring down bad banks, we not only would cripple the ability of criminal and international rogue actors to access the international financial system, but would be sending a clear message to others in the banking world that they would not be immune from our glare, especially if they did business with the same or similar nefarious actors. I decided to call our campaign the "Bad Bank Initiative."

And our focus on banks would pay off, largely thanks to a recent change in the culture of finance. Before 9/11, even though banks were subject to laws, regulations, and sanctions, they were mostly passive players. They were unlikely to scrutinize their customers and their possible criminality closely unless they were doing so to fulfill government mandates or investigations. When they were caught doing business with criminals or sanctioned regimes, they were subject to costly fines—but even so, this was at times viewed as a cost of doing business.

After 9/11, this attitude shifted. Banks were no longer willing to get caught facilitating terrorist financing. They feared permitting even a whiff of illicit financial activity into their systems. Just a week after 9/11, with the acrid smell of burning steel still in the air, bank leaders and executives met with Treasury representatives, the FBI, and Justice Department officials in a skyscraper in downtown New York to pledge their support and offer any assistance necessary to respond to the 9/11 tragedy. This spirit of cooperation would pervade for months, manifesting itself in myriad ways.

But there was more than patriotism at work. This response ultimately had to do with the banks' bottom lines. Reputational risk was now a central part of a bank's calculus. The CEOs of the major banks in the United States and the rest of the world saw a government investigation or sanction of a bank's operations as detrimental to their ability to do business—especially if it had any hint of terrorism attached to it.

New USA PATRIOT Act provisions required more due diligence about the funds coursing through financial institutions and greater scrutiny of customers opening new accounts or making cross-border transactions. Banks recalibrated their decision making, determined to head off damage to their reputations before it was too late. The industry ramped up compliance systems, hired new internal investigators, and spent hundreds of millions of dollars ensuring that they were not doing business with terrorists or other types of suspect actors. This was a fundamental transformation of how bankers viewed their bottom lines. And they did this with good reason.

President Bush's terrorist financing executive order had opened the door for banks to be branded as terrorist financiers and for their assets to be frozen, even if they had no specific intent to provide material support to known terrorists or terrorist groups. Indeed, we had already targeted a few banks for such designation—and their names were permanently tarnished once they appeared on the sanctions list. Moreover, their operations were scrutinized, and their very existence threatened. Ultimately, banks ran the risk of not only being tarred by the US government but of having their licenses pulled by the US or New York banking authorities—a virtual death sentence. No bank wanted to run the risk of being cut off from the US banking system.

Regulators and prosecutors began to train their eyes on banks and their anti-money-laundering and sanctions compliance. One after another, major banks were subjected to investigations and major fines, making headlines. The effects cascaded in the banking world. On May 10, 2004, the Swiss banking giant UBS agreed to pay a $100 million civil monetary penalty in agreement with the US Federal Reserve and Treasury's Office of Foreign Assets Control for financial facilitation of transactions with Cuba, Libya, Iran, and Yugoslavia during the periods when those countries fell under strict US sanctions.

On August 17, 2005, the Office of the Comptroller of the Currency (OCC) and the Financial Crimes Enforcement Network (FinCEN) announced a $24 million fine of Arab Bank PLC. Arab Bank was a major financial institution based in the Middle East with assets (as of the end of 2004) totaling $27 billion. The government alleged that Arab Bank was willfully blind to the suspicious nature of transactions connected to individuals and companies subject to asset freezes and with ties to terrorism—especially those tied to Palestinian groups. Transactions coursing through the bank's New York operations were particularly thrown into question. The civil monetary fine was preceded by an OCC enforcement action requiring Arab Bank to shut down wire transfers through New York and forcing the bank to convert its New York branch to an uninsured agency office. Arab Bank's ability to operate through the United States on its own was clipped, and it would be further hounded by lawsuits lodged by victims of terrorism.

Other examples would follow, with growing fines against banks as the US Treasury, myriad banking regulators, and prosecutors grew less forgiving of lax anti-money-laundering practices and purposeful stripping of information on bank and wire transfers to hide the origins and destination of funds.

One example in particular demonstrates the dynamics that would define the landscape for our Bad Bank Initiative. On May 13, 2004, the Treasury rocked the Washington banking establishment. That day, the OCC and FinCEN fined Riggs Banks in Washington, DC, $25 million for willful violations of suspicious activity and currency transaction reporting and for failing to establish an adequate anti-money-laundering system. Long a revered Washington institution, Riggs served a long list of distinguished clients, especially foreign diplomats and embassies. After 9/11, Riggs had come under the microscope in part because of its lax anti-money-laundering controls related to foreign embassy and diplomatic accounts—and, in particular, its banking relationship with Saudi Arabia and Equatorial Guinea. Riggs had built the premier banking business, catering to embassies and foreign diplomats and officials. In other times, the traditional winks and nods of private bankers with privileged customers would have been accepted as the norm. Unfortunately for Riggs, these were not normal times.

Regulators found that the bank maintained inadequate controls and checks on high-risk accounts and transactions, had failed to file suspicious activity reports on $98 million worth of transactions, and had failed to detect and report suspicious cash, monetary instrument, and wire activity by the Saudi and Equatorial Guinean governments.

The $25 million fine may have seemed small relative to Riggs' assets, which at that time amounted to approximately $5.8 billion. Nevertheless, it destroyed the bank's reputation and operations. Riggs was forced to close the accounts it held for most of the embassies in Washington. This triggered a crisis as embassies scrambled to find new banks to take their accounts.

Some countries, such as Equatorial Guinea, Saudi Arabia, Sudan, and Angola—often oil rich and nondemocratic ones—struggled to find banks willing to take their business. It was a tense moment. Regardless of tight US sanctions, these countries argued that the Vienna Convention for Consular Affairs requires the United States to provide financial services to all embassies. As soon as the fine was announced and it became apparent that Riggs would be closing all of its embassy bank accounts, we began fielding concerned calls at the Treasury. From our conversations with banking compliance officers, we already knew that banks were not eager to take on these embassy accounts, especially given all the negative press and attention Riggs was receiving and the compliance risks and scrutiny now attendant to holding certain accounts.

The embassies wanted us to order banks to open accounts for them, but the banks sought assurances that they would not be targeted if they took on the banking business of a former Riggs accountholder. Since the US government could neither force banks to take on this business nor guarantee that banks would not be given additional scrutiny, we were in a tight spot.

A crisis was averted after the State Department and Secretary Snow made some reassuring calls to ambassadors and the CEOs of Citibank, JP Morgan Chase, and other big banks. Wary bank executives were reluctant, but ultimately willing, to take on the embassies' business (at a premium, of course).

As Riggs' reputation crumbled, it was forced not only to shed its now-radioactive embassy banking business, but to sell its operations outright. A buyer emerged—PNC Bank out of Pittsburgh—and Riggs was no more. An established Washington institution had been destroyed because of its lax money-laundering controls, a deficiency that looked very suspicious under the post-9/11 regulatory and enforcement spotlight.

The scramble that followed the Riggs fine was not an isolated problem, but a reflection of changes taking place in the banking community. We had realized in 2003 that a new banking ecosystem had emerged. This was now an environment in which banks were acutely sensitive to their reputations and the risks of doing business with suspect individuals and entities under the international regulatory and enforcement microscope. Banks were willing to cut financial and commercial relations with rogue regimes, criminals, and terrorists, given the right conditions. And they were willing to do it on their own.

This new ecosystem also relied on a globalized financial infrastructure. The system connected all international actors—states and nonstates—with its leading node in the United States—New York. New York serves as the most important financial center in the world, and the dollar serves as the global reserve currency and dominant currency for international trade, including oil. The twenty-first-century financial and commercial environment had its own ecosystem that could be leveraged uniquely to American advantage. In this system, the banks were prime movers.

Simple as it was, this strategic revelation was revolutionary. We understood that this shift had already occurred and that we could build strategies around it. We could prompt banks to make decisions to cut off banking relationships, isolating rogues from the international financial system—and we could rely on the business decision-making of the banks themselves to do the heavy lifting. The key to managing the ecosystem was to ensure that illicit and suspect financial behavior continued to be thought of as detrimental to the efficient workings of the international financial system. Rogue and criminal actors needed to be branded by their own illicit activities and isolated by those who wanted to be considered legitimate financial players. With the United States defining those parameters, we had the ability to lock rogue actors out of the system as never before. This would now be our driving paradigm and approach. And Congress had already provided us the ideal tool in Section 311 of the USA PATRIOT Act.

When President Bush signed the Patriot Act on October 26, 2001, the provisions of Title III did not receive close scrutiny by the press. Almost without anyone noticing, it gave the secretary of the treasury, among other things, the ability to designate foreign jurisdictions, institutions, types of accounts, and classes of transactions as "primary money laundering concerns." The Treasury was empowered to impose countermeasures against these primary money-laundering concerns and to compel US financial institutions to take certain specified steps to guard against the possibility of facilitating the financial activity of designated entities. These steps ranged from additional recordkeeping to outright closure of accounts. The secretary of the treasury was also permitted to impose conditions on foreign bank accounts in the United States.

The Treasury did not lack for powerful tools, many of which we had already been utilizing to full effect. The power to freeze the assets of individuals and entities was the nuclear option in Treasury's arsenal. Treasury also had the ability to notify banks and other institutions with public advisories and reports, putting the banking community on notice about specific risks or trends of concern. But Section 311 gave the secretary of the treasury a middle ground. Institutions could be identified as risky from an anti-money-laundering perspective—in essence, a threat to the integrity of the financial system. This definition was wide open, and there would be no need to prove criminal culpability. The broad parameters and relative ambiguity of Section 311 gave it enormous reach in the newly reputation-conscious banking world.

Treasury was now armed with all the weaponry it needed to go to war. We had access to SWIFT data to gather financial intelligence; we had identified the unique contours of the new financial system that would be our battleground; and we now had our stealth financial weapon. With Section 311, we would be able to identify bad banks and label them as "primary money laundering" concerns. We would then apply countermeasures to signal to the banking community how these designated institutions should be treated. In all cases, the secretary of the treasury called for the closure of all correspondent accounts, thereby cutting off access to the US financial system. Where possible, we would coordinate such actions with international partners.

Although we could only directly affect bank activities in the United States, the intended effect would be global. Even though most bad banks had few or marginal dealings in the United States, Section 311 would immediately make them radioactive to reputation-conscious banks worldwide.

The intent of this strategy was to drive the private sector's isolation of these banks, placing the onus on banks to police their own system. It would also place added pressure on the criminals and rogue regimes that were relying on those banks to do business globally. Rather than directly imposing restrictions on these groups, this strategy was designed to cut off these bad actors from the financial system by making them financial pariahs. The banks they were using would be designated, but the activities they were facilitating and the actors involved would fall under the spotlight. Section 311 gave us a tactical tool against specific targets, but it also allowed us a broader mechanism to manage the banking environment by bringing what the Treasury was watching and worried about into the public light.

By 2003, when we met to launch the Bad Bank Initiative, we had already used 311 twice against jurisdictions. The first targets were Ukraine and Nauru, an island nation in the South Pacific. We published the proposed rule to label both of these countries as primary money-laundering concerns on Christmas Day of 2002, responding to a call for "countermeasures" by the FATF, reports that neither financial system was well regulated, and suspicions that they were both deeply compromised by Russian organized crime. Frantic to remove the label, the Ukrainian Parliament, within a month, enacted new anti-money-laundering provisions. Nauruans responded even more quickly. The country moved within days to implement legislation responding to US concerns, and the offshore banks registered in Nauru began to close.

When we took action against Nauru, to some, it seemed like we were merely swatting a fly. But importantly, the Treasury had proven the power of Section 311 to affect not just the designated jurisdiction but all the banks doing business in it. It was a domestic regulatory action with enormous international impact.

I knew what needed to be done and the tool to be applied. Now our small team at Treasury simply had to implement the initiative.

We decided to divide the world into regions and issues of concern in our effort to identify banks that were facilitating multiple types of illicit financing relevant to our national security. In other words, this was not a campaign designed around specific categories

of illicit activity, but instead around nodal banks that were facilitating a range of illicit activities posing a risk to the national security—
those helping transnational organized crime groups, terrorist
organizations, drug traffickers, proliferation, sanctions evasion,
counterfeiting, and/or other types of criminality. Some bad banks
were already evident to us, but we had not yet dug in.

The assignment I gave to my team was simple: find the key
banks or networks of banks that should be targeted because they
were important to transnational illicit financial activity of import to
the United States. Whether it was Southeast Asian drug trafficking,
Caribbean money laundering, Eurasian organized crime interests, or
funding for terrorism, we would need to come up with targets that
would have a demonstration effect on the banking world and
against our enemies.

This initiative had the elegant virtue of accomplishing multiple
strategic goals at once—for the US government, the Treasury, and
our office. In the first instance, it would allow us to highlight and
isolate illicit financial behavior. The banks targeted and their nefarious customers would have trouble doing business efficiently once
we hit them with a 311. A series of these actions would increase the
pressure on banks to police the financial system and to guard
against the kinds of activities we would be identifying. Banks would
not want to touch the radioactive clients and their activities we targeted. We would be doing this with a unique Treasury tool in fur-
therance of a core Treasury goal—to protect the integrity and safety
of the US and international financial system from illicit fund flows.
By doing this strategically and with the right targets, we would
inject Treasury into the heart of major national security debates,
giving policymakers yet another tool around which to devise pressure campaigns and affect actors seemingly beyond US reach. With
the strategic application of our unique new tool, we would prove
the importance, value, and power of the new Treasury.

The team branched out and began its work on this project—
among the dozens of other tasks and trips I had continued to pile on

their workloads. There was enthusiasm for the project, but some trepidation about what we were about to do. Soon after the team was unleashed, however, some targets emerged.

DerGarabedian struck first, identifying two banks in Burma (Myanmar) controlled by a well-known drug-trafficking organization in the Golden Triangle called the United Wa State Army. These were targets with great value because they were banks controlled by a known drug-trafficking organization that were facilitating recognized illicit activity, namely, drug trafficking and money laundering. They were also operating in an under-regulated banking environment run by a military junta already under US sanction. This action could be leveraged as another pressure point against the regime.

We moved quickly. On November 18, 2003, the Treasury Department designated Myanmar May Flower Bank and Asia Wealth Bank for facilitating drug trafficking in Southeast Asia. This 311 was not limited to just the banks—the treasury secretary also designated Burma as a primary money-laundering concern, since the country lacked a basic set of anti-money-laundering laws and regulations.

The country's first response was defiant. On November 21, 2003, the Burmese government issued a statement noting, "The US government has been criticizing and condemning almost every institution in existence in Myanmar, and now is the time and the turn for Myanmar financial institutions to be accused of wrong doing." Even so, Burma responded to US actions by revoking the operating licenses of both designated banks. Then, just two weeks after Treasury's proposed 311 rule was published, the Burmese government announced new money-laundering rules designed to respond to US and other international concerns. Officials made attempts to demonstrate the seriousness of their actions.

The 311 actions had worked—and the Bad Bank Initiative was underway.

Next up was the Commercial Bank of Syria (CBS). Traci Sanders had scoured the classified, law-enforcement, and open-source information to build a case against the Assad regime's all-purpose bank. The timing worked well. The Bush administration was beginning to debate how to implement the Syrian Accountability Act, which President Bush had signed into law on December 12, 2002.

The interagency debates were led by Elliott Abrams, who was in charge of Middle East policy and global democracy issues at the National Security Council, and Deputy Assistant Secretary of State Philo Dibble. I was invited to the meetings at the Eisenhower Executive Office Building as the senior Treasury representative. I sat quietly at first, listening to the debates, which focused on how aggressively to implement the provisions of the act. Much time was spent on what could be done to restrict exports and investments in Syria—with most of the discussion centered on the use of traditional tools to sanction those who were doing business there. One question was whether to restrict the shipment of spare aircraft parts to Syria—they were necessary for Syria's commercial airline fleet but would also likely be used for a different purpose—retrofitting airlines that were being used to transport weapons and military equipment to and from Iran. The options for trying to influence Syrian behavior via this act seemed limited.

I recognized the opportunity to inject 311 into the debate. After listening for some time, I suggested that we could put another tool on the table that would complement the steps required under the act. Section 311 could spotlight the illicit activity and money-laundering problems in the Syrian banking system—and add pressure, and perhaps costs, to their financial transactions. It was clear that most of the people around the table didn't quite understand what 311 was or why it even mattered, but Abrams understood it immediately and wanted to utilize this tool to help give whatever we announced some teeth. I had found an ally in Abrams. We proceeded with the preparation of the 311 package and got it ready for publication.

On May 11, 2004, Treasury designated the Damascus-based Commercial Bank of Syria, along with its subsidiary in Beirut, the Syrian Lebanese Commercial Bank, as primary money-laundering concerns. FinCEN explained that the Commercial Bank of Syria was used by criminals to facilitate or promote money laundering and by the Assad regime to engage in sanctions evasion and terrorist financing. This was an all-purpose bad bank being used by a regime considered to be rogue by the US government. At the same time, President Bush signed an executive order authorizing the Treasury to block the property of certain persons and imposing a ban on exports to Syria.

Shortly after President Bush's announcement, Syrian Prime Minister Muhammad Naji al-Otari said sanctions would "not have any effect on Syria" and called on the United States to "reverse its decision and not provoke problems between the two countries."[1] Nevertheless, Syrian financial officials clearly understood the potential impact and seriousness of this action. Ghassan al-Rifai, the Syrian minister of economy and foreign trade, admitted that US actions would have a "negative impact" on Syria's economy.[2] In spite of their public protestations, the Syrian government wanted to get out from under the 311 action, and quickly. A Syrian delegation came to Treasury to lobby Danny Glaser and me personally, but the only way to undo the 311 would be for Syria to enact anti-money-laundering laws and stop evading sanctions and funding terror. Glaser would later visit Damascus to discuss the 311 action and Syria's need to reform its anti-money-laundering system. With the withdrawal of US Ambassador Margaret Scobey from Damascus in February 2005, the Treasury interactions were some of the last diplomatic face-to-face meetings American officials had with the Assad regime under the Bush administration.

In May 2005, Syria strengthened its existing Anti-Money Laundering Commission, but it wasn't enough. Hawaladars remained unregulated, borders were porous, and corruption was still rampant. It was clear that the Syrian financial officials were handcuffed by the policies of the Assad regime. Despite some desire to cooperate, the Syrians were not prepared to do all that was necessary to lift the 311 rule. We would keep the 311 in place.

We would target other banks as well. Jeff Ross next focused his attention on the First Merchant Bank of the Turkish Republic of Northern Cyprus, which was the subject of intense law-enforcement investigation for its role in facilitating Russian and Turkish organized criminal and narcotics-trafficking activity. On August 24, 2004, the Treasury designated this bank as a primary money-laundering concern under Section 311.

On the same day, the Treasury designated InfoBank in Belarus as an institution of primary money-laundering concern. Anne Wallwork had found a bank that had helped the autocratic regime of Alexander Lukashenko launder money and game the international sanctions regime as well as the Iraqi Oil for Food program. InfoBank provided accounts and lines of credit for transactions with Saddam Hussein and his regime. As with the Burmese banks, this target proved strategically important because it not only exposed a bad bank facilitating a number of illicit activities, but also highlighted the use of the institution by a rogue, autocratic regime for its own profit. This would become part of an ongoing campaign with Europe to pressure and isolate the regime of Lukashenko, the last dictator of Europe. In 2012, the Treasury would use Section 311 against another Belarus-based financial institution—JSC CredexBank—as an institution of primary money-laundering concern.

From 2003 to 2005, the Treasury targeted banks in Burma, Syria, Latvia, Cyprus, and Belarus. Each case demonstrated that designations could spotlight nefarious activities, leading the international financial system to ostracize those institutions. The 311 actions could also be withdrawn if the targeted banks and jurisdictions made necessary changes.[3] These actions also raised the diplomatic stakes with each of the countries involved. The actions were not silver bullets, but they tempered the environment and created a sense in the banking community that something new was afoot.

By 2003, our long-term strategy was becoming clear. For Treasury's new powers to remain effective, we needed to draw clear lines between the legitimate financial world and the rogues who sat outside of it and tried to misuse or circumvent the financial system. This meant expanding the reach of anti-money-laundering and counter-terrorist-financing standards and practices around the world. There were three main elements to this strategy: bringing China and Russia into the anti-money-laundering fold; expanding the reach of anti-money-laundering rules and principles to new parts of the world that now mattered in an era of globalized finance; and empowering and building the capacity of the private sector as the gatekeeper of the financial system. This was the inclusionary complement to the exclusionary strategy of the Bad Bank Initiative.

First, we needed to bring China and Russia into the fold of the leading financial centers to give them a stake in the legitimacy, transparency, and defense of the international financial system. This was already happening naturally as both economies grew and became entangled by commerce and financial arrangements with the rest of the world—including through their banks. This meant that we needed to incorporate both countries into the Financial Action Task Force system deliberately—and make sure that they felt they had a leadership role in maintaining international standards. This would be a difficult and delicate task, because we had to preserve the apolitical and technical nature of FATF's work while giving China and Russia a sense that they were vital members of the club.

With Russia, this was particularly problematic. Russia had been a center of money laundering and illicit financial activity for years, with a banking system unaccustomed to the anti-money-laundering strictures of most of the world. The Financial Action Task Force had blacklisted Russia in 1999 for its lack of anti-money-laundering laws and measures. Organized crime, the global arms trade, corruption at the highest levels, and a willingness to do business with rogue states made the Russian commercial and financial systems a problematic intersection of illicit financial flows.

Russian President Vladimir Putin knew it was important for Russia to remove the money-laundering stain for the future of the Russian economy and for national prestige. This was a symbol of Russia's exclusion from the legitimate financial world, and Putin wanted to return it to legitimacy and power. To deal with this issue, he assigned a close and trusted colleague of his from the early days of his political career in St. Petersburg, Viktor Zubkov. Zubkov was a friendly Russian official with a no-nonsense style and thick, well-groomed hair. He knew he had the backing of Russia's most powerful man, but he also knew he had to deliver. The business of money was a serious and dangerous game in Russia, and it needed to be handled by someone with access and credibility. We knew we could work with Zubkov and that he had the power to make real changes if he determined they were important. We engaged with Russia and Zubkov on several levels, knowing this was an opportunity to bring Russia into the fold.

Ted Greenberg, the garrulous former head of the Department of Justice's anti-money-laundering section, took on the task of working with the Russians in a methodical way to reform their laws and systems to get off the FATF's blacklist. His goal and ours—though it was opposed by some within the US government and the international community—was not only to help Russia rehabilitate itself but to have Russia enter the exclusive club of the key financial jurisdictions that had a responsibility for the anti-money-laundering system. This was an aggressive plan, but one that Greenberg took on with gusto, with frequent trips to Moscow to meet with Zubkov and other Russian officials. Greenberg soon became indispensable to Moscow's entry into the FATF, acting as a veritable guide for Zubkov as well as someone with the cudgel to improve the Russian system. The Russians listened to Greenberg.

When Presidents Bush and Putin ordered that both countries work closely together on counter-terrorist-financing and anti-money-laundering issues, I also started working with Zubkov. We were charged with reporting to both presidents on the steps we were taking to improve cooperation and work together. In 2004, in preparation for one of these reports, I led a US delegation to Moscow, accompanied by Danny Glaser, to meet with Zubkov and his team. We had started to see the Russian government exert more control over the banking sector and impose anti-money-laundering controls where none had existed previously.

It was often hard to tell, however, if Russian law-enforcement raids and arrests were driven by political agendas and oligarchic power plays or were truly attempts to uphold the law. Prosecutions had been used to silence critics and to undercut challenges to power. This had been the history of the Putin era. Mafia-style killings were not infrequent, and organized crime maintained a major stake in being able to house and move money through Russian banks. Even so, it appeared to us that Zubkov and the Russian central bank were beginning to take our concerns seriously, particularly when it came to the money laundering that occurred in unlicensed banks, casinos, and organized crime's financial deals. On the eve of our visit, the Bank of Russia revoked the licenses of two banks, Kredittrrust and Sodbiznesbank, with Russian authorities engaging in a vicious firefight when they raided Sodbiznesbank.

When I met with Zubkov in his Moscow office, he struck me as a serious player who had real reforms in mind. No doubt, he knew that the raids and revoked licenses proved this point. He needed to be responsive to Putin, and I knew this meant he had to be responsive to our concerns. We would meet for all-day meetings—but the most productive sessions came at mealtime, when Zubkov was more comfortable conversing. Over lunch at his favorite Moscow restaurant between delegation meetings, he, Glaser, and I talked about what we could do together. Zubkov was a wonderful host—finding greater pleasure in the open banter of lunchtime—lubricated by several shots of Russian vodka—than in the formal conference room back at his office. I'm a lightweight when it comes to drinking, and after two vodka shots, with more obviously coming, I turned to Glaser to whisper, in some despair, "I can't do this anymore. We have more meetings this afternoon." Glaser whispered to me, "Just eat a lot of bread." One more was my limit, and I stopped trying to match the Zubkov pace.

The "Zarate-Zubkov" reports would lay out concrete steps that the United States and Russia were taking together to counter terrorist financing and money laundering. There was an important convergence of interests on these topics and on bringing Russia's banking system into the camp of legitimate financial systems. Importantly, with Zubkov, we would map out that engagement, which included Russia's eventual inclusion in the FATF, with real reforms and enforcement of anti-money-laundering laws. Russia would also be given a feather in its cap by leading the establishment of an FATF-style regional body, called the Eurasia Group, which would include Belarus, China, Kazakhstan, Kyrgyzstan, and Tajikistan. This would be an important way for Russia to demonstrate that, along with China, it was leading the anti-money-laundering reforms in Central Asia. Zubkov presided over the inauguration of the Eurasia Group in Moscow in October 2004.

Zubkov would continue to press for reforms—with frequent trips to meet with FATF evaluation teams. The Russian central bank would also continue to target the illegal practices of unlicensed banks; it revoked many licenses and enforced new anti-money-laundering controls. In September 2006, two gunmen shot and killed the first deputy chairman of the Bank of Russia, Andrei Kozlov, on the grounds of the Moscow Spartak football club. Kozlov, who had returned to the central bank in 2002, was leading the charge to revoke licenses and investigate banks engaged in money laundering. The week before his death, Kozlov advocated for stiffer criminal penalties for bankers convicted of money laundering.

At the Berlin Plenary meeting of the FATF in June 2003, Russia would be voted into the exclusive FATF membership. This was a major achievement for Greenberg, who had shepherded the Russians through the process and led US engagement, as well as for the German FATF president presiding over this important moment. This was a signature achievement for Viktor Zubkov, who led Russia's delegation to the FATF, and for Putin, who had removed the financial scarlet letter from Russia's reputation and been accepted into the elite anti-money-laundering club in one fell swoop. In September 2007, Putin named Zubkov Russia's prime minister in a "technocratic" pick that surprised much of the world. For those of us who knew Zubkov and the importance of the work he had done for Russia and President Putin, it was an understandable choice. Zubkov remains close to Putin and serves now as his first deputy prime minister.

The work of bringing China into the FATF club was equally important, but delayed. Although the Chinese worked closely with the Russians in the East Asia FATF-style regional body, they were less aggressive in working with the FATF to join the body than the Russians had been. The Chinese had often been reluctant to work with the FATF and its Asia/Pacific Group because of the presence of Taiwan in that body. Hong Kong was a member jurisdiction in the FATF, but China proper remained on the outside. The FATF sent delegations to work with Beijing on passing anti-money-laundering laws and bringing the Chinese banking system up to international standards. For the Chinese and the FATF, the most important group then became the mutual evaluation team of experts, which would pore over Chinese laws, interviewing dozens of Chinese regulators, prosecutors, and officials in order to understand the status of the Chinese system and compare it to the international anti-money-laundering standards. The most important member of that team was Paul DerGarabedian from the US Treasury, who spoke not just for the United States but for the international technical experts sitting in judgment of the Chinese anti-money-laundering system.

On June 28, 2007, the FATF accepted China as a member after years of engagement in a financial diplomatic dance that included Chinese adoption of new laws and practices. For China, this was an important moment. China was joining the ranks of those who stood at the center of the legitimate financial world. As it turned out, it did so on the eve of a financial crisis that would put it even closer to the center of that world. It would also put China at the table as the

FATF developed counter-proliferation-financing standards that would impact its companies and banks directly.

We were also trying to expand the FATF standards and writ into the Middle East and North Africa. Through the FATF and close partners such as the French and British, we worked to establish a Middle East and North Africa (MENA) FATF-style body. This was critical, because we needed the countries in this region to take ownership over the regulation of their financial systems and to find indigenous ways to do it effectively—especially to address terrorist financing risks. We had often heard the complaint that the standards being foisted onto the region were not sensitive to cultural practices or to modes of doing business that were not well adapted to Western models of regulation. This was a way of allowing the region itself to determine how the global anti-money-laundering and counter-terrorist-financing systems could be applied in the region. This was important when trying to decipher how best to interpret sharia law and how its practices dovetailed or diverged from common international anti-money-laundering and counter-terrorist-financing standards. This related not just to the field of Islamic finance but also the application of criminal law for terrorist financing and accounting principles and practices.

Glaser and I traveled to Manama, Bahrain, at the end of November 2004 to attend the inaugural meeting of the MENA FATF. Bahrain, which styles itself as a center of Islamic financing, was pleased to host the meeting and to serve as the headquarters for the new organization. Bahraini Finance Minister Abdullah Saif welcomed the observer countries, including the United States, the United Kingdom, and France, as well as the fourteen member countries: Algeria, Bahrain, Egypt, Jordan, Kuwait, Lebanon, Morocco, Oman, Qatar, Saudi Arabia, Syria, Tunisia, United Arab Emirates, and Yemen. Glaser and I would use the occasion for diplomatic bilaterals with most of the delegations, including the Syrians, as we continued to raise the concerns we had laid out earlier over Section 311. The first MENA FATF president was Dr. Muhammad Baasiri, the head of the Lebanese Financial Intelligence Unit, and the vice president was Mahmoud Abdel Latif of Egypt. The executive secretary was a Saudi official.

The reach of the FATF universe was now established, with regional-style bodies in every corner of the globe—and the two missing global players, Russia and China, in the fold. Only India, which was delaying making improvements in its financial regulatory system and still unwilling to submit to FATF standards and reviews, remained outside the system. In June 2010, India finally joined FATF as its thirty-fourth jurisdiction and took a seat as a rule-maker and judge of international anti-money-laundering, counter-terrorist-financing, and counterproliferation standards.

The expansion of our efforts was not limited to governments. On the contrary, we knew the effectiveness of Treasury tools depended first and foremost on the ability of the private sector—most importantly, the banks—to serve as the gatekeepers of the financial system. It was not enough for American or Western European banks to have compliance systems and enhanced due diligence procedures in place to ensure the identity of their clients and the legality of the funds coursing through the system. We needed to expand the reach of good corporate citizenship to encompass more regions and more banks—widening the domain of the legitimate financial world and the actors willing to protect the system. We decided to expand the "Buddy Bank" system, which would involve creating a series of "private-sector dialogues" in key regions. The Buddy Bank Initiative involved a mentoring system among banks that would facilitate information sharing, collaboration, and private-sector capacity building between more sophisticated banks and those that required some assistance.

I assigned this task to Ryan Wallerstein, the second person I had hired into EOTF/FC to serve as an executive assistant and a jack-of-all-trades. Wallerstein was a twenty-something graduate of Columbia University's Graduate School of International and Public Affairs who had already completed a successful stint as a marketing professional in New York City. He had no government experience, but he was a hard charger who walked and talked with supreme confidence and was willing to take on any task on a moment's notice. Our office didn't lack confidence, but the mission I gave him to expand the Buddy Bank system required his style of braggadocio and marketing skill.

A major challenge was finding a way of convincing foreign financial institutions, especially those in high-risk jurisdictions, to adopt similar anti-money-laundering standards and practices in their day-to-day transactions and business. The dialogue provided a platform to further shape the global financial ecology. The dialogues were established between US financial institutions and those from MENA, South America, and Eastern Europe. Meetings and conferences between select institutions allowed foreign banks to develop new relationships with potential correspondent partners in the United States. It also allowed the US institutions to teach their foreign counterparts about the requirements they had to meet in order to become trusted correspondent partners. The banks were allowed to talk to each other about the standards to be applied to justify the risk of doing business, especially with banks that touched at-risk jurisdictions in the Middle East or South Asia.

Of course, with the "light footprint" of the US Treasury's oversight of the mentoring relationships, the unspoken implication was that learning and practicing good financial behavior would help the foreign banks avoid the regulatory steps and sanctions that had begun to sting banks around the world. The Latin American banking organization FELEBAN (Federación Latinoamericano de Bancos), which had an interest in shoring up remittance accounts and access to the American markets, was the first to take on the notion of creating partner banks. In November 2004, I traveled to Guatemala City for its annual conference and delivered a speech that laid out the basic framework for the Buddy Bank Initiative. The FELEBAN leadership liked this idea and decided to try to implement it.

Meanwhile, the notion of a private-sector dialogue took off in the Middle East, with banks worried about their vulnerabilities and a set of banking officials willing to run with the idea.

Soon, the Buddy Bank Initiative began to evolve into regional private-sector dialogues. The US MENA Private Sector Development (PSD) program took on a life of its own, and a follow-up conference was held in 2006. Timothy Geithner, who was then the head of the New York Federal Reserve Bank, and Tom Baxter, the New York Federal Reserve's general counsel, were the hosts. Under the guidance of Chip Poncy and Danny Glaser, Wallerstein took the MENA PSD model and planned private-sector dialogues in Latin America and Eastern Europe. The first Latin American PSD was held in Washington, DC, in 2006. The PSD in Eastern Europe was held in Riga, Latvia, that same year. The PSDs continue today as a mechanism for the US government and financial institutions to engage collectively with the private sector and regulators for key regions.

With this initiative, we had achieved two important goals. We had begun to expand the set of actors who were tied to the legitimate financial system. More importantly, we moved the conversation further into the realm of the private sector, where the risk calculus needed to include the high risk of doing business with rogue and suspect actors. In so doing, we had conditioned the foreign financial sector to hearing directly from the US Treasury.

For Treasury, this was the start of a new approach that promised to resurrect Treasury's role as a national security player. We were defining legitimate financial activity and actors. And there was much still to come. Two of our candidates for Section 311 action would form the cornerstone of financial pressure campaigns larger than anything seen before. We were ready to target two bad banks that were financial conduits for the most dangerous rogue regimes in the world—Iran and North Korea.

These would ultimately prove to be the most important and defining acts of financial warfare launched by the new Treasury.

7

"The Mother of
All Financial Investigations"

By the winter of 2003, war with Iraq appeared inevitable. Saddam Hussein seemed not to realize until the bitter end that the Americans were actually coming to Baghdad. It wasn't until March, on the very eve of war, that he decided to move his money.

US airstrikes on Baghdad were just hours away when Saddam dispatched a handwritten note to the governor of the Central Bank of Iraq. Personally delivered by Saddam's son, Qusay Hussein, and Iraq's finance minister, Hikmat Ibrahim, the message was succinct:

Top Secret
In the Name of Allah, the Compassionate, the Merciful
His Excellency the Governor of the Central Bank of Iraq
This letter gives authorisation to Mr. Qusay Hussein and Mr. Hikmat Ibrahim to receive the following cash amounts:

    1. Nine hundred and twenty million US dollars.

    2. Ninety million euros.

This is to protect this money from American aggression. Please execute promptly.
(signed) Saddam Hussein
President
March 19, 2003[1]

Bank employees scurried to gather the cash from the vaults. As they did so, they kept detailed records of the withdrawal, often by hand and in large ledgers. All told, the cash filled 236 boxes, each neatly packed, numbered, and marked with a banker's note indicating its contents. Witnesses reported that three or four truckloads of cash were driven out of the central bank that day. Some of these boxes of cash were hidden throughout Baghdad and the rest of the country. Some were taken into Syria, where the money would support the fleeing Baathist elite and the insurgency to come. And similar withdrawals were taking place across the region on the eve of war, as Iraqi embassy officials realized what was happening and made withdrawals from the banks where their funds were held.

In Washington, Pentagon planners had devised strategies for a possible cyber-attack to disrupt the financial infrastructure of the Iraqi state. The purpose would have been to erase the value of Iraqi holdings before the regime had the chance to hide its money. But these cyber-weapons were never used. Just as past treasury secretaries had balked at disruptive interference in the financial system, the Treasury feared that the consequences of disrupting electronic financial records would overwhelm any short-term benefit to capturing or destroying Saddam's assets. If the United States took any action to undermine trust in the integrity of the financial system, the whole system might collapse.

Instead, we launched a conventional asset recovery effort as the bombs fell on Baghdad. On March 19, 2003, the United States invaded Iraq. The next day, Secretary of the Treasury Snow announced that the US government would hunt Saddam's assets and ensure they were preserved and returned to the Iraqi people for the reconstruction of their country. President Bush signed Executive Order 13315 authorizing the confiscation of nondiplomatic Iraqi government assets in the United States. At the same time, the United States vested $1.7 billion in Iraqi assets and placed them in a New York Federal Reserve account for reconstruction pursuant to the International Economic Emergency Powers Act.[2] The international community began to act to freeze Iraqi assets. On April 3, 2003, the Bank of England revealed that it had frozen $648 million in Iraqi assets in British banks. It was time to find and recover the Hussein regime's assets—hidden in Iraq and abroad.

Despite over a decade of international sanctions, the Hussein regime had managed to accrue billions of dollars. The international community had sanctioned Iraq after its invasion of Kuwait in 1990, initially focusing on keeping Hussein from gaining access to Kuwait's resources. The sanctions regime evolved over time. The international community put a strict blockade on trade with Iraq in the hopes of strangling the regime and preventing it from arming itself, whether with weapons of mass destruction or conventional weapons. But like most autocratic regimes facing embargo-like sanctions, the regime of Saddam Hussein found a way to game the system and survive as the ordinary people suffered.

Oil was Iraq's escape valve because it was a central income generator for the Iraqi people and important to the international economy. Beginning in the early 1990s, the Iraqi government entered into trading agreements with Jordan, Turkey, and Syria to sell Iraqi oil to each of these countries outside of the international sanctions that were in place. The United Nations Security Council—including the United States and the United Kingdom—agreed to allow Iraq to trade with its neighbors, in part to alleviate the effects of the sanctions on those countries. The trade deals allowed Iraq to trade oil for up to $3 billion per year. But these trading relationships provided a way for Iraq to circumvent the sanctions.

In each country, the proceeds of the oil sales were split between a trade account and a cash account. Most of the funds (60 to 75 percent) were placed in the trade accounts. Under the trade protocols, the Iraqi government was required to use the money in the trade accounts to purchase goods from vendors in the particular partner country. The money from the cash accounts (25 to 40 percent of oil sale proceeds) was transferred to bank accounts in Jordan and Lebanon—usually set up in the names of front companies or individuals to further disguise the movement of the funds. Eventually, this cash was deposited in bank accounts controlled by the Central Bank of Iraq, Rasheed Bank, or Rafidain Bank. After this, it was withdrawn in the form of cash and transported back to Iraq. When the money reached Baghdad, it was deposited into the vault at the Central Bank of Iraq.

In April 1995, the United Nations altered the sanctions regime in a fundamental way to allow for the sale of Iraqi oil when it created the Oil for Food (OFF) program.[3] The aim was to allow the country to feed itself with the proceeds of its oil exports. Iraq could export oil at fair-market value and be paid in escrow, with its new line of credit allowing the government to purchase food and medicine. What the United Nations actually created was a trading regime that allowed Saddam Hussein a new mechanism to pump money into his regime and profit personally. The Iraqis manipulated the price of oil and humanitarian goods, collecting surcharges and kickbacks on each exchange. From 1997 to 2001, Saddam and his regime raised $10.1 billion in OFF-related illegal revenues.[4]

Saddam used the revenue to pay his loyalists, the army, and himself. He spent lavishly on his pleasure palaces in Baghdad, which were built with the kind of faux luxury reminiscent of a gaudy nightclub in Atlantic City. A 1999 State Department report estimated that Saddam had spent over $2 billion on fifty new palaces since the first Gulf War.[5] Saddam would order the purchase of teakwood from Burma, in violation of sanctions, for use in his palaces. Those palaces would soon become the dormitories and offices of the US troops and officials who would occupy Iraq. Saddam also used money to buy allegiances and build relationships with those who were willing to skirt international sanctions to profit from the trade in Iraqi oil. Although years of harsh sanctions had successfully contained some of his most grandiose and dangerous regional ambitions, Saddam, like many other autocrats, had learned to use the system to his full benefit.

The Iraqi regime established elaborate front companies and wantonly abused the immunity of the diplomatic courier system to deliver currencies and goods in diplomatic pouches from the international market to Baghdad and Saddam's inner circle.[6] The Iraqis accumulated the money from Saddam's various schemes at Iraqi embassies, or deposited it into bank accounts in the region, later to be withdrawn in cash. This cash was then transported back to Iraq, and some of it was deposited into the vault of the Central Bank of Iraq. Iraq's embassies became a hub for managing Iraq's money movements, commercial relationships, and acquisition programs.

Money also bought weapons and restricted technologies. The Iraqi Intelligence Service was heavily involved in the international illicit procurement network during the sanctions period. It set up front companies in Iraqi embassies worldwide to make contact with business officials for sales and investments in Iraq and the acquisition of dual-use technologies. According to the Duelfer Report, which in 2004 delineated the findings of the US government's investigation into the issue of weapons of mass destruction in Iraq, Iraq's illicit procurement program was so successful that it undermined regional support for sanctions enforcement.

Saddam also used the sanctions system and the OFF program specifically as strategic, diplomatic leverage. The OFF program gave him enormous influence over those in the international system who were hungry to make money in Iraq. In negotiations with the United Nations, Iraq won the right to determine who its customers and vendors would be. The Iraqi government manipulated the selection of companies who received contracts and "vouchers" for the program to increase its influence in international politics and to push for further easing of the sanctions regime against it. It also sought elaborate kickbacks from the buyers in exchange for the opportunity to do business with Iraq. All of this defanged the effects of the sanctions.

Like many dictators, Saddam did not organize and control every element of his financial empire directly or by simply doling out cash. Instead, he offered his sons, Uday and Qusay, along with other family and tribal members and loyal ministers, business opportunities and the corruption attendant to that trade. Like a Mafia don, he allowed control of different industries and sectors within his country. He handed the most lucrative commercial sectors—such as the religious tourist trade and cigarette smuggling—to his sons.

Underlying the corruption and profligacy of the regime was a corroded economy and society. Little was invested in infrastructure or the people, while investment and bank accounts worth hundreds of millions of dollars were maintained in Switzerland, Dubai, and Beirut. Not much was done outside the control of the Iraqi regime, and the country's assets were used as Saddam's playthings. In his tyrannical regime, the assets of the state were his to invest or spend as he liked. The ones who suffered were the Iraqi people, who were issued ration cards and were beholden to the whims of the government for their food and fuel supplies.

The goal of the US government was to recover as much of this money as possible and return it to Iraq for reconstruction and recovery. The tricky part was finding it. In this case, it was embedded in front companies and accounts controlled by Hussein's cronies and family members. Once it was found, we needed to use diplomatic, regulatory, and legal tools to get it back to the Iraqis.

There was nowhere else in government for this work to be done than at the Treasury Department. Treasury had a track record of freezing and recovering stolen assets through the Office of Foreign Assets Control, the ability to access vast amounts of financial data, and the international networks and connections to ensure that the assets could be found and returned. Right after the secretary announced that Treasury would take on this role, on March 20, 2003, George Wolfe, the deputy general counsel, approached me to take on the role of leading the asset recovery efforts for the secretary and the US government. Wolfe would be headed to Iraq shortly after this to be Treasury's principal representative. I was flattered but deeply reluctant to take on a wartime global asset hunt. Still reeling from the creation of the Department of Homeland Security and the emasculation of Treasury's Office of Enforcement, our small group was already overtaxed and trying to maintain our focus. This was likely going to be a mammoth task on top of what we were already doing to counter terrorist financing, expand the anti-money-laundering system, and isolate rogue actors from the financial system. I initially said no to the suggestion, but Wolfe and the secretary convinced me to take on the project, and so we did. As I would soon learn, the work we would do to recover Iraqi assets would help to shape the way we waged financial warfare beyond the borders of Iraq.

Treasury quickly put together a small team to seek out three types of assets. First, we needed to find the cash the regime had taken from the Central Bank of Iraq and other Iraqi banks, because this was money that the regime and its allies would otherwise use to survive and fight our troops. Second, we would try to capture existing Iraqi state assets abroad and in Iraqi banks, using the Chapter 7 (mandatory) obligations of UN Security Council Resolution 1483 to freeze and repatriate the money. Finally, we would attempt to uncover hidden or layered assets that Saddam, his family, and his cronies had nested outside of Iraq. The last objective would require painstaking investigative and intelligence work. The regime had used proxies, fronts, and multiple bank accounts to move assets beyond the reach of the sanctions regime.

Estimates of Saddam's wealth varied widely, with some reports saying he had acquired upward of $30 billion to $40 billion since the 1980s.[7] But the rumors of his existing wealth and holdings did not paint the full picture. His wealth was largely wrapped up in the state's assets—there was a fundamental admixture between Saddam's assets and those of the Iraqi government. He also used much of the country's asset flow to maintain power, to build allegiances inside and outside of Iraq, and to buy the materiel he and his military needed to rule with an iron fist.

Our first job was to find the cash that had been withdrawn from Iraq's central bank on the eve of war. As US soldiers fanned out throughout the countryside, they were followed by investigators specifically tasked with turning up the missing cash. Within days, the soldiers and investigators began to find boxes of cash hidden in safe houses and storage containers. Within two months of the invasion, 191 of the 236 original boxes had been recovered, totaling more than $850 million in US dollars and 100 million in euros.

Perhaps unsurprisingly, the full amount withdrawn from the Central Bank of Iraq was never recovered. Some of the cash had most likely been distributed among loyalists in Iraq or shipped across the border to Syria. One story that persisted—though it was likely apocryphal—was that a truckload of cash containing some of the March 19 withdrawals sat parked under a large tree near a farmhouse owned by one of Saddam's relatives. US imagery identified the truck as a possible military vehicle hiding from overhead surveillance, and warplanes targeted it for destruction. When the truck was hit with the American missile, the cash scattered high into the air and burned along with the wreckage.

But the hunt was only getting started. We quickly realized that, for this effort to work, we would need investigators in the field—investigators who could question witnesses, or collect and analyze financial records. I turned to the only investigators we still had in the Treasury Department—IRS criminal investigators. IRS special agents are the best financial forensics investigators in the business. All of them carry accounting degrees along with their guns and badges. It had been Treasury agents who had convicted Al Capone for tax evasion. We would rely again on the same agents to hunt Saddam's assets.

Nancy Jardini, a no-nonsense former prosecutor and accountant, was the deputy chief of the Internal Revenue Service–Criminal Investigation Division (IRS-CID). I called Nancy and asked her if the IRS could put together a group of agents willing to go into Iraq and around the world to find Saddam's hidden assets. Jardini, who would become chief in January 2004, was ready to take an enormous chance, along with the IRS leadership—understanding the importance of the effort but also the real danger for her agents and agency. She put out the call for willing volunteers, unsure what kind of response she would get. We would need seasoned agents willing to go into a war zone. There would be bank records and wire transfers to be analyzed from the Central Bank of Iraq as well as Iraq's primary commercial banks, Rafidain and Rasheed; trade and commercial contracts to be deciphered; and sources, former regime elements, and money men to be interviewed.

By noon of the same day, IRS-CID had received responses from some of the most senior agents from around the country—totaling a page and a half of names of volunteers. Many of these were grizzled veterans with experience investigating the financial underworld of drug-trafficking organizations and international organized crime networks. Some had made careers as undercover money launderers, working against some of the most dangerous criminal organizations in the country to get at their money. The IRS leadership was surprised at how many were willing to go into a war zone, without much clarity as to where they might be going and what they would be doing. They were patriots and hungry to help in Iraq.

One of the first volunteers was an IRS agent named Scott Schneider, a former US Army intelligence officer who had become an accountant and a hard-charging IRS agent. Schneider spoke the two languages that were critical for a civilian agency heading into a Middle Eastern war zone for the first time—Arabic and "military." He understood how the military worked—the jargon, processes, and command structure that make it tick. This would prove critical as we designed an asset recovery effort alongside the war fighters. Schneider was joined by Treasury analyst Pat Conlon, a longtime analyst who had deployed to the Balkans during his career to hunt leadership assets. Conlon was one of the few Treasury employees who understood what a war zone looked like.

The immediate goal on the ground was to find and lock up assets so as to weaken the remnants of Saddam's power base and to keep the money from being used to fund a war against our soldiers. Our financial "jump teams," led by IRS agents, were ready to deploy within hours, if needed, to pursue leads and look for Saddam's hidden treasure. Department of Homeland Security agents were also on these teams, and the FBI and other analysts assisted.

We worked with an interagency collection of key actors. The group was small, but it included dedicated analysts from the intelligence community; State Department officials, including Assistant Secretary of State Tony Wayne, his deputy Steve Simon, and Ambassador Joseph Saloom; and Jody Myers, who was detailed to the National Security Council from the Treasury. The analysts and investigators began to map out where the assets might be, with a focus on those assets still controlled by Saddam, his family, and his cronies. Wayne and Saloom mobilized our embassies to work with the Iraqis and host governments to implement UN Security Council Resolution 1483 in finding and freezing Iraqi assets. Customs, Secret Service, and FBI agents would prove pivotal on the ground to provide expertise and support. Treasury lawyers, such as John Vardaman, would later go bravely into Iraq, following George Wolfe into the war zone. Vardaman would end up bunking with others in the throne room of one of Saddam's palaces, sleeping next to a mural depicting Scud missiles headed toward America.

We sent Scott Schneider and Pat Conlon into Iraq in May 2003. Upon their arrival, they were given camouflage uniforms with the identifying label "Treasury" stitched across the top left part of their shirts. Schneider and Conlon's first job was to get access to key financial documents and identify the right witnesses and detainees in custody to interview. They hitched a ride to the Central Bank of Iraq almost as soon as they arrived and collected as many documents as they could.

They soon found there was no lack of documents. Over the next few days, the investigators were confronted with rooms full of documents that the military had already found and collected as quickly as possible. The papers were stuffed into big duffle bags and poured out of files and boxes. The first order of business was to determine which documents might be valuable.

In the early days of the Iraq War, the central bank had been looted like other government ministries, buildings, and museums in Baghdad. With the regime toppled, the security infrastructure crumbling, and Saddam and his sons on the run, there was little law and order in the city. The looters were not interested in documents and files, however—they were interested in getting access to the vault. By the time American officials arrived, it was clear that someone had tried to break through the massive steel vault door with a grenade launcher. Not only had the attempt failed, but the blowback from the explosion in the relatively small room apparently killed the bank robbers.

The Iraqis had kept good financial and commercial records. The ledgers, account files, and contracts may have represented corrupt deals or embedded kickbacks and over-invoicing, but the flow of funds and the nature of the trades were diligently memorialized. The bank documents gave the investigators leads and a picture of how the Iraqis were doing business. They showed where money was wired and when cash was withdrawn. The identities of those who would know something about the deals were revealed by their signatures. The bank statements gave company names and the names of those who were in control of bank accounts, which could lead the investigators to front companies and the people who were complicit with the Iraqis. The financial records—yet again—proved to be a valuable source of leads and irrefutable evidence.

Eventually, the central bank employees, many of them government technocrats and economists with no political affiliation, returned to work. Some of them, along with other Iraqi bankers, who had moved money for Saddam by necessity, proved invaluable in directing and guiding the investigators to key documents and deciphering the meaning of others. They also helped to identify key bankers and accountants in neighboring countries on whom they had relied to move and hide money.

The Treasury team was most interested in talking with those who would know how the money was handled and how the trade deals were designed. This meant interviewing the ministers of oil, trade, and finance, the governor of the Central Bank of Iraq, and a number of deputy ministers, as well as Saddam's business associates. These were the people who would understand the inner workings of Iraqi money management and decision making.

The interviews took place in a secure location inside the perimeter held by the military at Baghdad International Airport. Large canvas tents were propped up by thick wooden poles to allow for interviews of those deemed not to present a risk of flight or injury to others. The investigators and the detainees sat in folding chairs, with folding tables in between them. It was suffocating, hot, and dusty inside the tents, which were placed right on top of the dirt. It was an unpleasant place to meet, but it was the space that was available.

Most of the officials the Treasury team needed to interview were older politicians and bankers. None of them had been mistreated, but each man appeared downtrodden and tired as he arrived at the tent. Most cooperated, at least to some degree. Schneider had been trained as an interrogator, and Conlon was an analyst by training. They knew how to build a relationship with a detainee, and they treated the detainees—most of whom were older than them by a couple of decades—with respect.

As is so often the case in detainee interviews, each initially deflected responsibility and attention from their own role and pointed fingers at Saddam, his sons, and the most senior officials. Truly useful information was much less forthcoming. Yet, over time, the Treasury team began to make headway with the detainees. In the growing heat of the Iraqi summer, Schneider determined that the most attractive commodity was simply a cold drink. A refrigerated bottle of water or cool Coca Cola proved to be enough to unlock the memories of many detainees tired of suffering in the heat. After the IRS shipped a large refrigerator to Iraq, Schneider and Conlon became very popular. The detainees would get cold drinks in return for their time. It wasn't long before they were rewarding the investigators with real information that filled the gaps in our knowledge about the true nature of the Iraqi economy and the location of Saddam's assets.

It was clear that the Oil for Food program and the trade in oil were the primary vehicles for generating huge amounts of money for the regime. Saddam and his relatives controlled the key smuggling industries—from cigarettes to dual-use military equipment—and they and their trusted proxies helped to manage the money that sat outside of the country. Tariq Aziz, Saddam's foreign minister, and his son controlled some of the oil deals with Western companies, illegally evading sanctions, and were sure to take their fair share of kickbacks from the contracts. Investigators had found correspondence laying out details about the transportation of oil, along with a list of Iraqi-controlled oil tankers. Money that was not kept in the country was usually being used in trade to circumvent the sanctions and to pay for loyalties and services abroad. The money would collect in the trading accounts and find its way into banks in Beirut, Dubai, and Switzerland.

Based on the information that was emerging from documents and detainee interviews, we were soon able to send our financial jump teams into countries like Jordan and Syria to recover assets. The IRS had assembled an all-star collection of adventurous graybeard investigators who were willing to grab their duffle bags and laptops and go overseas on a moment's notice. Two of them, Alan Schick and Larry Kaiser, were veterans of financial investigations throughout the country but had their greatest takedowns in Southern California, where they had posed as money launderers for cartels and entered the inner sanctums of these organizations. Schick was a burly man with a neat beard and a deep, raspy voice. Kaiser was a slim, lanky Wisconsin native with thin white hair who liked to talk. Both could look deeply into the eyes of a suspect and judge truthfulness just as easily as they could decipher the spreadsheets and accounts of illicit financial dealings.

Schick made his way to the Central Bank of Jordan and Jordan's Ministry of Finance. We knew that the Jordanian banks had handled upward of $600 million in Iraqi trade per year, if not more. Jordanian merchants were trading openly with Iraq, and Iraqi fuel tankers crossed the border daily to deliver Iraqi oil.

In the early days of his investigation in Amman, Schick was at the US embassy when Secretary of State Colin Powell visited and met with the ambassador and the embassy team. The secretary was there to be updated on all that was happening in Jordan related to the Iraq War and other matters. When he met Schick, Powell asked him how the investigation was going. In Schick's usual gruff yet jovial manner, he said simply, "This is the 'mother of all financial investigations.' It's just like any other tax case, but with just a lot more zeroes at the back of the numbers." Powell smiled, seemingly assured by the quick assessment.

Eventually, Schick and the investigators and analysts identified more than 1,600 Iraqi-controlled accounts in eight Jordanian banks.[8] The agents obtained and reviewed bank files and statements relating to these accounts and identified front companies with accounts in Jordan. Finding enough copiers and scanners to capture the information was a challenge. The investigators learned that money managers in some Jordanian banks, including a banker in Jordan who was considered "Saddam's money launderer," had handled the deals and helped to move the money into accounts around the world—especially into Beirut. Schick also learned that the day the war started, two senior Iraqi generals had attempted to withdraw $50 million in Iraqi assets from Jordanian accounts. Though they had signature authority over the accounts, a Jordanian central bank official refused to allow the withdrawal and ordered the accounts frozen. These same Iraqi generals then traveled to Beirut to withdraw assets. There, they were successful, withdrawing $33 million from Iraqi bank accounts. The generals then sent the millions in cash via courier to Damascus for safekeeping.

The Jordanians did not hesitate to freeze Iraqi assets. They provided the US agents with access to relevant files and accounts. Overall, there was almost $300 million left in Iraq's trading accounts in Jordan. But although the Jordanians were cooperative, they were concerned that Jordanian merchants and the Jordanian government would be left holding the bag with Iraqi debt still outstanding. According to their estimates, the amount of this debt reached approximately $1.3 billion. They wanted the accounts reviewed to determine the validity of the claims filed against these monies. I would later visit Amman to negotiate for the return of the frozen Iraqi assets, which would eventually find their way back to Iraq.

We also needed access to Iraqi accounts in Syria. We knew the Iraqis had used Syria as a major commercial hub. In 1999, an oil pipeline repair there proved to be a major income generator for Saddam. The Iraqi oil trade was worth billions of dollars, and much of that money flowed through Syrian and Lebanese banks. In particular, the Commercial Bank of Syria (CBS), a major Syrian bank, and its Lebanese subsidiary were used to help maintain the accounts necessary for the trade between Iraq and Syria during the Oil for Food years. We also knew the Iraqi embassy in Syria had been used by the former regime to move money in and out of the country. Syria remained a safe haven for Saddam's retreating Baathist allies. Finding Iraqi money in Syria was critical.

But Syria and the United States were on unfriendly terms, and the Assad regime in Damascus was not going to open the door to Syria's banks simply because we asked. There was growing tension between Washington and Damascus, with talk of pulling the American ambassador in Damascus, Margaret Scobey, given the increasing divide between the countries. Nevertheless, the Syrians did not like the idea of their banking sector being targeted.

We met with Syrian government and banking officials in Washington and in Bahrain. The Syrians were willing to talk about the concerns we had raised about the lack of money-laundering controls in Syria. Though tensions were mounting, they were willing to allow our investigators into Syria to look at the Iraqi bank accounts and records.

So we walked into Syria with our financial jump team. Larry Kaiser, along with Mike Bridgeman, another seasoned financial investigator, visited Damascus. The agents knew they would be carefully watched. At the hotel, Kaiser had noticed that his bags and computers were being searched every day while he was out. On the third day, he decided to leave a note on his computer for the Syrian agents searching his room. It simply said, "Meet at the bar at 5 pm." The note was intended to let the Syrians know that he knew he was being watched. It would also put the Syrians a bit on the defensive—they would wonder if this might be an attempt to recruit them as intelligence sources. That evening, Kaiser strolled through the lobby looking at the men seated in the lounge of the bar. He recognized a couple of them as men he had seen several times around the hotel and their rooms. He had already surmised that they were likely following him and his colleague. He decided not to approach them, but he walked through the bar to let them know he was now watching them.

Kaiser wanted to get to the Iraqi embassy, since we knew how important the embassy had been in controlling the flow of money in and out of Iraq. Kaiser, Bridgeman, and an Iraqi audit official decided to pay a visit and simply ring the entrance bell to see if they would be admitted. An armed Iraqi guard answered the door. Kaiser, through his interpreter, explained who he was and what he was doing. He showed the guard his credentials, and the guard brought them in. Kaiser and the team talked to the chargé d'affaires and inquired about the embassy's cash stores, knowing that the Syrians had frozen the embassy's bank accounts. After forty-five minutes, the chargé admitted that the embassy was using cash to pay the embassy's expenses. He then gave them a ledger, where all the payments were recorded by hand. The ledger showed a cash balance of approximately $13 million to $16 million on hand. The investigators were then led to a small room with a standing safe and eight AK-47s leaning against the wall. The chargé d'affaires opened the safe and showed them piles of cash neatly stacked—mostly hundred-dollar bills, most of them newly printed and wrapped in shrink wrap. The agents were somewhat incredulous but methodically took samplings of the serial numbers of the bills and sent the numbers back to the Federal Reserve. American officials, in concert with the Iraqis, later took possession of the cash and transported it to the Central Bank of Iraq in Baghdad. They seized approximately $13 million in total. The new bills found in the safe were later traced to a shipment of dollars from the multinational banking and financial services company HSBC in London to a bank in Beirut.

The Syrians gave Kaiser and the team access to Iraq's trade and cash accounts, along with some accounts from the CBS. They were not trying to hide much, since so much of the trade with Iraq had been well known to the world. It was no secret that the Iraqi oil pipeline had been flowing for years before the war began in 2003. The investigators had access to piles of records. The files and transfers revealed about $3 billion in trade over the course of three years, with $1 billion kept in the trade and cash accounts at any one time. In March 2003, just before the war, the accounts contained almost $1 billion. As the war started, the accounts began to be emptied, and only about $200 million was left.

The Syrians claimed that the withdrawals had been legitimate payments to Syrian businesses and vendors owed by the Iraqis. They provided the investigators with invoices and paperwork to validate their claims, but the vast bulk of the assets seemed to have been simply withdrawn by the Syrian government. Despite our best efforts, we were never able to determine what happened to most of that money. We suspected that the Syrians used it to help pay for Saddam's generals and allies who settled in Syria—and perhaps later to fuel the insurgency. We would continue to find evidence of Syrian complicity in evading sanctions.

We also had plenty of new information about the schemes that
Saddam and his sons had used to maximize their profits. For
instance, Uday and Qusay controlled the tourist industry in Iraq.
Although Iraq was not a place that Western tourists went, it was a
leading destination for Shiite pilgrims visiting Muslim holy sites and
mosques. The tourist industry was worth at least half a billion dollars a year. Following the leads they had gathered about this source
of income, Treasury officials used its designation authorities under
Executive Order 13315 to name a tourist company serving as a
front for the former regime, submitting its name to the United
Nations 1518 Committee to ensure that its assets were frozen
worldwide.

We also saw that the regime used an international commercial
and procurement system to gain access to weapons and equipment
prohibited under the international sanctions. IRS agents and intelligence analysts focused their attention on Iraqi front companies
operating in Dubai. The banking and commercial facilities of Dubai
made it one of the most vibrant commercial and cultural crossroads
in the world. Unfortunately, the same facilities that allowed for
legitimate business also provided an infrastructure for illicit financial networks.

The Iraqis used a front company called Al Wasel & Babel to procure weapons for the Iraqi regime, primarily from Russia. On April
15, 2004, we made what we knew about Al Wasel & Babel public and
designated it as a front company for Saddam's regime, thus ensuring
that its assets anywhere in the world would be captured, and that
those doing business with the company would be forewarned to stop.
With the war and the investigations of Iraqi business underway, Russian transactions and other weapons procurement programs with the
Iraqis stopped. When informed of the success of the financial investigations by the Treasury teams, one CIA officer in the region said,
"Wouldn't you know, the IRS comes to the Middle East and finds all
the espionage."

The investigations began to reveal more information about the role of Iraq's diplomatic corps in profiteering. The IRS agents determined that the former Iraqi ambassador to Russia had stolen $4 million in Iraqi assets that had been entrusted to him. The money was in Russian banks. The agents thoroughly documented the witness accounts and helped the Iraqis present the information to an Iraqi court. The court then ordered that the money be seized and transferred to Iraq. The Russian government moved to freeze the assets, and on August 2, 2004, the Treasury designated this ambassador and submitted his name to the UN 1518 Committee.

The Iraqi ambassador to Switzerland in the 1990s, Barzan al-Tikriti, who was one of Saddam's half-brothers, had served as the principal money manager for the Saddam regime in Switzerland and Europe. He had also served as head of the Iraqi Intelligence Service from 1968 to 1983 and had spent nearly a decade living in Geneva representing Iraq's interests at UN bodies and with the Swiss. He had facilitated the movement of assets for the regime, and he had used front companies and nominee accounts to shelter money while siphoning payments to Saddam's family members and cronies. Investigators found a letter from Barzan to Saddam that listed the main Iraqi accounts held in Europe, with key beneficiary information. Companies such as Logarcheo in Switzerland and Montana Management, headquartered in Panama, were used as fronts to move money and make purchases and investments. The Treasury designated him and moved with the Swiss government to freeze his assets and the properties and equity he controlled. Switzerland was able to act quickly, using an administrative, executive power to freeze assets, especially once the United Nations acted. In January 2007, Barzan was hanged for committing crimes against humanity for his participation in the Dujail Massacre of 1982.

We worked closely with the countries in the region to recover and return assets. One case in particular captured our attention. It provided an important opportunity to return a signature Saddam asset to Iraq. We had found one of Saddam's private jets, a Falcon 50, sitting in Jordan. The Iraqis had used a front company called

Aviatrans Anstalt, registered in Liechtenstein, to purchase the jet. When we found it, it was not in good shape. It needed some repairs and refitting. Its value had been diminished, but it carried great symbolic value for the new Iraqi government. We worked closely with the Liechtenstein government, and its newly formed financial intelligence unit, run by René Bruelhart, along with the Swiss and Jordanian governments to seize the jet and related assets, and they were returned to the Iraqis. In 2005, the Falcon 50 flew back into Baghdad's international airport accompanied by Romania's ambassador to the United Nations, who was head of the Iraqi sanctions committee. It was an important symbolic moment.

Overall, the jump teams conducted hundreds of interviews all over the world and reviewed tens of thousands of documents. Along with analysts and diplomats, they helped to identify thousands of bank accounts and other assets held in more than twenty countries located in Europe, the Middle East, Southeast Asia, and elsewhere.

Finding and freezing assets was not enough. Asset recovery is only partially completed once the accounts and assets are found and frozen. The real work often begins when the assets need to be repatriated to the host government. There are legal questions of proof that the assets—liquid, hard, or real—should be returned to the ownership and control of the state. Claimants may challenge the ownership, or creditors may attempt to attach the assets for claimed debts. There are diplomatic and political considerations, with countries often not wanting to return the assets, or opting to use them as leverage to gain concessions. And there are always questions of financial integrity. To whom will the assets be returned, and will they simply be stolen or pilfered again by new officials who now control a government? For what purposes will those returned assets be used?

The Iraqi asset recovery effort was helped enormously by UN Resolution 1483. It was intentionally crafted to mandate the freezing of Iraqi assets and included a provision requiring the automatic repatriation of those funds. This meant that all UN member states were obligated to return any assets they froze and needed to find a way within their respective domestic legal systems to make this happen. Importantly, the resolution also indicated that all the funds were to be returned to a single, transparent account, the Development Fund for Iraq (DFI). The DFI would be opened and held at the Federal Reserve Bank of New York.

We had identified almost half a billion dollars of Iraqi assets in Lebanese banks, and we suspected there were more assets in Beirut. We had been in discussions for weeks with the Lebanese government to negotiate the return of the assets.

As I left for the hotel after long meetings in Amman in late 2003, I received a call from Gary Edson, the deputy national security adviser for economic affairs. By then, the National Security Council, under the leadership of Condoleezza Rice, had taken over coordination of US activities in Iraq, and Edson was coordinating all the economic issues. I enjoyed working with Edson, but others found his aggressive, rough style difficult to handle. He suffered no fools, but he was ruthlessly effective at his job.

Edson told me that an Iraqi delegation had just left Beirut, confusing the question of the return of frozen Iraqi assets. Getting the Lebanese banks to return the assets would not only be a significant repatriation, but would have a positive demonstration effect in the region for other banking centers. Edson promised that a delegation from the White House would come to Beirut to discuss the matter. Little did they know it would be a delegation of one. I was now traveling alone and would need to be ready when I landed to put the repatriation of assets from Beirut back on track. I did not know who I would be meeting with to discuss asset recovery in Lebanon.

When I landed, in the evening, a young US embassy officer, Jen Sublett Gavito, met me at the airport. We jumped into two bullet-proof black Suburbans and made our way out of the airport to go to downtown Beirut and await word of our meetings. On the highway, we passed by the Hezbollah-controlled neighborhoods, with our security detail noting that we would stay clear of those streets. In the Maronite Christian neighborhoods, colorful Christmas lights adorned buildings and homes.

Gavito told me that I would be meeting with Prime Minister Rafik Hariri, who had heard that I was coming at the direction of the White House and requested to host the meeting at his palatial home in the heart of Beirut. I grew quite nervous about meeting him. Hariri had been a transformational figure in Lebanon and a major political force, having served as prime minister from 1992 to 1998 and then again starting in 2000. He was a business tycoon whose fortune gave him enormous power and influence inside and outside of Lebanon. It also gave him the ability to reshape the face of Beirut after years of war. His construction projects and other investments had fueled a renaissance in Beirut, with rebuilt neighborhoods; new, fashionable shopping districts; and hip cafés full of young couples. He had begun to resurrect Beirut again as the Paris of the Mediterranean.

Hariri was legendary, the seminal political figure in Lebanon's fractious politics, which had been defined by ethnic and religious divides that were sharpened after years of civil war. He and his party represented the Sunnis of Lebanon, and he was the principal foe of the Syrian forces still occupying the country. He was the chief political adversary of Lebanese President Emile Lahoud, who was supported by the Syrian regime and Hezbollah. Hezbollah purported to represent the country's Shia population. A major political force and a "state-within-a-state" militia, the terrorist organization despised Hariri, his political force, and his close international ties to countries such as Saudi Arabia, France, and the United States. Most troubling to Syria, Hezbollah, and their benefactor, Iran, was that Hariri represented a Lebanon that longed for freedom—freedom from Syrian military occupation, from constant conflict with Israel, and from turmoil within Lebanon. Hariri was the most powerful man in Lebanon in a sea of sharks.

We had not been summoned yet to the meeting, so we made our way to a Starbucks set on the Mediterranean seaside. As we parked and entered the two-story coffee shop, I was surprised at what I saw. The Starbucks was humming, full of a young, hip crowd. Young men and women were mingling, checking their cellphones, and working on laptops. On the second floor, I looked at the vibrant seaside scene and the dark Mediterranean beyond the window-panes. As we drank our coffee, I marveled at how this could easily have been a scene from Los Angeles or Seattle. Then we got the call—the prime minister was ready to meet. We made our way quickly to the Suburbans and headed straight for Hariri's home in the heart of Beirut.

As we entered his home, we were escorted to a large office that doubled as a meeting room, where Hariri and our ambassador and deputy chief of mission were waiting. I walked in and greeted Hariri as he stood at his chair. I could tell that the ambassador was anxious, since we had never met in person and had not coordinated our message before the meeting. I sensed that everyone in the room was surprised that I had arrived alone—and that I was not an older man. Hariri graciously invited me to sit next to him and offered me Swiss chocolates from a bowl sitting on the table in front of us. I took one, and we paused so Hariri could watch an evening news broadcast on the big-screen TV in the corner of the room. He was listening intently to the news coverage of Lebanese President Lahoud's visit to Damascus to meet with Bashir al-Assad, which included footage of them walking together after their meetings. In a surreal moment, we watched as the news broadcast shifted to a report on Hariri's meetings that day and showed footage of him, too. I watched Hariri watch himself on his own big-screen TV.

We then began our discussions, as staff brought in more food. Hariri was pleased to receive me and asked me to pass his warm regards to Condoleezza Rice, for whom he had great respect. I told him I would and that I brought our deepest regards from the White House. I then spoke about the need to move toward repatriation of Iraqi assets found in Lebanese banks. I noted that this would be an

important step for both the Iraqis and the Lebanese, especially for
its banking system. Beirut banks could be seen as leading the banking world by repatriating the assets. The move would serve as a
clear demonstration effect for other banks holding Iraqi assets. He
was well versed in the issue and knew the amount of assets in question. In the middle of our discussion, Lebanese Finance Minister
Fouad Siniora came in to join the discussion. Fortunately, Siniora
and I had met on numerous occasions in the past, so he knew who I
was and added a sense of familiarity to the meeting. Siniora and
Hariri were close allies, and Siniora, too, would later become
Lebanon's prime minister.

Hariri understood our position but expressed concern about the
Beirut banking system's exposure to liabilities as a result of repatriating too quickly. There would be opposition by merchants,
bankers, and those claiming to be owed by the Iraqi government.
He suggested calling his friend Kofi Annan, the UN secretary general, to get a new UN resolution that would clarify the obligation to
repatriate assets, suggesting that it might build in immunity for
banks and jurisdictions doing so. I argued that this might be a confusing step, since the obligations under UN Resolution 1483 were
already clear, with the requirement and manner of repatriation
spelled out neatly. The most important next step was moving to
repatriate those assets that undeniably belonged to the Iraqi state.
The new Iraqi government could then resolve any claims against
their assets through a separate process. If we allowed claims—real
or not—to get in the way of repatriation, we would never see a
penny sent back to Iraq.

After over an hour of discussion, Hariri seemed pleased and convinced that the assets needed to be returned. There would need to
be some work within the Beirut banking world and the Lebanese
commercial sector to allow this to move forward, but he and Siniora
seemed resolved to get this done. The Syrians did not like the idea
of assets being returned—in part because it isolated them further
and portended a day when their leadership assets might be chased

and frozen in the Beirut banking system. We chatted a bit longer and then ended the meeting.

As we exited Hariri's home, a crowd of reporters met us with the bright lights of their television cameras. Some of the reporters wondered what the meeting was about, and some plainly asked, "Who are you? Where are you from?" I was happy to remain anonymous as we slipped back into the black Suburbans and sped away to the ambassador's residence. Our mission was complete in Beirut. We were back on track to see the return of Iraqi assets. I knew I had just had an encounter with an important historical figure. Little did I know just how important.

In October 2004, Hariri would resign as prime minister, feeling constrained in his role by the Syrian- and Hezbollah-backed political forces. Instead, he would work behind the scenes for change, perhaps wielding more independent power as he sat behind the throne. His enemies knew just how powerful he remained. On February 14, 2005, Hezbollah and Syrian operatives packed a Beirut street with 2,200 pounds of explosives, killing Hariri in his motorcade along with twenty-one others. They had known his route and planned extensively—creating mass destruction and a massive crater where the explosives and Hariri's car had once been. This followed a string of assassinations of pro-Western and anti-Syrian figures, including journalists, security personnel, and politicians, that continues to this day.

Hariri's death spawned a new movement, the March 14 coalition—named after the date of a mass rally that took place in Lebanon a month later to protest both the assassination and Syrian occupation. With popular displeasure with the Syrians growing, the Assad regime was forced to withdraw Syrian forces from Lebanon. Saad Hariri, the slain leader's son, along with French, Saudi, and American diplomats, pressed for an accounting. A special tribunal was commissioned to investigate the murders, and after months of wrangling, the prosecutors issued a report. Evidence pointed to Hezbollah and Syrian direction and involvement in the attack.

Hezbollah had attempted to undermine and stop the tribunal, attacking those who were involved, disputing the facts, and, ultimately, trying to cast blame for the assassination on Israel. After this event, Hezbollah further eroded its credibility within Lebanon, especially in 2008 when the terrorist group turned its guns on fellow Lebanese during an internal conflict. The organization has continued to throw its support behind the regime of Bashar al-Assad, even after the escalation of conflict in Syria in 2012 between the government and rebel forces and the assassination of Lebanon's security chief, Wissam al-Hassan, who was a key pro-Western figure in the March 14 coalition.

At this point, we were making progress. However, all of the efforts to recover assets began to change complexion as the insurgency took hold inside Iraq.

American and allied forces and the Iraqi government faced a full-fledged armed insurgency by 2004. Al Qaeda in Iraq, aided by the broader Al Qaeda network, began to see the US presence in Iraq and the perceived injustice of US forces "occupying" another Muslim country as a major opportunity. Added to this violent mix was Iranian support for allied Shia militias, which were threatening Americans, attacking Sunnis, and undermining the authority of the new Iraqi government. Thus, by 2006, we were fighting multiple fronts in Iraq. Meanwhile, we were trying to avoid a sectarian civil war and build the capacity of the Iraqis to handle their own security, economy, and politics. At the heart of this effort was an attempt to cut off the flows of funds that fueled the groups fighting US troops in Iraq.

The Iraqi Intelligence Service had been a major financial facilitator for Saddam, and its former operatives were in the middle of fomenting the insurgency. Khalaf al-Dulaimi, a former intelligence officer and a key money manager for Saddam's regime, helped to operate some of the front companies that Treasury identified. He had held money for the regime and wheeled and dealed on its behalf. When Dulaimi was designated by the United States and the United Nations, most of the assets that he controlled were frozen, much of it by Switzerland. Dulaimi, however, made his way to Syria with some money and allies to help maintain the Baathist resistance to the United States and the new Iraqi government. He and others found safe haven in Syria and used their prior networks to begin to fuel the insurgency. Dulaimi did not need access to major accounts or sums. Even a few thousand dollars went a long way to ensure instability in Iraq. Amazingly, Dulaimi has challenged the freezing of his assets in Switzerland, arguing before the European Court of Human Rights that he was not afforded due process before the UN and Swiss orders to freeze them took effect.

With this shift taking place, we began to focus less on asset recovery and more on cutting off flows of funds to the insurgency. Recovery was well underway, but we would now also direct our efforts to border checkpoints and airports, where cash would be moving into the country in satchels and suitcases en route to the insurgents within Iraq. We would begin to turn our attention as well to the criminal activities—such as hostage taking, oil smuggling, and bank robberies—that Al Qaeda in Iraq and other insurgents would employ to raise money while sowing fear.

I sat down with US Central Command (CENTCOM) leadership—at Treasury and then later when I served in the White House—and we discussed what an operational financial task force would look like. We took cues from the cooperation logged to date between the Pentagon and the Treasury Department on asset recovery and counterterrorism. Treasury had built strong relationships with the military after 9/11, sending OFAC analysts to sit with the combatant commanders and their intelligence units in the Pacific, in Europe, and at targeting centers in the United States.

This effort was of even deeper relevance to the military than what we had done together so far, since the money flows we were trying to freeze or stop this time were heading into Iraq to kill soldiers. It did not take much to convince the military leadership that this mattered. Questions to detainees about financial backing and money flows now moved up the list for the military interrogators. Our designations and diplomacy became focused on shutting down the foreign fighter pipeline from North Africa and the Gulf and the related financial pipelines from Gulf donors and other financial supporters.

By 2006, we would stand up the first interagency task force focused on wartime insurgency financing. The force would target "threat finance"—a military term meaning any money flows representing a threat to US military personnel and interests. Called the Iraq Threat Finance Cell, it would be run by CENTCOM and the US Treasury and would focus on recovering documents, gathering financial data, and creating the actionable intelligence necessary for the military to go after the financial underbelly of the growing insurgency. The analysts and agents of the finance cell would find the courier routes, financial frauds and bank robberies, and oil-skimming and corruption schemes that fueled attacks against the coalition. Soldiers now gathered ledgers, contracts, and documents to fill intelligence dossiers on suspected financiers, while Treasury continued to identify networks sending money into Iraq to support suicide attacks and Al Qaeda. The rat lines of recruits from Saudi Arabia, Libya, Morocco, and other parts of the "jihadi" world were funneled through Damascus International Airport en route to the Iraqi battlefields. This had become the battlefield of choice for Al Qaeda. With their presence came flows of funding that we needed to disrupt both inside and outside of Iraq.

Our original mission, asset recovery, had come to an end, but we had channeled our strategies into a legitimately new military innovation. The model of threat finance cells (TFCs)—tracking an enemy's assets and using them as a key vulnerability—began to take hold. In Afghanistan, with a rising Taliban insurgency in 2007 and 2008, we moved to create an Afghan Threat Finance Cell in Kabul. This one would be led by the Drug Enforcement Agency under the visionary leadership of Mike Braun, the chief of the DEA's expeditionary and intelligence-driven Strategic Operations Division (SOD). The DEA had already been tracking and arresting Taliban narcotics traffickers. The trick now was to combine those efforts with the military's capabilities and Treasury's tools. What emerged was a new capability in Afghanistan to exploit financial information and the money and corruption tied to the opium trade to target the Taliban and its Al Qaeda allies. This model would animate policy discussions within the Department of Defense and at Special Operations Command as officials determined how the United States could leverage this brand of financial warfare to its benefit.

In the years since we created the Iraq Threat Finance Cell, "threat finance" has become a part of the military's vernacular and doctrines. The key counterinsurgency generals, David Petraeus and Stanley A. McChrystal, along with Admiral Eric T. Olsen, in charge of Special Operations Command, would begin to adopt this terminology and devote military resources to helping stem suspect financial flows in and out of war zones. This term now animates the military's thinking and planning against America's enemies, and it has embedded itself in the broader US national security lexicon.

For our small team at Treasury, the Saddam asset hunt had initially seemed like a departure from the work we had already been doing to combat terrorist financing and isolate rogue states. However, in reality it dovetailed with that work and served to animate new thinking about a different kind of target—the high-end, all-encompassing corruption of kleptocracies, regimes engaged in widespread and endemic corruption, often serving the personal gain of the leadership. We had now seen how a regime could game the international system for profit. Saddam's activities corrupted not only his own society but also those that came into contact with Iraq's economy and touched its money. The international system had never before been adequately prepared to deter kleptocracy or to address its effects and aftermath. Though corruption was often pervasive in third world countries, it was often the first world banking centers and high-end real-estate markets that served as the welcoming refuge for leaders' assets. Our work in Iraq had created an effective roadmap for recovering assets. It required cooperation with other governments and with the banking world—and it worked—yet with the new post-9/11 financial environment and the tools we had refined, we were capable of doing more.

Soon I would leave Treasury to join the National Security Council, but I would remain a silent partner within the White House. From there, we sketched out a means of globalizing the lessons we had learned from the Saddam asset hunt to inoculate the international community from the perpetuation of kleptocracy. We would not be able to stop corruption cold, but we could make rogue leaders think twice before wiring millions of dollars to an offshore bank account—and banking executives think twice about taking the money of "politically exposed persons."

On August 10, 2006, President Bush issued the 2006 National Strategy to Internationalize Efforts Against Kleptocracy. There was little fanfare, but those in the anticorruption world noticed and saw its effects. When he launched the effort, President Bush made the most comprehensive statement on kleptocracy of any president to date:

> For too long, the culture of corruption has undercut development and good governance and bred criminality and mistrust around the world. High-level corruption by senior government officials, or kleptocracy, is a grave and corrosive abuse of power and represents the most invidious type of public corruption. It threatens our national interest and violates our values. It impedes our efforts to promote freedom and democracy, end poverty, and combat international crime and terrorism. Kleptocracy is an obstacle to democratic progress, undermines faith in government institutions, and steals prosperity from the people. Promoting transparent, accountable governance is a critical component of our freedom agenda.

. . . Our objective is to defeat high-level public corruption in all its forms and to deny corrupt officials access to the international financial system as a means of defrauding their people and hiding their ill-gotten gains.[9]

This strategy statement set the stage for greater prosecutorial focus on corruption overseas; provided for stronger anticorruption measures and more targeted financial intelligence gathering against rogue regimes; and authorized an increase in diplomatic efforts to gain support on this issue from close partners such as the United Kingdom, Transparency International, and the World Bank and to work with them to create new anticorruption initiatives. Eventually, the World Bank would begin its own Stolen Asset Recovery (StAR) Initiative. The Egmont Group of Financial Intelligence Units would create a specific group to focus on high-end corruption, while the Financial Action Task Force would devote more anti-money-laundering attention to the need for heightened financial scrutiny of "politically exposed persons" (PEPs). Switzerland would begin to take the lead on asset recovery in Europe, creating higher standards for its banks and acting more quickly than most other countries to freeze and repatriate leadership assets. Switzerland also launched the "White Money Initiative" to ensure the integrity and reputation of its financial system.

Ultimately, the hunt for Saddam's assets revealed crates full of cash, hundreds of Hussein front companies in the Middle East and Europe, a web of thousands of accounts, and the farce of the Oil for Food program. All told, we identified over $5 billion in assets, returning almost $3.5 billion to Iraq, and stopped the flow of millions more in suspect assets. More importantly, we had further shaped the international environment to reject the flow of corrupt capital and to view high-end corruption as part of the swamp of threats to the integrity of the financial system.

Treasury had reshaped the financial battlefield—attacking Al Qaeda's finances, isolating bad banks, and conditioning the international financial system to reject rogue capital. As focused as the government was on terror and Iraq, we knew the Treasury tools and this new power would also be used to confront other authoritarian regimes that opposed the United States and its allies, including Syria, North Korea, and Iran.

Treasury's vision of financial warfare was continuing to evolve. In Iraq, we had seen the danger of a kleptocracy undaunted by traditional sanctions. In our ongoing fight against the flow of illicit capital, we recognized that we would need to draw clear lines between the legitimate financial world and the rogues who sat outside it and tried to misuse or circumvent the financial system. Soon enough, Treasury would have the opportunity to marshal the tools and experience we had accumulated to attack these rogues in ways they never expected.

8

RESURRECTION

Since the creation of the Department of Homeland Security, our team at Treasury had fought hard to make its presence known. Having survived a period of institutional turmoil, we had begun to flourish, seeing results from our new initiatives on bad banks and Iraqi assets. Though others sometimes misunderstood the work we were doing, we were confident of its importance and centrality to national security. By employing legal and economic tools, we were creating a new kind of financial warfare in the service of American interests. It was time we reconceived how our team should be organized.

First, we had to address the weaknesses inherent in the department. Most glaring was Treasury's lack of intelligence capabilities. In spite of its post-9/11 relationship with SWIFT, Treasury remained something of a passive consumer of intelligence. Its intelligence office was little more than a message center that delivered packets of information from the intelligence community to offices in the Treasury. This was a nineteenth-century model in dire need of an update for the twenty-first century.

Together with Aufhauser, we developed the concept for a new office that would correct these problems and amplify the work already underway. Aufhauser would soon craft the framework for the new office, which we simply called the "white paper." He laid out three pillars of a revitalized function at the Treasury Department: an empowered policy office; a financial crimes enforcement arm; and a new intelligence function. The paper envisioned a reconstituted, more muscular Treasury office capable of reshaping the US government's prosecution of financial warfare. Aufhauser insisted that he be the one to draft this white paper, and it was important that he did. The paper needed the credibility of the Treasury's general counsel behind it to gain traction.

The first prong of our reimagined Treasury team—an empowered policy office—would build on what we were already doing in the Executive Office of Terrorist Financing and Financial Crimes (EOTF/FC). We would continue our work using financial diplomacy to set and build standards for the legitimate financial system and to execute financial warfare campaigns. This office would also include the work of the Office of Foreign Assets Control (OFAC)—which administered sanctions programs—and of the Financial Crimes Enforcement Network (FinCEN)—which served as the ligament of information sharing between regulated financial institutions, law enforcement, and other departments. And it would include the Treasury's Executive Office for Asset Forfeiture (TEOAF), which was responsible for handling the hundreds of millions of dollars of seized assets that our law-enforcement efforts produced.

The second prong would be a new Treasury financial crimes enforcement office. Treasury may have retained some law-enforcement capability, in the form of the Internal Revenue Service–Criminal Investigative Division (IRS-CID), but Aufhauser and I believed that this wasn't enough. Treasury needed a law-enforcement capacity focused specifically on financial crimes. This would give Treasury additional leverage and an ability to drive law-enforcement tools and focus on criminal and enemy nodes and networks of financial relevance. We envisioned Treasury agents with Treasury badges investigating money laundering, counterfeiting, sanctions evasion, and various other financial crimes.

When the Department of Homeland Security was established, I

proposed that Treasury be left with "1811s" from the relevant departing agencies to focus on financial crimes enforcement. That idea died a quick death, with decision makers having little appetite for pursuing even more bureaucratic changes. It was felt that another law-enforcement body in Treasury would compete with the myriad other law-enforcement agencies in the federal government. Yet we did not wish to create another FBI or undermine the new Department of Homeland Security. We wanted a US government law-enforcement focus on illicit financial flows to be integrated into the one department whose central concern was money. A law-enforcement effort would complement the multiple tools Treasury already had at its disposal in targeting illicit financial networks—freezing orders, regulatory actions with banks, and financial intelligence.

The third prong of the new architecture of Treasury would be a full-fledged intelligence office. There was a genuine need for Treasury to be able to manage, develop, and use its own intelligence products. The dependencies in Treasury on the intelligence community were deep; it was clear that if the department was to control its own use of financial intelligence, it needed a real intelligence shop that could task, manage, and analyze financial information. The office would manage the Terrorist Finance Tracking Program with SWIFT and work to integrate the financial intelligence within the Treasury's orbit internally and with other intelligence agencies. Importantly, this office would convert intelligence into information that the Treasury could use to wield its various powers and authorities. The Treasury Department and the discipline of financial intelligence had grown up, and there needed to be a home for this function at the Treasury.

This office would use Treasury information, tools, authorities (official and unofficial), and relationships around the world (with finance ministries, central banks, and other members of the financial community) to focus entirely on financial crimes, illicit networks, terrorist financing, and other matters relating to finance that affected national security. It would not be orphaned within the department, but instead would be one of three offices and functions within the Treasury that warranted an undersecretary. This way of structuring the office would send a clear signal that this was an office with the full support of the Treasury and Capitol Hill and give it a senior seat at the table on national security issues. This office would give institutional permanence to Treasury's role in national security—apart simply from the campaign to counter terrorist financing.

The white paper became the blueprint for the new office. Art Cameron, a savvy career legislative affairs professional at Treasury, took the white paper with him to Capitol Hill. The Senate Banking Committee, led at the time by Senator Richard Shelby, a Republican from Alabama, maintained jurisdiction over Treasury's many functions tied to banking. Shelby and the committee had shown a keen interest in Treasury's role in sanctions enforcement and the campaign against terrorist financing since 9/11. The committee's focus was driven in large part by anti-money-laundering experts, such as senior staff members Steve Kroll and Steve Harris. Kroll had been the general counsel for Treasury's FinCEN and understood the importance of financial intelligence and of Treasury's capabilities. In the post-9/11 world, Kroll, Harris, and their colleagues would become critical to Treasury's work and relationship with Congress because they understood how important it was to the anti-money-laundering and national security mission.

Cameron would bring me up to the Hill to discuss the idea of a new office and our functions in relation to DHS. In general, there was steep resistance in Congress for anything new that seemed to duplicate what DHS was now doing. We had to explain that this was to be an office built on the inherent Treasury authorities and powers we were already wielding. We just needed more firepower. Slowly but surely, the idea began to gain traction.

Cameron saw an opening in the fact that Senator Shelby was not only the chairman of the Banking Committee but a key member of the Senate Permanent Select Committee on Intelligence. Perhaps Shelby would be the key to getting new legislation on the Hill through the intelligence committee, rather than through banking. This hunch turned out to be correct. Creating the new office through the intelligence committee would prove less controversial and more easily managed. Cameron worked with Shelby's staffers to insert Treasury's new "Office of Intelligence and Analysis" (OIA) into the draft intelligence authorization bill. This was the start. OIA would be the intelligence arm of the office outlined by Aufhauser's white paper.

By the winter of 2003, all of the behind-the-scenes work was done. Now we needed the secretary of the treasury's official sign-off. John Duncan, Treasury's assistant secretary for legislative affairs, walked into the secretary of the treasury's office on the third floor to make the pitch. Well-respected as a wise man of Washington's political world, Duncan was in charge of all of Treasury's congressional interactions and relations. He was Cameron's boss and had helped to manage expectations on the Hill and in the Treasury as to what was achievable. When Duncan talked, people listened. This time, he explained with calm clarity the opportunity presented in the intelligence authorization bill and asked Secretary John Snow whether he supported the creation of a new intelligence office at the Treasury Department.

Secretary Snow was aware that this was not a project being driven out of the White House or the administration, but instead by Congress. Indeed, there was little appetite within the White House to create yet a new organization within the Treasury. Even within Treasury, which had suffered cuts as a result of the Homeland Security transition, there was little enthusiasm for a bigger office committed to isolating rogue financial behavior. There was a risk of upsetting the White House and other members of the president's cabinet by not coordinating this decision. But Congress had presented the option, and there was no time for the usual protracted policy review. Snow knew that Treasury and the administration would be worse off if he said no, left with the legal responsibility but not the capability to fulfill its mission, despite all the good work already being done.

For Snow, it wasn't a difficult decision. After listening to Duncan and his chief of staff, Chris Smith, and asking some questions about how committed the Congress was to this mission, he looked at Duncan and Smith and said, "Let's go for it. This has my support." With that simple direction, Duncan had what he needed. Duncan and Cameron would give Senator Shelby and his team on the Hill the green light to move forward with the new office.

On December 8, 2004, Congress created Treasury's new Office of Intelligence and Analysis, to be overseen by an undersecretary and run by an assistant secretary. This would make the US Treasury Department the first finance ministry in the world to have an arm with an active intelligence function. It would be part of a new Treasury office, which had not yet been given a name, that would oversee all three prongs of the new office we had envisioned. OIA was the intelligence cornerstone.[1]

The new legislation specified that the new assistant secretary should "build a robust analytical capability on terrorist finance by coordinating and overseeing work involving intelligence analysts in all components of the Department of the Treasury, focusing on the highest priorities of the Department, as well as ensuring that the existing intelligence needs of the OFAC and FinCEN are met; and . . . provide intelligence support to senior officials of the Department on a wide range of international economic and other relevant issues."[2] We had looked around the intelligence community for someone to create this new intelligence capability at Treasury while integrating Treasury into the broader intelligence community. We ultimately turned inward to Janice Gardner. Gardner, a Japanese American and well-respected longtime CIA analyst, had been serving as Secretary Snow's intelligence briefer and principal liaison with the CIA for a couple of years. She knew the Treasury and had been paying close attention to what we were building. We respected and trusted her. Gardner agreed to resign from her position in the CIA and join the senior leadership at the Treasury Department.

By the time her successor, senior professional Leslie Ireland, another longtime CIA analyst, took over in 2010, the Treasury's OIA was producing original intelligence reports and analysis. In addition, the assistant secretary of the treasury had become the director of the National Intelligence Manager office for the entire intelligence community for "threat finance." The Treasury Department was now leading in the financial intelligence game. It had come full circle.

We would combine this new intelligence office with the existing Executive Office for Terrorist Financing and Financial Crimes that I was running, and my position would be elevated to the assistant secretary level. We would now have a robust office dedicated to attacking the financial networks of our enemies. This would become the hub for the new brand of financial warfare. Snow would later reflect that this was the most important decision he made during his tenure at the Treasury Department.

The public affairs professionals got into the game, with Rob Nichols, Tony Fratto, and Molly Millerwise Meiners offering ideas for the new office's name. This was no longer the old "Enforce-ment" office. Nor were we attempting to build a law-enforcement agency to compete with the Department of Justice. And it was more than the Executive Office for Terrorist Financing and Financial Crimes. The name needed to imply an intelligence function as well as the role we had already staked out in national security. Nichols and Meiners felt that the office had to have "Terrorism" in its title, since it was born out of the campaign to counter terrorist financing and would continue to lead the charge for Treasury against Al Qaeda. I had wanted the office name to signal that it was doing more than just countering terrorism—and thus advocated for inclu-sion of the terms "Financial Crime" or "Financial Integrity." These were seen as too vague. The name also needed to highlight the Treasury intelligence function.

The name we settled upon was "Office of Terrorism and Financial

Intelligence" (TFI). It was clean and simple, even if it didn't capture everything the office was doing or would accomplish in the coming years. Now all Treasury needed was an undersecretary—and soon enough, the secretary found someone who seemed a solid fit—Stuart Levey.

Levey was a well-respected lawyer who worked as the principal associate deputy attorney general, an important position in the Office of the Deputy Attorney General. In the early days after 9/11, he had overseen immigration issues, terrorist tracking, and other thorny legal issues for the Department of Justice. He did so with great professionalism and without much fanfare. A couple of years later, he took on the portfolio of terrorist financing for the Department of Justice, which gave him an insight into Treasury's role and capabilities.

Levey had not always been sympathetic, and frequently he had gone to battle against me and the Treasury in interagency meetings or policy decisions. He was always fair, but he was also tough. He had built a reputation as being smart and reliable. Even when we fought, I liked his grit and good faith.

In particular, Levey had never liked the Treasury's perceived intrusion into the FBI's role as the lead on terrorism investigations in the United States. The existence of the Treasury law-enforcement initiative Operation Green Quest, led by Customs and assisted by the IRS-CID and the Secret Service, had been a thorn in the side of the FBI. The FBI did not like the competition and confusion that a separate law-enforcement effort seemed to create. With Green Quest moving aggressively on cases against illegal money-service businesses, charities of concern, and tax avoidance by suspect individuals like Abdurahman Muhammad Alamoudi, there was real competition in town. Levey heard the complaints, and he didn't like the apparent interference with the FBI or the potential crossed wires on intelligence operations.

Once the decision had been made to move Customs and the Secret Service to the Department of Homeland Security, the fate of

Operation Green Quest was sealed. The Department of Justice did not want to replicate the law-enforcement fights it had with Treasury with a new behemoth department with parallel law-enforcement powers and resources. Levey set out to kill Green Quest—a legacy of Treasury's traditional enforcement efforts. He negotiated a deal with the new leadership of the Department of Homeland Security that gave the FBI explicit primacy over any cases that touched upon terrorism or terrorist financing. Levey had delivered for the FBI. The signature law-enforcement effort launched by the Treasury after 9/11 was no more.

When the White House's Presidential Personnel Office called Levey in early 2004, asking him to consider becoming the undersecretary of the treasury, he was somewhat skeptical. Hadn't Treasury's authorities and efforts largely been transferred to the Department of Homeland Security? Hadn't he just put a stake through the heart of one of Treasury's signature counter-terrorist-financing efforts? He didn't quite know what was being created, or whether it was intended to compete with the Department of Justice. In some ways, his healthy skepticism made him the ideal candidate.

Levey started making calls, and he spoke with me and others about what the new office was and what we intended to do with it. I explained to Levey that our mission was about leveraging Treasury's tools and capabilities in the national security issues facing the country. Treasury's ability to design and execute broader financial campaigns to protect the United States and to isolate rogues in the financial system could not be done anywhere else. And this was about more than just freezing the assets of terrorist suspects in the United States or initiating investigations. This was about leveraging Treasury's authorities, information, and powerful suasion capabilities to prompt the international financial system to reject business dealings with rogue actors of all stripes. This was a new power that could be wielded to great effect.

After reflection, Levey took a leap of faith and decided to lead the new office at Treasury. The vanquisher of Green Quest would

become the head of the new Treasury office. I was ecstatic to have
him on board—as an ally and to provide needed senior help in the
interagency and overseas work. We had done all we could with the
small group we had assembled and had proven the value of the work
that could be done from Treasury. We were all exhausted from fending off bureaucratic battles and were looking forward to having more
firepower. Now it was time to grow the office, and Levey was ready
to lead it. Later, Levey would kindly reflect that he was called upon
to coach a group of all-stars who were already playing the game.

The stage had been set. It was time to replicate the paradigm we
had established for a new brand of financial warfare.

TFI's work would be shaped by the tactics we had used in the past
to attack terrorist financing: targeted designations, pressure on
banks, law-enforcement investigations, international cooperation
built on UN sanctions obligations, and the development of international norms and capacity building to isolate rogue financial behavior. What made this approach effective was that it focused on illicit
activity that could infect the international financial system. Our
efforts to stop terrorist financing, isolate money laundering, and
battle kleptocracy had revealed that the enemies of the United
States used many of the same systems and networks to evade detection and move money around the world. With the tools and know-
how we were developing, we could serve national security objec-
tives while protecting the integrity of the international financial system from tainted capital.

On a long plane trip in 2003, I took out a scrap of paper and
mapped out what I thought should be the framework for the paradigm. Along the top of my sketch I listed the various illicit financial
activities tied to national security issues of concern: terrorist financing, rogue states, drug trafficking, organized crime, kleptocracy, and
proliferation of weapons of mass destruction. These categories over-
lapped in a number of ways. Along the left side, I laid out our prin-

cipal tools: targeted financial designations, information use and sharing mechanisms, UN Security Council resolutions and treaties, and Financial Action Task Force standards and regulatory focus. There were other tools—such as criminal statutes and prosecutions—that I did not include. I was delineating the various aspects of a financial warfare architecture—which I believed should not focus on classic country programs (like our sanctions often were), but on systems and networks. We could only impact these systems and networks by using the full array of Treasury tools and influence. The sketch was a mess, but it gave form for me to the new financial-warfare paradigm that had emerged and was to come. I saw this as a complement to what we were doing with the Bad Bank Initiative and a natural expansion of the work that we had done to establish new, more aggressive ways of attacking terrorist financing.

The chart was instructive. It was clear that proliferation and organized crime could be attacked financially far more aggressively than we were attacking them at that point, especially considering the outsized impact of both on national security and their reliance on illicit financing. Importantly, the issue of proliferation was a systemic way of addressing our deepest concerns and threats from rogue states—particularly Iran, North Korea, and Syria. We had to think big and build a new framework for addressing these problems.

The United States had not ignored proliferation financing. A sanctions program was in place, and President Bush had launched the Proliferation Security Initiative (PSI) in 2002 to improve coordination with our willing allies in the interdiction of suspect shipments. Much more could be done, however. The US government's experience with proliferation—the most critical installment of which involved the network of Abdul Qadeer (AQ) Khan—had taught us that proliferation was driven by profit. Nationalist interests may well come into play, but money was ultimately the grease as well as the engine of the international weapons proliferation system—which gave TFI an opening to make a difference.

AQ Khan—known as the father of the Pakistani nuclear program—had fashioned the most expansive proliferation network we had ever seen, and he had done so to make money. He sold nuclear secrets and parts to rogue regimes like Libya, Syria, North Korea, and Iran. His proliferation business, which operated throughout the Middle East and Asia, relied on Swiss financial facilitators as well as manufacturing facilities in Malaysia and South Africa.

The financial network that supported AQ Khan helped to fuel both his operations and his capabilities. AQ Khan relied on the Swiss engineer Friedrich Tinner and his sons Urs Tinner and Marco Tinner to facilitate much of his global financial networking. Authorities were familiar with the Tinners. In the mid-1990s, UN inspectors had supplied documents to Swiss authorities alleging that Friedrich Tinner had sold Saddam Hussein parts for a bomb fuel production line. Tinner denied knowing where the parts had been sent, and the Swiss dropped the investigation. Another investigation found suspicious money transfers from a Dubai currency exchange used by the 9/11 hijackers to Marco Tinner's Swiss bank accounts and companies. The Tinner family denied having any knowledge of a 9/11 connection. Swiss magistrate Andreas Müller, however, said in 2010 that she believed Marco should face money-laundering charges. The money in question, $12.5 million, came from Urs's work for AQ Khan's company, Scomi Precision Engineering (SCOPE), in Malaysia, and AQ Khan's middleman, B.S.A. Tahir. Urs claimed he had stopped working for Tahir because he had not been paid for months.

The legal battle following their arrests in 2003 exposed the Tinners' possible ties to the CIA. The family was ultimately suspected of assisting the CIA in tracking and disrupting AQ Khan's network in return for millions of dollars. The Agency reportedly approached the Tinners in the 1990s to request that they supply information about AQ Khan and introduce flawed equipment into their shipments to him,[3] even though Swiss law prohibits cooperation with foreign intelligence. In 2007, the Swiss Federal Council canceled the investigation into the Tinners' CIA connections and destroyed evidence of their participation in AQ Khan's network. Ostensibly, this was to prevent the theft or spread of sensitive nuclear technology. But a 2009 report by the Swiss parliament suggested that both decisions were the product of US pressure.

Investigation into the Tinners' involvement with AQ Khan lasted from 2008 to 2010 and also exposed unspecified allegations of forgery, money laundering, and pornography.[4] In 2011, the family agreed to plead guilty to charges of nuclear smuggling to expedite their legal proceedings and limit the publication of sensitive details; the deal limited their prison terms to five years. The Tinners were found guilty of supplying illicit materials and information to Libya's nuclear program as part of the AQ Khan network in September 2012. They received suspended or shortened prison sentences because of their role in the US investigation, but had to pay substantial fines.

The 2003 interception of an AQ Khan shipment bound for Libya and the American invasion of Iraq prompted the Libyan government to disclose and renounce its nuclear weapons program. The AQ Khan network was exposed and dismantled, leading to revelations about the advancement of weapons of mass destruction programs in Libya, North Korea, Iran, and Syria. AQ Khan made a public confession about his illicit activities the following year and was placed under house arrest.[5] AQ Khan later declared that this confession was coerced by the Pakistani government. The declaration by the Islamabad High Court in 2009 that AQ Khan was again free to move about the country was met with concern in the United States. That year, the US State Department sanctioned three private companies and thirteen individuals for their involvement in AQ Khan's network, citing the need to "provide a warning to other would-be proliferators."

The damage had been done, however, with a global proliferation network having spread nuclear know-how and technology to the worst regimes in the world. North Korea would continue to march toward nuclear capability, with its first test in 2006; Syria developed a nuclear power plant, based on North Korean designs and assistance, that was suspected of having a military purpose (it was destroyed by Israeli fighters in 2007); and the Iranians continue their cat-and-mouse game with the international community while expanding their nuclear program. We are still dealing with the fallout of AQ Khan's proliferation network.

Treasury needed to find a way of disrupting and deterring the financing of proliferation networks in the future. If we could disrupt proliferation networks, we could undermine rogue regimes. We would need to employ all the tools at our command and reshape the international financial landscape to reject proliferation financing.

We crafted an executive order intended to give the secretary of the treasury the power to identify and freeze the assets of anyone involved in or facilitating the proliferation of weapons of mass destruction—to include financial institutions—as well as of any entities owned or controlled by those involved. There was skepticism and little enthusiasm for this approach, at first even within the Treasury Department. But, critically, the new OFAC director, Bob Werner, a former Supreme Court law clerk and Treasury lawyer, was on board. He was a staunch supporter of the idea and established a unit to focus on proliferation financing. Werner understood exactly what we were trying to do with Treasury's powers to isolate the front companies and banks facilitating proliferation of weapons and dangerous materiel. He would continue to serve as a chief ally in his role at OFAC and later as director of FinCEN. Stuart Levey made phone calls to the Silberman-Robb WMD Commission (officially the Commission on the Intelligence Capabilities of the United States Regarding Weapons of Mass Destruction) to ensure that this executive order and a new financial approach to proliferation were included in its recommendations.[6] President Bush signed Executive Order 13382 on June 29, 2005. The key financial tool to go after proliferation finance had been created—and it would be the cornerstone of our financial campaigns directed at those engaged in proliferation finance.

The State Department helped to shape the international environment with the passage of a new UN Security Council resolution, 1540, adopted in April 2004. The resolution obligates countries to prevent the support, financing, creation, and proliferation of weapons of mass destruction. At the same time, we launched an effort at the Financial Action Task Force, led by Chip Poncy, to make proliferation financing an area of focus for the world's principal anti-money-laundering body. We wanted to build recognized standards of conduct for banks and other financial institutions to address the concerns surrounding proliferation. Poncy would lead that effort for years, doggedly building consensus and technical expertise in the international body.

By 2006, FATF was debating new standards and methodologies tied to countering proliferation finance and money laundering. We would amplify the impact of these efforts by pushing for UN recognition of the standards and findings of FATF. These efforts would soon be recognized and adopted by the United Nations Security Council, which referenced FATF's work in its nonproliferation resolutions tied to Iran and North Korea. By the time the new anti-money-laundering standards were updated and adopted in Paris in February 2012, the FATF standards—the de facto requirements on the international system—were known as the International Standards on Combating Money Laundering and the Financing of Terrorism and Proliferation.

As we worked to expand this initiative, I always kept my original sketch folded in a small stack of notecards in my shirt pocket. It would grow crumpled and frayed over time, but I held onto it anyway. The ideas that were embedded in the work to come had first come together on that piece of paper.

Before leaving the Treasury Department for the White House in 2005, I had thought about turning the chart into a memo for Secretary Snow—as a roadmap of sorts. I didn't do so, in part out of respect for Stuart Levey, who was now running the Office of Terrorism and Financial Intelligence at Treasury. Also, I knew that from my new position on the National Security Council staff, I was well positioned to help Levey and the Treasury steer their efforts as needed. The new paradigm was already in motion. The memo I had once envisioned for Secretary Snow, I would write later that year for President Bush.

The Treasury had been resurrected. With the new Office of Terrorism and Financial Intelligence, it could now begin to use the paradigm that had been established in the terrorist financing campaign to full effect to attack rogue and enemy financial networks of concern. There was now a permanent address in the US government for the execution of all-out financial warfare.

Part III

FINANCIAL FURIES

9

"Killing the Chicken to Scare the Monkeys"

The Treasury had been training its financial sights on the ripest of rogue state targets: North Korea. The regime in Pyongyang was guilty of virtually all of the illicit activities we wanted the international financial system to reject. To generate funds, the Kim dynasty had become the quintessential criminal state. To access and move these funds, it relied on access to the international financial system. This was its vulnerability. We had only to determine how to exploit it.

In early 2003, while looking for vulnerable bad banks, we noticed a small bank in Macau that was facilitating a range of illicit financial activities, including transactions for the North Korean regime. I assigned an analyst detailed to the Treasury from the intelligence community to produce a detailed sketch of North Korea's links to international finance based on the best intelligence and open-source information available. Within a few weeks, she came back to me with a map of North Korean financial links. As soon as I flattened out the big chart of North Korea's financial infrastructure, I knew this would become our financial battle map.

Showing the banks most closely involved with North Korea and the countries where North Korea had significant financial links, the chart signaled national origin with flags next to each bank and institution. Chinese flags and links dominated the map, as might be expected. Still, I was surprised to see that even an isolated pariah state like North Korea maintained significant connections to major banks. To do business abroad, North Korea was using front companies and banks in places like Vienna, Russia, Singapore, Hong Kong, Beijing, and Macau. This meant it had international financial exposure that we could target and exploit. With this insight, our strategy to find Pyongyang's financial Achilles' heel began.

North Korea's economy was already inherently vulnerable to the new brand of financial pressure we were wielding. Since the Korean War, the international community, led by the United States and its allies, had isolated North Korea with classic state-driven trade sanctions. Little trade or commercial activity existed between North Korea and the rest of the world. Sanctions blocked North Korea's import of luxury goods and foreign currencies while channeling trade to specific and tightly controlled economic zones along the South Korean and Chinese border. China was North Korea's most important economic lifeline—serving as its principal trading relationship—with China benefiting from access to North Korean mines and the influence the economic relationship gave it with Pyongyang.

North Korea's economy was mismanaged into deep poverty in the 1990s and early 2000s, with little legitimate economic activity generated from within. Despite a short-lived warming of relations in the late 1990s between North and South Korea—and the United States—North Korea had remained isolated from the global market, running a trade deficit of more than $1 billion per year. This imbalance, combined with the scarcity of foreign currency in North Korea, further isolated the country's fragile economy and stunted its economic growth. Cycles of devastating famine had taken a severe toll. Yet, even while the North Korean people continued to starve to death, the regime and the military remained well fed and funded.

The Kim dynasty constructed an economy built for regime survival. The egomaniacal leadership had maintained an appetite for luxury goods and required substantial capital to pay senior members of the government and other supporters to sustain their own control. The regime also needed funding to pay for its nuclear program and missile ambitions. The North Koreans relied heavily on trade with China, along with remittances from South Korea and the "Chosen Soren," a pocket of Korean immigrants in Japan.

To circumvent international restrictions and compensate for its failed economy, the North Korean rulers had constructed a criminal money-making machine. The government and its secretive military and intelligence units developed sophisticated counterfeiting and smuggling operations worldwide that were designed to transport fake products into global markets.[1] Front companies and trade offices would become hubs of North Korea's commercial relationships in places like Hong Kong and Macau. North Korea's embassies, diplomats, state-sponsored companies, and intelligence services together constituted an elaborate illicit distribution network for counterfeit and illicit goods.

The regime of Kim Jong Il assigned "Office 39"—a special unit of the North Korean military and intelligence services—to raise funds abroad, using diplomatic posts and front companies to build business lines and launder illicit proceeds. The counterfeit products were sold to international organized crime groups, and the proceeds then funneled back to North Korea through shell corporations, formal diplomatic accounts and pouches, and the personal holdings of senior North Korean officials. It was estimated that the North Koreans had collected revenues of between $550 million and $700 million per year from the sale of counterfeit cigarettes and narcotics.[2]

The most brazen North Korean illicit financial activity was the counterfeiting of US $100 bills. These were the highest-quality counterfeit US bills in the world. The Secret Service had dubbed them the "supernote." Most bank tellers and commercial enterprises could not tell the difference between the supernote and genuine US currency. The paper, ink, and printing for the fake currency made the supernotes almost identical to real bills.

The supernote was first detected in 1989 by a Filipino money exchanger in Manila, who felt the counterfeit bills and knew from his tactile experience with US currency that something was not right.[3] The Secret Service investigates all types of counterfeit currency—but most of it is of poor quality and has little chance of undermining confidence in the US dollar. The investigators for the supernote found that it was a different breed altogether.

As Secret Service agents began to talk to banks and money exchangers around the world, they found more instances of the supernote popping up in locations as far flung as Taiwan, Yemen, and Peru. A pattern began to emerge. Wherever there was a North Korean presence or link, the supernote appeared. Surveillance photos of North Korean officials passing supernotes in banks and casinos revealed direct connections between the note and the regime in Pyongyang. Currency forensics reinforced the conclusion that North Korea was producing the bills. By tracking each instance of the supernote, the Secret Service traced the currency straight back to North Korea.

The counterfeit $100 bill had proved quite useful to North Korean agents and diplomats—especially when big-ticket cash transactions and imports were necessary or illicit deals with organized crime figures were consummated. The regime even used supernotes to buy genuine currency. North Korean agents and front companies would sell the notes at a discount—for $70 or $80 per note—typically to foreign buyers. The buyers would get the full value of the supernotes when they introduced them into the financial system, and the North Koreans got real foreign currency in return. The trade in counterfeit currency had brought the North Koreans closer to Asian criminal triads as well as to the Irish Republican Army (IRA). One well-known IRA member, Sean Garland, worked directly with the North Koreans to help move supernotes in Ireland. Garland, a wanted Irish leftist and terrorist organizer, visited the North Korean embassy in Moscow and returned to distribute millions of dollars of supernotes through his criminal network in Dublin. It had been estimated that the North Korean government earned $15 million to $25 million per year from the counterfeiting.[4]

The experts at the US Bureau of Engraving and Printing and the US Secret Service tried to stay one step ahead of the counterfeiters by changing the type of printing and the special features of US currency. Much of US currency is held outside of the country, with citizens in many countries around the world—where local currencies are volatile or governments can change currency policies on a whim—holding onto dollars like an insurance policy. More than two-thirds of the $800 billion of US currency in circulation is held abroad.[5]

The confidence in the dollar and its widespread use makes it valuable to hold. Whenever a new version of US currency is introduced, the Treasury devotes resources to explaining the changes in places like Russia, where a significant number of US bills are held. The $100 notes, with the famous Ben Franklin profile, are often the preferred denomination. The new "big head" $100 notes—so-called because the picture of Ben Franklin takes up more of the space on the currency—had special security features intended to make it almost impossible to counterfeit.

The North Koreans had made an industry of producing new lines of counterfeit notes to match the new bills and security features introduced by the Treasury. Over the years, the North Koreans have issued several series of the fake currency to account for changes in the style and security features of the "Benjamins" and to improve the quality of the counterfeit. Pyongyang imported high-quality industrial printers, the same kinds of intaglio presses used by the US Bureau of Engraving and Printing, to manufacture US dollars. The counterfeiters were using the same kinds of paper as the United States, with the right mix of cotton and with the same optically variable ink used by the United States. They used specially designed plates to create near-perfect replicas.

The currency experts at the Secret Service showed me samples of supernotes compared to the real thing. Minute differences between the fake currency and the real notes could only be detected with a magnifying glass when looking at very specific security features on the bill. Mike Green, the National Security Council's senior director for Asia Affairs during the Bush administration, described the Secret Service's presentation on the supernote to him in 2001 as the most interesting briefing he had heard, noting that "all [the Secret Service] wanted were the [currency] plates back." Pyongyang had become a full-scale industrial counterfeiter of US currency.

The counterfeiting of these notes and the undermining of confidence in the US dollar were unacceptable. Under international law, counterfeiting the currency of a country qualifies as a proxy attack on its national integrity and sovereignty—and a *causus belli* to justify self-defense. This international doctrine reflects the importance of the integrity of currency to countries and their economies as well as the use of counterfeiting as a form of financial attack throughout history. During World War II, the Nazis forced Jewish artists to replicate US and British currency as part of an operation seeking to undermine the Allied economies. This effort was never implemented, however, and most of the bills were dumped underwater. From this perspective, North Korea has been engaged in financial warfare by undermining the integrity of the US $100 bill.

Moreover, Pyongyang ran major drug-trafficking operations and was a source of illicit proliferation of missile and nuclear technology—engaging in both for the purpose of generating funds and preserving the regime. Abdul Qadeer Khan worked closely with North Korea to build and export centrifuge and other nuclear technologies. North Koreans helped to design the nuclear facility in Syria that was destroyed by the Israelis in 2007 and were advising the Syrians.[6]

Our team sought a way to squeeze the regime financially that would stop its illicit financial activity, impede its proliferation of nuclear technology, and end or slow its own nuclear program. Again, a financial tool of isolation could help give teeth to our diplomacy. It would also demonstrate Treasury's importance on one of the thorniest national security problems facing the United States.

Our strategy was straightforward—we would tighten and close North Korea's remaining access to the banking system. This approach came directly from the Bad Bank Initiative, which was well underway and serving its purpose. Already we were uncovering and isolating key financial institutions facilitating a full range of illicit financial activity—from drug trafficking and money laundering to terrorist financing and sanctions evasion. Now we would add North Korea to the target deck.

Pyongyang was dependent on banks to do business. It had a domestic bank, Tanchong Commercial Bank, which the regime used as its primary financial institution and a trading company doing business with the world. It facilitated much of the proliferation activity with the North Korean company KOMID (Korean Mining and Development Corporation). It also relied on Daedong Credit Bank, the only foreign-owned bank in North Korea. These banks helped give the North Koreans access to other banks and the international financial system. And the regime and its networks relied on banks outside of North Korea for accounts, credit, and access to international trade finance and wire-transfer services. Despite their economic isolation, the North Koreans had to be able to access and move capital outside of North Korea's borders—especially if they wanted to proliferate missile and nuclear technology and profit from illicit activity.

The network of banks was the key to our battle plan. All we needed was the right bank to target—one that was assisting the North Koreans to evade sanctions and engaging in illicit financial activity in its own right. As we had learned from past initiatives, by incapacitating that bank, we would effectively make doing business with North Korea toxic to the private sector. We wanted North Korean financial activity to be rejected like an infection by the antibodies we had built up in the international financial system.

The bank of choice was Banco Delta Asia (BDA). BDA was a Macau-based bank held by the Delta Asia Group (Holdings) Ltd. and controlled by Stanley Ho.[7] Macau was historically a crossroads for maritime commerce and trade, finance, and people—and in recent years had become a major international gambling center. In Macau's growing casino industry, billions were invested and spent annually. Pods of "whales"—high-value gamblers—visited Macau from around Asia and the rest of the world. For many years, local operators and investors, like Stanley Ho, dominated the Macanese casino market. Major American and international casino moguls, such as Steve Wynn and MGM, had major properties or planned investments in Macau. This booming former colonial enclave of China is now four times as large as Las Vegas, producing more than $23 billion a year in revenues.[8] With this cash and flow of goods and people from around the world came illicit trade, smuggling, and money laundering. Macau was known as a jurisdiction with lax money-laundering controls. Officials would look the other way as the economy prospered on the backs of both legitimate and illegitimate commerce. It was an ideal place for the North Koreans to do business.

BDA would become the most important bad bank we would identify as part of our Bad Bank Initiative. It provided an ideal access point for North Korea into the international financial system. With little oversight in Macau, North Korea was able to pay a fee to the bank in exchange for access to its financial network. BDA was not the only bank doing business with North Korea. The regime also used the Bank of China, among others. But BDA handled a large sum of financial transfers for North Korea and most of the regime's precious metal sales as well as cash deposits and withdrawals. The bank allowed North Korea to open bank accounts, wire and launder money, and deposit bags of cash—genuine or counterfeit. North Korea was dependent on BDA—which meant BDA was the perfect target.

Because BDA was a small, private bank, its isolation was unlikely to have much effect on the United States. Chinese interests would certainly take notice, but were unlikely to deem action against BDA a direct assault on the financial sectors of Beijing or Hong Kong. The isolation would, however, send a message to the rest of North Korea's bankers. Given a choice, banks doing business with North Korea would abandon that country's business to avoid the stigma and financial sting of US regulatory action. The volume of business they did with North Korea and the related profit margins did not make it worth the risk. Targeting BDA would force Chinese banks and others to choose in favor of isolating North Korea for their own self-interest, even if Beijing didn't like it. Perhaps the most important potential strategic impact of this plan would be that we would be employing the unwitting assistance of China to isolate North Korea. It was a strategy reflected well in an ancient Chinese proverb: we had found a way to "kill the chicken to scare the monkeys."

In 2004, we started work on a Section 311 regulatory package— readying the designation of BDA as a primary money-laundering concern to cut off any correspondent banking relationships in the United States. Importantly, we would not actually be freezing any accounts or transactions. Instead, our action would send a message to the international financial community that this bank was a financial pariah because of its illicit business with North Korea. The market would take care of the rest. As it turned out, this move would ultimately prove to be the most important Section 311 action we would ever unleash.

At the same time, David Shedd, a senior director at the National Security Council who was responsible for intelligence policies, called me into his corner office in the Eisenhower Executive Office Building next to the White House to read me into a sensitive project. Shedd, the son of a missionary who had grown up in South America, was a longtime intelligence professional. We had become friends, but he was dead serious about his job and very matter-of-fact when it was time to get down to business. From his influential position managing sensitive intelligence issues for National Security Adviser Condoleezza Rice and the National Security Council, Shedd was a seminal figure in shaping the post-9/11 development of the intelligence community.

When I arrived in his office, Shedd shut the door and proceeded to tell me that there was work underway regarding North Korea that needed Treasury's input and help. I would be the only Treasury official read into the program for now. To my surprise, he told me that a small group at the State Department had already been leading an effort to look at North Korean illicit financial activity. He didn't give me many details, but he advised me to meet David Asher, a senior adviser to the assistant secretary for East Asian and Pacific Affairs. Unaware that such an effort was underway, I was eager to find out what the team at State was doing.

A few days later, I walked into a small conference room at the State Department, unsure what to expect from the department's efforts, or from Asher. An Oxford PhD and hedge fund strategist, Asher was a protégé of deputy secretary of state Richard Armitage and an expert on East Asia and global financial and trading systems.

Asher and his trusted and longtime intelligence analyst and economist from the Bureau of Intelligence and Research (INR), William Newcomb, were sitting at the table and welcomed me warmly. When I met them, Asher had a grin on his face, while Newcomb's deep voice and thick glasses clashed with his soft demeanor. Asher started by complimenting the work we had been doing on terrorist financing, noting that he had been watching our campaign from afar. Then, taking on the air of a mad professor, Asher described for me what he and Newcomb had been doing.

Asher explained that in December 2001, Deputy Secretary Armitage had authorized James A. Kelly, assistant secretary of state for East Asian and Pacific Affairs, and him to organize a closely held campaign to curtail North Korean illicit activity. Meanwhile, the president wanted to develop a new means of negotiating with North Korea. Mike Green, who helped to develop a road map for this new means of negotiation, recalls that President Bush had said, "You're just rearranging the deck chairs on the *Titanic*. I want something big." Offering rewards for good behavior clearly wasn't working. Green wanted Asher to look at the supernote problem and develop a strategy to counter it that was tied to the plans for diplomatic engagement with North Korea.

What Asher developed, with the help of Newcomb, was a broad assessment of the North Korean illicit financial networks. His theory was that these financial flows were important sources of funding for the regime. Newcomb, a trained economist, dug into the data. He uncovered interesting anomalies in North Korea's economy and balance of trade, and they began to shape his view on the importance of the illicit flow of funds to the regime. Though North Korean industrial output had fallen dramatically, and the trade deficit typically ran at around a billion dollars per year, the North Korean economy had not collapsed. It was surviving, and it was not suffering from inflation. As Asher would later put it, "North Korea had a mysteriously large black hole in its trade accounts. . . . Some dark matter, in effect, had to be filling the void."[9] That dark matter was illicit financing.

Asher had settled on the goal of stemming the illicit funding streams into Pyongyang. To do that, he wanted to use law enforcement—including the FBI and the Secret Service—in an unprecedented way. They would go after the North Korean networks, especially those tied to criminal networks abroad. The goal was to create an international enforcement model that would bring greater credibility and cooperation internationally to the efforts to shut down North Korean illicit financial flows. Once the illicit networks and activities were identified, the campaign to squeeze Pyongyang became less about politics and more about enforcement of the law. It would certainly be easier to convince foreign governments to make arrests and shut down front companies if the organizations involved were violating local criminal laws. This model was different from the classic campaign that relied primarily on political or diplomatic motivations and suasion to convince allies to act. If we could stop these flows and shut down the networks, it might provide much-needed leverage to diplomats seeking a nuclear deal at the six-party talks that had begun in August 2003.

As Asher continued his flurry of a presentation, Newcomb passed one of his large white binders to me to show me the data and links they had begun to find. I sat there and listened—amazed. I was in shock at the scope of the intelligence effort underway and the nature of the endeavor. I had been skeptical of their work at first, but the binders and the documents in them demonstrated that they had data to back up what they were concluding. They and the intelligence community had been doing their homework and knew what they were talking about.

As the briefing proceeded, I felt as though I had found two long-lost brothers—both of whom were viewing the world through the same lens I was. Just as exciting was the fact that their work coincided neatly with the work we had already begun on North Korea's banking relationships. I was already thinking about how our work on BDA could fit into their strategy. I had found in Asher and Newcomb a broader diplomatic and national security platform into which to inject our tools and financial isolation strategy against North Korea.

When they finished, I took a moment, sat back, and told them how impressed I was with their efforts and approach. I then leaned forward and offered my own little briefing. I explained the research we had been doing into the banking relationships of the regime, and I emphasized the importance of squeezing North Korean access to foreign bank accounts. The banks needed to be at the center of our approach. I explained the Bad Bank Initiative and how Section 311 permitted us to target rogue financial actors. This was different from the campaign against terrorist financing that they were already aware of, but it built on it. I then mentioned BDA as our next 311 target and told them how designating BDA might affect North Korea's access to the international financial system.

Asher and Newcomb were clearly intrigued. Though Section 311 was new to them, they were certainly focused on BDA. They invited me to participate in the small interagency group dedicated to the North Korea Illicit Activity Initiative, and I eagerly accepted.

At the first meeting I attended in late 2003—and thereafter at each meeting for nearly two years—I would explain the range of Treasury powers available, how the intelligence and law-enforcement cases we were building could be leveraged to isolate an illicit financing regime, and the possible use and impact of Section 311 against Banco Delta Asia. Most of the people in the room were aware generally of our sanctions powers, but had no experience with Treasury's tools, and so did not see what more we could do to a country that had been economically sanctioned and isolated for decades. For most in the group, what I was telling them—that targeting Banco Delta Asia, a private bank in Macau with little activity in the United States, would really impact North Korea, even though we were not sanctioning the country with anything new and would not have multilateral support for whatever we were planning— seemed counterintuitive.

The talk about our ability to use Section 311 to force an isolation of North Korea's broader illicit financial network seemed almost fanciful to them and disconnected from what the US government could actually order or control. Yet, as I assured them, this wasn't about classic sanctions or freezing assets, or even arrests or seizures. It was a modern act of financial warfare intended to isolate North Korean commercial and illicit activity from the international financial system using the subtle power of regulation and financial suasion.

A year later, the group would be taken over by the National Security Council, which brought the effort (now called the North Korean Illicit Finance Action Group, or NORKAG) into the White House orbit, with David Shedd leading the meetings and Asher serving as his deputy. National Security Adviser Condoleezza Rice and Deputy National Security Adviser Steve Hadley asked Shedd to make sure the efforts were well coordinated, while Asher tried to push for more actions to squeeze the North Koreans.

Besides making the case to the interagency group, I soon began to brief Treasury's leadership and others in the Treasury Department about the consequences of the possible 311 action. My principal concern was that the key leaders be aware of the impact this action could have on US relations with China. Targeting BDA would not only put Macau in a negative spotlight—Chinese banks would instantly realize that they might be next on the target list. The move would be sure to upset the Chinese government. The chairman of the New York Federal Reserve Bank, Tim Geithner, and the bank's longtime general counsel, Tom Baxter, were worried that the action would have unintended consequences with the Chinese. But Geithner didn't object, and Treasury Secretary Snow remained confident that we could manage any Chinese fallout. The Chinese banks would have to adapt to the reality that we would no longer tolerate North Korean financial criminal behavior. Snow, in meetings with the president and his cabinet counterparts in the Situation Room, would later describe the Treasury tools that could be brought to bear on North Korea, highlighting the purpose and workings of the 311. Defense Secretary Donald Rumsfeld pooh-poohed the notion that this kind of action could work. Nevertheless, President Bush was quite interested in and engaged with on this idea, and certainly preferred it to a military solution. Any pressure we could engineer would give our diplomats more leverage to press for a nuclear deal.

What emerged from our collaboration was a pressure campaign against the North Korean regime that consisted of three distinct stages. The first had begun in 2002 and was well underway. This stage involved investigative and intelligence operations targeting specific elements of North Korea's criminal networks. Treasury would play a role in the second stage, which would involve cutting off certain funding routes used by the regime. Our use of Section 311 action against BDA would serve as the catalyst for this stage of the campaign. The third and final stage would amount to an explicit effort to hunt down North Korea's leadership assets and shut down the engines of its illicit financing, such as Office 39. The pressure would increase with each stage as we tightened the vice on the country's financial escape routes around the world.

The first stage had already produced results, largely because of the cooperation that took place between intelligence and law-enforcement agencies and diplomats from various nations. Investigators scrutinized Golden Star Bank in Vienna, Austria, and determined that it had been not only the primary financial center for North Korean business in Europe but the front for a variety of covert and fraudulent businesses that generated foreign funds for the regime. In 2003, the Austrian authorities quietly shut the bank down and disallowed its operations. But the pressure on North Korea's overseas banking access was just beginning.

In April 2003, Australian authorities tracked a North Korean cargo vessel as it illegally entered Australian waters. Members of the Australian special forces, among the best in the world, later stopped and raided the *Pong Su* as it attempted to flee into international waters. What they found was revealing. The *Pong Su* had attempted to smuggle 150 kilograms of heroin into Australia. The shipment was tied to the Asian narcotics trade in Southeast Asia and Australia. Some of the *Pong Su* crew members had been offloaded, and they had already been arrested on shore in possession of large amounts of heroin. The drug-trafficking state had been caught red-handed. The *Pong Su* was impounded, and, in 2006, it was sunk by the Royal Australian Air Force in a military exercise. The world was now plainly on notice of North Korea's drug-trafficking and smuggling role.

Treasury contributed to stage one by making a public case about North Korean counterfeiting, with the primary intent being to make it harder for North Korea to acquire the equipment and materials it needed to upgrade its counterfeiting operation. I contacted Ron Noble, the secretary general of Interpol and a former treasury assistant secretary, an impressive, articulate law-enforcement official who had helped oversee the old Treasury Enforcement office and agencies in the late 1990s—including the Secret Service. We had developed a close relationship with Noble right after 9/11, when we agreed to share information about terrorist financing designations that would be fed into Interpol databases. We ultimately worked with Noble to tie Interpol's travel notice system to the travel ban required for terrorists and financiers designated under United Nations Security Council Resolution 1267.

I brought in the two leading Secret Service investigators on the supernote cases, who gave Noble a briefing on the counterfeit bill. We made it clear that we knew North Korea was producing these notes at will. Noble, who was quite familiar with the Secret Service's expertise, suggested that we think about an "Orange Notice" to the private sector coming from Interpol, which would advise the key industries impacted—especially the producers of large-scale industrial printers—of the contours of the cases and our concerns. This would conceal the full scope of our cases but nevertheless aid in constricting the environment in which the North was operating. The Orange Notice, published in March 2005, warned the international community and the private sector not to sell banknote production equipment to North Korea.

At the same time, we wanted to put direct pressure on the private sector. Sam Bodman, the deputy secretary of the treasury, sent a letter reminding German printing companies of existing US laws and sanctions and explaining the concern we had about North Korea's demonstrated and wanton counterfeiting of US currency. These companies, whom we suspected of selling equipment to North Korea, were now on notice of what we suspected. We were slowly but surely shaping the environment to isolate North Korean activities.

All the while, the Secret Service and the FBI were successfully disrupting North Korea's organized crime connections inside America—specifically, the counterfeiting operations on both the west and east coasts. The Secret Service had been uncovering the networks and the organized crime groups that were using supernotes and possibly acting as pass-throughs for the North Koreans. At the same time, the FBI was digging into significant additional organized crime activity, with a focus on the growing ties between Asian organized crime and La Cosa Nostra—the Mafia—in the

United States. The FBI had deep expertise in bringing down mob families in the United States and cracking Asian triads, and its agents had begun to see signs of counterfeiting—of both cigarettes and currency—in the dealings of the groups. In a globalized criminal world, criminal networks were willing to collude with counterfeiters for profit and market access. It was a marriage of convenience. Though there was tension regarding who would lead the investigations, the Secret Service and the FBI would begin to work together on two major cases that would lead to the discovery of even deeper links between North Korea and organized crime.

The cases were known by their operational names, "Royal Charm" and "Smoking Dragon." On the East Coast, the Royal Charm investigation was underway, with the FBI using "a false-front Mafia group in northern New Jersey, reminiscent of the one on the hit television show, the Sopranos," to uncover North Korean illicit financial ties. Kim Jong Il was a fan of *The Sopranos*, so the agents used the allure of the Italian Mafia as bait.

On the West Coast, the FBI had launched Smoking Dragon to investigate Asian organized crime activity—including the import of counterfeit goods into California. The investigation soon discovered that the organized crime network on the West Coast was engaged with the group on the East Coast.

We would sit down often with Department of Justice senior officials, led by Bruce Swartz, who was managing these cases and ensuring that they were integrated with the North Korean strategy. They and the investigating agents were concerned that a public action like a Section 311 designation would spook the organized crime figures and signal that we were watching the flows of illicit funds through Macau, where there was significant organized crime presence and activity. Some of the financial activity in Macau was tied directly to the organizations and activities under investigation. We agreed not to move forward with the BDA 311 until these cases were brought to fruition. It wasn't yet clear when the State Department and the White House would want to unleash BDA.

In early 2004, it appeared the cases would be brought to a conclusion during a wedding in New Jersey. The wedding would bring
together many of the key figures in organized crime who were
being taken down. It was a scenario right out of *The Sopranos.*
The wedding became the key event around which all the law-
enforcement team's efforts turned. We agreed to wait until after the
wedding to launch the 311. The "wedding" was in reality a grand
sting operation, and arrests were planned for those traveling from
around the world to attend. It took place on August 22, 2005, and
officers arrested fifty-nine people as they arrived.

The undercover operations targeting North Korean illicit activity
in the United States found counterfeit cigarettes and counterfeit
pharmaceuticals along with more than $4 million in supernotes.
These were operations befitting of the country known as a "Mafia
state." Stage one was coming off without a hitch, and the law-
enforcement barriers to action had been lifted. Now all we needed
to get before putting stage two into action was the consent of the
diplomats. During almost two years of discussions, we had been sitting on the 311, waiting for a moment that wouldn't upset the
applecart that was the six-party talks.

In my last meeting as a Treasury official in May 2005, I went to
Foggy Bottom to meet the new assistant secretary of state for East
Asian and Pacific Affairs, Chris Hill. Hill was a distinguished career
diplomat who had seen negotiating success in the Balkans in the
1990s and had been ambassador to South Korea. Condoleezza Rice,
who was now secretary of state, believed that Hill would be the one
finally to broker a deal with Pyongyang. She wanted a breakthrough, and Hill was brought in to make it happen. He was driven
by his single-minded focus on getting that deal—but this single-
mindedness would also be his greatest deficit. As our long-standing
State Department contacts, David Asher and Jim Kelly, stepped
aside to make room for Hill and his team, it soon became clear that
Hill did not much appreciate the campaign of constriction that we
had spent so much time building.

When Hill arrived, he was forty-five minutes late. He apologized and noted that he had been with the secretary, and we proceeded to talk about the work underway in the illicit financing field. We went around the table to explain who we were and what we were working on that impacted North Korean illicit financing activity. The intelligence representatives gave their briefing on the state of North Korean finances and illicit activity. The State Department representatives explained the diplomacy and outreach it had built around the issue of North Korean illicit financing. The Department of Justice described its ongoing investigations in very general terms, without a hint in the broader group that they were close to making arrests. When my time came, I could see that Hill was either distracted or uninterested. I went on to explain the 311 action we had ready to go and told him why we thought this was a critical part of the pressure campaign, but it was clear that Hill, like so many of his colleagues, had little understanding of the strategic impact that this brand of financial warfare could have.

We had set the stage for what promised to be the greatest demonstration of Treasury's most potent financial weapon to date, but as I left the meeting, I was somewhat demoralized. I was leaving Treasury to serve as the deputy national security adviser. Asher, who had worked so hard on this campaign, was literally sitting on the sidelines and on his way out of the State Department. And Hill seemed uninterested in moving our plan forward. BDA would need to wait for another day—and fortunately, that day would come.

10

The Awakening

The time for action came on September 15, 2005. After getting the go-ahead from the State Department and the White House, the Treasury Department launched a direct financial assault on Pyongyang unlike anything the North Koreans—or anyone else—had ever seen. Simply by publishing a Section 311 regulation advising US banks to end relationships with BDA, a small, private bank in Macau, the United States set powerful shock waves into motion across the banking world, isolating Pyongyang from the international financial system to an unprecedented degree. The North Koreans didn't know what hit them.

The Section 311 regulation labeled BDA a primary money-laundering concern and described the bank's role in facilitating North Korean drug trafficking, counterfeiting, and nuclear technology, not to mention related money laundering in the hundreds of millions of dollars.

It exposed the illicit activities of the "Soprano State" and Banco Delta Asia as one of the key banks it was using to launder its dirty money, deposit its counterfeit currency, and engage in smuggling and front operations: "Banco Delta Asia has provided financial services for over 20 years to multiple North Korean government agencies and front companies that are engaged in illicit activities, and continues to develop these relationships. In fact, such account holders comprise a significant amount of Banco Delta Asia's business. Banco Delta Asia has tailored its services to the DPRK's [Democratic People's Republic of Korea's] demands. . . . Banco Delta Asia's special relationship with the DPRK has specifically facilitated the criminal activities of North Korean government agencies and front companies."[1]

In a single stroke the bank was converted into a financial pariah in the US and international financial system. The tool we had been using to such great effect against bad banks since 2003 would now demonstrate its full potential.

The North Koreans certainly did not expect such an action. The regime had endured decades of financial isolation and sanctions while retaining the comfortable lifestyles expected by the leadership and military, even though they only did so at the expense of the vast majority of North Koreans. But this was something new. Unlike previous sanctions, the Section 311 regulation acted like a public financial indictment of the bank and of North Korea's illicit financial activity. Once news of the regulation circulated around the banking world, it sparked a chain of market-driven rejections of North Korean accounts and transactions. The taint of Section 311 unleashed financial furies the likes of which the regime had never experienced.

It began in Macau, where authorities shut down BDA and froze almost $25 million in North Korean assets held by fifty-two separate account holders. Depositors who feared for their own assets quickly made a run on the bank. Traders were instantly concerned that similar investigations would implicate the Bank of China, Seng Heng Bank, and other international markets. In a matter of days, BDA was being attacked from all sides. Reeling in the aftermath of the Treasury action, BDA sought the government of Macau's assistance in maintaining basic cash flow, which was running $60 million to $75 million short.[2]

The BDA board of directors abdicated its administrative and managerial responsibilities over the bank and gave governing authority to a Macau government-appointed committee. The Macau government appointed a three-member committee to take control of the bank and return its operations to normal as soon as possible. On September 30, 2005, a BDA spokesman said that all DPRK accounts had been closed.

The ramifications of cutting off BDA were just beginning. The compliance officers and general counsels of other international banks with North Korean clients quickly realized the reputational risks they faced. Austria had previously shuttered the only North Korean bank operating in Europe, Golden Star Bank. Now that the Treasury appeared to be openly hunting banks associated with North Korean illicit activity, no bank wanted to be seen as Pyongyang's financial lifeline. There was no interest or business reason to wait around to be the next target for the US Treasury. The volume or value of North Korean business to any particular institution or country certainly was not worth the risk.

In Singapore, Hong Kong, and other banking hubs around the world, regulators and compliance officers began to close or freeze North Korean bank accounts and transactions, subjecting North Korean individuals and entities to intense financial scrutiny. Millions of dollars' worth of assets were frozen or locked out of the banking system. Officials in key banking and commercial centers recognized the broader implications of this action and its impact—these kinds of targeted actions against dirty money could expose them to scrutiny and liability, costing them billions of dollars. As noted by Mike Green, then senior director for Asia for the National Security Council, "They weren't comfortable with this. Today it's North Korea, next it could be Iran and Burma that had billions in their systems."

In China, officials were not sure exactly what had happened, let alone how to respond. We had given ample advance warning to officials at the People's Bank of China about our growing concerns over North Korean illicit financial activity. Secretary Snow had spoken with the central bank governor, Zhou Xiaochuan. According to

Snow, the Chinese were not surprised and did not react to the asser-
tion that there was North Korean illicit capital coursing through the
Chinese banking system. The day before the 311 announcement,
Secretary Snow had even made a courtesy call to let the Chinese
People's Bank know what was coming. Even with these warnings,
Chinese officials had not anticipated the gravity of this action or its
ripple effects, including within the Chinese financial system.

Nevertheless, Chinese state-run banks reacted to the regulation
just like other banks. They, too, were worried about appearing to be
facilitating North Korean illicit financial activity, and they began to
close and scrutinize North Korean accounts and transactions. Chinese banks wanted access to New York and wanted to be perceived
as legitimate international financial institutions. Soon after the
Treasury's 311 action was made public, the Bank of China in Macau
froze all North Korean accounts. Despite the consternation of Chinese officials who wanted to support North Korea, market forces
compelled Chinese banks to make a choice—appear legitimate by
scrutinizing North Korean illicit financial activity in their banks, or
risk appearing like a financial rogue and losing access to the US
financial system. Officials ultimately came down on the side of protecting the Chinese banks, and on July 25, 2006, the Bank of China
announced that it had frozen accounts relating to North Korean
transactions in BDA.

The 311 action revealed an important cleavage in the Chinese
system. On the one hand, the Chinese financial system and actors
had clear economic and financial interests that required them to
preserve the perceived legitimacy of their system. They wanted
Chinese banks to be accepted by the United States as serious actors
on the right side of the line of financial legitimacy. On the other
hand, Chinese Ministry of Foreign Affairs and political officials
were not pleased that this issue was interrupting the diplomatic
dance with North Korea. On March 16, 2007, the Chinese foreign
ministry spokesman, Qin Gang, expressed his "deep regret" that
the United States had issued such a ruling. Meanwhile, the Chinese

foreign ministry and political establishment campaigned to unwind the BDA action and return the North Koreans to the six-party talks.

Perhaps the most important lesson was that the Chinese could in fact be moved to follow the US Treasury's lead and act against their own stated foreign policy and political interests. The predominance of American market dominance and financial power had leapfrogged traditional notions of financial sanctions. It was a lesson the Chinese certainly would not forget.

The Section 311 ruling had an impact that lasted well beyond its initial effects. On February 16, 2006, Banco Delta Asia terminated its business with DPRK entities and requested that the United States remove its financial sanctions against the bank. In April 2006, Daedong Credit Bank—the only foreign-owned bank operating in North Korea—announced that its revenue had been cut in half by US actions. On September 7, 2006, reports emerged that Koryo Asia Ltd., a British investment company, was going to purchase Daedong Credit Bank. And in August 2006, Vietnamese banks shut down North Korean accounts. Finally, on December 26, 2007, the East Asia Commercial Bank—which had functioned as a correspondent bank to North Korea—instructed its Pyongyang customers to close their accounts within a week.

US Treasury Secretary Henry Paulson later explained in a speech that "worldwide, private financial institutions decided to terminate their business relationships with the designated entities, as well as others suspected of engaging in similar conduct. The result is North Korea's virtual isolation from the global financial system. The effect on North Korea has been significant, because even the most reclusive regime depends on access to the international financial system."[3]

A country that found itself able to manage under international sanctions for decades was now under a new financial assault whose basis was North Korea's own illicit financial activity. Banks around the world made a simple decision not to touch tainted North

Korean capital. The North Koreans may have been dismissive of the action, at the beginning. However, within about four weeks, they realized they had a major problem on their hands.

About a month after the Section 311, the North Koreans called the State Department through their UN offices in New York expressing a desire to talk. According to Victor Cha, the Georgetown University professor and National Security Council director charged with handling North Korean policy, this was a first. To his recollection, the North Koreans had never called the United States first to talk about anything. Something had happened.

As soon as it dawned on the North Koreans that what they had been hit with was no ordinary sanction, they went on a diplomatic offensive. On center stage was the removal of the financial pressure campaign. The focal point of their demands was the unfreezing of the $25 million in the fifty-two accounts in Macau. Every conversation began and ended with the same question: "When will we get our money back?"

For most American foreign policy and national security experts outside of the Treasury Department, the ripple effects of this regulatory action were far beyond what they would have expected. Those who were aware of Section 311 tended to think of it as working like traditional sanctions—and it was accepted wisdom that sanctions had little effect on the North Koreans. The method of its effectiveness was hard to understand. The financial isolation did not come from a classic trade-based sanction or law; nor did it derive from a UN sanctions resolution. The bank had no assets in the United States, and the United States had not frozen $25 million. Instead, the essence of this power came from banks' decisions to stop doing business with North Korea—prompted by the Treasury's unilateral 311 action. It was clear that something new had happened. In the words of then CIA director Michael Hayden, "This was a twenty-first-century precision-guided munition."

Even those who had long been involved in discussions to apply financial pressure against North Korea were surprised at the scope of the impact of the regulatory action. In the words of an intelligence veteran with over two decades of experience working on illicit financing, "We had anticipated a single or a double. This was a home run." In meeting after meeting from 2003 to 2005, I had explained to the small group of North Korea policy experts, led by David Asher at the State Department and later the National Security Council's David Shedd, what the potential effects of this action would be. In those meetings, neither my deputy, Danny Glaser, nor I had wanted to overstate the impact of the proposed 311 regulatory action against BDA. We remained conservative in our estimates of what might happen and how banks would respond. Still, we attempted to be absolutely clear that this would have a serious, real-world ripple effect that would usher in the first wave of North Korea's financial isolation.

For national security professionals in Washington, the strategic impact and effects of these actions were a revelation. Victor Cha describes a conversation in the winter of 2005 at the six-party talks: "After much ceremonial toasting with Chinese baiju, an inebriated member of the North Korean delegation leaned over to us and mumbled, "You . . . you Americans finally have found a way to hurt us."[4] As Cha would later describe it, "It was a smash in the mouth, a slap in the face. When they first heard about the action, they just thought it was another sanction, but four weeks later they realized what had hit them. It really got the North Koreans to sit up and notice that this was a tool they'd never seen before, and frankly, it scared the shit out of them."[5] For perhaps the first time, the scales were lifted from the eyes of the national security community to the devastating potential of this brand of financial warfare.

I witnessed all of these effects and reactions from a privileged position in the White House. From that vantage point, I watched how Treasury's handiwork was perceived in the top echelons of US government. In a meeting shortly after the BDA action in the fall of

2005, my new boss, Steve Hadley, the quiet and brilliant national security adviser, said that no one had anticipated the remarkable effects from the Treasury action. I looked at him and said directly, "We did." He looked surprised, but listened intently as I explained why we knew this action would work against North Korea. I explained that the strategy against North Korea and the effects of the BDA action derived directly from the changing shape of financial power and suasion since 9/11. What happened to North Korea was absolutely according to plan and was part of a natural evolution in the use of US financial power.

Remarking that he had never heard the issue explained this way, Hadley asked me to write a memo to the president explaining what had transpired. I did just that—detailing how the very nature of financial pressure and suasion had been reshaped after 9/11 into a sharper and now essential tool for US national security. I wrote a second memo in 2008, updating the president on the use of these powers to pressure and isolate rogue actors in the international financial system.

The early promise of Treasury's financial suasion had now come to full fruition. A power that fell uniquely to the Treasury Department—Section 311—had been used against a target that was uniquely suited to Treasury's work—a bank—to influence a constituency that was uniquely part of Treasury's expertise—the international financial community—to protect the US financial system. This was the moment of awakening to the power of the Treasury Department and the point of graduation for the Treasury Department. Treasury regained its seat with the national security heavyweights. This was the coming-of-age of a new era of financial pressure and warfare. The tools that our small team at Treasury had created had now been unveiled to a wider audience.

This was the high-water mark of the campaign, however, and based on what followed, one might even conclude that Treasury's power had worked too well. Our supercharged financial pressure campaign had leapfrogged the stages of the three-part financial campaign. The unexpected success would lead to new friction between those who ran the financial pressure campaign and the diplomats. Already skeptical of Treasury's plans, Chris Hill and others at the State Department would soon come to see our handiwork as an outright hindrance to diplomacy.

Soon, government agencies would be at cross-purposes, disagreeing about strategies and goals. In contrast, the North Koreans knew exactly what they wanted—restoration of their ability to access the international financial system. They would soon take full advantage of fissures on the US side to reverse the effects of Treasury's targeted strike.

STEPHEN JAFFE/AFP/Getty Images

President George W. Bush (L) walks to the Rose Garden with Secretary of State Colin Powell (C) and Secretary of Treasury Paul O'Neill (R), September 24, 2001. Bush had just signed Executive Order 13224, which marked the start of the campaign against terrorist financing. He declared, "Today, we have launched a strike on the financial foundation of the global terror network. . . . We will starve the terrorists of funding."

SHAH MARAI/AFP/Getty Images

A money changer and his customer exchange dollars for Afghanis at the money exchange market in Kabul, Afghanistan, October 8, 2003. The Afghan economy has long relied on cash, money exchangers, and the use of the traditional *hawala* money transfer system, all of which came under intense scrutiny after 9/11.

The author (dressed for business, not combat), in front of a C-17 cargo plane on a Treasury delegation trip through Afghanistan and South Asia. Searching for ways to staunch the flow of terrorist and illicit funds, Treasury officials took numerous trips soon after 9/11 to war zones, crisis areas, and banking centers.

David Aufhauser, Treasury's General Counsel, speaks at a press conference at the Treasury Department regarding terrorist financing efforts and designations, soon after 9/11. Aufhauser played a key role coordinating counter-terrorist financing actions and policy. Behind him is Richard Newcomb, the longstanding Director of the Treasury's Office of Foreign Assets Control (OFAC), a small and sometimes secretive office that manages the US government's sanctions programs.

Secretary of the Treasury John Snow speaks at a Treasury press conference announcing the joint US–Saudi "designation" of four branches of the Saudi-based Al Haramain organization for funding al Qaeda. Such designations targeted individuals, companies, and associated properties with the intent of shutting them out of the US financial system, thus making it nearly impossible for them to engage in legitimate financial activity. This designation was intended to demonstrate tangible US–Saudi cooperation and ultimately resulted in the closing of Al Haramain, then the largest Saudi charity. From left to right, Assistant Secretary of State for Economic and Business Affairs Tony Wayne, Ambassador-at-large for Counterterrorism Cofer Black, Secretary Snow, the author, and Adel al Jubeir, then Foreign Affairs Adviser to the Saudi Crown Prince (later King) Abdullah and later Saudi Ambassador to the United States.

Frances Fragos Townsend, President Bush's Homeland Security and Counterterrorism Adviser, meeting with Saudi King Abdullah bin Abdulaziz, on June 21, 2006, in Jeddah, Saudi Arabia. Townsend became the principal interlocutor with the Saudi government on counterterrorism.

IRS-Criminal Investigative Division agent Scott Schneider and Treasury analyst Pat Conlon at an airfield in Baghdad, Iraq, May 2003. They were the first Treasury agents deployed to Iraq to hunt for Saddam's assets and set up the logistics for linking Treasury's efforts with the US military. Their uniforms are labeled "Treasury."

Treasury analyst Conlon in Baghdad amidst the piles of financial records collected from the Iraqi Central Bank in the spring of 2003, soon after the American-led invasion. These financial documents, along with local interviews and an international effort, formed the basis for locating and recovering more than $3 billion of Saddam Hussein's assets.

The Riggs Bank, circa 1921, on Pennsylvania Avenue in Washington, DC, located across from the US Treasury. Riggs was a longstanding and storied banking institution servicing high-value clients and many foreign embassies in the city. It had once billed itself as "the most important bank in the most important city in the world." After 9/11, Riggs was investigated for lacking anti-money-laundering controls and failing to apply necessary due diligence to high-risk accounts and customers. Riggs closed in 2005, sold its assets to PNC Financial Services, leaving numerous embassies temporarily without a banker. The building became a PNC Bank.

The author (L) and Stuart Levey at their confirmation hearing before the Senate Banking Committee on July 15, 2004. Both assumed leadership roles in the new Office of Terrorism and Financial Intelligence at the Treasury Department, established in 2004. The new office— referred to as "TFI"—would become the center of the Treasury and US government's financial warfare efforts.

US Deputy Assistant Secretary for Treasury Daniel Glaser (L) and US Assistant Secretary of State Christopher Hill (R) hold a press conference at a hotel in Beijing, March 19, 2007. By deploying Section 311 of the USA PATRIOT Act, the Treasury stunned North Korea in an action against Banco Delta Asia in Macau, which resulted in Pyongyang's isolation from the banking system. US officials then attempted to unwind the financial pressure, with the goal of inducing North Korea back to the six-party talks.

Osama bin Laden and Ayman al-Zawahiri reading the 2006 *New York Times* article about the US Treasury's Terrorist Financing Tracking Program. The story revealed a secret program the Treasury department had established soon after 9/11 to work with SWIFT, the international bank messaging network based in Belgium, to track and disrupt suspected terrorist financing networks. The story caused a firestorm of controversy.

President George W. Bush meets with his senior leadership in the Oval Office on November 9, 2006, to discuss the financial constriction campaign against Iran. Treasury's Undersecretary for Terrorism and Financial Intelligence Stuart Levey (standing center) led the briefing, which focused on choking Iran's banking sector and finding ways to isolate the regime's illicit activities from the financial system. Participants included clockwise, Jared Weinstein (president's aide), Secretary of State Condoleezza Rice, Stuart Levey, Deputy National Security Adviser Elliott Abrams, the author, National Security Adviser Stephen J. Hadley, Homeland Security Adviser Frances Townsend, Director of National Intelligence John Negroponte, Chief of Staff Josh Bolten, and Vice President Dick Cheney.

Stuart Levey, Undersecretary of the Treasury for Terrorism and Financial Intelligence, meeting with German officials at the US Embassy in Berlin on July 6, 2010. Levey traveled throughout the world during his tenure for both the Bush and Obama administrations explaining how rogues—especially the Iranian government—were moving and hiding money through the financial system.

Photo by Mark Wilson/Getty Images

Secretary of State Hillary Clinton and Treasury Secretary
Tim Geithner announce new financial measures against
Iran at the State Department on November 21, 2011.
This included the use of Section 311 of the Patriot
Act against the Iranian Central Bank, an important
move intended to spur the private sector and other
governments to break off transactions with most
businesses in Iran. Congress would follow with
legislation strengthening existing sanctions.

Photo courtesy of the US Treasury/Chris E. Taylor

John Brennan, President Obama's Homeland Security and
Counterterrorism Adviser at the ten-year 9/11 commem-
oration held at the Treasury Department. Brennan, who
would later become the Director of the CIA, spoke about the
critical role played by the Treasury to attack Al Qaeda and
terrorist networks. Brennan's presence at the gathering
reinforced the accepted importance of the Treasury to core
national security issues after 9/11.

11

PUTTING THE GENIE
BACK IN THE BOTTLE

A throng of press was ready to pounce, cameras and microphones in hand, in the lobby of the opulent Hotel St. Regis in Beijing. The lobby was abuzz with their excitement. Daniel Craig, the famed British actor who is the latest to play the role of James Bond, was staying in the hotel. The reporters were fixated on the hotel elevators and exits like predators waiting for their prey to emerge. And Craig did emerge. He came out of one of the elevators and walked through the lobby, trying his best to hide his identity with a hat and sunglasses. He walked quickly, heading toward the rear exit. Nothing happened. There was not a flash of a camera to be seen, nor any question or comment uttered. No one pursued him. Though they saw the famous actor, the press simply ignored him. Instead, the cameras and microphones were waiting for a different Daniel—Daniel Glaser, a deputy assistant secretary of the US Treasury.

Glaser, a career Treasury civil servant and lawyer, had been sent to Beijing in March 2006 by Secretary Paulson, at the direction of President Bush, to sit down with the North Koreans and resolve the "technical issues" of the Banco Delta Asia crisis. The North Koreans refused to return to the six-party talks unless the financial pressure was eased and the approximately $25 million in frozen assets unfrozen. Glaser was there to negotiate the fix, and all of Asia was watching.

Glaser, a barrel-chested, balding thirty-eight-year-old, looked like a younger, smaller version of Richard Armitage, the famed, weightlifting deputy secretary of state under Colin Powell. Glaser started his career as a lawyer for the Secret Service and later rose into the policy ranks of Treasury's Office of Enforcement. He had become a pillar of Treasury's policy and international work, especially after 9/11. He did not suffer fools lightly, and he frequently remarked that the Treasury Department was the most prepared and technically proficient of any agency in the US government, if not the world. I had made Danny my deputy because there was nobody better in the business. He was someone I could trust. He was a true professional and took his role as a Treasury official and expert as a defining feature of his identity. He also became a close friend.

Glaser, a veteran of sensitive financial diplomatic negotiations and the head of the US delegation to the Financial Action Task Force (FATF), had received overseas attention in the past, but never anything like this. Neither had the Treasury press representative, Molly Millerwise Meiners, who was watching it all from the lobby. Meiners was a striking green-eyed, twenty-six-year-old native of Michigan who had quickly become a seasoned public affairs specialist traveling around the world. She had worked with me—and then later with Stuart Levey—on the Treasury Department's financial pressure campaigns and some of the most sensitive of issues, such as our dealings with the Saudi government. Meiners had been dispatched to accompany Glaser and had already advised Glaser to ditch his usual hard-rock T-shirts and Wayfarer sunglasses for the duration of the trip. There was too much press attention and too much at stake in this mission.

As Glaser emerged from the elevator, the reporters immediately surrounded him, blinding him with camera flashes and peppering him with questions. Meiners jumped into the middle of the throng and pulled Danny out and to the door, as the press followed quickly behind. Hurrying into the embassy van, they escaped their pursuers—for the moment.

The members of the press were principally from Asian outlets, primarily in China, Japan, and South Korea, and they knew these negotiations were critical. Before the six-party talks could resume, the financial pressure on North Korean illicit activity had to be resolved. For the first time, the United States had real leverage with the North Koreans.

It was difficult, however, for US representatives to press their advantage when the action against BDA was so widely misunderstood. Commentators, analysts, and even many US diplomats habitually referred to the campaign of constriction alternately as a sanction, a freezing action by the Treasury, or a technical law-enforcement action. It was none of the above.

No one had ever seen this kind of measure before—a domestic proposed regulation that impelled the private sector to isolate rogue financial behavior. The tendency was to liken the measure to a classic state-based sanction. And for most in the diplomatic corps, this meant a classic state-based sanction like those of the 1980s and 1990s, which were often trade-based, reliant on UN authorities to have effect, or focused squarely on the assets of key political leaders. Experience with traditional sanctions had taught diplomats that their coercive impact was determined largely by political decisions. But these were not classic sanctions that could be turned on and off like a light switch. What the State Department had a hard time grasping was that Treasury had unleashed the financial furies.

We had not frozen anything; nor had we obtained a UN sanctions resolution to isolate North Korean activity. This was a new brand of twenty-first-century financial warfare. The only real cure was for the North Koreans to stop engaging in illicit activity and cease using the banking system to launder their funds. What the North Koreans wanted was an antidote. And unfortunately, our diplomatic team was only too eager to give it to them, if only they could achieve some kind of "resolution."

The trouble was that the various actors involved, including within the US government, had different perceptions of what "resolution" meant. For Treasury, the underlying illicit activity needed to be resolved. Because the 311 action was based on underlying North Korean criminality, the pressure could not be credibly unwound until the illicit financial behavior was resolved. For State Department diplomats, such as Chris Hill, and the Chinese foreign policy and political establishment, resolution meant lifting the financial pressure and unfreezing any North Korean assets. Hill had been assigned this job by Condoleezza Rice, and his mandate was to forge an agreement with the North Koreans. It was little wonder that he had been displeased when the BDA action halted all progress in the six-party meetings. The BDA action was seen as an unfortunate interlude that had complicated talks at a moment when progress seemed to be taking place. The State Department wanted a calming of the tension and a return to talks.

Not long before, negotiations had been moving in a positive direction. In September 2005, the North Koreans had agreed to eventually dismantle their nuclear program and allow the return of monitors from the International Atomic Energy Agency (IAEA). This concession would be made in return for food aid, normalized relations with the United States and Japan, and resumption of peace negotiations between North and South Korea. After the BDA action was launched, prospects for this deal being implemented were slim.[1]

The Japanese and South Koreans were heartened by the BDA action. They appreciated the willingness of the US government to pressure the North Koreans and the creative effects of US actions. The Japanese took it as a signal to take additional steps of their own to tighten the financial screws on Pyongyang. They saw resolution of the case to include a wholesale resolution of Japanese grievances with North Korea—including the thorny and emotional issue of Japanese abductees who were yet unaccounted for. For America's allies, the BDA action was not a one-off step but part of a broader strategy to change North Korean behavior and the dynamics of diplomacy. Resolution could not be complete unless a number of other issues were addressed.

North Korea matched its diplomacy with a show of martial defiance. On July 4, 2006, North Korea launched ballistic missiles, including a Taepo Dong 2, a missile capable of targeting the West Coast of the United States.[2] On October 6, 2006, North Korea conducted its first nuclear test, which was quickly condemned by the United States and the United Nations.[3] The North Koreans were thrashing about in an effort to seek relief from the financial shackles and made it their priority in negotiations. By November 1, 2006, an uneasy agreement had been reached to move forward on the next round of six-party talks, with North Korea's foreign ministry announcing that it was returning to negotiations "on the premise that the issue of lifting financial sanctions will be discussed and settled."[4] There arose some debate as to whether the BDA action had prompted North Korea to test its nuclear weapons. Many experts, including Victor Cha and Mike Green, argued that North Korea had been marching toward a test regardless of the BDA action. According to Cha, "they would have done a test anyway, sooner or later."

In the end, President Bush saw this as a moment when we could use our leverage—to get the North Koreans back to the table. So it was that by 2007, the United States had prepared a plan to help the North Koreans unfreeze and transfer the assets held in Banco Delta Asia.

Now it was up to Glaser to finalize a resolution. He was put in the unenviable position of negotiating with the North Koreans on the "technical" matters tied to resolution of the BDA matter. Diplomats tended to think of this as little more than paperwork. Those of us who had designed the 311 action and the financial pressure campaign knew better.

What few outside of Treasury understood was that it was impossible to put the genie fully back in the bottle. The Section

311 action had unleashed the private sector to isolate rogue financial behavior—like antibodies in the international financial system, rejecting the virus of North Korean contact and business. Our
move against BDA had been an act of systemic inoculation, not a
singular political act that could be easily reversed. There was no
on-off switch to this kind of pressure, and unwinding would prove
problematic. This was a lesson that Chris Hill and the State
Department would learn the hard way.

The North Korean embassy in Beijing was perhaps the most important diplomatic post for the DPRK, given the central importance of
the country's political and economic relationship with China.
Everything about the embassy building was intended to convey a
sense of grandeur emblematic of North Korea's view of its own
power, its resistance to the rest of the world, and the majesty of the
Kim dynasty. For Glaser and the three other young Americans who
made up the delegation, it was comically gigantic.

When Glaser entered the embassy, he was led to a room where
the discussions would be held. It was a gymnasium-sized room,
with a huge multicolored mural on the wall of a crashing wave on
the North Korean shoreline. The table set up was overly large for
the group that would assemble. Later in the discussions, the North
Korean hosts would place a giant bowl of candy on the table. The
unrecognizably large pieces of candy were wrapped in fluorescent
paper and looked like cartoonish props from *Willy Wonka and the
Chocolate Factory*. One of the North Korean delegates, who was likely
an intelligence operative, repeatedly offered the Americans candies
from the bowl—digging his unusually thick, large hands into the
mix like claws. The delegation soon began to refer to this official
affectionately as "Meathooks."

This was not the first time Glaser had met with the North Koreans. He had participated in a first round of technical discussions in
New York, and a technical working group had been formed to

resolve the underlying concerns about North Korean illicit financial activity. The negotiators had learned to respect the Treasury delegation. At one point in the negotiations, the North Korean lead negotiator revealed his respect for Glaser in a characteristically North Korean way. He told Glaser, "You are like a pockmark on someone's face that is bothersome and annoying at first but which one gets used to over time." He would later reveal that there were two officials that the North Koreans had initially hated—Glaser and Stuart Levey. Now, it was only Stuart Levey they hated. Glaser made a point of ensuring that this tidbit was cabled back to the State Department.

In these negotiations, the North Koreans were attempting to pull off a very clever strategy—and the stakes were high. As Victor Cha noted, "the North Koreans were on the ropes, they were scared." Their goal was to shift the onus back to the American side to "resolve" the problem of the financial pressure. They first fixated on the approximately $25 million of assets frozen by the Macanese authorities in BDA. From the perspective of a nation—even one as economically hobbled as North Korea—this was not very much money at all. Secretary Paulson—who had previously been at the helm of Goldman Sachs—was often called the "$700 million man" because of his immense accumulated wealth. In this light, the amount of frozen BDA assets seemed like a rounding error. When briefed on the North Korean demands, American senior officials would often ask if the briefers were misstating "million" instead of "billion." Twenty-five million dollars seemed a small price to pay to bring the North Koreans back to the six-party talks.

But the North Koreans knew exactly what they were doing. The amount of money wasn't the issue—they wanted the frozen assets returned so as to remove the scarlet letter from their reputation. The North Korean connection to the international financial system had been shattered, their ability to do business paralyzed. They had no intention of changing the nature of their illicit financial activity. The release of the money became a proxy for the first step in restoring their ability to do business with banks. And they knew they could only do this with America's help.

The frozen money drove the agenda, and it was clear that nothing would change until it was unfrozen. Unfortunately, what few seemed to grasp was that the United States had not frozen any money—nor did it have any jurisdiction to release it.

There were three fundamental problems with focusing on the frozen money as the point of resolution. This point—that the United States had not frozen anything—was the most basic of these. A misperception that prevails, even among experts to this day, was that the US Treasury had ordered North Korean assets nested in BDA to be frozen. This revealed a fundamental misconception of what had happened and what type of resolution was feasible. The Section 311 action—as had been described within the US government over the course of two years—was not a freezing order. Instead, it was a domestic regulatory action to cut BDA off from the US financial system.

The United States didn't control the market reaction. It simply prompted it. In this case, the Macanese authorities froze the assets as a prophylactic regulatory step to aid in their investigation of BDA. They needed to contain the damage.

The false assumption, therefore—prevalent even within the US government—was that the United States could quickly issue an unfreezing order. This was dead wrong and mechanically impossible. With the United States agreeing to resolve the issue, it committed itself to resolving quite complicated legal and financial regulatory matters—and to using US diplomatic and financial capital to release pressure on the North Koreans. Chris Hill certainly didn't realize this at first, and he became increasingly frustrated by how seemingly complicated the unwinding had become. Despite the close relationship between Secretary Paulson and Secretary Rice, this pernicious misunderstanding became a major source of tension between the Treasury and State departments.

A second misperception—and one of which the North Koreans

took full advantage—was that the assets in the bank all belonged to the North Koreans. They did not. Out of the 52 accounts, 35 of them, worth $13 million, were determined to be legitimate accounts; 17 of them, worth $12 million, were tied to illicit activity. Not all of them were held officially by the North Korean government. Most were held by other owners and interests (most related to the North Korean regime). The DPRK wanted the entirety of the assets to be unfrozen.

Regardless, the number of accounts and accountholders created additional legal complications. Separate agreements had to be negotiated with the accountholders that weren't obviously North Korean state institutions. Those accountholders had to agree to have their frozen assets in BDA unfrozen and returned to the North Korean state. The North Koreans were trying to take full advantage of the confusion by laying claim to assets that were not obviously theirs.

The final problem with fixating on the return of the $25 million was that it confused what the North Koreans really wanted and divorced the 311 action from the underlying illicit financial activity that was the focus of the financial pressure. Return of the assets represented both a first step to restoring North Korea's financial reputation and a means of shifting the debate from the topic of what other actions might be taken to isolate North Korean financial activity. The North Koreans had no intention of taking any steps toward actual reform, so they needed to find another way to signal to the financial community that they were once again relatively safe to do business with. They believed that if the assets were returned in full to Pyongyang via international banks, it would serve as a signal that their assets were no longer toxic and could be touched again without fear of subsequent Section 311 actions. This was what the North Koreans really meant by "resolution"—and it had little to do with the actual money being frozen.

As a result, Glaser's talks with the North Koreans appeared to be hopeless. The North Korean negotiators did little more than read from scripts. They were in no position to seriously address American concerns over counterfeiting of US currency, money laundering, drug trafficking, or the smuggling of counterfeit cigarettes. Glaser also was not in a position to promise anything permanent or to suggest that he could orchestrate any deals, especially when the actors that were impacting North Korea's access to the international financial system were the banks themselves. Glaser would return again and again to Beijing—four times in the span of two months—in his attempts to resolve this matter.

The North Koreans remained insistent, however, that the assets needed to be unfrozen before any talks could continue. The State Department wanted this issue resolved—regardless of the status of the 311 action. One way or another, it seemed that the United States was going to help with the return of the assets. Glaser was called back once again to Beijing in early March 2007 to help manage the financial diplomacy that was still in process. Now the problem would be managing the return of the money to the North Koreans. The DPRK did not want to simply "pick up" the $25 million at BDA in Macau. Nor did Pyongyang want to be put in a position of inadvertently admitting some form of wrongdoing by showing up at BDA's doorstep to collect a cashier's check. The North Koreans demanded nothing less than an act of reintegration into the financial system—a first step in allowing them full access to the system. The $25 million would have to be wired back to a bank in Pyongyang. Glaser's problem was that no bank in their right mind would even touch such a transaction without ironclad assurances from the US Treasury that they would not be subject to some form of sanction or additional attention in the future.

Just as confusion had plagued the initial response to the BDA action, an unnecessary misunderstanding arose once again to divide the US government's response. When Glaser and his team arrived in Beijing, the assembled State Department team informed him that the issue had already been resolved. The Chinese had agreed to transfer the money back to North Korea through a Chinese bank. In the White House, I had heard the same report given in the Situation

Room. None of this made any sense, since it had been clear that the Chinese did not want to be implicated or drawn directly into the resolution of this matter. They, too, were worried about the taint of North Korean accounts and the reputational impact this could all have on Chinese banks.

Nevertheless, the State Department team assured Glaser that it was all resolved, and that there would be a press conference the next day to announce the agreement. Glaser reviewed the proposed resolution, and sure enough, it did not make sense to him. The idea of the Chinese agreeing to use one of their banks to transfer the money back to North Korea ran counter to everything Glaser had heard from the Chinese directly. They did not want to be in the middle of this transaction—that much was clear.

At one in the morning, Glaser met with Tom Gibbons, one of Chris Hill's deputies, and raised concerns. He questioned whether the right elements of the Chinese government—namely, the central bank and finance ministry—had signed off on the deal.

Gibbons responded by going into attack mode. "Why are you causing problems?" he said. "You are going to crash the entire deal!" He lashed out, saying Glaser was purposely trying to scuttle the six-party talks and calling Glaser's motivations and professionalism into question. He accused Glaser of having his own agenda and noted that "everyone in Washington knows what you are trying to do." It was the worst verbal assault Glaser had endured in his career.

As had been the case with the State Department all too often, this attack was divorced from the realities and complications of the deal being discussed. The State team was single-mindedly fixated on getting a deal at all costs. Any impediment to talks, whether frozen assets or Glaser himself, had to be removed. Hill and his team's mission had come straight from Secretary Rice and the president—to forge a deal. But this was a complicated situation that was not in the diplomats' control. Without a clear understanding of how American financial power had been used in this case, they found it all too easy to ascribe underhanded bureaucratic, personal, or political motives to Treasury officials who seemed privy to the secret world of financial transactions.

At last, Glaser broke down in tears, and Gibbons left the room. The direct assault on Glaser's motivations and the pure fatigue and frustration of the negotiations, along with the thousands of miles of travel he had logged over the past few days, contributed to the emotional response. Most acutely, Glaser felt isolated—as if no one understood what was really happening or wanted to listen. Meiners, along with Jennifer Fowler and Amit Sharma of the Treasury Department, tried to calm him, but he could not be consoled. The delegation had never seen the steely jawed, confident Glaser so emotionally shaken. The small Treasury delegation felt alone and isolated—caught in a game of high-stakes diplomacy and under attack by their own side.

Glaser asked the delegation to get Stuart Levey, the relatively new undersecretary of the treasury and Glaser's boss, on the phone to get guidance and protection. When Levey heard Glaser's shaking voice and his account of what had happened, he was livid. Levey had already been upset about the diplomats' actions over the course of the past several months. Chris Hill had not only appeared to misunderstand the leverage Treasury had given him, he was besmirching the Treasury Department to the White House and others to excuse diplomatic missteps. For Glaser to be treated this way was the last straw. Levey called Secretary Paulson to ensure that he and Secretary Rice were aware of this incident and to say that Glaser would be called back to Washington unless Hill made amends. Glaser talked to Paulson, who reassured Glaser that he had his backing in Washington. This broke the sense of utter isolation for the delegation. Paulson would later call Secretary Rice to inform her of the incident. Secretary Rice then instructed Chris Hill to apologize and fix the mess.

While these calls were being made in Washington, a debate ensued within the Treasury delegation in the hallways and rooms of the Beijing hotel. The team from State still had their agreement, which they intended to publicize in spite of Glaser's fundamental concerns. Should Glaser even participate in their press conference, when he knew it was likely not going to work? Would he be putting Treasury's credibility on the line to go along with this plan when he knew Hill was leading the US government into a diplomatic mess? Meiners argued that the delegation should go home and allow the State Department to put its own credibility on the line. After calming down, Glaser decided to be the good soldier and participate, but he knew that what Hill and he were announcing would not survive the complications of unwinding the 311 action.

After about two hours of sleep, Glaser awoke to meet Chris Hill and the State delegation for breakfast. Cordial and businesslike, Hill and Glaser shared breakfast together without mention of the incident the previous evening. The press conference would be an important moment for Hill, signaling that pesky issues like the BDA action were being resolved, and allowing the real work of the six-party talks to resume. Hill held the press conference. Glaser knew Hill was making a big mistake, but he joined him at the podium anyway and announced the following:

> The United States and North Korean Governments have reached an understanding on the disposition of DPRK-related funds frozen at Banco Delta Asia.
>
> The DPRK has proposed the transfer of the roughly $25 million frozen in BDA into an account held by North Korea's Foreign Trade Bank at the Bank of China in Beijing.
>
> North Korea has pledged, within the framework of the Six-Party Talks, that these funds will be used solely for the betterment of the North Korean people, including for humanitarian and educational purposes. We believe this resolves the issue of the DPRK-related frozen funds.[5]

When the press conference ended, Glaser was dispatched to see his counterparts in the Chinese government before going home. He sat down with officials in the Chinese central bank and finance ministry—to receive a scolding. The Chinese finance officials demanded to know why US negotiators were now attempting to unwind the BDA action. They saw this as a moment to insulate the Chinese banking system from North Korea's illicit financial activity. They could not understand why the United States, which had rightly argued for the protection of the international financial system and the isolation of BDA, would now try to convince Chinese banks to help BDA and the North Koreans with unsavory bank transfers.

As Glaser would note later, "It was one of the most embarrassing meetings I've ever endured, but it was also one of my proudest moments. While I was being scolded and lectured, I was thinking to myself, 'Good for you guys.'" The Chinese were graduating into the legitimate financial world, and their disparagement of the US Treasury officials was a signal that they would not allow their financial system to be toyed with for political reasons—by Beijing or Washington.

Glaser knew the saga was not over. Almost as soon as he landed in Washington, he received a call from Secretary Paulson. The Chinese central bank had put a stop to the deal, and there would be no Chinese bank involvement in the transfer of the frozen North Korean assets. President Bush was pressing and had asked Paulson, "Where is your team?" Paulson had said authoritatively, "They're on the plane." After the call, Paulson called Glaser and ordered, "Get on the plane!" Paulson insisted that the Treasury team needed to be on the next flight to Beijing regardless of whether they had visas. Meiners got a call too. Paulson was aware that Meiners had scheduled time to go wedding-dress shopping with her mother, who was flying into town that week. When he called her directly, he apologized for the imposition and thanked her for her work on behalf of the department and country. He underscored the historic nature of this work, as Meiners cried quietly on the other end of the line and prepared to travel again.

The delegation was back in Beijing within seventy-two hours of having returned to Washington. This time, Paulson sent along his chief of staff, James R. Wilkinson, a veteran of the State Department who was trusted by Secretary Rice and known to Chris Hill. Wilkinson was there to keep the State Department honest and to be the eyes and ears of the secretary of the treasury.

The frustrating negotiations with the North Koreans resumed once again. Wilkinson dealt on a daily basis with his North Korean counterpart, a man with gold front teeth who was named Mr. Chang. But the Treasury delegation was constrained in what it could offer. As a banking regulator itself, the Treasury did not want to be seen negotiating a deal for the transfer of the frozen assets. Furthermore, the Treasury representatives certainly did not want to signal that there would be automatic safe harbors against regulatory action for any jurisdiction or institution involved. No secretary of the treasury would be willing to promise this. As with the embassy banking crisis after the fall of Riggs Banks, it was up to the State Department to find banks willing to do risky business.

Chris Hill spent weeks trying to find a bank that would help in the transfer of the assets. At the end of the day, it would need to involve an American institution. Involving an American institution to assist in the transfer of money back to North Korea was the only way institutions would agree to touch North Korean assets. It was also ideal for North Korea, since the United States would be directly validating a banking transaction with Pyongyang. At one point, Wachovia seemed to be a willing participant, but without assurances against future sanctions or regulatory actions, the bank declined to get involved. It wasn't worth it.

At last, in the late spring of 2007, the New York Federal Reserve Bank, accustomed to handling sensitive transactions and dealing with foreign sovereign counterparties, agreed to help. The New York Fed was the last and most important resort for an international transaction of this nature—and could transfer assets between central banks. Tom Baxter, the legendary general counsel who had started his career at the Fed by helping with the return of Iranian assets after the hostage crisis in 1979, was enlisted by Tim Geithner to fashion a mechanism for the transfer of the assets. The mechanics were crucial to this act of high-end technical financial diplomacy.

The United States had found a Russian bank in Vladivostok, Far Eastern Bank, that held an account for the North Korean Foreign Trade Bank and was willing to help with the transfer of assets—but only if it was assured that it would not be sanctioned or targeted as a result. The Russians also needed a mechanism to receive the assets from Banco Delta Asia, since they did not have an established banking relationship with BDA. This meant that Russia's central bank would need to be involved. American Ambassador William Burns—who would later become Secretary of State Hillary Clinton's deputy—provided assurances to Russian government officials that the United States would not act against the private Russian bank or the central bank. President Bush and Russian President Vladimir Putin discussed the issue at the G8 summit in Germany and agreed to make this work. Baxter began designing a multistaged global transfer of toxic assets, with the Federal Reserve serving as the ultimate financial middleman.

In June 2007, Banco Delta Asia transferred the $25 million to Macau's central bank, the Macau Monetary Authority. Once these assets were transferred, the Macanese authorities sent the money to the Federal Reserve Bank of New York. Then the Fed sent the assets to the Russian central bank, which then transferred the assets to the Far Eastern Bank. Finally, the Far Eastern Bank transferred the $25 million into the account of the North Korean Foreign Trade Bank. The money was back in the North Korean regime's hands. The transaction was done—unwinding one of the most significant asset freezes in modern history. The price for North Korea's return to the six-party talks had been paid in full.

The unwinding had been a hard-fought endeavor. But if the

State Department's hope had been to secure a deal with North Korea, there was a problem. We had prematurely given up the financial leverage that could have provided even more fundamental diplomatic leverage. It had been a unique moment where the United States had the opportunity to alter the overall dynamics with North Korea and China. Instead, we had tried to put the genie back the bottle, at the cost of American credibility and leverage.

What's worse, unwinding the BDA action undercut our own financial weapon. Section 311 worked as an expression of Treasury's ability to protect the financial system. If the pressure could be lifted simply for diplomatic reasons, it would suggest that the decisions being made about the isolation of North Korean financial activity were simply political decisions. To use American credibility to give the North Koreans a pass on reforming their illicit financial behavior would deeply damage our ability to use the same tool to squeeze the North Koreans or others in the future.

The better move at the time would have been to force the North Koreans to resolve the issues with the Macanese and Chinese authorities directly—which would have entailed a more elaborate process of cleaning up their illicit financial activity. It would have forced banks to review their accounts and reveal to regulators where the DPRK was nesting assets. The North Koreans would have had to respond to a chorus of actors—not just to the United States, but to the legitimate financial world. The United States could have stood back and acted as the defender of the global financial system—in the process making more specific demands, such as for the printers and plates used to counterfeit US $100 bills to be turned over.

Instead, we allowed ourselves to be transformed into North Korea's agent, resolving the problem they had created. We took what were quintessentially multilateral effects of a domestic regulatory action and turned it into a unilateral American problem to solve. The North Koreans had expertly turned the tables. We were outmaneuvered at the height of international pressure and gave up our leverage.

This was not an act of bad faith. Chris Hill and Secretary Rice wanted to conclude a deal, and so they pushed for a resolution of the frozen assets and an unwinding of the pressure. The president agreed, reasoning that the North Koreans were on the ropes, and it was a good idea to return to the negotiating table while we were in a position of strength. This was not a faulty instinct—but it was premature. All along we had designed the financial pressure campaign to provide leverage for our diplomacy and to force the North Koreans to make some hard choices. We had not forced them to make all of those choices yet. We had given up the opportunity to force the Chinese to make some hard choices as well with respect to their financial dealings with North Korea. The pressure had been on Beijing, too, but we relieved it for them. We cashed in on BDA too soon.

As a result of this episode, many around the world began to perceive that our efforts to "protect the financial system" with our "conduct-based" financial pressure were just a Trojan horse for political and diplomatic interests. When convenient, we would abandon our concerns about the integrity of the financial system and the illicit financial activity by rogues. Tactics that had previously been effective because they were perceived not to be politically driven now fell prey to precisely that accusation.

Allies who had supported our actions felt betrayed, as if they had had the rug pulled out from under them. Adversaries took note that they could maneuver their way out from financial pressure. In particular, the North Koreans learned a lesson about diversifying their holdings and access points to the international financial system. Over time, they would cultivate new banking and financial relationships, largely through new commercial relationships and mining deals with Chinese companies and merchants. They would find ways to enrich their regime and to continue to access the financial system. They would not be overreliant on a Golden Star Bank or Banco Delta Asia the way they had been in the past.

The fixation on the release of the assets had also shifted the debate away from why the international financial community had clamped down on North Korean accounts to begin with. North Korea continued to engage in illicit financial activity—including counterfeiting of the US $100 bill—and this issue was not resolved. Instead, it was left to a technical working group led by the Treasury Department, which still meets to this day. There has been no transfer of the counterfeit plates or any indication that North Korea has stopped its illicit activity. Those issues remain unresolved.

The BDA action was intended to be the start of a financial pressure campaign—not the end. The environment was set for the isolation of North Korean regime assets around the world—to include scrutiny over leadership assets and practices used to finance and prop up the DPRK government. Losing sight of this action as part of a broader campaign may have been the biggest opportunity cost of the unwinding of the BDA action. We let the North Koreans—and the Chinese—off the hook. This would be a lesson in forfeiting our financial leverage too early without guaranteed benefits.

Even so, for the Treasury officials involved, this was a critical case study that demonstrated the power of American financial tools. "Our financial tools are sometimes the most powerful weapons our government has to help change behavior," said Jim Wilkinson. "At the end of the day after this transaction, the diplomacy is moving forward and the world now sees just how powerful Treasury's financial tools really are."[6] The quest for the "next BDA" would echo for years in every national security crisis of import in the White House Situation Room.

In the future, Treasury officials, the State Department, and the White House would ensure that any financial pressure or coercive diplomatic campaign would not split the US delegation. Financial pressure and diplomacy can diverge dramatically if they are not managed carefully—especially if the parties don't understand why and how the financial pressure works. The Treasury and State departments needed to be in lockstep if such a powerful campaign were to be launched again—and if an unwinding were to be managed properly. Stuart Levey learned this lesson well. He would apply it as he looked to the next large-scale initiative: the financial assault on Iran.

12

REVELATION

Ever since Treasury's press secretary, Tony Fratto, had been read into the classified and closely held SWIFT program, he had prepared for a leak. We had constructed the program to help track terrorist financing legally, effectively, and in secret. But we assumed all along that the program would see the light of day. Fratto knew the call would come. When it did, he was surprised it had taken so long.

The Treasury Department and officials involved in Europe made a serious attempt to keep the program quiet and to limit those with knowledge of its operations. But we always knew that the program would be revealed. From the outset we designed the program to ensure that it would stand up to legal and public scrutiny. The mechanics of the program were far more open than those of a classic intelligence operation. More foreign officials—especially more of those who were not traditionally in the intelligence business—were aware of the program than had been the case with any other highly sensitive counterterrorism program. The backlash that had come in 2005, when the *New York Times* reported the existence of the White House's highly secret Terrorist Surveillance Program (TSP), had been a searing experience. Not just the US government, but SWIFT executives, too, were nervous. The SWIFT officials feared their cooperation would be construed in the same critical light.

This is what Fratto and the small group of public affairs professionals "read into" the program had prepared for since 2002. Fratto and his predecessors Michele Davis and Rob Nichols had crafted a communications plan that anticipated the inevitable leak—with detailed questions, designated phone trees, and anticipated lines of attack and counterarguments to use with reporters. The communicators held three tabletop exercises with SWIFT officials and Treasury's European counterparts so that all of them would understand their roles and the various pitfalls of a poorly coordinated response. Fratto had made two trips to the historic SWIFT chateau in Brussels to work with the company's senior officials on the communications plan until they felt comfortable with it and were ready to respond.

In 2006, Fratto picked up a call from *New York Times* reporter Eric Lichtblau, and he knew the time had come. Lichtblau was coy, mentioning only that he was looking into a possible story about Treasury acquiring data from SWIFT. He made it sound like he didn't know much, but alarm bells went off for Fratto. He understood that a call like this would not have happened unless Lichtblau, who had won a Pulitzer Prize for his TSP piece, already had a story in mind. Lichtblau had begun to dig around and was asking other people questions about SWIFT as well. SWIFT communicators called Treasury press representative Molly Millerwise Meiners to let her know that *New York Times* reporters were sniffing around a story. In the conversation with Lichtblau, Fratto was able to discern that the *Times* had its hooks into the story and would ride it to the end. From the tenor of the conversation he could also tell that the *Times* thought the Treasury was doing something illegal—perhaps even stealing the financial data. Fratto did not reveal anything about the program, but he agreed to talk with Lichtblau again, since the *Times* would not be publishing a story without first talking to the Treasury Department.

Quickly, Fratto and the architects of the program put the response plan into motion—Fratto called Dan Bartlett, the communications director at the White House, while others called their counterparts throughout the US government. Fratto assembled a group that included Stuart Levey, Molly Millerwise Meiners, and Treasury lawyers to determine the course of action. The team believed that the story the *New York Times* was constructing was flat-out wrong—there was nothing illegal about the SWIFT program. They hoped to convince the *Times* that the program was legal, effective, and appropriate—this would be our one chance to kill the story.

Josh Bolten, the president's chief of staff, convened a meeting in his bright and spacious office just down the hall from the Oval Office. All of the administration's key senior stakeholders on this issue were present, including Vice President Cheney, White House Counsel Harriet Miers, National Security Adviser Steve Hadley, and Treasury Secretary Snow. The options on the table were straightforward—try to shut the *New York Times* out by not cooperating at all with the story; work with Lichtblau and his editor to try to convince them to not publish the story; work with them but try to shape the story in a favorable light; or hand the story to another publication.

Secretary Snow and the Treasury staff made the case for working with Lichtblau and the editors at the *Times* to try to convince them that they really didn't have much of a story and the program they were investigating was legal, effective, and constrained in its application. Fratto did not want to be caught behind the story and knew that if it came out with inaccuracies and false assumptions, it would be a disaster for the Treasury, the administration, and SWIFT, jeopardizing the program itself. He also realized that the story could leak anyway, given the reporter's ongoing inquiries to experts and officials in the United States and Europe about the program. I agreed wholeheartedly with Fratto and my former Treasury colleagues.

At every opportunity and every meeting I attended, we argued that this was a program worth defending vigorously and publicly if necessary. If the *New York Times* decided to publish the story, we should demand that it defend its decision and its reporting. Yet at the same time we knew that we were likely fighting a losing battle. The senior leadership could already tell that Lichtblau and his fellow reporter James Risen, who was also working on the story, thought they had found another TSP-like program worthy of front-page revelation—and perhaps another Pulitzer Prize.

Stuart Levey became the primary interlocutor with the reporters. In a back-and-forth dialogue, Levey focused on explaining the legal framework and the responsible handling and tracking of the SWIFT data accessed. He encouraged Lichtblau to consult an outside national security legal expert to test his proposition that the program was illegal. The *Times* reached out to David Kris, the well-respected national security lawyer who had run the Foreign Intelligence Surveillance Act (FISA) review process at the Department of Justice during the early years of the Bush administration. Kris, who would later become President Obama's assistant attorney general for the National Security Division, reviewed the SWIFT program for the *Times* and determined that it was legal and that there were no inherent problems with its legitimacy. Levey, who knew Kris well from their days at the Department of Justice, knew what Kris had told the *Times*. The program as designed and implemented was legal—there was no story.

After several weeks, Lichtblau came back to Fratto. It was clear that the reporters had not found what they were looking for with the program. The Treasury was not stealing the SWIFT data out of the air and misusing the financial information therein. This wasn't a massive fishing expedition into the world's financial data. It really was an effort by the US government to target and track terrorist financing as understood by the American public. As long as the methods were legal, there didn't seem to be much basis for a story. But it seemed as though the *New York Times* was going to publish it anyway—potentially endangering a crucial source of financial intelligence for Treasury and exposing the SWIFT board to public scrutiny.

Even though it still was not clear what the story actually was, to Levey, and the rest of us who had worked with the program, the risk was clear. Exposure in the *New York Times* threatened the very existence of the program and our most effective method of tracking terrorist financing through the banking system. It would also stir up European anger at SWIFT and European central bankers aware of the program. Fratto demanded to know why this was still considered a story, but Lichtblau simply demurred and said it was in the editors' hands now.

At the same time, Josh Meyer from the *Los Angeles Times*, who had been covering Treasury stories for the paper and had taken trips with us abroad, called the Treasury Department asking questions about a relationship with SWIFT. The *Los Angeles Times* reporters did not have enough to pursue a story on their own, but it was clear that they were searching for whatever the *New York Times* investigation was stirring up.

There was little hope of stopping the story, but the administration tried. Bill Keller, the editor of the *New York Times*, agreed to a meeting with Treasury Secretary Snow. Snow and his team made the case for the legality of the program and its utility, while explaining the damage the revelation could do with our European partners and to SWIFT itself. Snow offered a separate briefing with Treasury's enforcement lawyer assigned to the program. But Keller listened politely, asked a few perfunctory questions, and ended the meeting. It was apparent that Keller had already made up his mind, and that he was going to publish the story regardless of what was said in that meeting.

The 9/11 Commission cochairs, Lee Hamilton and Thomas Kean, both appealed to the *New York Times* not to run the story. Even Senator Russ Feingold, a Wisconsin Democrat known for his defense of privacy and civil liberties and his ardent opposition to the Bush administration, was convinced of the value and legality of the program and was asked to call the *New York Times* to intervene. Yet all who tried to convince the *Times* were rejected politely.

In the end, part of what drove publication was competition between papers, since the *New York Times* wasn't the only paper to have uncovered the SWIFT program. Levey was in Italy when he got word that the *Los Angeles Times* had the story, too. This would accelerate publication and trigger the *New York Times* to publish. Levey and spokesperson Molly Millerwise Meiners flew back immediately, understanding that they would have to move quickly.

The call came in to Fratto that the *New York Times* was going to run the story. Once this was clear, the communications team decided to meet with the reporters from both the *New York Times* and the *Los Angeles Times* again before they published their articles. At the same time, the Treasury Department called Glenn Simpson at the *Wall Street Journal*, a seasoned journalist who understood the banking world and had followed the issues of money laundering, terrorist financing, and organized crime for many years. When Meiners spoke to Simpson, she told him, "Bring your laptop." The Treasury intended to give him background on the program to allow him to publish a competing story. There had been no promise made to the *New York Times* not to speak to other reporters if the *Times* decided to publish the story, though Lichtblau would later complain to Fratto.

Glenn Simpson's story in the *Wall Street Journal* was published the same day as the articles in the *Los Angeles Times* and the *New York Times*. Simpson, who had covered Treasury after 9/11, had long been aware of Treasury's program with SWIFT data but had elected not to publish it. He had lived in Brussels and had even met the SWIFT chairman, Lenny Schrank, once, testing him out and inquiring about any information sharing with the US government. Schrank had played it coy, but Simpson knew that there was an arrangement and a program in place.

Yet Simpson had not even approached his editors with the story at the time—because he didn't think there was a story. For Simpson, the program was legal, unobjectionable, and in line with what the administration said it was doing to track terrorist financing. From his years of reporting on international organized crime and money laundering, Simpson knew that the banking world was subject to reporting requirements, suspicious activity reports, and a full regimen of otherwise intrusive regulatory scrutiny that made cross-border transactions fair game under the right circumstances. He felt the SWIFT program was in line with this historically intrusive regulatory system. From his point of view, this program was not infringing on anyone's civil liberties, and there was no journalistic reason to expose it. When his editors heard that the *New York Times* story was imminent, it was not difficult for Simpson to put together a story on short notice. He already knew about the banking world, SWIFT, and how Treasury was likely using the data.

In contrast, the *New York Times* reporters came to the subject assuming that the SWIFT program was being run just like the NSA surveillance program that the *Times* had already revealed. Their lack of sophistication in understanding the international financial system and banking laws, and their related unwillingness to listen to experts inside and outside of government, added fuel to their fire. So it was that they decided to put in jeopardy one of the most valuable and legal counterterrorist tools the United States had at its disposal.

On June 23, 2006, the *New York Times* published its above-the-fold front-page story: "Bank Data Is Sifted by U.S. in Secret to Block Terror," by Eric Lichtblau and James Risen. On the same date, Simpson published his article for the *Wall Street Journal*, as did Josh Meyer and Greg Miller for the *Los Angeles Times*. All had raced to publish their stories online ahead of the others. The *Washington Post* also published a story about the Treasury program on June 23.[1]

Members of the administration at all levels blasted the *New York Times*. President Bush called the story "disgraceful." John Snow wrote in a June 29, 2006, letter to the editor of the *Times*: "In choosing to run its June 23 front-page article, the Times undermined a highly successful counterterrorism program and alerted terrorists to the methods and sources used to track their money trails."[2] In a hearing before the House Financial Services Subcommittee on Oversight and Investigations on July 11, Stuart Levey warned, "This disclosure compromised one of our most valuable programs and will only make our efforts to track terrorist financing—and to prevent terrorist attacks—harder. Tracking terrorist money trails is difficult enough without having our sources and methods reported on the front page of newspapers."[3]

Congress was outraged that the program had been compromised. On Capitol Hill, Senator Jim Bunning, a Republican from Kentucky, asked the attorney general to investigate the *New York Times* for treason. Representative Peter King from New York, the Republican chairman of the House Homeland Security Committee, called for an investigation of whether the paper's decision to publish the article violated the Espionage Act. Representative J. D. Hayworth, Republican from Arizona, circulated a letter to colleagues asking that the *Times's* congressional press credentials be suspended. Nevertheless, the *New York Times* and the other newspapers all stood by their stories.

There were many who later rationalized that the existence of the program was obvious and that the story was not really a revelation of anything secret. But if it was so obvious, why was it a front-page story? More importantly, why were there not more media inquiries before 2006, or savvy editorial writers or think tanks offering this as a good idea to use as a tool in countering terrorist financing? If it was so obvious, why then wasn't this part of a concerted effort prior to 9/11 to subpoena SWIFT data for legal purposes?

The reality was that this program had been innovative and legal and had operated well and in secret right under the noses of those who pretended to understand the issues of terrorist financing and terrorism. Before this revelation, terrorist organizations and networks didn't understand what we were seeing and tracking, although they knew we were tracking money flows. Most nonexpert observers had no idea what SWIFT was or how it functioned in the international financial system. Now they knew exactly what we were seeing—as did rogue regimes and every financial institution around the world.

In a lunch meeting in New York after the stories hit the press, *Times* editor Keller met with US intelligence officials, including CIA Director Mike Hayden. Keller was asked why he had decided to publish the SWIFT story when the program was legal and so important to the US government. With surprising candor, Keller said, "It was because the president was weakened by then." The attendees could not believe their ears as they heard this overt admission that there had been a political calculus to the decision making. When the US officials got back to the airport, still stunned by what Keller had said, Hayden turned to his aides and asked, "Did you just hear what I did?" There was no question that Keller had declared that the decision to publish was ultimately based on a political decision about the state of the Bush presidency.

To its credit, SWIFT stood ready to defend itself. Schrank and the board members had steeled themselves for years for the eventual revelation of the program. Its leadership felt that it had done everything that was legally required and responsible to limit the Treasury's access and use of its data. In a public statement, SWIFT explained, "The UST cannot simply browse through the data. They are only allowed to see data that is responsive to targeted searches in the context of a specific terrorism investigation. Data searches must be based only on persons, entities or related information with an identified connection to an ongoing terrorism investigation or other intelligence that the target is connected to terrorism."[4]

SWIFT also noted that its compliance was "legal, limited, targeted, protected, audited and overseen." In a statement on the matter, it said,

> SWIFT takes its role as a key infrastructure of the international financial system very seriously and cooperates with authorities to prevent illegal uses of the international financial system. . . . SWIFT negotiated with the U.S. Treasury over the scope and oversight of the subpoenas. Through this process, SWIFT received significant protections and assurances as to the purpose, confidentiality, oversight and control of the limited sets of data produced under the subpoenas. Independent audit controls provide additional assurance that these protections are fully complied with.[5]

A December 2008 report by French counterterrorism judge Jean-Louis Bruguière agreed, finding that "the U.S. Treasury Department complies with the strict use limitation and stringent privacy safeguards set out in the Terrorist Financing Tracking Report Representations and that TFTP has demonstrated significant value for the fight against terrorism, in particular in the EU." Although European sources said they were aware of 27,000 requests for data by the US government to SWIFT, they did not identify any violations by the parties involved.

The *New York Times* "public editor"—responsible for the journalistic integrity of the paper and journalism ethics—Byron Calame, initially responded to the chorus of criticism by defending Bill Keller's decision.[6] However, several months later, Calame changed his mind, issuing a piece entitled "Banking Data: A Mea Culpa":

> My July 2 column strongly supported The Times's decision to publish its June 23 article on a once-secret banking-data surveillance program. After pondering for several months, I have decided I was off base. There were reasons to publish the controversial article, but they were slightly outweighed by two factors to which I gave too little emphasis. While it's a close call now, as it was then, I don't think the article should have been published. Those two factors are really what bring me to this corrective commentary: the apparent legality of the program in the United States, and the absence of any evidence that anyone's private data had actually been misused.[7]

The mea culpa received little notice. The damage was already done.

In his July 11, 2006, statement before the House Financial Services Subcommittee on Oversight and Investigations, Stuart Levey said, in a discussion of SWIFT's data stream: "For two years, I have been reviewing that output every morning. I cannot remember a day when that briefing did not include at least one terrorism lead from this program. Despite attempts at secrecy, terrorist facilitators have continued to use the international banking system to send money to one another, even after September 11th."[8] That was now about to change. Those who were using the banking system for terrorism purposes were now fully aware of how the US government gathered intelligence about wire transfers. What's worse, SWIFT itself was thrust into the broader political debates, something it had long sought to avoid. Even if the relationship with SWIFT could survive, Treasury's ability to collect financial intelligence would never again be what it was.

A debate about the SWIFT program erupted in Europe, where deep sensibilities about government intrusion into personal data are paramount. The disclosure also began a diplomatic debate driven by a lack of understanding of the program and the privacy safeguards built into the system. As SWIFT was registered in Belgium, it soon came under legal and political scrutiny there for its decision to release information on European citizens. Many in the European Union raised concerns about the legality of the SWIFT disclosures to the US Treasury, although SWIFT responded by noting that it was legally obligated to disclose information because of US subpoenas.

Soon, SWIFT was facing legal challenges in European courts, and it became a frequent target for political attacks across the continent. In response to the unrelenting legal challenges, SWIFT argued that the solution was for US and European regulators to find a way to conduct counterterrorism operations while respecting European requirements for personal and financial privacy. To resolve some of these challenges, the United States and the European Union agreed to name a "high representative of the EU to the United States of America for the financing of terrorism," famed French judge Jean-Louis Bruguière, with an office in the US Treasury Department. They also allowed for the appointment of a European observer who could monitor the ongoing process and draw independent conclusions on the adequacy of privacy safeguards.[9]

The following summer, the US Treasury sent representatives to the European Union to describe "the controls and safeguards governing the handling, use and dissemination of data" under the TFTP.[10] Their description included information on the United States' legal basis for subpoenas, the limited nature of data sought, the role of an independent audit, and information on the data retention period.

As the program came under assault, some European officials ran for the hills, while others protested that they had not understood the extent of the program. What most did not appreciate was that the United States had become the global intelligence hub for tracking illicit financial activity, thanks to its ability to tap financial data in conjunction with the best and deepest types of other intelligence. Losing access to the SWIFT data would be deeply damaging to that work.

Stuart Levey launched an effort to shore up the program, making public statements and meeting with officials throughout Europe. In one meeting, he met with a senior official of a country where the political leaders were critical of the program and had stated that they did not see its value. In preparation for his meetings, Levey had ordered every piece of SWIFT data and analysis that had been passed to that country to be printed out in hard copy. He wanted to have it with him for the meeting. Levey met with the official and talked about the value of the program to both countries. Applying a showman's sense of timing." Levey then pulled out the foot-high stack of SWIFT-related reports that had been shared with the government and plopped it onto the table in front of the official. Levey asked directly, "Do you want us to stop giving you this? If not, you need to be a part of the conversation. Talk to your politicians."

In March 2009, the European Parliament called for a more comprehensive EU-US agreement on data protection.[11] An EP resolution in September expanded on this call, requesting clear rules on the targeting and use of data, redress opportunities for European citizens, and a limit of twelve months on a cooperative agreement until a permanent one could be settled under the Lisbon Treaty.[12]

The EU-US agreement was reached that winter and encompassed limitations on data to be used, a prohibition on data mining, a data deletion requirement after five years, and a process of EU review. The Council of the European Union simultaneously declared that a future long-term agreement would be more explicit on principles of redress, data deletion, and third-party information sharing.[13]

The task of shoring up support would require constant attention, with the voices in opposition dominating the public space. On February 11, 2010, by a vote of 378 to 196 (with 31 abstentions), the plenary of the European Parliament rejected the 2009 agreement between the European Union and the United States to allow US law-enforcement authorities to have access to SWIFT data. The agreement had been negotiated between the EU Council of Ministers, the European Commission, and the US government to allow continued access to the database, a mirror copy of which had been moved by SWIFT from the United States to Europe. The liberal-minded European parliamentarians—now empowered in a post–Lisbon Treaty European structure—were making a point of asserting their power and their predilection to unwind Bush-era war-on-terror policies and programs. Among the parliament's concerns was the need for more stringent mechanisms of judicial redress. It also wanted more explicit rules on how data would be obtained, stored, and accessed.[14] Unfortunately, the parliamentarians were picking on the wrong program.

After months of debate in various nations, on June 28, 2010, rational arguments prevailed. The United States and the European Union signed an agreement on the transfer of data from the SWIFT program. The European Parliament had at last found a compromise. The main concession was that requests to SWIFT be "tailored as narrowly as possible in order to minimize the amount of data requested." In an interview with Spiegel Online, EU Justice Commissioner Viviane Reding said, "It is unquestionably correct that EU and US authorities fight against terrorism together. . . . But we must finally speak the same language when it comes to data protection, as well."[15]

The agreement stipulated that any US request for data be verified by Europol to confirm its targeted and justified nature for tracking terrorist activities.[16] The system also included provisions for an
EU-appointed overseer, a requirement for unused data deletion
after five years, and a redress procedure applicable to all people
regardless of nationality. In addition, it provided for a joint review
of its implementation and effects. The first such report from the EU
delegation was released in March 2011 and confirmed the adequacy
of data protection safeguards. Finally, the agreement promised US
assistance for the construction of an equivalent EU Terrorist Finance
Tracking System (TFTS).[17]

Yet even with an agreement in place, the program remains fragile. Considering the intense scrutiny it is now under, it has to be
managed carefully in financial and diplomatic circles. SWIFT could
decide at any moment to stop sharing the data, and if it did so, US
and global authorities would be blind to critical financial data.

For those of us at Treasury, the whole ordeal was a regrettable,
avoidable mess. The way the program was revealed—amid suspicious
and false assumptions of vast and unlawful data mining—
prevented the program from serving as a possible model for how governments should handle and use mass amounts of personally sensitive data in the future. Access to the information had been
cooperative and collaborative, with the private-sector actor in control
of the data. Straightforward and unambiguous legal tools were used
to justify access to the data. Constraint on the information accessed
and used was negotiated and strictly enforced. Perhaps to the disbelief
of most, we had built the program in a way that purposely blinded us
to possible links and significant suspect relationships—with increasing
layers of restrictions over time. Outside auditors confirmed the limited scope of use, and the private-sector actor had authority to stop
access to the data at any time if there was a concern that the negotiated parameters were being breached.

We had found a way of tracking financial transactions in a creative and important way. We had gone in through the front door in a completely legal and careful way, with due respect for civil liberties and privacy protection. We opened the program up to outside scrutiny, and there had been no evidence of a breach of the agreements reached with SWIFT. Indeed, the US government's Privacy and Civil Liberties Oversight Board (PCLOB) had been briefed on the program and was impressed with and supportive of the program and the model it established. Lanny Davis, the board's lone Democrat, noted that although he had doubts about the program going in, he "was impressed with the lengths to which these people have gone to avoid infringing on people's civil rights. . . . It was less of a concern than I expected."[18] He went on to say that, "based on what I've seen so far in both programs [banking and NSA], I think they have struck the right balance [between fighting terrorism and ensuring civil liberties]." The protocols we used could still be a model for how to limit the government's use of data in a world where the need for data analysis for purposes of national security must be balanced with the maintenance of privacy protections and civil liberties. But if it is to become a model, the existing program needs to survive.

For SWIFT, the revelation of the program brought unwanted scrutiny and attention, though Lenny Schrank and the rest of the SWIFT leadership always knew the program would eventually be revealed and their decisions likely questioned. SWIFT had always billed itself as an apolitical company whose messaging service provided a safe and secure communications backbone for the international banking system. With SWIFT reaching the front pages of the newspapers, this was all now at risk. This attention would land SWIFT in the heart of new debates as policymakers scanned the landscape for ways to isolate rogue financial actors. As pressure on Iran increased, European and American politicians would put access to SWIFT squarely into the debate about isolating Iranian banks. In 2012, for the first time ever, SWIFT unplugged designated Iranian banks from its system, in accordance with a European directive and under the threat of possible US legislation. The European Union agreed that "no specialized financial messaging shall be provided to those persons and entities subject to an asset freeze." SWIFT complied with the regulations, but getting pulled into the policy debate about isolating rogue regimes and banks crossed a political Rubicon for the Brussels-based organization.

Now, its bank members, including banks from China and Russia, are questioning whether SWIFT is merely a political tool of the West. Alternative networks—and the ease of Internet communications— challenge SWIFT's hold on its position as the core global banking communications system. Already, the Iranians have resorted to using the Internet and faxes to send messages to brokers and banks as a means of replacing SWIFT messages. With SWIFT's messaging format available for free, the system can be replicated outside the system that SWIFT manages. These imitations are not as efficient or secure as SWIFT's system, but they are workarounds that will no doubt evolve and improve over time. They could represent the emergence of alternate financial networks and tools—tools that could organically create an alliance of financial rogues operating to evade the strictures of the formal financial system.

And SWIFT officials worry that the threat of expulsion from the SWIFT system will become part of every international security debate. If forced banishment from the SWIFT system could be used in the Iranian context, why not use this same threat against Syria, North Korea, or any other state or financial institution that falls under the reproach of the major powers? Who should make these decisions on behalf of the international financial system? Now that financial exclusion is seen as a principal tool of coercion, SWIFT executives fear they will get pulled into such debates continually. They hope the Iranian case can be explained as an extreme, one-of-a-kind situation, and that this will be the last time they will be injected into the debate on international security concerns. But it may be too late.

The potential for more exclusion raises the more fundamental question of whether inclusion in the international financial system—where established rules and monitoring can at least be applied—is better than blanket exclusion for rogue actors, where alternate means of communicating and financing will inevitably develop. Should exclusion from the financial system be the first instinct and policy step, or the most extreme of measures?

For Treasury, there was a thin silver lining to the story. The revelation of the program gave context and detail to the idea of a Treasury Department with real intelligence value and relationships that were critical to national security. The arrangement with SWIFT could only have been arranged and managed by the Treasury Department. The program put Treasury at the center of a key national security program. At the highest levels of government, the Treasury Terrorist Finance Tracking Program was a point of pride. It was a program that had been run well, was effective, and could be defended without question publicly. President Bush would often speak of this program and the grave error the *New York Times* had made in revealing it. President Obama and his administration would fiercely defend it in the face of European criticism.

For those in the bureaucracy who had questioned whether the Treasury Department had anything tangible to offer the intelligence community, this program was proof positive that it was an important and necessary player in the post-9/11 environment. For all the problems that attended its revelation, the program helped to explain precisely why the US government's finance ministry housed an intelligence and analytic shop—the only one in the world.

13

The Constriction Campaign

Iran would be our next target. Treasury had demonstrated that its tools and the financial information at its command could be leveled against the most serious national security threats we faced. Like North Korea, Iran presented a significant challenge. It appeared to be marching toward a nuclear weapons capability. The United States needed leverage to affect Tehran's calculus.

For years, sanctions and trade embargoes had been the tools of choice to deal with the perceived threats from Iran, including state-sponsored terrorism and the proliferation of missile technology. Iran had been under American sanctions since the Iran hostage crisis of 1979. Over time, the sanctions had become more layered and restrictive—both to punish the regime and to isolate it. Soon after the hostage crisis, President Carter signed an executive order banning Iranian oil imports. The order also froze $12 billion in Iranian assets in US and overseas banks. There was a brief thaw in January 1981, when the United States and Iran signed the Algiers Accords releasing most of the frozen assets, lifting the trade embargo, and allowing for future resolution of asset-related disputes. But a variety of executive orders and legislation followed for the next two decades, from trade restrictions in the late 1980s on "dual-use" technologies, in response to Iran's budding nuclear program, to prohibitions of American involvement with the Iranian petroleum industry, due to Iran's sponsorship of terrorism.

The sanctions had not proven successful in undermining the regime or halting the Iranian policies and practices that the United States was attempting to confront. But after 9/11 we entered a new period of financial warfare, and the Treasury Department had proven that a different kind of financial campaign could produce results. Stuart Levey wanted to use these tools to isolate Iran.

For months, a group of us within the department debated the basic questions. Could the same tools that we had used to isolate Al Qaeda from the formal financial system and to shock the regime in Pyongyang be leveraged to attack the Iranian regime? Could the international financial environment be engineered and conditioned to reject Iranian commercial and financial behavior? Could the new brand of financial warfare be waged successfully against Tehran?

Unlike North Korea, Iran was not a commercially isolated nation. Though it had been subject to US sanctions for years, the Iranian government and business sector had continued doing billions of dollars' worth of business every year with the rest of the world. The sixth largest supplier of energy resources to the European Union in 2012, the country retained deep commercial and financial ties with economic powers such as Germany and South Korea and represented an important market for Europe and Asia. Neighboring countries, including the United Arab Emirates and Turkey, had even deeper commercial and financial ties with Iran. In spite of the sanctions, even US companies with foreign subsidiaries had no trouble selling American goods to Iran. Likewise, Iranian businessmen and companies did easy and open business in most parts of the world.

Most important, Iran had oil. Oil provides instant access to markets and business relationships between companies and countries. The business of extracting, selling, and transporting oil brings with it an array of business relationships and financing needs. Oil also creates ties to an international market addicted to the flow of crude from the Middle East. Oil remained Iran's trump card.

In the face of economic pressure, Iran often threatens closure of the Straits of Hormuz—through which one-fifth of the world's oil is transported—as a way of spooking the oil markets and fending off Western pressure. The mere threat of stopping oil production or shipments sends shudders throughout oil markets, especially for countries deeply dependent on Iranian oil. The world's dependence on oil was Iran's ultimate defense against financial pressure.

Yet I was still convinced that Iran was inherently vulnerable. Although it was certainly a harder target than North Korea, which was more isolated and less sophisticated commercially than Iran—and didn't have oil—Iran was dependent on its international connections in the global financial and commercial system. The same ties that gave Iranian businesses access to foreign markets created dependencies for them in the international financial system.

What's more, the Iranian oil market was not immune from international pressure. Global oil trading occurs in US dollars, and therefore, any deals for Iranian oil had to be priced and transacted in dollars. There had to be some dollar-clearing function—the ability to convert any transaction into dollars—in order for Iranian transactions with foreign counterparties to occur.

Perhaps most important, when we carefully analyzed the Iranian banking sector and the movements of suspect financing, we saw a glaring vulnerability. The Iranian banks that were critical to Iran's business operations abroad were also linked to the country's illicit financial activity. Iranian banks such as Bank Saderat, Bank Melli, Bank Mellat, and Bank Sepah had a deep international presence in places like London, Frankfurt, Tokyo, Beirut, and Dubai. They were important for Iran's business ties and relations, providing lines of credit, correspondent accounts, and account access around the world to Iranians and their customers. Yet these banks were also hubs for illicit financial activity, with each bank facilitating a different aspect of Iran's overseas activity that fell under international scrutiny.

Bank Saderat—and its branch in Beirut—was the central conduit for Iranian financing to Hezbollah in Lebanon. It was easy for the regime in Tehran to send tranches of financing to its proxies in Lebanon, because it could simply transfer money through the head-quarters of Bank Saderat in Tehran to its Lebanese branch. Banks Melli, Mellat, and Sepah served as facilitators of proliferation deals for companies that could supply dual-use technologies and for countries, like North Korea, that were willing to sell parts and technology tied to missile and nuclear weapons systems. These banks had branches in the key banking centers in Europe, the Middle East, and Asia and were the preferred banks for doing business abroad with nuclear suppliers and proliferators, although unwitting companies dealing with Iranian front companies and cut-outs used them as well. Eventually, the central bank of Iran, known as Bank Markazi, would also begin to look like a commercial bank for Iranian interests, and it, too, was willing to serve as a banking hub for Iranian illicit activities. The Iranian regime was using Iran's banks to move money for illicit and suspect purposes. Its reliance on the international financial system made it vulnerable to financial isolation—and Treasury could take full advantage of this vulnerability.

In 2003, we identified Bank Saderat as a principal target in our Bad Bank Initiative. We had direct and convincing evidence that Bank Saderat was being used as the bank of choice for transactions taking place between Iran and Hezbollah, with the branch in Beirut serving as the central conduit for support to Hezbollah's activities in Lebanon. We were not the only ones to focus on Bank Saderat—this was a bank that Israel would consider bombing during its war with Hezbollah in 2006, considering its central importance to Hezbollah's financing. For our purposes, it was susceptible to being targeted surgically with Section 311 of the Patriot Act. The new tools we had under Section 311 raised the possibility of completely shutting down the bank. Such a move would hurt both Iran and Hezbollah, affecting both their financial operations and their international connectivity. It would serve as a shot across the bow to the Iranians—beginning the targeting of their financial sector—while also warning Beirut bankers to cease doing business with Hezbollah.

The action would be a conditioning step to spark greater financial scrutiny globally against Iran, Hezbollah, and their banking allies.

Before we could use this strategy, however, we needed to prove that it could work. When we first presented the idea to the Deputies Committee of the National Security Council in 2004, we had not yet used Section 311 against BDA or North Korea, and few outside the Treasury could imagine the effects. The NSC deputies were also concerned about inadvertently affecting global oil prices without gaining much in return. The decision to target Bank Saderat and undertake a new kind of financial campaign against Iran would have to wait for another day. That day arrived in February 2006.

In February 2006, Stuart Levey had hitched a ride on Secretary of State Condoleezza Rice's plane, during another of her marathon trips to the Middle East, in the hopes of making the pitch for a new financial campaign against Iran. Rice had already been briefed on what Levey was going to present, but she wanted to hear it for herself. She called Levey to the front of her plane on the last leg of the trip. Levey had been waiting for this moment. With Secretary Rice were her closest advisers, including Department of State Counselor Philip Zelikow, Jim Wilkinson, and NSC Deputy National Security Adviser Elliott Abrams.

Rice welcomed Levey into her cabin and gave him the floor. Levey explained the nature of this new form of financial pressure in the post-9/11 period, taking care to differentiate it from historical efforts to isolate Iran from the rest of the world. The campaign to constrict Iran's banking system and economy would not be a classic trade embargo. It would not matter if Iranians could buy Wrigley chewing gum on the streets of Tehran. Instead, Treasury could mount a targeted financial campaign attacking Iran's banks. The Iranians' use of their financial and commercial system to advance their nuclear weapons program and to support their military and intelligence operations would be their Achilles' heel.

The financial campaign would squeeze Iran's ability to access the international financial system in stages—actually feeding off of Iran's attempts to evade the program's heightened scrutiny. This would take some time, patience, and coordination within the US government and with allies—but, if staged properly, it could work. Diplomacy, while a necessary component, would not be the leading mechanism for Iran's financial isolation. The driving principle would be the same as what had been justifying the isolation of illicit financial activity since 9/11—the protection of the integrity of the international financial system. This would unfold in stages, and the international environment would need to be conditioned to reject doing business with Iran. It would not be a financial shock-and-awe campaign. Instead, it would take time, using a series of coordinated steps. If anything, this campaign would look more like a financial insurgency than a traditional sanctions program.

We would target Iran's banks by using Iran's own conduct—its proliferation activity, support for terrorist groups and Shia militias, and lack of anti-money-laundering controls, as well as the secretive nature of the regime itself—as the cornerstone of our campaign. Iran's suite of suspect activities and attempts to avoid international scrutiny would spur the private sector to stop doing business with Iran. No reputable bank would want to be caught facilitating Iran's nuclear program or helping it make payments to Hezbollah terrorist cells around the world.

What Levey was proposing was a virtuous cycle of isolation that would reduce Iranian access to the international financial system more and more over time. The more the Iranians tried to hide their identities or evade sanctions, the more suspect their transactions would appear and the riskier it would become for banks and other financial institutions to deal with them. Gradually, bank accounts, lines of credit, and correspondent accounts would be shut down. Like prey caught in a boa constrictor's lethal embrace, Iran's own actions to avoid scrutiny and obfuscate transactions would lead to greater financial constriction.

Already the Iranians were unwittingly deepening their greatest vulnerability. They were blending legitimate business transactions with illicit ones by funneling them through similar conduits. The Iranian regime often tried to hide the nature of its transactions and the identities of the Iranian government entities involved. They used front companies, cut-outs, and businessmen to acquire items and goods abroad that were hard to acquire, that were sanctioned, or that were tied to their nuclear ambitions or their weapons programs. At the same time, the Iranian military was taking greater control of the nation's economy. Importantly, the predominant economic player was Iran's Islamic Revolutionary Guard Corps (IRGC), the elite military and security unit founded in 1979. The IRGC had gained more power and influence over time as the protector and exporter of the revolution and reported directly to the Supreme Leader, Ayatollah Ali Khamenei.

The IRGC—with its vast network—had embedded itself into more industries within Iran, ultimately building what has been called a veritable business empire.[1] Its control of "charitable" foundations—known as *bonyads*—with access to billions of dollars of assets in the form of mortgages and business interests for veterans of the Iranian military—served as the baseline of its economic power, along with its ability to construct infrastructure through a corps of engineers. The reach of the IRGC's economic empire now extends to majority stakes in infrastructure companies, shipping and transport, beverage companies, and food and agriculture companies.[2] In 2006, the corps took over the Iranian telecommunications sector, and it has also begun to oversee more elements of the nation's energy sector, including the development of pipelines and the valuable South Pars oil field. Some estimates note that the IRGC controls between 25 and 40 percent of Iran's gross domestic product (GDP).[3] The IRGC is deeply involved in building Iran's infrastructure, pursuing projects such as deep-water ports and underground facilities important to Iran's defense and economy. These projects and industries give the IRGC political power and access to profits and capital.

The IRGC is an economic juggernaut, with responsibilities relating to the development of weapons of mass destruction, missile systems, and overseas operations. It is deeply involved in the Iranian nuclear program, and its international arm, the Qods Force (IRGC-QF), is responsible for providing support to terrorist proxies and exporting the Iranian Revolution. Between them, the IRGC and its Qods Force are responsible for all the activities—weapons proliferation, terrorist support, and militant activity—for which Iran has been sanctioned in the past.

From Treasury's perspective, this blend of activities created the ultimate vulnerability, particularly the blurred lines between legitimate industry and support for Iran's nuclear program and terrorist groups. The nefarious nature of the activities, tied with the IRGC's attempts to hide its hand in many of its economic dealings and operations, made Iran's financial activity inherently suspect. Iran was making itself a prime target for the kind of financial isolation that fed off of the suspect conduct of rogue individuals, companies, and countries.

The financial campaign Levey envisioned would focus not on squeezing the trade and economy of the populace, but instead on the financial infrastructure of the IRGC and the regime's profits. The actions were not intended to punish the Iranian people, and this was not an embargo intended to punish Iran for political delicts. The financial campaign targeted suspect Iranian financial and commercial activity in order to protect the international financial system from Iran's illicit financial activity. The system had to be inoculated from the Iranian virus.

An argument would be made directly to banks and companies around the world that it was too risky to do business with Iran, since no one really knew who was lurking behind corporate veils, pulling the strings, and accessing bank accounts and funding in Tehran. Would a bank be willing to risk its reputation by doing business, even inadvertently, with the IRGC or the Qods Force? Could their compliance officers guarantee that they knew who was behind their Iranian customers and transactions? Was trade with Iran worth the risk of access to American markets and banks?

Rice liked Levey's plan. Having noted the success of the BDA action, she and Treasury Secretary Snow and then later Secretary Paulson, along with National Security Adviser Steve Hadley, had been discussing how to increase the financial pressure on Iran. Levey's plan had the virtue of not relying on the consent of the United Nations. The campaign offered a new avenue for leverage against the Iranian regime. Rice asked Levey what he needed from her to get this done. Levey, stung in his fierce battles with Chris Hill during the BDA episode, spoke plainly: "I need your direct support, and I need to do this in concert with the State Department." She agreed, and with that Levey prepared to launch an all-out assault against the Iranian regime.

Levey would later brief President Bush in the Oval Office about the details of the campaign. Steve Hadley had kept the president apprised of the ideas behind the campaign and had been working hand-in-hand with Paulson and Rice to ensure close cooperation among the members of the president's cabinet. Treasury Secretary Paulson was a major advocate for the campaign. The former Goldman Sachs CEO was willing to use his deep credibility with his former colleagues in the financial world, in addition to his access to finance ministry and central bank officials around the world. In many ways, Paulson had the ideal background for the job. The former Wall Street executive could convincingly make a case to fellow bankers about the danger of doing business with Iran. When Paulson talked, financial leaders around the world listened.

When Levey and Paulson came to the Oval Office, there was no question about the president's support. Bush wanted the financial pressure campaign to impede Iranian progress toward a nuclear capability and to increase the fissures within the Iranian system. The ultimate goal was to force the question within Tehran as to whether proceeding with a nuclear program was worth the economic costs and isolation. The president gave the effort his blessing.

Paulson, Rice, and Hadley would keep the president updated on the stages of the plan.

In 2006, the campaign would be launched as a dual-track program combining diplomacy and financial pressure. Secretary Rice turned to Undersecretary of State R. Nicholas Burns to drive diplomatic pressure against the Iranians via the United Nations and engagement with Iran through our European partners. By early 2006, the administration had decided to seek negotiations with Iran along with the Permanent 5 members of the United Nations plus Germany ("P5 plus one"). The United States created that negotiating group in January 2006, in hopes of using diplomacy and negotiations as a way to end the Iran nuclear threat while keeping the use of financial pressure and measures in play.

Pressuring the Iranians to answer serious, lingering questions about their nuclear ambitions was a major goal. Burns's job was to align the international community with American interests in order to pressure and isolate the Iranians diplomatically—with the ultimate aim of seeking a negotiated agreement on the nuclear program. The United States and its partners made a public offer to Iran to negotiate on June 1, 2006, in Vienna at a meeting of the foreign ministers of the group. When it became clear that Iran would not accept that offer, the United States turned to the use of an all-out financial pressure campaign.

Treasury—led by Levey—would launch the financial pressure campaign marshaling and driving the private-sector isolation of Iranian financial and commercial activity. Levey's job was to stage the financial assault on Iran's banks and its financial system—in large part by demonstrating to CEOs and compliance officers around the world that the risk of doing business with Iran was too high. Iranian obfuscation was too ubiquitous to be handled through normal compliance efforts. Trade with Iran was valuable, but it was far outweighed by the importance of access to American markets, companies, and technologies. It was better to stop doing business with Iran altogether than to risk facilitating Iran's support for terror or its development of a nuclear program. Levey and Burns became a dynamic duo on the Iranian account.

Burns would lay out a diplomatic choreography to get international buy-in for sanctions, with a growing level of pressure on different sectors of Iran's economy over time. He would rely on our European partners but wanted to leverage the United Nations as well. Burns began negotiations for a UN Security Council resolution to sanction Iran for its suspect and unexplained nuclear activity. Many doubted whether a sanctions resolution could be passed at all. The negotiations bogged down, with China and Russia, both traditionally averse to applying sanctions, wearing down the other members of the Security Council and watering down the sanctions. What Burns expected to take a few weeks to negotiate took months to get through the Security Council. A first set of sanctions against Iran passed unanimously—but painfully—in December 2006. They did not include everything the United States wanted, but they were an important start to set the stage for further diplomatic isolation of Iran. In total, Burns and Rice would negotiate three sanctions resolutions with more and more diplomatic and financial bite from 2006 to 2008 as Iran demonstrated an unwillingness to deal openly with the international community.

The initial meager results taught Burns an important lesson. The United States could not rely exclusively on the United Nations to pressure Iran. With the Chinese and Russians blocking tough sanctions, and the delay likely to accompany any follow-on sanctions rounds, he began to look more and more to Levey to provide the leverage and diplomatic ammunition he needed to pressure the Iranians.

Early on, Burns asked Levey to explain the financial pressure strategy to his foreign ministry counterparts. By May 2006, it was clear to the United States that the diplomatic outreach and offers to Iran were not being met in good faith from the Iranian side. The Russians and Europeans, with US blessing, had offered to assist Iran with the development of a civilian nuclear program with the enrichment of uranium handled outside of the country. Those offers, along with pledges of economic and diplomatic integration, were spurned by Iran. It was time to pressure the Iranians in earnest with a new financial and diplomatic campaign of isolation.

Burns would visit capital after capital—often bringing Levey with him to meet his foreign ministry counterparts. It was important for foreign ministry officials to understand the United States' thinking about using financial suasion and financial tools to isolate the Iranians. This would require diplomatic coordination, and it would be most effective if there was international cooperation at every level. The diplomats could help by formulating appropriate sanctions and actions to match what the United States was doing— through the European Union and domestically—and could reinforce the quiet message being sent to their banking communities. Ideally, the dual tracks would reinforce each other, with Iranian isolation deepening both diplomatically and financially.

Getting the French on board would be critical. Meanwhile, the British were sympathetic, and the Germans seemed like they would follow begrudgingly, depending on what other countries decided. Burns invited Levey to join him in Paris on May 2, 2006, to meet with European counterparts engaged on the Iran issue. This would begin a diplomatic offensive with the three European powers that were engaged with Iran. We wanted to make sure they understood the path the United States was taking with its financial pressure. It was also a way of demonstrating the importance of the Treasury campaign to the United States and the close coordination between the Treasury and the State Department. There had been divisions over North Korea, but there would be no daylight between the State and Treasury departments on Iran.

Still, laying the groundwork and choreographing the steps were not easy tasks. Deputy National Security Adviser James Jeffrey coordinated the two tracks among a small deputies group from the State Department, Treasury, the Department of Defense, the intelligence community, and the National Security Council staff. In weekly meetings in the White House Situation Room—often twice a week—the players would lay out the steps being taken to pressure the Iranians and discuss what to do next. Jeffrey, a former Marine and a highly regarded, no-nonsense career diplomat who had already served as US ambassador to Albania and would later be named ambassador to Turkey and then Iraq, would manage the meetings with tough-minded pragmatism. The two tracks would sometimes diverge or come into tension, with the pace of financial pressure often slowed by negotiations for UN Security Council resolutions and the reluctance of close partners to shut down commercial and financial relationships with long-standing Iranian clients and customers. Questions would often arise over whether the United States should drive the actions or attempt to build a crescendo of coordinated international actions. The campaign turned out to be a mix of both—with Burns managing the international engagements—but the reality was that the United States would need to force the debate and drive the financial isolation of Iran. No other country had the means, the clout, or the political will to take the difficult first steps to drive the private-sector isolation of Iran.

And that's what Levey brought to the table. Levey began his meetings with bank officials around the world with a briefing on Iranian illicit activity and how it coursed through the international financial system. He would take this argument from board room to board room, often meeting with bank CEOs before and after meeting with foreign government counterparts. Steve Hadley called it the "whisper campaign," because the mission entailed meeting quietly with bank executives to explain the risks of doing business with Iran. At the heart of these meetings was a presentation on what Iran was doing with front companies and layered financial transactions to facilitate activity that was considered either illegal or risky.

Levey had perfected a similar pitch while he and Danny Glaser were chasing North Korean assets after the Section 311 action against Banco Delta Asia. These stops—in countries such as Vietnam and Mongolia—had convinced government and banking officials alike that maintaining or establishing banking relationships with the North Koreans was a dangerous business.

Levey now began an Iranian financial roadshow—but with a broader mandate and a global scope. His new assistant secretary, Pat O'Brien, a no-nonsense former Department of Justice official, added his voice to the chorus internationally. Secretary Paulson had argued in favor of going straight to the banks with the pitch and helped to open many doors to bank chairmen and CEOs. He also made a point of putting the issue of Iran's suspect financial activity on the agenda of his meetings with foreign government officials and banking friends with whom he met. In 2007, Paulson set up a special meeting with his G20 finance-minister counterparts to discuss Iran. With usual Paulson candor and in his halting cadence, Paulson laid out his concerns at this meeting about Iran's illicit activity. One would expect such talk from the director of the CIA or FBI, but to hear this coming from the former CEO of Goldman Sachs and the treasury secretary caused officials to take notice. The treasury secretary was speaking a new language of national security that resonated with the CEOs of the world's biggest banks and businesses.

Levey would meet over one hundred times with bank officials around the world. At each stop, he made the case that doing business with Iran was too risky—because the banks could not be sure they knew who they were doing business with. Levey insisted on meeting directly with each bank's CEO, knowing that the CEO would have little awareness of the risks in play and ultimately would be the one to make the costly decision to close accounts and unplug Iranian clients.

For each country and institution, the Treasury team would provide specific tidbits of data about Iranian transactions through a bank. The briefing packets would have general information about the Iranian economy, structure, and financial system. The packets would contain information about how the Iranian government and the IRGC used front companies and obfuscation to finance and acquire what they needed for their military and nuclear apparatus. The briefing would conclude with an explanation of what was happening in the bank and how the Iranians were hiding their activity. This would inevitably be a surprise to any bank CEO, though some banks would be caught later trying to hide transactions with Iran. These meetings not intended to be an accusation of complicity, however, but a wake-up call to lift the veil of Iranian financial activity and raise suspicions.

On one occasion, Levey had compiled information about Iran's use of a German bank to move money for acquisitions for their operations, potentially for the nuclear program. When Levey met with the bank's CEO and chief compliance officer, he asked them if they knew what was happening in their bank. The compliance officer seemed confident. The CEO less so and worried about what was to come. Levey then calmly explained what the US government knew about Iranian financial transactions and the use of cover payments and front companies to hide the real purpose for their banking. The IRGC was using bank accounts in Europe to acquire nuclear equipment and to develop its missile systems while lining their leaders' pockets. Levey went on to explain that most banks did not realize this, but that it was happening. The banks thus far had had no way to know what was transpiring through Iranian front operations and accounts. Levey then put a file on the table that contained documents detailing those types of transactions happening in that very bank.

After absorbing this revelation, the CEO was stunned, the compliance officer sheepish and worried. The CEO took the documents and thanked Levey for the information. He said he would take the information under consideration and look into the matter. The meeting was over, and it had its effect. The bank began to close its accounts with Iranian customers and curtail its business with Iran. The quiet campaign was working without any government decree or international mandate.

There was much consternation in the banking community and

among foreign government officials in response to this approach. Bank executives in money centers around the world took Levey's briefings to be not-so-subtle threats of sanctions and enforcement actions to come if the banks did not conclude their business with Iranian clients. Some bankers—perhaps in a response reinforced over time by financial lore—recall an angry Levey pounding the table and threatening dire actions. Levey, a mild-mannered lawyer, does not recall pounding any tables, but does remember offering up an explicit warning of Treasury attention to come. The real effect was to expose Iranian behavior and to signal that it would not be ignored, especially if Iranian money was flowing through the banking system. The US Treasury Department was feared and respected for what it could do, which made bank executives listen and act.

Foreign government officials often did not like the fact that an American official was meeting with private institutions without their approval. In the case of countries that relied on the capital markets and banking sector as a major sector of their economy, there was particular resentment, especially since many of these banks were the most important private-sector companies in those countries. They also did not like the effects. Regardless of what the host government did or did not do, the banks had to listen to the Treasury Department and consider the risks attendant to doing business with Iran. It became common, without any official action at all from the governments in countries where banks were located, for banks to simply close accounts and begin to minimize their dealings with Iranian businesses. This was the ultimate application of American financial power extraterritorially—and it relied on the decisions and actions of the private sector.

The campaign was beginning to have an impact. The Swiss banking giants UBS and Credit Suisse announced in 2006 that they would stop or curtail their business with Iran. Other banks and companies would soon follow, including the European banking giants ABN Amro and ING. In 2007, Germany's second-largest bank, Commerzbank, ended its dollar-clearing transactions with Iran.

These meetings were not the only step the Treasury needed to take. The Treasury also needed to set signals and guideposts for the private sector. To this end, a series of designations was designed to build like a financial crescendo, creating an international financial environment that would begin to reject, for its own sake, the risks of doing business with Iran. US executive orders would identify and target finance that supported terror and proliferation, which would be matched with designations at the United Nations.

Then Iran's banks were exposed and targeted—one at a time. On September 7, 2006, the Treasury cut off Bank Saderat from the international financial system, pulling its ability to rely on a particular type of transaction exemption (the "U-turn" exemption, described later) to access the US banking system. Thus began the campaign to cut off Iran's banks from the international financial system. The final rule noted: "Bank Saderat has been a significant facilitator of Hizballah's financial activities and has served as a conduit between the Government of Iran and Hizballah, Hamas, the Popular Front for the Liberation of Palestine–General Command, and Palestinian Islamic Jihad. To cut off Bank Saderat from the U.S. financial system, OFAC is making three amendments to the ITR [Iran Transaction Regulations] that effectively prohibit all transactions directly or indirectly involving Bank Saderat." The next day, the bank was designated as a terrorist financing institution under Executive Order 13224.

The Treasury next hit Iran's Bank Sepah and its UK affiliate, Bank Sepah International PLC in London. The bank was designated in January 2007 under the counter-proliferation-finance executive order for providing financial services for Iranian entities engaged in proliferation activities. It designated Bank Mellat in October 2007, as well as the Mellat-linked Mellat Bank SB CJSC (Armenia) and Persian International Bank PLC (United Kingdom) (and later, in 2009, First East Export Bank in Malaysia), under the same authorities. Mellat and its subsidiaries were being singled out for their role in assisting the development of Iran's nuclear program and for banking the Iranian entities that were attempting to acquire sensitive materials. In December 2008, Treasury similarly designated Bank Melli, along with its subsidiaries and affiliates Arian Bank (Afghanistan), Bank Kargoshee (Iran), Bank Melli Iran ZAO (Russia), Future Bank (Bahrain), and Melli Bank PLC (United Kingdom).[4]

The Treasury then began to use its authorities to hit other banks doing business with Iran. It designated Banco Internacional de Desarollo, CA (Venezuela) and the Export Development Bank of Iran in October 2008. The Treasury Department was making the case officially that Iranian banks were entangled in proliferation financing—a threat to both the integrity of the financial system and global security. It was also sending a clear signal that it would go after banks willing to cross the red line of doing illicit business with Iran.

The financial pressure campaign continued to mount, with more designations and private-sector outreach. The UN Security Council unanimously passed three resolutions focused on Iran's nuclear program as engagement faltered and leaders around the world looked for options between diplomacy and war. As of 2012, the US Treasury had targeted sixteen Iranian banks.

The campaign of financial isolation evolved quickly and began to target more than just Iranian banks and the military offices and front companies that were part of the broader proliferation network. In early 2006, Levey and the Treasury team began looking carefully at two sectors that would prove to be critical nodes for the Iranian proliferation networks as well as the broader economy: shipping and insurance. They were essential elements of Iran's access to the international financial and commercial systems. Iran's shipping line—Islamic Republic of Iran Shipping Lines (IRISL)—provided the means for Iran to ship weapons, parts, and equipment tied to its proliferation program and to support Hezbollah and other terrorist groups. In 2007, an Iranian ship was stopped off the coast of Israel delivering crates full of weapons to Hezbollah and Hamas. Though ships were not the only means of moving weapons or materiel—the Iranians also used planes and trains—they were the most efficient. IRISL and its subsidiaries would therefore become targets of US and UN actions.

On September 10, 2008, Treasury designated IRISL and eighteen of its subsidiaries under Executive Order 13382. The State Department press release noted:

> In order to ensure the successful delivery of military-related goods, IRISL has deliberately misled maritime authorities through deceptive techniques. These techniques were adopted to conceal the true nature of shipments ultimately destined for MODAFL [Ministry of Defense and Armed Forces Logistics]. Furthermore, as international attention over Iran's WMD programs has increased, IRISL has pursued new strategies to maintain commerce which also afford it the potential to evade future detection of military shipments, including: Falsifying shipping documents in order to hide the true end users of shipments; Employing the use of generic terms to describe shipments so as not to attract the attention of shipping authorities; and Creating and making use of cover entities to conduct official IRISL business.[5]

Treasury also determined that shipping and commercial insurance were critical to most of Iran's primary overseas engagements. For a ship to take part in legitimate commercial trade, it needed insurance—likely from Lloyds of London or major German maritime insurers. Ships without insurance could not legitimately carry goods, sail, or dock. Importantly, the insurance companies relied on the banking system to transact deals and needed to know the nature of the activity they were insuring. It was the very business of insurance companies to evaluate risk by determining what was being carried, where it was coming from and where it was going, and who was sending and receiving it. The more aware these companies were of Iran's true activities, the higher the valuation would be of risk—and the costlier the insurance would become.

Levey's visits expanded beyond bank headquarters and began to include insurance company CEOs and officers. These meetings, and the UN resolutions targeting Iran, highlighted the need for insurance executives to be suspicious of what was being insured for Iran as well as the importance of applying additional due diligence— common requirements by this time in the banking world. This was a natural expansion of the due diligence requirements that had arisen after 9/11. The Iranians found themselves squeezed on all sides, and the ripple effects of their financial constriction began to emerge. Even US officials were surprised at how effective these measures were and the impact they were having on Iran's ability to do business around the world.

On July 31, 2006, the UN Security Council adopted Resolution 1696, requiring Iran to suspend its enrichment and reprocessing activities as well as its construction of a heavy water reactor—in addition to adhering to steps required by the IAEA board of governors. On March 3, 2008, a new unanimous resolution, UNSCR 1803, called for vigilance over financial dealings with Iran. The United States imposed targeted financial measures against Future Bank and made the relevant information publicly available.

With each designation and official action, the US government attempted to expose the work of the IRGC and its Qods Force and their use of financial and commercial vehicles to support their activity. The intent was not just to raise diplomatic concerns about the progress of Iran's nuclear program, but also to pressure the banking world to suspect any financial transactions dealing with an Iranian bank or business.

On March 30, 2007, the State Department designated Iran's Defense Industries Organization (DIO) under EO 13382. This step was part of the United States' implementation of UNSCR 1737. The State Department press release noted:

> DIO was sanctioned previously by the United States for WMD or missile-related activities under the Iran and Syria Nonproliferation Act (ISNA), the Arms Export Control Act, and the Export Adminis-

tration Act. DIO also has been identified by the IAEA as involved in centrifuge component production for Iran's nuclear program. A June 2004 report from the Director General of the International Atomic Energy Agency (IAEA) on Iran's implementation of IAEA resolutions noted that Iranian authorities acknowledged that composite rotors for use in P-2 centrifuges had been fabricated in a workshop situated on a DIO site.[6]

The most important set of coordinated actions against the Iranians was put into place on October 25, 2007, when the State Department designated the IRGC and Iran's Ministry of Defense and Armed Forces Logistics under EO 13382. The press statement said, "The U.S. Government is taking several major actions today to counter Iran's bid for nuclear capabilities and support for terrorism by exposing Iranian banks, companies and individuals that have been involved in these dangerous activities and by cutting them off from the U.S. financial system."[7] The Treasury also designated nine IRGC-affiliated entities and five IRGC-affiliated individuals as derivatives of the IRGC, Bank Melli and Bank Mellat, and three individuals who were affiliated with Iran's Aerospace Industries Organization (AIO). It designated IRGC-QF for its material support and Bank Saderat as a terrorist financier. There was no question that the United States was upping the financial ante on all parts of Iran's economy.

The designations and regulations—coinciding with and prompting other international actions—were accompanied by additional financial diplomacy. On February 5, 2008, Levey again visited the Arabian Gulf to meet with officials and bankers in Qatar, Bahrain, and the UAE. His meetings in these and other capitals and financial centers had a single purpose. He sought cooperation and argued for voluntary steps by the banks and private-sector actors to cut Iran off from the international financial system.

It was also critical to weaken Iran's ability to deal comfortably in the oil markets. We were trying to strike a balance—making it very costly for Iran and its oil customers to do business while not spooking the oil markets and spiking prices. A key point of access for the Iranians, still allowed under US law, was the "U-turn" financial transaction. For a number of years, this provision had existed as a realistic function of the oil markets. The world needed Iranian oil, and oil was transacted in dollars. The U-turn provision allowed for dollarized oil transactions through the US banking system—without the money ever sitting in a US bank or the bank serving as the originator or destination financial institution in the transaction. The transaction could literally do a U-turn from abroad, just transiting the United States to convert the transaction into dollars and then sent back out of the country. The decision was made to end this exception, despite concerns that oil prices would spike or the oil markets would be disrupted. Getting rid of the U-turn exception would cut off any dollar-clearing transactions for Iranian oil through New York.

On November 10, 2008, the United States revoked authorization for U-turn transfers involving Iran. This simple regulatory fix had an important impact. It now meant that the banks and institutions in Europe, the Middle East, and Asia facilitating the financing for Iranian oil deals could no longer access and use their American correspondent relationships to clear the dollar. With oil transactions traded and monetized in dollars, this was crippling to normal transactions for the Iranians. It made it costlier and more cumbersome for the Iranians to get their oil to market, and it added uncertainty into the Iranian oil markets for those considering long-term investments. The Iranians and their financial backers would adapt, beginning to engage in regional transactions using local currency or bartering for the oil (trading oil exports for the return of consumer goods). On December 3, 2008, the Treasury added to this pressure and expanded the list of companies identified as being owned or controlled by the government of Iran to include the National Iranian Oil Company, Naftiran Intertrade Company Ltd., and Naftiran Intertrade Company Sarl.

The European Union—led by a more aggressive French government under President Nicolas Sarkozy—began to follow with important EU regulations and designations that paralleled US actions. The banking communities in London, Frankfurt, and Amsterdam were not necessarily enthusiastic actors, but they had to react to the realities of the new environment. The risk calculus was changing, and doing business with Iran was becoming a costly venture, given the potential for sanctions within the European Union and by the United States. That sense of vulnerability would only grow, despite the allure of business opportunities in Iran being filled by others like the Chinese and Russians.

By now, it was not only the federal government in the United States that was waging a campaign against Iranian finance. The Manhattan District Attorney's Office, led by the legendary Robert Morgenthau, began to investigate banks for lack of compliance with US banking restrictions and attempts to evade those controls by hiding the nature of financial transactions. In January 2009, a British institution, the Lloyds TSB Group, paid $350 million in fines after it was found to have ignored US sanctions on Iranian institutions and dollar transactions.[8] Morgenthau began to wade aggressively into waters that Levey and the Treasury Department thought to be their province. But the New York banking authorities have ultimate say in who does business and how in the New York banking system—a great power that would lead to conflicts of jurisdiction again and again.

Morgenthau became a leading voice on the issue of illegal Iranian financial flows through New York's banking system. He was out to expose it and stop it by punishing those banks that appeared complicit in allowing the Iranians to access New York banks. He became noticeably passionate about the role that the Venezuelan banking system was playing as a back door into the US financial system by the Iranians. He was willing to use investigations and prosecutions to stop illegal access to the US markets, but he was just as willing to use his bully pulpit and the threat of future sanction by New York prosecutors as a sword of Damocles over the heads of bankers. In one of his final speeches as district attorney in May 2009, Morgenthau noted the problem of evasion of financial controls against the Iranians and highlighted the role of Venezuelan banks in this complicity.[9] In a 2009 op-ed piece in the *Wall Street Journal,* Morgenthau argued that "in the past several years Iranian entities have employed a pervasive system of deceitful and fraudulent practices to move money all over the world without detection. The regime has done this, I believe, to pay for materials necessary to develop nuclear weapons, long-range missiles, and road-side bombs. Venezuela has an established financial system that Iran, with the help of Mr. Chávez's government, can exploit to avoid economic sanctions."[10]

This work of conditioning the environment also included bringing the full weight of the Financial Action Task Force—the global anti-money-laundering standard-setting and evaluation body—to bear on Iran. If Iran was to be isolated financially, the FATF had to be engaged to pass judgment on Iran's anti-money-laundering and counter-terrorist-financing system. Danny Glaser and Chip Poncy, who had become two of the most well-respected financial diplomats and money-laundering experts in the world, took charge of the effort for the United States to restart the old FATF process to blacklist problematic countries—which had proven effective in the past to spotlight money-laundering havens around the world. Even so, that process had raised criticisms of an unfair process targeting easily identifiable and politically vulnerable states. Glaser and Poncy set out to create a credible process within the FATF system that scrutinized the Iranian regime—using not just the anti-money-laundering standards but also the counterproliferation and counter-terrorist-financing standards that Treasury had pushed in the FATF after 9/11.

If the Iranians were found to be outside the bounds of the legitimate financial system or failing to cooperate or comply with accepted international standards, then there could be consequences. In the past, those consequences took the form of "countermeasures" that the FATF would declare necessary to protect against the systemic failings of the jurisdiction being evaluated. In the post-9/11 era, the notion of countermeasures took on added significance, because the United States and other countries had developed tools to isolate an offending jurisdiction from the legitimate financial system and make investment and business in that jurisdiction suspect.

Poncy and Glaser knew their efforts would take time, as it required building consensus among thirty-three jurisdictions that now included Russia and China. FATF also needed time to engage directly with the Iranian government. A methodical process would have to be followed, but it was a process that would bring the relevant financial and regulatory actors into line with the broader themes that the United States was echoing in the conference rooms of the big banks. Iran represented a systemic risk to the integrity of the financial system. Iran's secretive and reluctant nature made this process look like an enveloping trap for the Iranians. With each letter from the FATF seeking answers, the Iranians would fail to respond, or respond flatly without substance, just as they did with the UN nuclear watchdog, the IAEA. The lack of full cooperation engendered more suspicion and questions. Iran was sowing its own financial isolation.

Amid this campaign to put increasingly greater financial pressure on Iran, there emerged an unexpected opportunity to hit Iran hard and directly. In 2008, lawyers and others searching for Iranian assets became aware of what appeared to be more than $2 billion in Iranian assets in a Citibank account held by Clearstream. Clearstream Banking is a clearinghouse for financial trades and provides comprehensive international securities services. It was formed by the 2000 merger of Cedel International and Deutsche Börse Clearing. It is now a subsidiary of Deutsche Börse and acts as a clearinghouse and depository for bonds, securities, and equities. The institution has around 2,500 customers in 110 countries and completes more than 250,000 transactions daily. It holds an annual average of 11.1 trillion EUR in assets.[11] Acting in accordance with US and EU sanctions, Clearstream had closed or blocked all of its Iranian customer accounts by November 2007.[12] It was not clear in this case why these particular assets had gone unnoticed or unmoved, but with the additional scrutiny over Iranian assets, they emerged. The $2 billion was sitting undisturbed in an account.

Importantly, the assets belonged to the Iranian central bank, so successfully freezing or attaching them in some manner would affect Iranian reserves. Aside from the $12 billion in Iranian assets that had been frozen in 1979, this would be the largest freezing of Iranian assets in history. Capturing these assets, however, might undermine Clearstream and destabilize the international financial system at a moment of growing fragility. Actions taken too aggressively in the financial system might also send a signal that the United States was becoming a hostile environment in which to invest and nest capital. In the words of Secretary Paulson, the US government needs to respect the "magnificent glass house" of the financial system. Any perceived misuse of American financial prominence and power could destabilize and destroy the fragile system while making the United States a less attractive environment in which to invest.

In the end, the assets would be frozen, but not by the Treasury. Instead, lawyers for victims of terrorism who had previously brought actions against Iran as a state sponsor of terror acted on the information. In June 2008, a judge in the US District Court for the Southern District of New York used the information to freeze over $2.25 billion in Clearstream assets held in a Citibank account. Citibank denied having had any knowledge that the funds could be Iranian. Clearstream likewise denied that the funds were the Iranian government's and immediately began to engage in legal battles to release the money, successfully regaining $250 million within one month.

To Deputy Secretary of the Treasury Robert M. Kimmitt, this was an important event. Kimmitt was a veteran national security professional and powerful Washington lawyer—having served in the Reagan administration's National Security Council as the executive secretary and general counsel, and later as a senior policy official at the State Department and ambassador to Germany. He had deep experience in the sanctions and export control world—and knew that the most effective financial sanctions were multilateral in nature. Without an international framework for action, Kimmitt knew the United States would end up disputing with its friends and allies instead of hitting rogue regimes with sanctions. As deputy to Secretary Paulson, Kimmitt was a perfect national security and Washington complement to Paulson's Wall Street credentials.

Kimmitt was pleased the Iranian assets had not escaped. He had seen such assets get away from the United States in the past. In January 1986, the United States had placed sanctions on the Qaddafi regime in Libya but did not construct an immediate asset freeze mechanism as part of the sanctions. At the time, Kimmitt and other officials had watched as Libyan assets in New York—almost $3 billion worth—were transferred from Manufacturers Hanover and Chemical Bank and Bankers Trust to London. Eventually, the British courts allowed the funds to be released—in the minds of many, cynically preserving London's role as an Arab banking capital. The United States had let the money slip through its hands then. Kimmitt and others in the US government were satisfied to see the Iranian Central Bank's assets frozen by the courts this time.

The legal battles over these assets are still playing out. In February 2012, Iran's central bank—Bank Markazi—asked a New York judge to dismiss the pending suit freezing the assets and enforcing collection by the victims of the $2.7 billion. The bank claimed that such actions were unlawful under the US Foreign Sovereign Immunities Act. There is also legislation pending in Congress to allow the victims to access the frozen Iranian assets. As of the writing of this book, the litigation continues and the legislation remains under consideration. Regardless, a significant amount of assets were caught in the US legal system. The Iranian assets were not lost, and another financial pressure point had been pushed.

Iran's isolation was growing. By the end of the Bush administration, the Iranians were feeling the pressure and knew they were facing a financial assault unlike anything they had seen before. As of 2008,

Iranian leaders were already issuing public statements decrying the sanctions as ineffectual. But there was no doubt that the measures were starting to squeeze in unexpected ways—with Iran finding it difficult to access the international financial and commercial system. Something was different.

On September 14, 2010, former Iranian president Akbar Hashemi Rafsanjani urged the Iranian Assembly of Experts to recognize how painful the sanctions were. He said, "Throughout the revolution, we never had so many sanctions [imposed on Iran] and I am calling on you and all officials to take the sanctions seriously and not as jokes. . . . Over the past 30 years we had a war and military threats, but never have we seen such arrogance to plan a calculated assault against us."[13]

In the midst of the pressure, the Iranians realized they were under a financial attack of a new kind—and they noted that there was now a Treasury official dedicated to the financial assault on Iran. Levey's name was becoming synonymous with the isolation of Iran—making him a household name in the banks and finance ministries of the world. The Iranian government followed his every movement and would often shadow his meetings and follow him into the capitals and financial centers he had just visited. They were trying to contain the damage, but they were losing. Iran was growing more isolated financially in the legitimate financial system. Within the government, Levey was seen as the creative financial warrior whose engagement was helping to give the United States a tool it had not had in many years with Iran. The United States now had the leverage it had previously lacked.

The core question that remained was what the endgame of this campaign would be. Would there be a limit to the ability to use this kind of financial pressure to isolate the Iranian regime and its economy? Was the real goal of this campaign complete strangulation of the Iranian economy—moving it from a gradualist and targeted constriction campaign into a maximalist, traditional embargo by effect? Was there a final bullet in this financial arsenal?

The final bullet in the targeted financial campaign was the central bank of Iran itself. We had designed the financial pressure to lead to the isolation of the Iranian banking system and the central bank. Targeting Iran's central bank would be the last—and most extreme—step we could take against the banking system. Given the importance of the central bank system to the functioning of the international financial system, isolating Bank Markazi would have dramatic effects. Though it operated as a traditional central bank, holding currency reserves, it also acted as a commercial bank, picking up the slack for those banks that had begun to be excised from the international financial system. Over time, we knew that the central bank was opening accounts for designated Iranian companies and serving as a correspondent bank and pass-through for the Iranian banks that had been designated. Bank Markazi was the financial conduit of last resort for the Iranian financial system.

One additional weapon we held in reserve was targeting the oil sector. Commercially, oil was the final point of access to capital and the international markets. The question remained how to best attack Iran's oil markets to weaken Iran's ability to use it as a sword and shield against the financial pressure. Part of the answer was to make it harder for Iran to find investors in its oil fields, more costly for it to obtain new equipment, and too difficult for it to ship oil in and out of the country. Another answer was to dissuade those who were exporting refined petroleum to Iran to end those relationships and to sell elsewhere. This would leave Iran with a one-way oil market, given its dependence on refined oil imports. At the end of the day, though, the major challenge was to weaken Iran's ability to sell its oil for the currency, credit, and goods it needed to develop its nuclear weapons program. These steps were yet to come.

In this regard, the question remained how far the United States was willing to go to isolate the Iranian economy globally. There was a fragile balance that tempered and counseled against a financial blitzkrieg, but Iran's nuclear clock was ticking, and it was growing more and more isolated. But before we could take any final steps, there was a change of US administrations, which brought with it a possible shift in strategies.

President Bush would later note that he was particularly disappointed to have left the Iranian problem unresolved before the end of his tenure. Even so, his administration had set in motion a financial constriction of Iran unlike any other. Bush left office having created an international environment that was successfully isolating Iranian financial and commercial activity. The Treasury had saved the last bullet in the financial pressure campaign, and the administration handed over the constriction playbook. The Obama administration gladly assumed the playbook and elected to keep the same Treasury team in place that was prepared to continue the same campaign. The campaign would continue—but it would be delayed.

Part IV

ADAPTATION

14

DUSTING OFF THE PLAYBOOK

The 2008 election returns had been decisive. Barack Obama had won a historic election and was riding a wave of domestic and international popularity. In the final months of the year, Bush administration officials busied themselves with tying up loose ends and crafting transition documents in anticipation of leaving the government. President-elect Obama's transition team was preparing to govern and determining how to fill the senior seats in the executive branch. Then Stuart Levey received a call he was not expecting.

The call came in December from Tim Geithner, representing President-elect Obama's transition team. Geithner, the governor of the Federal Reserve Bank of New York, was tagged as the likely secretary of the treasury and was already expected to become an indispensable member of the Obama administration. Geithner and Levey had met when Levey had first joined the Treasury Department in 2004, and they had developed a respectful working relationship. Even so, he certainly wasn't expecting Geithner to make a pitch to keep him on board.

Geithner was polite but cut to the chase. He told Levey that the Obama team was impressed with Treasury's work to pressure rogue actors—especially Iran. The president-elect wanted him to stay on board to continue what he was doing. Though it was understood that the Obama team would want to keep continuity in certain positions, this call was a surprise. Levey had served in the government for both Bush terms—first at the Justice Department and then at Treasury. Levey asked Geithner for some time to reflect and to talk to his wife.

The Obama team did not wait long. The next day, Rahm Emanuel, who was close to the president-elect and understood to be in line to be White House chief of staff, called Levey and told him again that the president-elect wanted him to stay on board. Emanuel noted that it was important for the country to continue the good work at Treasury that everyone on both sides of the aisle respected.

Levey had one principal concern and demand for Emanuel. If he stayed in his position, he did not want to be treated as a political pariah in an administration that had made no secret of its disdain for the Bush team it was replacing. Levey knew that to be effective, he needed access to the White House in addition to support from his secretary. He was assured he would get all the support and access he needed—and that his work and voice would not be muted. After some conversations with family and close colleagues, Levey called Emanuel back within forty-eight hours. He accepted the president's offer.

For Levey, this was a validation of the work he and his team had done. For Treasury, it was an assurance that the Office of Terrorism and Financial Intelligence and the work that had been done for eight years would survive the transition. For those around the world who knew what Treasury had become and could do, this was a signal that America's policies would not shift radically and that Treasury could be expected to use its powers for national interests. With Levey remaining in his position, the Treasury would remain at war, and its functions would become an ensconced part of the US government's approach to national security. Next to Secretary of Defense Robert Gates, Levey, as Treasury's undersecretary for terrorism and financial intelligence, would be the highest-level Bush political appointee to transition to the new administration.

Considering the acrimony between the Obama and Bush administrations, it is notable that the post-9/11 policies of financial pressure and sanctions had not fallen prey to the usual games of political football in Washington. Treasury's work had been supported and extolled—in part because it tended to bring little controversy compared to other national security issues and seemed to most to be effective. The US government's work on terrorist financing, for example, was the only activity given an "A" or "A–" rating in 2005 by Thomas Kean and Lee Hamilton, co-chairs of the 9/11 Commission. In January 2009, in a letter to the Senate Foreign Relations Committee, Geithner wrote, "I agree wholeheartedly that theDepartment of the Treasury has done outstanding work in ratcheting up the pressure on Iran, both by vigorously enforcing our sanctions against Iran and by sharing information with key financial actors around the world."[1]

In fact, the kind of power that Treasury wielded was precisely the type of "smart" approach the new administration and its foreign policy advisers had been arguing for as a refreshed approach to foreign policy. Ever since 2004, prominent think tanks had trumpeted the concept of "smart power" as a way of promoting US interests softly in concert with other countries and institutions.[2] The mantra emerging was that the United States needed to be less unilateral in its use of force and in its promotion of its national security interests. There were other tools and multilateral means by which to achieve America's foreign policy goals.

The subtle, smart financial measures Treasury was already using fit neatly into this model of "smart power," though its use was often unilateral and coercive in its intent. The experts assessing what Treasury had been doing already marked this approach as a new brand of coercive diplomacy.[3] The playbook on the use of smart financial power had bipartisan support.

As the new president took over the White House, a core foreign policy question for the administration was how to apply pressure against America's adversaries while also abiding by Obama's campaign pledge to reach out with an open hand to the regimes in Pyongyang and Tehran. This idealistic rhetoric quickly collided with difficult realities. Governing is different from campaigning, and designing a foreign policy to meet the realities of the threats and the conditions of the world is the job of a president. With the financial pressure campaigns against both North Korea and Iran—and with sanctions on other countries like Burma, Sudan, and Cuba—there was a desire to reevaluate their effectiveness and consider whether a more aggressive and open diplomatic outreach could shift the landscape. The assumption from the White House seemed to be that a change in tone and diction—and the very person of the president—might create a diplomatic breakthrough. To give this approach time to work, the White House decided from the beginning of the new administration to pause the financial pressure campaigns on North Korea and Iran.

The pause did not last long for the North Koreans. The regime quickly rebuffed any attempts at outreach and met American diplomatic messages—sent secretly from President Obama to Kim Jong Il—with bellicosity and belligerence. On April 5, 2009, North Korea launched a three-stage Unha-2 missile over the Sea of Japan, triggering a cascade of diplomatic crises, to include condemnation by the UN Security Council and North Korea's withdrawal from the six-party talks that had been scheduled for April 13 and 14. Tensions only worsened when North Korea tested its second nuclear device on May 25, 2009.[4] The region continued on a near-war footing as the crisis continued to boil. In March 2010, a North Korean submarine sank the South Korean ROKS *Cheonan*. Alarmingly, the crisis escalated later that year when North Korean artillery units bombarded Yeonpyeong Island in the Yellow Sea. North Korean recalcitrance clarified matters: the administration had no choice but to resort to the economic pressure playbook.

The administration worked with counterparts to obtain Security Council Resolution 1874. Passed on June 12, 2009, the resolution tightened sanctions on North Korea; called on member states not to provide financial assistance to North Korea, except for humanitarian purposes; and authorized increased scrutiny of North Korean shipping, among other things. The administration's envoy for sanctions, Jim Steinberg—filling a new role at the State Department—began to work the diplomacy of the six-party talks and sanctions. He paid visits to Tokyo and Seoul to coordinate on next steps, even as the North Koreans refused to rejoin the talks. Steinberg helped to synchronize the actions of the United States, Japan, and South Korea amid the rolling crises triggered by the North Korean nuclear test and military provocations. Steinberg and Levey would travel together to Beijing, Seoul, and Tokyo to talk about sanctions on North Korea. Levey meanwhile was also trying to take the temperature of our allies on their willingness to cut ties with Iran. The Treasury would steadily increase the financial pressure on North Korea, designating companies and banks supporting its ongoing illicit activities.

Still, the North Koreans had learned the lessons of the BDA action and had begun to diversify their channels of financing. They were relying more heavily on the Chinese for cover. There would likely never be another opportunity to isolate the North Koreans from the banking system the way BDA had. We had let that moment pass, allowing the financial noose around North Korea to loosen. The lack of additional steps to target North Korean nodes, along with the final deal with North Korea, which included lifting the "state sponsor of terrorism" label, had taken the air out of our tires. It was hard to fill them up again.

China had learned its lessons, too, and had taken steps to avoid being cornered financially again. Traditionally it had been an economic outlet for North Korea. Now China had begun to increase its trade and commercial activity—especially in the mining sector—with North Korea, giving Pyongyang access to more goods, financing, and an outlet for economic activity, even as other international activity was squeezed.

With Iran, the Obama administration still held out hope that outreach and offers of direct talks could shift the balance and allow for a breakthrough. Diplomatic messages were sent to Tehran about the United States' willingness to negotiate. The president sent letters directly to Supreme Leader Khamenei to offer negotiations.[5]

As part of this strategy, the financial pressure campaign that had been launched in 2006, and that had gained steam in the following years, was put on hold. Levey was instructed to hold his powder dry while the administration attempted to reach out to the regime in Tehran. Meetings with bankers, designations of Iranian entities, and enlistment of partners to isolate Iranian financial activity stopped. Iran's central bank remained an ultimate target, but Iranian shipping lines, front companies, and agents continued to operate. Without being squeezed harder, Iranian money continued to flow.

There had been a natural momentum to the constriction campaign, but to continue to work, the environment had to be constantly tended. Levey knew that the strategy had been working and would later reflect that the campaign had built "momentum" that was lost in this period. But the new team in the White House did not want to upset the apple cart if there was a diplomatic deal to be had. Those trying to make a deal with another rogue regime once again saw the financial pressure as an impediment to diplomacy instead of its complement and enabler.

Problems quickly emerged with the new approach—starting with an all-too-flippant dismissal of the recent history of negotiations with Iran. The new American outreach seemed to ignore European views on the state of negotiations and diplomacy with Iran. From the French, British, and German points of view, European countries had been engaged in intense, good faith negotiations with the Iranians for years. They had had direct talks with the Iranian negotiators and had put concrete deals on the table along with the United States that would allow the Iranians to pursue a peaceful, civilian nuclear program—to no avail.

This approach also disregarded the diplomatic environment in

January 2009. The Iranians had traditionally responded positively to negotiations and concessions only when pressured to do so by the circumstances. The negotiated end of the Iran-Iraq War, for example, came only after a decade of pain, enormous loss, and obvious stalemate. The experience of the 1979 revolution had instilled a belief among the clerical regime that it was best to project strength in the face of pressure and take advantage of any sign of weakness from its enemies. The US attempt to engage in outreach at a moment of increasing international pressure was seen as a sign of weakness by the Iranian side and a moment to buy time.

Another problem was that the reset and outreach by the United States seemed to shift the burden of persuasion back to the West at a time when the burden of proof was on the Iranians to explain their nuclear ambitions. A series of Security Council resolutions had decisively placed responsibility for the stalemate on the Iranians, but the new administration seemed to now be saying that the United States had been to blame for lack of progress diplomatically—even though the offer for assistance with a civilian nuclear program had been explicitly on the table. This was an unfortunate and costly diplomatic shift. The United States had to demonstrate that it was reaching out in good faith at a moment when it was well aware that the Iranians were continuing to expand their secret nuclear capabilities.

In the administration, there was an all-too-familiar assumption that the financial pressure could simply be turned on or off like a light switch. Unfortunately, the kind of global constriction campaign launched against the Iranians needed to be maintained and managed—like a garden infested with weeds. What was needed was a commitment to taking continual action against an evolving set of financial and commercial targets to keep the Iranians from finding a way to access the international financial system even as they attempted to adjust to the changing rules of the game.

This diplomatic respite also undermined the credibility of the stated reason for the financial isolation—to protect the international financial system against Iran's illicit financial activities. Suspension

of financial pressure appeared to be an admission by the US government that the financial measures against Iran were really just driven
by geopolitics. This made the financial pressure campaign seem
much less urgent to bankers and CEOs around the world. They
would be less willing to listen and more able to throw up barriers to
action, because they would believe the actions were just political
machinations from Washington.

Most observers have rationalized that this attempt at outreach
was a necessary step, because it demonstrated the new administration's seriousness to engage and showed that the United States was
not the impediment to a deal. They also argue that European cooperation could not be reached without such overt diplomatic steps
taking place and that a lessening of the pressure was therefore
inevitable. This view discounts the fact that the Europeans were
already cooperating aggressively. They were following the US lead
on imposing sanctions and pushing for tougher resolutions at the
United Nations.[6]

This view also too easily dismisses the power of the new president. President Obama had just been awarded the Nobel Peace
Prize, and he came into office on a wave of unprecedented popularity and expectation. He could have articulated and recast the reality
and nature of the diplomatic environment—asserting that the West
had offered Iran real and concrete offers in the past and would continue to keep those offers open—without damaging the perception
that he was reaching out to Iran, without dismissing past diplomatic
efforts, and without forgoing the advantages of the diplomatic environment in 2009. His articulation of the reality of the situation with
Iran could have set the record straight and maintained the parameters of the relationship in our favor.

Finally, those who justify this approach completely overlook
what the administration could have accomplished if it had continued to increase the financial pressure on Iran. The financial campaign did not have to be suspended while President Obama
stretched out his hand to the regime in Tehran. The Obama

administration had framed its engagement with Iran as a step-by-step diplomatic dance, with an ascending scale of confrontation. Sanctions and financial pressure came in the middle of that dance—after engagement and before other options (presumably military). Aside from giving Iran more time, by dismissing the diplomatic engagement that had occurred before January 2009, this framework precluded the new administration from thinking about financial pressure as one part of a broader campaign to build leverage against the regime, with elements of that campaign working simultaneously and in conjunction with each other to create mounting pressure against Tehran. Using multiple strategies simultaneously could have helped at the negotiating table, or could have even led to regime change in Iran. But the mullahs knew the steps to this dance. They had watched the West's efforts to make a deal with North Korea for years, and they knew they could use this stage of diplomatic maneuvering to buy more time. The strategic ambiguity of "all options on the table" had therefore been undermined by the tactical predictability of the Obama administration strategy.[7]

Most troubling, the administration had seen a potential dialogue with the regime as a goal in and of itself. This way of thinking foreclosed opportunities to build multiple sources of leverage. The administration's muted response to the Green Movement opposing the fraudulent 2009 election was a case in point. On June 12, 2009, elections were held in Iran, and Iranian President Mahmoud Ahmadinejad was pronounced the winner, with 62 percent of the votes cast. But the election process was riddled with irregularities, and street protests and a vocal opposition to the regime emerged, lasting for months. The clerical regime cracked down viciously, arresting and torturing protesters and movement leaders, terrorizing family members, and using the Internet to engender suspicion.

Internal dissent and a call for real democracy within Iran had emerged at last in a tangible way, but the United States was absent.

When it became clear that US support was not forthcoming, many of the protesters chanted, "Obama, Obama, are you with us or them?"[8] Though there was an obvious desire not to inject America into the middle of domestic Iranian protests, the administration misread the moment. There was no answer from the new president to an emerging Persian Spring, and this temporizing made it all too clear that President Obama saw the movement in Iran as a complication to outreach, rather than a strategic opportunity. At the moment of greatest fragility for the regime, we were not only silent, but failed to pressure Iran financially.

Meanwhile, the administration's outstretched hand was being met with a slap. The Obama team's patience had run thin. The diplomatic messages went unanswered, and the Iranians continued to develop their nuclear program. By the time the United States and its partners revealed the secret nuclear facility at Qom on September 26, 2009, there was no question that the diplomatic entreaties were not working. This was the final straw for the administration, which now had no choice but to go into pressure mode again. President Obama made the pivot clear: "We have offered Iran a clear path toward greater international integration if it lives up to its obligations, and that offer stands . . . but the Iranian government must now demonstrate through deeds its peaceful intentions or be held accountable to international standards and international law."[9]

At the end of the day, more financial breathing space meant the Iranians had more time to manage the pressure and develop its nuclear program. Reflecting on the pause in financial pressure on Iran, Stuart Levey conceded that it took longer to restart the pressure, once Treasury was given the green light to do so, than even he thought would be the case.[10]

To restart the campaign, the Obama administration dusted off the playbook and followed the two-track program of using both pressure and diplomacy that had been set out in 2005 and launched in 2006. Those of us who knew the plays and understood what could be done to further increase the pressure on the Iranian regime were calling for Levey to be unleashed. Levey was waiting.

In the Situation Room in the fall of 2009, President Obama hosted a meeting to discuss Iran policy. Levey was there to provide a briefing on options for restarting the financial pressure campaign. He was prepared to lay out for the president the sectors of the Iranian economy that could be squeezed and what could be done to squeeze them. The main areas of Iranian economic vulnerability were well known and had already been targeted—the oil, shipping, insurance, and banking sectors. There had been much discussion and debate over the utility of focusing on Iran's refined oil imports. Levey explained his skepticism of this view. Pressure on refined oil imports would not be a harsh blow to the Iranians, in part because they were building new refineries to replace lost imports. The insurance and shipping sectors would be more important pressure points. Targeting these areas could cripple Iran's ability to engage in international commerce. But Levey emphasized that the most crucial target would continue to be the banking sector.

Levey explained that there were still a handful of significant banks doing business with the Iranians—and these banks were actually increasing their exposure to Iranian companies and accounts. Located in friendly countries in Europe and Asia, these banks could be targeted and convinced to end their business with Iran. If the United States did this, it would accelerate the Iranian regime's isolation from the international financial and commercial systems. The banks were the connective tissue for that system. Without banks to accept Iranian business, the Iranian economy would begin to suffocate. Without insurance, it would be hard for Iranian ships to trade. This was a financial pressure campaign premised on attacking the enablers of Iran's connectivity to the rest of the world.

Levey argued that these steps could be taken right away. Each line of pressure would reinforce the next. If a company stopped investing in Iran, or an insurance company stopped insuring Iranian oil exports and shipping, then banks would be more reluctant to keep doing business with Iran. Shuttered bank accounts, suspended lines of credit, and canceled investment contracts would follow, signaling that the private sector was trying to protect itself from risk. With all lines of pressure working together to restrict Iranian access to legitimate channels of commerce and finance, a virtuous circle of increasing pressure could once again begin. Iran would feel the effects, and its economy would suffer significantly. Levey and the Treasury Department were ready to launch at any time.

Susan Rice, US ambassador to the United Nations, objected to launching the program right away without UN action. She noted that it would be better and more likely to obtain cooperation with our partners if we had another UN Security Council resolution mandating tougher sanctions on Iran. The old orthodoxy that declared the need for multilateral steps at all points, and UN support from the start, reared its head again. She and others did not realize that much of Iran's financial isolation had come not on the heels of government decisions but as a result of the reputational risk and calculus made by the private sector.

Though the financial isolation Levey was describing resulted more from private-sector risk calculations than from multilateral agreement among nations, there was no question that another UN resolution with some teeth would help. Many countries could not act to freeze assets or seize suspect shipments without the international legal authority provided by such resolutions. A resolution would also give added weight to the message of Iran's isolation from the world—which certainly would echo in the boardrooms of the major banks and insurance companies. But Ambassador Rice seemed to forget the lessons from the Iran sanctions resolution negotiations that had already occurred during the Bush administration. The negotiations would take much longer than planned, and they would be watered down over time. She was confident that she could get this done in a few weeks. Instead, it would take several months.

The president commented that he liked Levey's presentation—especially the idea of finding a way to excise the Iranians from the remaining banks doing business with them. Levey grinned. But the president wanted to get a UN resolution and then move to the Treasury plan. This was not an unreasonable approach, but it meant delay. To make this approach most effective, the president also needed the Europeans to follow the UN resolution up with tougher measures on implementing financial and trade restrictions between the European Union and Iran. President Obama made sure Secretary of State Hillary Clinton understood that this was a priority.

The decision was made. The administration would begin the two-track pressure campaign. Levey and the Treasury were ready to use the power of designations, regulations, and outreach to banks to recondition the financial environment. They focused heavily on isolating the Iranian banking sector, but redoubled their efforts on the shipping and insurance sectors. They would launch the program after the resolution was passed.

It took months of effort, but on June 9, 2010, the United Nations Security Council passed Resolution 1929, which built on the three earlier Iran sanctions resolutions and imposed new sanctions on Iran. Though this resolution was not unanimous, it was important, because it upped the pressure on the Islamic Revolutionary Guard Corps (IRGC), naming the IRGC as a threat, and heightened scrutiny of Iran's shipping lines, air transport, banks, and companies. The administration had wanted this resolution to validate the additional pressure to come, which was viewed by many in Washington as "unilateral" without the cover of UN action, and it succeeded in doing that.

With the new resolution in place, the Treasury Department again focused aggressively on the weak links of the Iranian regime. Treasury and the intelligence community had focused their collection and analysis on the key financial nodes and sectors for the Iranians. Starting that summer, Treasury began to unfurl a backlog of targets for the financial community and world to digest. The Office of Foreign Assets Control (OFAC) designated numerous entities as fronts for the IRGC and the government of Iran, putting the public spotlight again on Iran's attempts to use the international financial system for illicit and nefarious goals.

This focus included hitting those Iranian banks that continued to service the IRGC and the Iranian leadership and that had helped other Iranian banks, which had been designated earlier, to evade sanctions and scrutiny. On June 17, 2010, the Treasury designated the Post Bank of Iran for acting on behalf of the previously designated Bank Sepah. Part of the strategy entailed going after third-country banks that continued to do business with Iran. The Treasury had to make its perceived threats real on occasion—to give them credibility and to send clear messages as to what type of financial engagement with Iran would not be tolerated. In December 2009, it was announced that Credit Suisse would likely pay a fine of $536 million to settle accusations that it violated Iran sanctions. The US Treasury added the German-based European-Iranian Trade Bank AG to its blacklist in September 2010. In the summer of 2012, the British bank Standard Chartered paid a $340 million fine as a result of its hidden dealings with Iran.

The strategy to squeeze the Iranian banking sector would climax with two elements. The first was isolating the central bank of Iran—Bank Markazi—from the international financial system by declaring it—along with the entire Iranian banking sector—a primary money-laundering concern under Section 311 of the Patriot Act. Bank Markazi was serving as the commercial outlet for the Iranian banks that were already isolated, and it needed to be plugged if Iranian illicit financial activity was to be stopped. This 311 action would signal that there were fundamental systemic concerns about Iran's lack of controls and illicit financing in their banking system.

After years of debate over the wisdom and timing of the 311 for Bank Markazi, the Treasury Department pulled the trigger. This was the first use of Section 311 since Banco Delta Asia in 2005, and the first time a central bank was targeted. Treasury had attacked the heart of the Iranian financial system. In a solemn press announcement on the seventh floor of the State Department on January 23, 2012, Secretary of State Clinton and Secretary of the Treasury Geithner announced the new economic measures against Iran. Secretary Geithner explained the "311" action against the central bank of Iran and the declaration of Iran as a primary money-laundering concern. He cited the findings of the Financial Action Task Force that Iran presented a real risk and remained unresponsive to the international community's questions about its anti-money-laundering system. At the press conference in the State Department's Treaty Room, Secretary Geithner said, "The policies Iran is pursuing are unacceptable, and until Iran's leadership agrees to abandon this dangerous course, we will continue to use tough and innovative means to impose severe economic and financial consequences on Iran's leadership."[11] Treasury had taken a final shot at Iran's most important financial outlet—its central bank. The signal was clear. This was intended as a full financial strangulation.

The final element of the financial pressure campaign was squeezing those banks that continued to do business with Iran. The Treasury maintained a list of the banks that maintained business relations and activities with Iranian banks and entities. That became a target list for quiet pressure and enforcement steps to convince banks to stop doing business with Iran. Levey, along with Danny Glaser and Levey's new assistant secretary and former Treasury official in the Clinton administration, David Cohen, made it their mission to find those recalcitrant banks and cajole or convince them to reduce their exposure to Iranian business. The threat of the sanctions or regulatory measures that could destroy an institution's reputation and access to the US financial system was always in their back pockets. The Iranians once again began to follow the delegation of Treasury officials as they visited banking centers such as London, Frankfurt, Dubai, Beirut, Hong Kong, and Singapore. The Treasury was deploying again.

The Treasury continued its barrage of designations to shut off

Iranian shipping and air traffic from the international system. Treasury analysts identified 5 IRISL front companies and 27 vessels and updated entries for 71 vessels related to Iran's efforts to evade sanctions. In many ways, the designations appeared to be a game of whack-a-mole, because the Iranians often simply renamed their ships to evade scrutiny. The Iranian shipping line even tried to turn off radar tracking mechanisms to hide its ships.

But ships could be tracked and identified much more easily than assets. Before ports could accept vessels anchoring in their harbors and relying on their facilities, they needed to verify the identity and insurance coverage of the vessels—and had to determine whether they were violating any local laws or international obligations. Legitimate operators in major ports such as those in Singapore, Hong Kong, and Rotterdam paid attention to the lists and those docking, offloading, and using their facilities. This was a significant area of vulnerability for the Iranians—in part because the shipping of weapons and proliferation-related items exposed their underlying activity. On March 17, 2011, Malaysia, South Korea, and Singapore conducted arms seizures of components deemed illegal under UN sanctions. On July 1, 2011, Maersk announced that it had decided to stop doing business with ships originating from the Iranian ports Bandar Abbas, Bandar Khomeini, and Asaluyeh, owing to the suspect ownership of the ports. In Hong Kong and Singapore, Iranian ships would be held in port or not allowed to offload because of lack of insurance and suspicions over their ownership and cargo. Writing in the *Financial Times* in August 2010, Levey argued that "some of Iran's most dangerous cargo continues to come and go from Iran's ports, so we must redouble our vigilance over both their domestic shipping lines, and attempts to use third-country shippers and freight forwarders for illicit cargo."[12]

This campaign simultaneously went after the insurance and reinsurance upon which Iran relied to engage in international commerce. Without insurance, the Iranians would find it hard to ship their oil and to dock their ships to trade. Lloyds of London announced it would stop insuring and reinsuring refined-petroleum shipments into Iran in February 2010. As European insurance giants Allianz, Munich Re, and Hannover Re committed to ending their business ties with Iran, it became clear that the insurance sector had declared its judgment on the risk of insuring the Iranians.

At the same time, Treasury identified twenty-two companies determined to be owned or controlled by the government of Iran. On June 22, 2010, Levey remarked to a Senate Foreign Relations Committee that this round of sanctions marked an "inflection point."[13] Treasury's war had been unleashed and was pressuring Iran on all fronts.

The Treasury Department and the White House were no longer alone in wielding these tools. In 2009, Congress began to play a more active role in the debate. For the first time since 9/11, Congress injected itself directly into the strategic use of financial sanctions and power, with legislative mandates that began to overpower the Treasury's program in strategy and approach. Many members of Congress had watched as Treasury's powers were developed and had seen how effective they had proven to be. Impatient with a gradualist constriction campaign, Congress wanted in the game.

Congress understood that the financial pressure had been successful because it had targeted the financial sector, but wanted to use that model to maximize the impact on Iran's economy. Congress wanted to send a clear message to banks and countries that continued to do business with Iran—especially those engaged in oil transactions—that they would be subject to financial sanctions and attention.

Despite the 311 action against Iran's central bank, Congress knew that the Treasury Department had yet to order the freezing of Bank Markazi's assets and did not prohibit foreign banks from doing business with Iran. The 311 was not good enough for Congress. Congress wanted more pressure, faster, and also wanted to squeeze the international oil markets that were feeding Iran's budget. Congress was focused on using the potential for sanctions against third-country banks still facilitating oil deals with Iran's central bank. It wanted to use financial isolation as a means of squeezing Iran's oil sector and income.

For the first time in nearly a decade, the Treasury Department found itself putting the brakes on congressional enthusiasm for the use of financial tools and sanctions against a rogue actor. Treasury was committed to a gradualist constriction campaign, but it wanted to avoid blunt steps that would upset the balance of the international financial system or cause allies in Europe and Asia to resist further cooperation because of perceived American threats or over-reach. Japan and South Korea relied heavily on imports of Iranian oil. Yet even the hint of congressional action had its effect. As negotiations on the language and scope of the House and Senate bills proceeded, the mere threat of sanctions on countries, companies, and banks for doing business with Iran tenderized the international environment, leading oil companies and banks to abandon their investments and their business with Iran. Most foreign companies disliked having to respond to political machinations from the United States, but they could not afford to ignore the coming mandates from Congress that had global effect.

On July 1, 2010, the Senate passed the Comprehensive Iran Sanctions, Accountability, and Divestment Act (CISADA) by a vote of 95–0. CISADA became a defining element of the sanctions regime against Iran. The act required the sanctioning of any foreign bank that continued to conduct oil-related transactions with Iran's central bank. That meant that a bank could not do business in the United States if it was transacting with Iran's central bank. CISADA once again put the focus of the international community on the banking sector as the lynchpin for squeezing the Iranians. Congress was making explicit the same calculus that had been at play all along throughout the financial constriction campaign: If you want to do business in the United States, you must stop doing business with Iran.

CISADA gave some wiggle room to countries with deep dependencies on Iranian oil by allowing the State Department to issue exemptions for countries that substantially dropped their imports of

Iranian oil.[14] Some of this dependency was relieved with the Saudis committing to the production of additional barrels of oil to help make up for the loss of Iranian crude on the markets. With these provisions, Congress created fear of secondary sanctions against non-American companies still doing business with Iran. On August 16, 2010, the Treasury issued the Iranian Financial Sanctions Regulations to implement CISADA.[15] On September 29, 2010, the United States revoked authorization to import certain foodstuffs and carpets of Iranian origin, pursuant to Section 103 of CISADA. The pistachio and rug rapprochement from the late 1990s had ended.

Quickly, the energy sector responded. On September 30, 2010, the State Department announced that multiple energy companies had reduced their ties to Iran, including the European oil giants Total, Royal Dutch Shell, LUKOIL, BP, Shell, and ENI. Investments in Iranian oil fields and sectors were withdrawn, with companies such as Reliance, Glencore, Trafigura, and Vitol ending deals planned in Iran. On October 15, 2010, Inpex announced that it was getting rid of its stake in the Azadegan development project. The State Department estimated that $50 billion to $60 billion in upstream energy-development projects (i.e., exploration and production) were terminated or put on hold.[16] In July 2010, Iran's gasoline imports were down 50 percent from May, according to the International Energy Agency, and according to Reuters they were down 90 percent in August from the previous year.[17]

The Europeans were not absent from this debate—in fact, in many ways, they had already begun an even more aggressive approach. The Europeans had signaled that they planned to pull the plug on Iranian oil imports altogether—a critical step for a continent both dependent on Iranian oil and suffering severe economic setbacks and crisis. The political commitment across the European Union for such an important step—a step that would have real effects on Iran's economy as well as potential backlash within Europe—was critical. The diplomatic and security environment was essential to this shift for the European Union. Their core members had been engaged in fruitless negotiations with the Iranians for years, and they had watched as the new president had been rebuffed when proposing additional talks. Meanwhile, the Iranians seemed to be playing for time while they marched toward nuclear capabilities outside the full gaze of the international community. Revelation of the Qom nuclear site in 2010 seemed to be the last straw.

With each passing month without diplomatic progress, there was a growing dread of war on the horizon. The extremist talk of annihilation of the Israeli state by Iranian President Ahmadinejad, along with his repeated Holocaust denials, heightened sensitivities in Europe about the unstable and dangerous nature of the regime in Tehran. In addition, the talk of preemptive war by Israel—which began to impact the public debate within Israeli society and in Washington, DC—made clear that more aggressive steps were necessary to avert war. Speaking to the American Israel Public Affairs Committee (AIPAC) in Washington on March 5, 2012, Israeli Prime Minister Benjamin Netanyahu said, "Israel waited patiently for the international community to resolve this issue. We've waited for diplomacy to work. We've waited for sanctions to work. None of us can afford to wait much longer. As Prime Minister of Israel, I will never let my people live in the shadow of annihilation."[18] The Israeli strategy was clear—it would use saber rattling to impel greater international economic and financial pressure. The world was moving into maximalist financial pressure mode on Iran to avoid war. Financial constriction needed to move to economic strangulation.

In April 2011, the European Union passed the mandate requiring an end to all Iranian oil imports by July 1, 2012. This was a clear line in the sand and a signal of European commitment. It also sent a ripple effect throughout the financial and commercial worlds. By 2012, Japanese oil imports from Iran had dropped by roughly 80 percent from the previous year.[19]

The Europeans also made it clear that the SWIFT messaging service had to be turned off for sanctioned Iranian banks altogether. The EU mandate required SWIFT to prepare to unplug the Iranian banks from the international financial messaging system. The only Iranian banks left connected were those that were not sanctioned and that were largely dealing in the trade of food and medicines. The Europeans were serious, and the pressure on Iran would not cease until there was a resolution of the underlying diplomatic issues. On May 19, 2011, the European Union designated entities associated with Iranian proliferation, resulting in over one hundred firms being placed on the EU list. On April 9, 2012, Hong Kong insurers warned that they could not provide full coverage to tankers carrying Iranian oil once EU sanctions took hold in July.

This isolation was also coming from jurisdictions that did not ordinarily bend to Western financial pressure. Unable to ignore the financial and commercial environment, India's central bank, in January 2011, banned local companies from doing business with the Asian Clearing Union (ACU), an exporter of Iranian oil. India had previously been Iran's largest trading partner in the ACU. The Reserve Bank of India noted, "In view of the difficulties being experienced by importers/exporters in payments to/receipts from Iran, it has been decided that all eligible current account transactions including trade transactions with Iran should be settled in any permitted currency outside the ACU mechanism until further notice."[20]

The European and international steps and actions were being matched in the United States. Congress again got into the action in late 2011, adding more financial restrictions. This time Congress focused on third-country banks and companies that continued to do business with Iran. These companies would risk their ability to do business in the United States. On December 31, 2011, the president signed the National Defense Authorization Act (NDAA), which contained additional provisions. US firms also pulled their third-country subsidiaries from Iran. A Congressional Research Service report found that Huntsman, Halliburton, GE, Caterpillar, Ingersoll Rand, KPMG, PricewaterhouseCoopers, and Ernst and Young had terminated relationships inside Iran.[21]

By July 2012, the combination of financial and commercial pressure on Iran was unprecedented. Its banks were isolated and largely unplugged from the global banking system; its oil exports to Europe were shut off; and the United States was putting enormous pressure on countries to end their commercial relationships with Iran. As a result, not only did the Iranians find it harder to bank or do business abroad, but their economy began to show serious effects as a result of shrinking investments and oil exports. Sanctions have reduced the amount of gasoline Iran imports by 75 percent.[22] The central bank's reserves have been depleted, with some reports suggesting that foreign currency reserves have fallen by as much as $110 billion.[23] Meanwhile, Iran's currency, the rial, has been battered, with confidence dropping at each turn of the screw. In September 2010, Iran's rial fell by about 15 percent when the UAE restricted banking transactions with Iran.[24] By the summer of 2012, the rial had fallen by 80 percent.[25]

The price of everyday goods increased significantly in Iran, putting pressure on an already unsettled populace. In July 2010, a two-week strike in Tehran and elsewhere within the country resulted when the government attempted to increase taxes on merchants, partly as a result of revenue constriction due to sanctions.[26] On January 6, 2012, in an interview on National Public Radio, an Iranian writer, Hooman Majd, reported that sanctions were impacting Iranian's daily lives: "Yeah, absolutely. [Y]ou feel them because . . . the price of goods goes up. The thing that you bought yesterday at a store—for example, an Oral B toothbrush, . . . or toothpaste—is suddenly not available in Tehran, because the sanctions have prevented the importers from bringing them in. But also, the price of goods in general, including even domestically-made goods and domestic products such as fruit, vegetables and stuff like that, have been rising almost on a daily basis. And people are feeling that."[27]

In October 2012, a major strike from currency traders and bazaar merchants followed the precipitous fall of the rial's value. Protesters hurled stones at banks and government buildings, with pressure building internally within the regime to forestall a new crisis and support the rial. This pressure on internal prices and Iranian's budgets may also be having an effect on Iranians' views of the value of the nuclear program. In July 2012, an Iranian television station conducted a live, televised poll of viewers about sanctions and the Iranian nuclear program. The commentary about the poll was that it appeared slanted in favor of registering popular support of the nuclear program in defiance of Western sanctions. The Iranian state TV station abruptly terminated the telecast when more than 60 percent of those polled stated they would prefer to abandon the nuclear program if that would end the sanctions.

The Iranian government has tried to downplay the effects of the financial pressure campaign, dismissing the effects and reiterating that such steps will not dissuade Iran from acquiring nuclear capabilities. On January 23, 2011, after talks in Istanbul stalemated, Ahmadinejad said, "You cannot make Iran back down an inch from its course as it is now a nuclear state."[28] On March 21, 2001, Ayatollah Ali Khamenei said, "The sanctions which the enemies of the Iranian nation have imposed have been undertaken with the intention of inflicting a blow to our country's advancement, prevent it from realising the outcome of its steady efforts. Of course, their intention will not materialize."[29]

The Iranians have no doubt made efforts to adapt. On October 29, 2011, National Iranian Oil Company deputy Mohsen Qamsari said that Iran had "reached new agreements for receiving money for Iran's oil exports" and that "Iran's central bank has different and diversified ways and methods for receiving its money from selling oil to India."[30] Iran has been developing bartering agreements and cash payments as a way of circumventing the use of dollars or banks.

But the reality of the effects has been reflected in the Iranian economy and even in what its leaders have sometimes admitted, regardless of their stated defiance. On May 12, 2011, a UN Security Council report found that Iran had attempted "circumvention of sanctions across all areas," but that Iranian businesses were nevertheless "increasingly cut off from international financial markets."[31] On February 16, 2011, in a television interview, Ahmadinejad claimed that UN sanctions on Iran's nuclear program had not affected the regime's economy, adding that they "may have caused prices to increase in a few cases, but they will decrease in the near future." Putting a positive spin on the sanctions, he said the sanctions were actually beneficial because they had allowed Iran to "attain self-sufficiency in many areas."[32] He followed this statement up on November 1, 2011, however, by admitting, "Our banks cannot make international transactions anymore."[33] In the face of the October 2012 economic riots, Ahmadinejad blamed the United States for causing the distress for the Iranian people and for waging an unprecedented, sophisticated "hidden war" against the Iranian economy.

The financial constriction campaign was working. Levey was confident that the initiative had regained momentum and would be successful, but after six years in the same intense job working for two different presidents and three different Treasury secretaries, he made the decision to leave his post. It was a sensitive moment in the campaign against Iran because Levey had become the face of the financial assault. The Iranians knew who he was and followed his every move. Banks watched for his approaching footsteps. Foreign leaders were often infuriated by Levey's presence or public comments. But they all knew and respected him. In a bilateral meeting between Secretary Clinton and British Foreign Minister David Miliband, Clinton introduced Levey as part of her delegation. Miliband stopped the conversation and asked, "Which one is he? I've heard about him but never met him." He was known in London and around the world, and his departure in the midst of pressuring Iran was a significant moment with potential pitfalls.

On January 24, 2011, Treasury announced Levey's resignation. Secretary Geithner noted that the change would have "no effect on policy."[34] It was perhaps a testament to Levey's reputation that the response from Mohammad Nahavandian, the president of Iran's

Chamber of Commerce, was that Stuart Levey's resignation was "good news" for Iran.[35]

Levey would continue to push against the Iranians until his last day on the job. February 2011 saw a flurry of designations and actions against Iranian entities. The Treasury Department was continuing its assault to isolate Iranian entities of concern. But perhaps Levey saved the best for last.

In the winter of 2011, Libya was consumed by civil war. After four decades of tyranny, Muammar el-Qaddafi battled his own people for the survival of his regime—and it was beginning to look like he might be toppled.

The administration was debating whether to impose comprehensive sanctions against Libya. Qaddafi had survived in the tribal society of Libya through a combination of wanton cruelty and strategic largesse. Calling himself the "King of Kings," Qaddafi used Libya's lucrative oil revenues to pay for loyalty, enrich his family and tribe, and sprinkle support to African and other leaders around the world. He had survived because he had access to money to protect his rule and was willing to kill his enemies and rivals or send them into exile. As rebels brought the fight to him, he retained access to billions of dollars in assets that he could use to buy mercenaries and political loyalty. To weaken and topple Qaddafi, it was necessary to go after his money.

Levey and Adam Szubin, the Harvard-trained lawyer and OFAC director, had prepared an executive order for a comprehensive sanctions regime against the Libyan state that would target and freeze the assets of its central bank, its sovereign wealth fund, and all of its state institutions with investments abroad. Ironically, Levey and Szubin, close friends dating back to their days together at the Department of Justice, had actually met Qaddafi in Libya. They had been part of a group of senior US officials visiting Qaddafi—usually in one of his Bedouin tents—to discuss a possible rapprochement between the two governments.

The rapprochement led to Libya's reintegration with the West after Libya gave up its WMD program in 2003. In the years that followed, the Libyans had invested in Europe and spread their money throughout the Western banking system. This made Libyan investments and institutions more vulnerable to sanctions than they would have been before its economic reintegration. Some estimates for the amounts Libyans held in various institutions and investments abroad topped $200 billion.

The intent behind Levey's executive order—like the freezing of Iraqi assets after Saddam Hussein had invaded Kuwait—was to keep the assets from bleeding away and falling outside the reach of US jurisdiction. If that happened, then the Libyan leader would have the opportunity to tap into reserves to buy allegiances internally and internationally and to pay for the defense of his regime with allied tribes and imported mercenaries. Even worse, as we had learned in the 2003 Saddam asset recovery effort, loose assets could also be used to spark and fuel a postregime insurgency.

Time was of the essence. Qaddafi, his family, and their senior advisers no doubt knew from past sanctions and the experience of recent years that their assets were in danger. They had been able to disentangle billions from the United States in the mid-1980s, to the consternation of American officials. But amid the tumult and fighting in Tripoli, Misrata, and Benghazi, they may not have realized how exposed they really were, or understood just how fast they needed to act. Treasury, however, did know, and wanted to act quickly before any assets disappeared from the Libyan accounts.

But Treasury was split. The undersecretary for international affairs feared the action would create instability in the markets at a time of European banking unease. This argument—which had been replayed over and over within Treasury during past crises—carried additional weight in the wake of the most serious financial crisis since the Great Depression. It was a serious argument, but Levey pushed back. The administration was looking for options to affect the dynamics within Libya, and this was a way to hurt Qaddafi. This time, Levey won the argument, and Tim Geithner agreed to move forward with a recommendation to impose an asset freeze and comprehensive sanctions.

Levey went to a principals meeting in the Situation Room that morning to take part in a discussion on Libya. He found no objections to the idea of sanctions or how they might work. Instead, there was deep interest in how much of Libya's money could be frozen. The same question that arises all the time in the sanctions and policy world appeared again. How much money could be frozen and announced? It was a tangible, attractive metric. Before he walked over to the White House, Levey had gotten the latest update from his OFAC specialists, who had been in conversations with bank officials in New York and their lawyers. They anticipated that there was $100 million in Libyan assets subject to US jurisdiction.

In the Situation Room, Levey told Tom Donilon and the others assembled that the Treasury expected to freeze about $100 million. This was not an insignificant amount and sounded like a solid figure, but those who were present knew it would not break Qaddafi's financial back. The modest amount of assets anticipated might not have the desired strategic and psychological impact for which all were hoping amid the ongoing fighting in Libya, and it would not allow the administration to argue credibly that this would hasten Qaddafi's demise.

The immediate concern from the State Department was that American citizens remained in Libya and had yet to be evacuated. If sanctions were imposed, Qaddafi could retaliate by holding the Americans in Libya hostage—or worse. The decision was made to prepare the sanctions package but to hold off on launching them or announcing anything. The risk of asset flight did not outweigh the risk to American lives.

Levey headed back to the Treasury Department knowing that this would be his last day on the job. His trajectory over the past decade had taken him from the Department of Justice to the

Treasury Department and into the heart of power in two administrations that had been diametrically opposed politically and in their worldviews. But in this new world of financial warfare, there was apparent continuity, and Levey represented exactly that. When he got back to his office on the fourth floor, he read an email from Adam Szubin, his longtime friend, with an update on the amount of Libyan assets that might be subject to US asset freezes. The note was clear but shocking—the amount subject to US jurisdiction and potential freezing was likely $27 billion. To underscore the amount and avoid confusion, the email ended with, "Yes, that's billion with a 'B.'"

This would be the largest single asset freeze in American history, coming at a critical time for Libya and American policy and standing in the region. It was too important an opportunity to miss. After taking a moment to reflect, Levey called over to Denis McDonough, the deputy national security adviser. "Denis, we have a bigger number," he said. Levey then calmly explained the numbers, knowing what the impact would be on the other line. McDonough told him to get the sanctions ready and to send the package over as soon as possible for clearance. It was time to freeze those assets.

Treasury sent a new executive order into the clearance process—one that by now was well worn and understood. There would be no objections or squabbling from other departments and agencies this time. Everyone knew what this action could mean, and the White House wanted this ready to go. The Treasury team did not know exactly what they had on their hands, but they realized they could be sitting on a historic asset freeze. More importantly, they had a clear shot at impacting the trajectory of the course of Libyan history—with the hopes of weakening Qaddafi quickly and saving lives.

Levey said his tearful goodbyes late that afternoon—ending his six-year tenure at Treasury. Like any other departing employee, he turned in all his equipment and Treasury badges. After serving through two administrations, the face of the new Treasury was departing—with the Libya executive order yet to be signed, and

Qaddafi's assets yet to be frozen. Levey was still worried that the assets could slip through US hands, but he had done everything he could. The sanctions program was in good hands at OFAC, with Levey's closest aide, Adam Szubin, running the day-to-day management of all the sanctions programs. Szubin and Treasury were poised to act as soon as the president signed the order. Levey decided to keep his cellphone in case someone needed to call him.

Someone did. As Levey left the Treasury for the last time and began driving home, Tom Donilon, the national security adviser, called him. Donilon was about to go into the Oval Office to explain the Libya executive order to the president. The president wanted to sign it. Donilon wanted to review the details and make sure he understood how the order would work and what might ensue. Levey pulled off the road and gave his last briefing to the national security adviser. The steps discussed would help to topple Qaddafi.

President Obama signed the order, and the Treasury sent out the order to banks to freeze all Libyan assets. Treasury launched its principal weapon against rogue actors—its ability to move the private sector to act. The lawyers and banks had been poised for this—following the informal, quiet conversations with OFAC and the Treasury over the previous days. They reacted quickly and went into overdrive, with lawyers working through the weekend to help their banking and financial clients find Libyan assets that might be in their systems. By the time Monday rolled around, it was clear that significant Libyan assets had been captured.

The number was bigger than expected. On February 25, 2011, the Treasury announced that it had frozen $32 billion in Libyan assets. This was a stunning amount. The Treasury was ecstatic, as was the White House. The White House trumpeted the action as a blow to Qaddafi and a signal that the end was near for his regime. It would be harder for him to pay mercenaries, to dole out payments for tribal loyalty, and to hold out, if it was clear he was running out of money. The amount of assets frozen by the US Treasury would eventually rise to $37 billion—the most assets frozen under any country program. The international community followed suit by finding and freezing $50 billion more.[36] Treasury had struck. Qaddafi could never have imagined that the Treasury officials he had met years before in his Bedouin tent would be the ones to squeeze his regime's finances like this. His days were now numbered. Levey drove home a conquering hero in the world of financial warfare, his reputation secured as champion of Treasury's centrality in national security.

The Treasury team that remained behind knew what it was doing. The reins were handed over to David Cohen, the assistant secretary under Levey. Cohen had learned from Levey how to make his way to major capitals to apply political and financial pressure against the North Koreans, Iranians, and Al Qaeda. The remaining team, including Glaser, Poncy, and Szubin, remained as the engine of Treasury's work.

The Treasury road show would continue, with attempts to convince banks and governments all over the world—including in Turkey, India, Russia, and China—to cut off their relations with Iranian banks and sanctioned companies. The State Department continued to issue sanctions of its own, the European Union kept up its own restrictive measures, and Congress pushed the Treasury and State departments to be even more aggressive. The pressure on Iran continued unabated from all quarters, and Iran's central bank remained a focal point for pressure and debate within the US government.

Fines and punishments continued to be meted out to banks that persisted in doing business with Iran. In August 2012, the New York bank examiner issued a report on Standard Chartered Bank's dealings with Iran. Its practice of stripping wire transfers of any information that would identify Iranian entities in transactions, in particular, was called into question. The report quoted a Standard Chartered employee in London who wrote in an email, in response to an

American colleague who had expressed concerns over the bank's practices with the Iranians, "Who are you [Americans] to tell us, the rest of the world, that we're not going to deal with Iranians?"[37]

The reality was that in the new age of financial pressure and a global financial system, American demands and practices applied globally. If Standard Chartered wanted to do business in the United States, it had to comply with US law. Before a hearing about its license to operate banking facilities in New York, Standard Chartered agreed, on August 14, 2012, to pay a fine of $340 million to New York authorities. Standard Chartered would still be allowed to do business in New York, but it had been whipped publicly and a pound of flesh had been exacted. In December 2012, the British banking giant HSBC would be hit with a record fine of $1.9 billion for money-laundering and sanctions violations, including financial dealings with Iran. The financial community was on notice.

Amid the deepening economic warfare loomed three fundamental questions that have been left unanswered.

First is the question of what we are trying to achieve with the financial campaign against Iran. Secretary of Defense Gates and Secretary of State Clinton stated that the goal of sanctions and financial pressure against Iran was to force the regime to make a calculated judgment. Is the nuclear program worth the costs and economic pain of financial and commercial isolation? The effects of this campaign were unprecedented and were putting pressure internally on the leadership. The movement toward a maximalist economic strangulation policy shifted the focus of the campaign from constricting Iran's ability to do business with the world to making the economic pain bad enough to force the abandonment of the nuclear program. This then shifts the focus to the economic pain of the Iranian people, and it assumes that the regime leadership will either splinter or be forced by its people to modify their position on developing a nuclear power capability.

The problem with this theory is that there is no evidence that the regime is willing to give up the nationalist and nearly sacred goal of gaining nuclear power to avoid further economic pain. There is also no evidence that the opposition in Iran would be willing to give up the nuclear program. Regardless, the regime has already crushed internal dissent without external objection, and regime leaders understand in the wake of the Arab uprisings that brute force and media and Internet blackouts can forestall revolution. Its assistance to the Assad regime in Damascus in crushing the Syrian uprising is yet another testing ground for this approach. The maximalist mode assumes that there will be a broader economic effect on Iran in which the pressure campaign follows an embargo model and relies on internal dissent and turmoil to force a regime decision.

Second is the question of how the United States will unwind the financial pressure if that becomes part of the diplomatic deal for Iran. As of the writing of this book, the hopes for a diplomatic breakthrough with Iran have fizzled. Talks in Istanbul, Baghdad, and Vienna have resulted in no real progress, and the International Atomic Energy Agency continues to issue reports warning of the unanswered questions and suspicious activities surrounding the Iranian nuclear program. Even so, if lifting the economic pressures becomes part of a package deal, what will this deal look like in practice? The Iranians begin any discussion about a deal with the demand to lift the economic pressure—often asking for an end to the SWIFT ban on dealing with sanctioned Iranian banks. With the type of financial pressure campaign Treasury devised, unwinding the sanctions—as seen in the North Korean case—is a complicated matter, and not subject to an on-off switch.

Unwinding the sanctions means much more than just convincing a foreign bank to unfreeze accounts, or withdrawing a designation or regulation. The financial argument at the heart of Iran's isolation has been that Iran is engaged in a host of nefarious and illegal activities that have been facilitated by its interactions with the international financial system. It is the threat to the international financial system of the illicit and suspect flows of money that is the baseline for Iran's isolation. No doubt, the deeper political measures and embargoes put in place in recent months—especially the European oil-import ban—have bitten hard into the Iranian economy. But Iran will not regain its access to the international financial system until it addresses the underlying concerns that drove its isolation in the first place—proliferation, support for terrorism, and development of weaponry and programs of concern controlled by the IRGC. These concerns will likely remain even if a nuclear deal is reached; therefore, the attempts to roll back the financial measures will be limited—without American cheerleading for reentry of the Iranians into the legitimate financial order. I don't think anyone has yet contemplated this problem or imagines that it will happen. If that is the case, can the easing of financial pressure as expected by Tehran really be put on the table?

Third, the fundamental question remains whether any of this economic warfare and pressure can slow the nuclear program and ultimately change the regime's calculus. Is there an economic silver bullet, and what would the last financial measure be that we could use before it was too late? On January 21, 2011, the Federation of American Scientists reported that Iran had increased centrifuge operations at Natanz by 60 percent over the past year. As Ivanka Barzashka, a researcher who studies nuclear weapons proliferation and international security policy, has put it, "Iran clearly does not appear to be slowing down its nuclear drive."[38] Director of National Intelligence James Clapper has noted that recent US sanctions "almost certainly have not altered Iran's long-term foreign policy goals."[39] An IAEA report published in the summer of 2012 again confirmed that the Iranians are continuing to expand their nuclear capabilities, with increasing numbers of centrifuges and facilities that have opened and expanded to handle nuclear research.[40]

Despite unprecedented financial pressure, Iran's nuclear march continues. Timing in this equation matters, and financial pressure and sabotage have certainly slowed Iran's ability to develop a nuclear program. Israeli Prime Minister Netanyahu has called for red lines for Iran's program before the Iranians reach a "zone of immunity" in which their nuclear capabilities allow them to develop a nuclear weapon at will—beyond the reach of airstrikes and disruption, likely underground or carved into mountains. The United States has stated that it will not allow Iran to obtain a nuclear weapon. The timing on when Iran may reach nuclear capability is in dispute, but at play is the idea that financial pressure and sanctions need more time to work. There are no indications, though, that the regime has changed its nuclear trajectory as a result of the economic pressure exerted thus far.

It is not clear that economic pressure can alter the calculus of a regime committed to nuclear capability as a central element of national power and international influence. As a result, it is best to assume that financial measures alone will not be able to change the calculus. Instead, it is critical that the financial pressure campaign be viewed as part of a series of actions and policies to change the regime's trajectory or the regime itself. The US government has to be clear about what it is trying to achieve in order for the strategies and measures to be directed with desired impact. Just as a missile has to be aimed, the financial measures used in the twenty-first century to isolate rogues need to be tailored to the strategic end state desired. This is even more important now that most of the key steps that can be taken to constrict the Iranian economy have been taken.

This is the fundamental question for the US government as it wields its economic power more aggressively in the service of its national security. Can this new brand of economic warfare stop the bombs and bullets of tyrants? In Syria, this has been the hope. There has been little desire from the Obama administration to intervene militarily to topple President Assad or to assist the revolutionaries and militants fighting the Syrian regime. Instead, the muscular, public alternative has been to pressure the regime with the use of financial pressure. Instead of issuing military orders, the president has signed executive orders to freeze the assets and restrict the travel of Syrian officials and entities.

Against Syria, this campaign has taken three main forms. First, the administration has wanted to demonstrate the underlying danger of Syrian behavior that touches the international financial system—proliferation, support to terrorism, corruption, and lack of money-laundering controls. In many ways, this approach leveraged the Section 311 action against the Commercial Bank of Syria in 2004 and the designation, in 2008, of Rami Makhlouf, Assad's corrupt relative who runs Syria's largest businesses. Those actions were salvos in an attempt to undermine the Syrian regime's economic resources and to signal a desire to peel away elements of Assad's coalition by going after corrupt figures tied to his regime. On August 17, 2011, President Obama issued Executive Order 13582, providing authority to "block" the property of the government of Syria ("blocking" generally means that transactions between US persons or entities and the entity in question, such as, in this case, the Syrian government, are prohibited), banning the export of US services to Syria as well as new investment in Syria, and banning the importation of Syrian-origin petroleum and petroleum products into the United States. Treasury identified five state-owned oil companies in Syria that are subject to the blocking.

Second is an effort to underscore the human rights abuses of a regime that has been waging a slow-motion massacre against its own people. The moral opprobrium of the Assad regime and the perception in the West that there are few good alternatives have caused the United States and Europe to lock arms to target Syrian officials and institutions in the financial realm. On April 29, 2011, President Obama issued Executive Order 13572, providing authority to block the property of, among others, persons determined to be responsible for human rights abuses in Syria, including those related to repression. On May 18, 2011, he issued Executive Order 13573, blocking the property of senior officials of the Syrian government, including President Bashar al-Assad. On April 22, 2012, he issued Executive Order 13606, providing authority to block the property and suspend entry into the United States of certain persons determined to have operated, or to have directed the operation of, information and communications technology facilitating computer or network disruption, monitoring, or tracking that could assist in or enable human rights abuses by or on behalf of the government of Syria. These executive orders have served as the United States' major public response to the Syrian abuses and atrocities.

Finally, the Obama administration has tried to tie the taint of Iranian and Syrian activity together. The Iranian and Syrian governments collaborate to support terrorism, proliferate weapons, and now to crack down on political opposition and protesters. On June 29, 2011, the Treasury Department designated Ismail Ahmadi Moghadam and Ahmad-Reza Radan, heads of the Iranian Law Enforcement Forces, for providing expertise to aid Syria's crackdown on civilians. The European Union followed on August 24, 2011, by designating the Qods Force for supporting Syrian security services to repress civilians. On October 12, 2011, the Treasury designated Mahan Air for helping the Qods Force to ship weaponry—especially to Syria. With the Iranians admitting IRGC support to the Syrians and Hezbollah admitting its support for Assad, these types of actions in the West will likely accelerate, with the United States and European governments attempting to underscore the atrocities undertaken by the Syrians and Iranians in concert.

These efforts have begun to be supported by Arab states that oppose Assad and want to accelerate his fall. The growing willingness of the Arab League to engage abroad and intervene—as seen with Qatari and UAE military forces assisting the Libyan rebels against Qaddafi—is now translating slowly into the financial battlefield. The Treasury and the Qatari central bank in fact collaborated to take a concrete step together against Syria. On May 30, 2012, Treasury designated Syria International Islamic Bank (SIIB), pursuant to Executive Order 13382, for acting for or on behalf of the Commercial Bank of Syria and providing services to the Syrian Lebanese Commercial Bank, both of which have been subject to US and international sanctions. The Qatari government acted with the United States and took steps to isolate SIIB from the Qatari financial system. Countries like the UAE and Saudi Arabia have quietly assisted in the isolation of these entities as well. This may become a more aggressive arena for action against the Syrians and Iranians.

The goals in taking these steps are to reduce Assad's power and quicken his fall. These measures are also intended to weaken Assad's coalition and to peel away supporters. Even so, the Obama administration has relied on the United Nations, in general, to legitimate US actions, and Russian and Chinese reluctance to support stronger measures and sanctions that bite has constrained the financial pressure campaign. The Obama administration has also been reluctant to take steps that might inadvertently fracture the Syrian political and social system in a way that makes the situation worse. This posture has made little sense as Syria devolves into civil war and sectarian camps prepare to fight to the death. The lack of US leadership and a consolidated international response has muted and hamstrung the responses of countries in the Arab League, and, most importantly, Turkey. The frustration of watching Assad slaughter his own people and destroy his own cities has been accompanied by hedging in countries unwilling to step ahead of the herd against the regime. With Russia and Iran supporting the Assad regime, and without a more creative and aggressive approach, it seems unlikely that further executive orders and designations will help.

This playbook is now well understood by our enemies and adversaries. New plays and strategies are needed to ensure that the tools of financial warfare remain sharp and effective. In Iran and Syria, the United States should launch preemptive asset hunts for the key leaders and selected proxies and allies. Traditionally—as with Sani Abacha in Nigeria and Saddam Hussein in Iraq—governments and banks have waited for the regime to fall before going after their looted assets. Preemptively launching asset recovery efforts would have the virtue of energizing the international financial community and activating all the tools of asset recovery before the regime falls. The threat of such preemptive efforts would also be a means of incentivizing regime allies to defect and to make deals.

We need to focus more attention on the convergence of financial networks of interest that are being leveraged by our enemies to raise and move money around the world. We also need to use the interest of the Arab states and legitimate financial centers to create positive incentives for the isolation of rogue actors—and rewards for those willing to act with legitimacy and transparency. Finally, we need to find ways of wrapping financial actors such as China and India into the legitimate financial order, putting these issues on their plate as policies of concern to them and not just the United States and the European Union.

Unless we have new plays in the playbook, our enemies and adversaries will work around and weaken America's financial power and tools. The financial battlespace is constantly evolving, with dirty money finding ways around the systems we have built to prevent the flows of illicit financial capital. Our enemies are smart and will continue to adapt, taking advantage of the growing complexity and sophistication of international financial systems. We, too, must adapt, or else dirty money will find new ways to flow and to threaten.

15

LEARNING CURVE

We had found new ways of using financial intelligence, tools, and campaigns to isolate rogue actors from the formal financial system. These efforts had yielded real-world results, and our enemies had felt the effects of financial warfare that they had not anticipated. The financial pressure we had put on terrorist, proliferation, and illicit networks had taken its toll on the funding mechanisms of those targeted. It was now harder, costlier, and riskier for them to raise and move money around the world.

This approach, however, is not a silver bullet. In the face of this pressure, the enemy has adapted, and illicit capital still moves. Where there is money to be made and moved, it will find a channel and agents to facilitate that movement. The networks have adapted by finding alternate ways to raise and move money, creating new tools of their own to avoid the pressure leveled by the formal financial system and the US Treasury. These adaptations and evasions form part of this new financial landscape—one with which the United States must constantly contend.

The huge used-car lots on the coast of West Africa seemed out of place. The images from space showed the car lots beginning to carve out acres and acres of coastline. The business of moving used cars from the United States into West Africa was growing fast. And so was the size of the lots. What had been created was a bustling trade zone in used cars that remains in business to this day. Though seemingly innocuous, the cars formed the centerpiece of an elaborate trade-based money-laundering enterprise run by the terrorist organization Hezbollah in concert with South American drug traffickers.

Hezbollah, the Lebanese-based terrorist group and political party, had always had a diversified balance sheet. It received hundreds of millions of dollars from Iran every year. Hezbollah used its social and charitable networks—along with media campaigns on its Al Manar cable station—to generate millions more. It also relied on trade-based money-laundering and business operations through sympathetic Lebanese and Syrian diaspora members around the world. Assad Ahmad Barakat, Hezbollah's South American treasurer, had embedded his trading companies and counterfeiting operations in the commercial hub of the Tri-Border Area to finance Hezbollah. In West Africa, a bustling Lebanese commercial class traded in everything from diamonds to furniture.

Hezbollah had always found ways to make money through trade, including through the drug trade. With the increased pressure on Iranian budgets and new scrutiny over banks that were being used to help finance Lebanese Hezbollah, such as Bank Saderat, Hezbollah's moneymen needed to fill a budget gap. The war with Israel in 2006, which destroyed much of Hezbollah's infrastructure and neighborhoods in southern Lebanon, also put stress on the group's bottom line. The Hezbollah leadership had passed out cash to those affected and promised to rebuild homes, hospitals, and schools. But Hezbollah required massive amounts of funding to support its extensive military apparatus and missile purchases, its patronage system and political program, and its expansive social and charitable network. Criminal activity was a lucrative and appealing option for increasing revenues. Drug trafficking and related money laundering was an avenue for raising and moving hundreds of millions of dollars. Hezbollah knew how to make and move money around the world, and understood how to make the drug-trafficking networks in South America and West Africa a principal source of revenue. The drug money was attractive, and it made for unusual bedfellows.

Ayman Joumaa, a designated and indicted narco-trafficker, ran a global cocaine distribution network that suited Hezbollah nicely. Joumaa was an all-purpose narcotics trafficker and money launderer. He would negotiate the sale and movement of multi-ton bulk shipments of cocaine from trafficking organizations in South America. He also knew how to launder the proceeds—upward of $200 million a month—using an intricate global money-laundering network he controlled. Joumaa used bulk cash smugglers to deposit drug proceeds into Lebanese money-exchange houses that he owned or controlled. The exchange houses had established accounts in the Lebanese Canadian Bank (LCB), with sympathetic members of the network in key bank branches. The money was deposited in the money-exchange house's LCB accounts to allow it to settle without having to be laundered further.

Joumaa and his network of drug traffickers and launderers would then use the US correspondent accounts to wire suspicious amounts of money to used-car dealerships in the United States. The recipients, often known drug dealers, purchased hundreds of used cars from approximately twenty US dealers and transported them to West Africa or other parts of the world. The proceeds from the sale of those cars were then transmitted back to Lebanon for Joumaa and Hezbollah to use. So the drug money was laundered through used-car sales, and the used cars themselves became literal money-laundering vehicles.

Joumaa also used a long-standing trade-based money-laundering system in Latin America that was known as the "Black Market Peso Exchange." He ordered money in the LCB accounts to be wired to Asian suppliers of consumer goods, such as refrigerators and electronics, who would then ship goods to Latin America for sale by trusted brokers or companies controlled by Joumaa and his associates. They then deposited the proceeds in their accounts in local banks and withdrew hard currency. That currency was deposited into accounts at the Lebanese Canadian Bank, with transfers back to accounts in Lebanon. Joumaa and Hezbollah thus profited from drug proceeds laundered through a well-established money-laundering operation in Latin America.[1] The money-laundering cycle was complete.

The US Treasury Department designated Joumaa and members of his network in June 2012 as terrorist financiers and drug-money launderers. David Cohen, the undersecretary of the treasury for terrorism and financial intelligence, stated that "the Joumaa network is a sophisticated multi-national money laundering ring, which launders the proceeds of drug trafficking for the benefit of criminals and the terrorist group Hizballah."[2]

More significantly, the US Treasury Department and the Drug Enforcement Administration exposed this money-laundering scheme by targeting the bad bank that was at the heart of the scheme. On February 27, 2011, the Treasury Department announced that the Lebanese Canadian Bank was being designated as a bank of primary money-laundering concern under Section 311 of the Patriot Act. The proposed rule laid out the public indictment of the bank, noting that LCB management had been complicit in allowing money laundering tied to international drug-trafficking networks run by Hezbollah from South America to Europe and the Middle East via West Africa. The bank allowed suspect cash transactions and wire transfers and was the favored bank for drug-traffickers' exchange houses.

The Treasury had been sparing in its use of Section 311 since the designation of Banco Delta Asia in 2005, but the designation once again proved effective. The proposed rule exposed LCB as a money-laundering bank worthy of isolation, the centerpiece of a sophisticated global money-laundering scheme that Hezbollah had helped develop, and the canary in the coal mine of the Beirut banking system as a refuge for mass amounts of illicit financing—for Iran, Hezbollah, and others evading the scrutiny of the legitimate financial system. The shock waves in the Lebanese banking system and for Hezbollah's financial managers were significant.

Hezbollah officials began to scramble to find alternate ways of holding and moving money, Beirut bankers began to calculate whether they might be next on the Treasury target list, and Lebanese officials worried about the potential targeting of their entire banking system. The Central Bank of Lebanon revoked the LCB's license in an attempt to contain the damage to the reputation of Beirut's banking system. Treasury officials have noted that the spotlight remains on the Lebanese banking system. In May 2012, David Cohen reaffirmed the Treasury's focus on the Lebanese financial sector, saying, "We've been very clear with the Lebanese authorities about this—we will do what we need to do to protect the U.S. financial system from that sort of illicit activity."[3] In addition, private advocacy groups—in particular, United Against a Nuclear Iran—have continued to push the Lebanese Central Bank, Congress, and the media to focus attention on the illicit financial activity coursing through the nearly fifty private Lebanese and foreign banks based in Beirut.

In August 2012, the United States seized $150 million in illicit funds from the then defunct Lebanese Canadian Bank's correspondent New York accounts. The bank was shut down, and its assets were sold off like scraps to other banks and investors.

Hezbollah has found a way to use global criminal and money-laundering networks to raise and move money—relying on South American drug networks, West African facilitators, used-car dealers in the United States, and moneymen and banks on three continents to help hide and launder the money. The US Treasury team and other authorities have tried to stay on top of these adaptations to keep Hezbollah scrambling for access to the financial system and sources of money. Unfortunately, Hezbollah is not the only target that has adapted to the Treasury's pressure.

Al Qaeda and its affiliates, too, have had to adapt. Since 9/11, Al Qaeda's overall budget and financial infrastructure have been hit hard. With Osama bin Laden—the symbolic center and fundraiser for Al Qaeda and Associated Movements (AQAM)—gone, the movement will have even greater difficulty raising money. The bin Laden documents found in the Abbottabad compound in May 2011 tell the story of an Al Qaeda core struggling financially and relying more heavily on its affiliates for funding. The intense counterterrorism and regulatory focus on funders, corrupted charities, front operations, and even banks used to facilitate financial flows to terrorist groups has served not just to disrupt but also to deter donations and support.

The Al Qaeda movement has adapted to this pressure, and its affiliates have grown more independent and innovative in developing self-funding mechanisms while individual members and cells use local means to raise necessary funds. The future of terrorist financing parallels the more fractured and localized nature of Al Qaeda itself and will present new challenges and opportunities for counterterrorism officials.

With a weakened and financially feeble Al Qaeda core, AQAM is relying more heavily on diffuse and localized funding schemes, often relying on criminal activities such as extortion, kidnapping, and financial fraud that provide fruitful sources of funding.[4] These activities, however, also expose networks and members to attention from local authorities and enforcement. We have already witnessed this evolution.

Al Qaeda in Iraq has siphoned oil, extorted businesses, and robbed banks—attempting to rob the Central Bank of Iraq on June 13, 2010—and engaged in a July 2011 online funding appeal. Al Qaeda in the Islamic Maghreb (AQIM), which had gained a territorial foothold in the northern part of Mali until being dislodged by French and African forces, has mastered the kidnapping-for-ransom business, taking European hostages and ransoming them to the tune of tens of millions of dollars a year paid for by governments and insurance companies. The revenue has proven so significant that bin Laden himself was contemplating moving Al Qaeda to rely heavily on kidnapping for ransom as the central funding source. This, along with AQIM's involvement in drug smuggling through the Sahel into southern Europe, has allowed AQIM to become a funding engine for the broader Al Qaeda movement, with support to Boko Haram, the Nigerian Al Qaeda adherents, and perhaps even other sympathetic groups emerging in North Africa, especially in the wake of the Arab revolutions.[5] In combination with the flow of new arms from Libya and the lack of governance and security in the region, the funding has allowed AQIM to expand its reach and lethality.

The Al Qaeda affiliate in Somalia, the Al Shabaab movement, created the most diversified and innovative funding method, a combination of taxes and checkpoint fees, diaspora remittances, and a charcoal trade–based money-laundering scheme to raise millions of dollars. Al Shabaab has generated $70 million to $100 million in revenue from its financial operations.[6] This should come as no surprise, as the Al Shabaab fighters have controlled key territory and trade in southern and coastal Somalia, including the lucrative port of Kismayo; can tap into flows of remittances from the wealthy, worldwide Somali diaspora; and rely on a committed cadre of savvy Somali businessmen, including Ahmed Jumale. Jumale, who remains at large and is at the heart of the Al Shabaab financial empire, had long before used the Al Barakaat network to help fund Osama bin Laden and the Al Qaeda network.

Jumale and his cadre have developed an effective financial infrastructure. The Al Shabaab tax system is simple and effective, levying taxes in six principal ways in the territory it controls: there is a tax on consumer goods in merchandise stores; a tax on businesses by size and profitability; a tax on the livestock and crops of farmers; a levy by acre on farmers; a 2.5 percent tax on corporate profits; and ad hoc military contributions. In addition, before being dislodged by Kenyan, Ethiopian, and African Union forces, Al Shabaab fighters operated mobile military checkpoints in vast swaths of territory where travelers were obliged to pay taxes for passage.[7]

Until late 2012, the port of Kismayo had been a major source of revenue, providing $35 million to $50 million in revenues, with $15 million coming from the trade in charcoal and sugar. For many years, the Al Shabaab business clique had outmaneuvered the Transitional Federal Government in Mogadishu, setting more competitive fees for the port of Kismayo than the government set for the port of Mogadishu and driving trade into Al Shabaab–controlled channels. The port of Kismayo, for example, imposed smaller import duties than the Somali government, with a fee of $200 on any vehicle rather than $1,300.[8] Most impressively, Al Shabaab has harnessed the trade in charcoal, which is exported from Somalia to wealthy Gulf states in return for sugar. Eighty percent of the charcoal produced in Somalia is exported to Gulf Cooperative Council (GCC) states, much of it in exchange for sugar from preferred traders who pay no tax to Al Shabaab.[9] The sugar is then sold at higher rates in East Africa, giving Al Shabaab profits in the millions of dollars. This explains why the United Nations has imposed sanctions on charcoal exports from Somalia—it was an attempt to cut off an important revenue source for the Al Shabaab moneymen. It also explains why it was a priority for Kenyan troops and allied forces to dislodge Al Shabaab control over Kismayo in 2012.

Because AQAM is seeking alternative financing sources and efficient vehicles for moving money, it will continue to develop relationships and operations that tie its financing to the infrastructure and operations of other organizations. Today, Al Qaeda in Pakistan relies on donations from sympathizers and supporters in the Persian Gulf and Arab states while also increasingly collaborating and sharing resources with Pakistani-based militant groups. For example, Al Qaeda is known to share resources and secure funding from Lashkar-e-Taiba, Pakistan's largest and most capable terrorist organization. In addition, Al Qaeda has sought to generate revenue from foreign recruits, charging tuition to radicals who journey from the

West to Pakistan for militant training and support.[10] This funding collaboration is happening between Al Qaeda affiliates. AQIM is funding and training Boko Haram members in Nigeria, and Boko Haram, Al Shabaab, and Al Qaeda are sharing funds and trading explosives.[11]

This adaptive collaboration is seen already in the case of drug trafficking, where AQIM has profited from the drug trade from South America through West Africa and the Sahel into Europe. In the past, Al Qaeda and groups like Lashkar-e-Taiba have benefited from alliances with Indian crime lord Dawood Ibrahim and his organized crime network. The overlaps between the criminal underworld, illicit financial activity, and terrorist operations and funding will continue to evolve as marriages of convenience emerge in common areas of operation. Focusing on key financial conduits, nodes, and networks that serve not just terrorists but transnational criminals will be critical for counterterrorism officials.

Although AQAM has been hurt financially, the old funding networks that sustained the Afghan and Arab mujahideen, Al Qaeda core, Islamists in Chechnya, Al Qaeda in Iraq, and other elements of AQAM still exist. Sympathizers, deep-pocket donors, and charities and other organizations remain, and they can be used to funnel money to sympathetic causes.

These networks have been weakened over time, but they have also been revitalized around specific causes important to violent Islamic extremists, such as the invasion of Iraq, the wars in the Caucasus, and sectarian fighting in Lebanon. Thus, galvanizing events, conflicts, or causes could help resurrect these established networks and the means by which they have justified support for Islamist causes and moved money transnationally, often relying on front companies, traditional hawala, and cash couriers. The deepening conflict between Sunni and Shia Muslims in countries throughout the Middle East and South Asia—along with the tumult of the Arab revolutions—is providing an opportunity for these networks to rejuvenate. Syria may provide the most fertile ground for a resurrection of the old financing and recruitment networks—out of the Arabian Gulf, Iraq, and North Africa—as extremists help to drive the fight against Assad in Damascus. Authorities then must maintain vigilance over these networks and financiers and ensure consistent oversight using existing measures to combat money laundering and terrorism financing.

On July 28, 2011, the US Treasury designated six Al Qaeda members operating in Iran. The designation was explosive in its accusation that these individuals had operated in Iran "under an agreement between al-Qa'ida and the Iranian government."[12] The designation noted that Al Qaeda operatives in Iran had played a critical financial role in facilitating donations and other funding streams to Al Qaeda's senior leaders in Pakistan, including Atiyah Abd al-Rahman. These Al Qaeda operatives utilized their perch in Iran to travel in the Gulf, raise funds, recruit members, and channel resources to Pakistan and other Al Qaeda operatives worldwide. Ezedin Abdel Aziz Khalil, Al Qaeda's representative in Iran, has brokered deals with the Iranian government for the release of Al Qaeda members from Iranian prisons, the transit of Al Qaeda members and families through the country, and the transfer of funds and resources to Al Qaeda in Pakistan and its global affiliates. According to the Treasury designation, Khalil required every Al Qaeda operative transiting to Pakistan to carry $10,000 to Al Qaeda senior leaders in Pakistan. These old networks can be rejuvenated, in the wake of conflict, with the aid of state sponsors, and with those willing to make deals with the devil against the United States.

All the while, new technologies and innovations in the storage and movement of money and value are reshaping the international financial landscape. This is especially the case in developing economies and communities without access to formal financial outlets, which are relying more heavily on mobile devices and mechanisms for storing and transferring money. The pace of growth of these systems in the developing world has been staggering. By 2009, the developing world accounted for three-quarters of the more than 4 billion mobile handsets in use.[13] Some studies estimate that there could be 1 billion users of mobile banking technologies by 2015. Prepaid cards, as an alternate way to store and transfer value, have gained momentum over the years as a replacement for standard currency transactions, with more innovation on the horizon. MasterCard and Sharjah Islamic Bank recently announced a deal with the UAE grocery store Sharjah Cooperative Society to issue a prepaid "Coop" card as an alternative to cash payment.

The development of online alternative currencies and new mechanisms for virtual barter will further open the Internet for potential exploitation by AQAM and its sympathizers. On November 23, 2011, Philippine police officers arrested four people for involvement in a $2 million remote toll scam that started in 2009. The cell had gained access to AT&T customer lines and telephone operating systems, "forcing the businesses to dial expensive toll numbers, which the men controlled," according to an Internet security website summary. The group thus hijacked the telephone infrastructure to collect funds from unwitting users.[14] These funds were then sent on to support Jemaah Islamiyah, an Indonesian-based Al Qaeda network, and Lashkar-e-Taiba.

Tracking the large volume of rapid and anonymous money flows around the world, and getting in front of new technologies to allow for lawful and appropriate tracking, will remain major challenges for law-enforcement, intelligence, and regulatory officials, especially because groups and individuals are able to hide and layer their identities and ownership interests. Digital currencies—replacing traditional currencies and the controls and chokepoints that attach to traditional international money flows—are emerging as efficient yet potentially problematic ways to raise, move, or hide illicit capital.

In many cases, the drive to evade the financial pressure of the United States has served as the impetus for new structures to profit from markets of opportunity and new relationships to subvert the legitimate financial system. The enemy has learned to adapt against the tools and methods used to pressure it financially. These financial networks often take advantage of opportunities and allies naturally present in the environment.

Importantly, money allows seemingly disparate networks and groups to blend their operations. Money—and the potential for profit—greases relationships that ordinarily would not exist. The grand global arms traffickers of this era, such as Viktor Bout and Manzar al-Kassar, the "Prince of Marbella" who supplied weapons to criminals and terrorists and is now serving a federal prison sentence in the United States, have proven this rule. They were willing to service any group or regime willing to pay the right price—often, as in the case of Bout, selling arms to warring sides in the same conflict. This principle of opportunistic profit and operations is now implicating the interactions of networks of all ideological stripes. There is money to be made, and there are logistical networks to be harnessed, to achieve criminal and political goals.

This blend of purposes is seen most clearly in the conversion of terrorist groups into drug-trafficking organizations—such as the FARC in Colombia or the Taliban in Afghanistan. According to Michael Braun, the former head of the Drug Enforcement Agency's Special Operations Division, the DEA has linked at least half of the Foreign Terrorist Organizations to the global drug trade.[15] Braun described these growing links vividly:

> If you want to visualize ungoverned space or a permissive environment, I tell people to simply think of the bar scene in the first "Star Wars" movie. Operatives from FTOs [Foreign Terrorist Organizations] and DTOs [Drug Trafficking Organizations] are frequenting the same shady bars, the same seedy hotels and the same sweaty brothels in a growing number of areas around the world. And what else are they doing? Based on over 37 years in the law enforcement and security sectors, you can mark my word that they are most assuredly talking business and sharing lessons learned.[16]

Ideology gives way to opportunity. The reason is money. Drug trafficking nets an estimated $320 billion annually, according to one source.[17] In 2006, it was estimated that Mexican and Colombian drug-trafficking organizations generated between $8.3 billion and $24.9 billion in wholesale drug earnings in the United States annually.[18] The FARC has raised $500 million to $600 million annually from its control of the cocaine trade out of Colombia and Venezuela,[19] and the Taliban makes between $70 million and $400 million a year from the opium trade.[20] Over time, the Taliban has increased its involvement in the heroin trade—it started by protecting opium fields, but is now also engaged in actual production and distribution. In 2008, the Taliban made as much as $50 million simply from opium harvesting and another $125 million from Afghan morphine base and heroin labs.[21] The amounts have grown exponentially as the Taliban has controlled more and more of the drug trade out of Afghanistan. A Taliban leader's drug ledgers recently revealed $170 million in heroin sales in less than one year.[22] Other groups, such as the Kurdish terrorist organization PKK (also known as Kongra Gel), made between $50 million and $100 million annually, according to a NATO report, though the Turkish government claims that the network makes closer to $615 million or even possibly $770 million a year.[23]

These connections allow groups to work together more broadly. The DEA, the FBI, and the intelligence community have focused more and more attention on the nexus between drugs and terror—with terrorist groups assuming the role of drug-trafficking organizations, and drug-trafficking organizations taking on the characteristics and violent methodologies of terrorist groups. The US Attorney for the Southern District of New York has merged its international drug and foreign terrorism sections because of the intimate link between the two.

In the most dramatic example of the potential operational convergence of terror and narcotics organizations, the US government revealed the disruption of an Iranian assassination plot in 2011 against the Saudi ambassador in Washington, Adel al-Jubeir. According to US officials, an Iranian Quds Force member—directed by the Iranian leadership—hired a DEA source whom they believed to be a member of the vicious Mexican drug cartel Los Zetas. The Iranians wanted to enlist Mexican drug hitmen to kill the Saudi ambassador and others in Washington, DC. The nexus between state-sponsored terror and drug traffickers' violence was nearly manifest in the nation's capital. America's enemies are finding each other—as a matter of convenience and opportunity.

Unfortunately, there is always a means to adapt around financial pressure and strictures when there is money to be made. The magnitude of illicit transactions is staggering. A 2011 UN study found that "all criminal proceeds are likely to have amounted to some 3.6 per cent of GDP (2.3–5.5 per cent) or around $2.1 trillion in 2009."[24] In Afghanistan, for example, $4.6 billion was declared as exports from Kabul airport in 2011, roughly equivalent to the entire budget of the Afghan government.[25] Crime can pay, making it an especially attractive avenue for fundraising for networks and groups with global ambitions. Where there is money to be made and moved, financial institutions will be implicated. Banks and financial intermediaries will continue to weigh the balance between making significant amounts of money while doing business with suspect customers and the need to apply the most stringent financial controls and standards on money flowing through their systems. We have seen this over and over with multinational banks, including, most recently, HSBC and Standard Chartered. There is little mercy for those targeted by regulatory authorities, investigators, and prosecutors. Institutions that attempt to evade sanctions and scrutiny in order to tap lucrative business lines or markets are taking huge risks—with their reputations and with their access to the US and global banking systems.

Evasion from scrutiny can take many forms. The Iranians have gone to great lengths to avoid the international financial and commercial pressures they are now facing. They have adapted their evasion over time—initially relying on Iran's central bank (Bank Markazi) to funnel the commercial banking deals and transactions not allowed through Iran's other designated banks. With the central bank now scrutinized and isolated, money has been moving through sympathetic banks—with banks in places such as Venezuela or China often being used to move money in an attempt to avoid American and Western scrutiny. In July 2012, the Treasury Department designated Kunlun Bank in China and Elaf Bank in Iraq for their continued transactions with designated Iranian banks. Noor Islamic Bank, partially owned by the government of Dubai, has been found to be a primary conduit for evasion of international sanctions on Iranian oil proceeds. Iran has most recently attempted to purchase smaller banks. Iran has also been aided by trading part- ners unwilling to clamp down on Iranian commercial activity. Iraq has frustrated the Obama administration by providing an oil and trading outlet for the Iranians as the United States attempts to squeeze the Iranians.[26]

But Western banks have not been able to resist the temptation of making money off of Iranian deals either—often oil or infrastruc- ture deals. Such banks have hidden the origin and destination of the transactions, often stripping wire information from banking transactions. This has been a common transgression cited by regula- tors against banks such as Standard Chartered, UBS, and HSBC. Iran has also tried to establish bartering agreements with countries that need its oil and are willing to offer goods in return—leaving out any dollar-clearing transactions. Iran has tried to hide its oil and goods— reflagging its ships, attempting to turn off the tanker tracking devices, and moving money in hard currency and gold across bor- ders to avoid the banking system.[27]

The Iranians are not alone in the evasion game. The North Kore- ans continue their illicit activity to fund their regime, selling and moving arms, missile technology, and counterfeit goods, including tobacco and pharmaceuticals, to rogue states and criminal networks. To do so, North Korea runs multiple state-owned businesses, collaborates with Chinese firms that can evade sanctions, and smuggles materials through criminal networks and diplomatic channels. They have used procurement networks as money movers and constructed elaborate smuggling routes and alternate-front businesses to continue illicit activity despite international sanctions. North Korean commercial deals with Chinese companies, driven by mining interests and development projects, have been quite useful in this regard. The movement of goods between North Korea and China has allowed for a network of businesses and brokers to develop and to move money and goods outside the gaze of the international banks.[28]

According to a 2009 UN report on the implementation of sanctions against the DPRK,

> while sanctions have clearly not stopped the Democratic People's Republic of Korea's nuclear programmes and trade in arms, they have made it more difficult and expensive for the country to pursue these. Nevertheless Member States continue to face numerous difficulties in implementing sanctions. The Panel has discovered loopholes and other vulnerabilities in shipping and transportation practices that the Democratic People's Republic of Korea and others have exploited, and notes increasing sophistication on the part of the Democratic People's Republic of Korea both in the establishment of shell and front companies and offshore financial agents, and in the proliferation of affiliates, substitutes and aliases intended to mask already designated entities and individuals.[29]

Evasion of international sanctions and financial restrictions—along with illicit trade—can evolve amid legitimate trading relationships. As North Korea's most significant ally, China acts as a major trading partner and a key source of food, arms, fuel, and other aid for the largely isolated state. It also serves as an outlet for the North Korean regime. China has an interest in ensuring North Korean economic stability. Any economic collapse in North Korea could foment instability along its border and unleash waves of refugees as well as risk foreign intervention by powers such as South Korea or the United States. About half of Chinese foreign aid is provided to North Korea.[30] Chinese arms sales to North Korea jumped to $4.32 million in 2009, the same year that China was the only exporter of small arms to North Korea.[31] North Korea, mistrusting of China's interest, must likewise continue to claim self-reliance while also engaging in something close to "normal" external relations.[32] As such, the economic relationship between the two countries, based on trade, foreign investment, mining contracts, special economic zones, and other measures, creates a delicate and important balance.

As such, China is the safety valve for the North Korean regime's finances, and their economic and commercial relationship is growing. According to the World Bank, China has supplied the majority of North Korea's food, and almost 90 percent of its energy imports, since the early 1990s.[33] Bilateral trade in 2008 reached $2.79 billion (a 41.3 percent increase from 2007) and exemplified the large trade imbalance between the two states. Chinese imports were valued at $2.03 billion, and North Korea's exports totaled $750 million in coal and iron ore.[34]

China is the largest foreign direct investor in North Korea (excluding South Korea's investment in the Kaesong Industrial Complex just across the border). China supplied $18.4 million of North Korea's $67 million in 2007 FDI (foreign direct investment), and $41.2 million of the $44 million invested in 2008.[35] China has reason to be attracted to North Korea's resources. North Korea holds mineral deposits potentially worth 140 times the country's 2008 GDP. Resources include coal, copper, graphite, iron ore, lead, limestone, magnesite, salt, tungsten, and zinc. Chinese and North Korean mining interests have developed a number of joint projects to develop iron ore, copper, gold, and coal to supply China with needed energy and raw materials while giving North Korea a source of committed capital, investments, and economic development. One report noted that "China Tonghua Iron and Steel Group (a state-owned but partially privatized enterprise) has invested 7 billion yuan (approximately $875 million) in developing the DPRK's Musan Iron Mine, the largest open-cut iron mine in Asia, with verified iron-rich ore reserves reaching seven billion tons."[36] North Korea and China have also committed to developing infrastructure and investment projects in special economic zones (SEZ) to attract foreign investment.[37]

Arrangements for evasion are not isolated to commercial deals or operations between two countries. Given the potential for lax enforcement of anti-money-laundering and transparency rules and principles in countries such as China, Malaysia, Russia, Qatar, and Venezuela (as well as the penchant of those countries' governments to oppose Western policies and interests, especially those that directly concern the United States), these places could serve as international financial outlets for rogue regimes and illicit nonstate actors.

In fact, the most interesting dimension of the threat comes in the development of alliances of financial rogues—those countries or entities targeted or isolated by the legitimate financial system but who work together to evade sanctions or access the financial system. These arrangements arise both by design and by happenstance, but they are an innovation and result of the intensified financial warfare waged by the United States.

The attempts to build workarounds to avoid the legitimate financial system have already been seen. Those wary of SWIFT's motivations after the decision to stop dealing with sanctioned Iranian banks have begun to develop online messaging alternatives among like-minded banks and financial institutions. Those wary of relying on dollar-clearing transactions have begun to establish bilateral or regional trading relationships that rely on local currencies or barter arrangements to bypass the traditional banking system. In addition, less rigorous financial centers and banks have been willing to pick up the business jettisoned by the legitimate banking world—risking the scrutiny of the US Treasury and others.

There have also been natural alliances between the rogue states targeted for isolation by Western countries and banks—namely Iran, North Korea, Syria, and Belarus—to avoid and skirt international scrutiny. The financial and commercial connections take many forms—often with a sharing of know-how and a shared attempt to avoid scrutiny. These countries use front companies and sympathetic financial actors to operate. On June 30, 2009, the US Treasury Department designated Hong Kong Electronics, a North Korean company, as a proliferator of nuclear weapons and ballistic missiles. This company was based on Kish Island, Iran, and had been transferring millions of dollars connected to the proliferation network from Iran to North Korea.

Venezuela, which has access to the American banking system and commercial ties to the United States, in particular via oil deals, has proven to be a problematic player among the rogues. Iran has been working with Venezuela to avoid sanctions, with frequent visits between the leaders of the two countries. Flights from Tehran to Damascus to Caracas have not been about meeting the burgeoning tourist traffic from Iran to Venezuela. These flights have symbolically tied these countries and allowed the movement of suspect individuals and goods. The late Venezuelan President Hugo Chávez reportedly sent diesel to Syria and worked with Iran to allow Iranian forces into Latin America.[38] Iran and Venezuela have sought to deepen their political, military, and economic relationship through bilateral agreements, foreign investment, and support for anti-American initiatives in global diplomatic forums.[39]

These ties are only likely to grow as countries under scrutiny or isolated by the legitimate financial system attempt to do business together outside the gaze of the United States and the strictures of the US dollar.

The last policy meeting I attended in the Oval Office with President Bush, in November 2008, was not about terrorism, but about the threat of international organized crime. Starting in earnest in 2007, we had been debating for months within the US government how to address the growing reach of organized crime around the world and the threat to US national security that it represented.[40]

Mafias and organized crime had always bedeviled law enforcement—from Al Capone to John Gotti. But the organized crime of the twenty-first century was a different breed. The age of globalized trade and investment had given well-funded criminal organizations the ability to access markets and embed in the legitimate commercial world like never before. It also gave them the ability to profit from the full range of illicit trade—from drugs and human trafficking to counterfeit Gucci bags and illegal logging.

At my request, the intelligence community produced an updated National Intelligence Estimate on the threat to national security posed by transnational organized crime, which was ultimately published in 2010. The United Nations also issued a threat assessment in 2010, finding that "organized crime has diversified, gone global and reached macro-economic proportions: illicit goods are sourced from one continent, trafficked across another, and marketed in a third. Mafias are today truly a transnational problem: a threat to security, especially in poor and conflict-ridden countries. Crime is fuelling corruption, infiltrating business and politics, and hindering development. And it is undermining governance by empowering those who operate outside the law."[41]

The famed and feared Yakuza from Japan, the Brothers' Circle from the former Soviet republics, La Familia in Mexico, the Asian triads throughout China and Taiwan, and the Sicilian Mafia have all profited and expanded their reach. They aren't alone. And they are ruthless. These groups are led by vicious businessmen who wield violent control over their extensive networks. They control more than just lines of business or swaths of territory. They often gain control of the governments they infiltrate or influence.

We realized that the reach and power of these groups was beginning to present risks to national security. Some of this risk had to do with the willingness of organized crime networks to do business with all comers and to deal in anything that could bring a profit. Groups in Central Asia and Russia could gain access to nuclear material—and could make a deal with the highest bidder to sell the radiological material. We had seen smuggling of nuclear material across the Georgia border on a couple of occasions in 2003 and 2006, enough to raise concerns that these groups presented a real threat of proliferating weapons of mass destruction to anyone willing to pay the right price.[42]

In addition, many of these groups had developed enough of a diversified capital base to wield control and influence over legitimate commercial ventures and industries. These were not just local mafiosos extorting small businesses. These were organizations running global enterprises, with companies controlling valuable markets, members of legitimate boards of directors, and a small army of lawyers and accountants ready to defend their interests. As stated by Treasury's David Cohen, "There is a dark side to globalization.... As our global economy and financial systems have grown more sophisticated and interdependent, they also have become more vulnerable to criminal organizations and their illicit financial activities."[43]

International organized crime syndicates have expanded the money-laundering operations that have helped fuel their growth and financial reach globally—making them more layered and using a variety of investment vehicles.[44] Such groups not only understand how to profit from the international system but also recognize that certain types of investments and influence can shield their activities and leadership from law enforcement and political pressure. Translated into a more aggressive posture, such groups and potential terrorist allies could see opportunities in controlling certain businesses or wielding influence over particular markets and states, distorting the political frameworks in which they operate through corruption, intimidation, and deepening influence.

Finally, these are groups that could influence governments, but given their connections to various regimes, they can also be co-opted and used by governments and leaders or their allies and sympathizers. The lineage of some of the organized crime members—for example, Russian organized crime's links to the old KGB, and Los Zetas' with former Mexican special operations troops—gives them unique insights, relationships, and influence within their home countries. The organizations—with their deep pockets, logistics networks, and ability to access specialized personnel, including computer hackers—give countries that are willing to deal with such groups an upper hand in the global marketplace. This arrangement allows for a group of nonstate networks that, if enlisted, can act as a proxy against the state's enemies.

We had focused on the nexus between organized criminal activity and terrorism for years. The arrests of the international arms brokers Manzar al-Kassar and Viktor Bout, along with the arrest of a series of Taliban narco-traffickers, demonstrated our willingness to use the reach of American law to prosecute international scofflaws who served as an operational nexus for terrorist and rogue networks. In 2008, US Attorney General Michael Mukasey announced a refocus on the new threats from international organized crime, noting networks' infiltration of strategic energy and minerals markets and exploitation of US and international financial systems. "Some of the most significant international organized criminals," Mukasey warned, "are also infiltrating our own strategic industries, and those of our allies, are providing logistical support to terrorist organizations and foreign intelligence agencies, and are capable of creating havoc in our economic infrastructure." He further noted that modern organized crime touched all elements of the economy and presented a host of threats, including "manipulation of securities markets; corrupting public officials globally; and using violence as a basis for power." He added, "These are the hallmarks of international organized crime in the 21st century."[45]

The November 2008 meeting in the Oval Office was about using the president's wartime economic powers to freeze the assets of organized crime figures around the world. Deputy Attorney General Mark Filip had been a champion of using these powers and Treasury tools to go after organized crime, and I was trying to do everything I could to help him. Ironically, the Treasury Department was less enamored with the idea of the president signing a new executive order targeting organized crime's financial networks. We had used these powers, delegated to the secretaries of treasury and state, for years against drug traffickers, terrorists, proliferators, and those engaged in corruption and human rights abuses. Should we now expand the power and program to target known organized crime groups and their business networks? In the Oval Office with the president was Attorney General Mukasey, Director of National Intelligence Mike McConnell, Secretary of the Treasury Paulson, Secretary of State Rice, National Security Adviser Hadley, Deputy National Security Adviser for International Economic Affairs Dan Price, and me.

The discussion was in-depth and respectful, with the attorney general arguing for the need to use these new financial tools to attack the financial infrastructure of organized crime groups. In many ways, as Filip and I had been arguing for weeks, this was the ideal tool to use against criminal organizations, which thrived on access to the international financial and commercial systems. We had seen the dramatic effect this isolation could have on drug cartels, which needed to launder their funds and operate businesses to gain the reach and impunity to operate at will. The tools had worked against terrorists and rogue regimes that were looking to access the financial system for profit and political goals. As these criminal groups grow more interconnected in ways that transcend national boundaries, such networks are gaining influence in strategically vital markets that could impact the accessibility to and stability of these markets. In addition, the ability of such groups to provide their infrastructure and expertise to others (including terrorists)—whether access to fraudulent travel documents or nuclear material—raises the specter of alliances of convenience and profit aligned dangerously against the United States.[46]

The reach of the Russia-based organized crime network of

Semion Mogilevich is a stark example of this point. In the late 1990s, Mogilevich gained control of a set of companies, including YBM Magnex in Philadelphia, that produced industrial magnets in Hungary and engaged in extensive securities fraud and money laundering. As a senior administration official told the *New York Times*, this represented the "first public demonstration of the manipulation and infiltration of world financial markets by Russian organized crime."[47] In a 2005 speech, FBI Director Mueller described Mogilevich's network as "engaged in drug and weapons trafficking, prostitution, and money laundering, and organized stock fraud in the United States and Canada in which investors lost over 150 million dollars," all from his headquarters in Budapest.[48]

These were organizations that had begun to embed themselves in the global marketplace, even in the United States. The same reason the financial tools would be so important to use against such networks made the prospect of a new executive order targeting organized crime potentially problematic. Those opposing issuing the executive order noted that it would be very hard to confine the scope of the order, and legitimate businesses could unknowingly and inadvertently get caught in the wartime executive powers. The Treasury Department was also worried that this new executive order would add uncertainty to the marketplace at the height of the growing financial crisis, while dissuading investment in the United States.

President Bush recognized the conundrum immediately—we needed to attack the financial underpinnings of the creeping reach of international organized crime, but we needed to do it carefully and thoughtfully. He also astutely realized that we needed a broader, more strategic approach to the problem. The president turned to us and directed that we draft a broader strategy—into which the executive order would fit—instead of handling the issue piecemeal. He was also worried about publishing anything this important in the tail end of the administration, potentially handcuffing the new Obama administration. He directed us to draft the skeletal strategy and hand it over to the Obama team. That's what we did over the holidays. When I met with John Brennan, who would assume the role of both deputy national security adviser and homeland security adviser for President Obama, I handed over the draft strategy in a red folder. Brennan took the folder and the issue seriously.

On July 25, 2011, the Obama administration issued its version of the transnational organized crime (TOC) strategy.[49] President Obama noted: "This Strategy is organized around a single, unifying principle: to build, balance, and integrate the tools of American power to combat transnational organized crime and related threats to our national security—and to urge our partners to do the same. ... While this Strategy is intended to assist the United States Government in combating transnational crime, it also serves as an invitation for enhanced international cooperation."[50] The strategy set out to break the economic power of transnational criminal networks and protect strategic markets and the US financial system from organized crime penetration and abuse. The principal goal was to defeat transnational criminal networks that posed the greatest threat to national security by targeting their infrastructures, depriving them of their enabling means, and preventing the criminal facilitation of terrorist activities.

At the same time, President Obama signed the executive order giving the secretary of the treasury the power to freeze the assets of organized crime groups and their financial facilitation networks. The order established a new sanctions program to block the property of significant transnational criminal organizations that threatened the national security, foreign policy, or economy of the United States. It also named the first groups to be subject to the financial isolation and scrutiny of this program: the Brothers' Circle from Eurasia, the Yakuza in Japan, the Camorra from Italy, and Los Zetas, the ruthless Mexican drug cartel. These groups are engaged in everything from drug trafficking and human exploitation to pirating commercial goods, enterprises worth billions of dollars in proceeds and business. The global and business diversity of these groups underscored the importance of using this financial tool against their economic interests.

The administration also proposed new legislative measures, including one to increase the visibility of financial assets and transactions to reveal beneficial ownership. This proposal, long championed by Chip Poncy at the Treasury Department, was in response to the problem of hidden criminal assets vested in the United States, without an ability to know who or what was invested in the country. Criminal assets could be housed or layered in front companies based in the United States, and US banks and regulators would be blind to the origins of the funds or the real owners of the assets. This financial regulatory loophole made the United States a vulnerable haven for smart criminals who knew how to hide their operations.

The globalization of trade and finance has altered the financial battlespace. The United States has used its global financial influence and power to isolate rogue actors. At the same time, those impacted by US financial pressure are adapting—using globalization and new technologies to their advantage. They evade pressure, and they profit from illicit trade and the opportunities to collaborate in commercial and financial marriages of convenience. These networks not only seek profit, however, but are attempting to circumvent and undermine US power and influence. This is how they can stay in business and make money. This is also what makes them a threat.

The use of these tools is not now confined to the United States. State and nonstate actors have learned from the financial campaigns we have unleashed over the past decade. They have seen how to use financial influence for national advantage, and they are beginning to use the same tools and techniques to extend their own influence. But these other actors in the international system may not be as restrained as the United States in protecting the international financial system. In fact, some of America's enemies and emerging competitors may have the United States and its vulnerabilities directly in their financial crosshairs.

16

THE COMING FINANCIAL WARS

In the summer of 2008, at the height of the financial crisis, Russian officials approached their Chinese counterparts with an intriguing proposal. The countries could band together to sell their holdings in US housing finance giants Fannie Mae and Freddie Mac. These government-sponsored enterprises (GSEs) owned or guaranteed over $5 trillion in residential mortgages and mortgage-backed securities, approximately 50 percent of the total mortgage market. The GSEs had accumulated approximately $1.7 trillion in debt, hundreds of billions of which were owned by the Chinese government alone. With the United States still reeling from the financial crisis already underway, a coordinated Russian-Chinese sale of GSE holdings could force the US government to use its emergency authorities and spend massive sums to keep Fannie Mae and Freddie Mac alive. Such a move would likely exacerbate the global economic crisis, causing an even deeper crisis in confidence in the US financial system and potentially a run on the dollar.[1]

Secretary of the Treasury Hank Paulson was informed of the proposal after the Chinese refused to go along with the plan. It was a harbinger of the increasing willingness of countries to use financial weapons to strike the United States. This and other uses of economic power and influence offer a glimpse into a new age of geo-economic competition emerging in the wake of the Great Recession of 2008.

The 2008 financial crisis was a major blow to American power. It caused a fundamental loss of confidence in the American financial system and capital model, shaking the foundations and perceptions of American economic power. In its wake, many countries and investors questioned whether dependence on New York and the US dollar should dictate their well-being and national fortunes. This sense of America's lost economic predominance has grown as the G7 has quickly given way to the G20 as the club of key economic actors. Meanwhile, countries such as China, Qatar, and Turkey have survived the crisis relatively well, invested widely, and prospered, while the US economy continues to limp along. The 2012 credit downgrade of the United States by Standard & Poor's is yet another signal that there was a loss of confidence in America's ability to address its most important fiscal challenges. The perception of economic predominance has been shattered.

This loss of perceived power has now been met with an increased willingness to use economic influence for national interests. We have entered a new era of financial influence where financial and economic tools have taken pride of place as instruments of national security. The conflicts of this age are likely to be fought with markets, not just militaries, and in boardrooms, not just battlefields. Geopolitics is now a game best played with financial and commercial weapons.

The new geo-economic game may be more efficient and subtle than past geopolitical competitions, but it is no less ruthless and destructive. Major and minor state powers, along with super-empowered individuals and networks, can harness economic interdependence to increase their global power status at the expense of their geopolitical rivals. So far, the United States has been at the cutting edge of this competition. But the fact that it was first to develop innovative and powerful financial tools to pursue its interests is no guarantee of continued success. Indeed, there is the potential for greater US vulnerability and decreased financial and economic leverage. Although the United States has had a near monopoly on the use of targeted financial pressure over the past ten years, this edge is likely to erode, leaving the United States both more vulnerable to external financial pressure and less able to use financial suasion as a lever of foreign policy.

The irony of the Russian proposal was that it echoed the methods the United States had been using against rogues. In the past ten years, the United States had demonstrated to the world—and to its competitors, in particular—that it was willing to leverage economic and market powers to influence international security. China and other countries have resented the use of this influence to affect their economic interests and influence. The powerful financial tools that the US Treasury has honed over this decade are now proliferating, particularly to major competitors. They have been and will continue to be used against the United States and its allies in the future, not only because of an increased foreign understanding of the means of financial pressure, but also because of a decreased reliance on the dollar and on American banks and the US financial system.

Importantly, the states and nonstate actors that the United States has targeted are inventing new means of avoiding sanctions. The United States has little influence over the separate financial and monetary systems that are emerging, particularly in the cyberrealm. Further, there are increasing efforts, including by some US allies, to limit the United States' unilateral leverage in the financial sphere.

These trends are weakening the ability of the United States to use its financial power to promote US national security interests. The evolving geo-economic environment has raised the stakes of international competition and new forms of financial warfare. The coming financial wars will reveal complicated and novel risks—both macrolevel challenges and microlevel threats—that the United States is not prepared to address. Nondemocratic state competitors capable of exercising full and complete control of their global capital activity and leveraging nonstate proxies have recognized the changing landscape and have adjusted their pursuit of national security accordingly. In order to catch up and regain its relative power position, the United States must redefine national security along economic lines and rebuild its foreign policy toolkit accordingly.

Glimmers of Financial War

As allies and enemies continue to question the shelf life of US economic predominance and the utility of an American-led capitalist system, challenger states with alternative political models and values are aggressively capitalizing on America's struggles. This moment has accelerated the challenges to US economic power, with countries like China becoming less willing to take a backseat to American financial dictates. The use of financial power in the twenty-first century is no longer just an American endeavor.

In particular, China's brand of state authoritarian capitalism appears to be an increasingly attractive alternative. Chinese strategists view economic influence as central to Chinese national security. Consequently, Chinese companies and state-owned enterprises (SOEs) benefit from state policies that subsidize their work and access to markets abroad. With this model, China has become the second largest economy, the world's leader in greenhouse gas emissions, and the direct challenger to American economic and political hegemony.[2]

China's hold on major resources is a central part of its power projection. China already produces 93 percent of the world's rare-earth minerals (and 99 percent of some of the most prized of such minerals), which are used in manufacturing numerous important products, including hybrid engines and solar-panel glass. As China solidifies and strengthens this near-monopoly market position, the incentives to use resource dominance as a political weapon will increase. China has sent signals that it is willing to flex its economic muscles for direct and relatively minor national security interests.[3]

In the wake of Japan's 2010 seizure of a Chinese shipping trawler captain, and in light of increasing tensions over China's claim of "indisputable sovereignty" over the South China Sea, for example, China banned the export of certain rare-earth minerals to Japan.[4]

The Chinese aversion to sanctions has given way to an open debate about the utility of unilateral sanctions and of leveraging market access in China to achieve national goals. In the wake of an American sale of new military equipment to Taiwan in 2009, Chinese officials threatened to sanction all American companies doing business in China. A Chinese official was reputed to have said that the Chinese had learned how to use such sanctions from watching the United States. No sanctions followed, but the Chinese had sent the message: they were now willing to restrict access to their markets to achieve a geopolitical goal.

Moreover, Russia has used its critical oil and natural gas supplies to both fill the Kremlin's coffers and exert political pressure. In 2006 and again in 2009, Russia shut off natural gas supplies to Europe through Ukrainian pipelines as part of an ongoing price and diversion dispute. The Russian government and Gazprom used Europe's dependence on Russian natural gas, which constitutes about 25 percent of all EU supplies, to extract concessions from Ukraine. The Russian government repeated this pattern with Georgia to pressure the Saakashvili government, cutting off all gas supplies and 25 percent of Georgia's electricity during the winter of 2006.[5] There is now speculation that Russia—through Gazprom—intends to purchase the Greek natural gas company DEPA as Greece conducts a fire sale of its public companies. DEPA is an important player in the Italy-Greece-Turkey Interconnector (IGTI), an alternate natural gas pipeline intended to circumvent Russian supplies into Europe.[6] This purchase would follow the same pattern by which Gazprom has acquired interests in the Balkans and Poland as a means of "plugging the holes" of alternate channels of supply in Europe. The Russians have never been shy about their desire to use their economic power for broader national interests. In 2007, Russian President

Vladimir Putin stated that the Russian intelligence services "must be able to swiftly and adequately evaluate changes in the international economic situation, understand the consequences for the domestic economy and . . . more actively protect the economic interests of our companies abroad."[7]

The United States and its companies, by contrast, remain reluctant to meld political and economic interests directly abroad. This is seen not only in the passive policies of the United States in Iraq and Afghanistan, but also in flaccid trade and investment policies that lack strategic purpose. Secretary of State Clinton showed an awareness of this broad deficiency in US policy and the global dynamic in a speech at the US Global Leadership Coalition Conference:

> The simple truth is if we don't seize the opportunities available today, other countries will. Other countries will fight for their companies while ours fend for themselves. Other countries will promote their own models and serve their own interests instead of opening markets, reinforcing the rule of law, and creating widespread inclusive growth. Other countries will create the jobs that should be created here, and even claim the mantle of global leadership. None of us want to see that happen, and I don't believe most of the people around the world do either.[8]

This timid trade policy of the United States reflects a long-standing structural divide between national security policies and the role of the US private sector in the international commercial and financial system. US economic reach and influence have been taken for granted as a function of the free trade paradigm that the United States helped to establish and the competitive advantages of US companies. This economic advantage and the international influence it provides are now in jeopardy. In a more competitive global environment, a passive policy that fails to connect national security and economic influence dooms the United States to diminishing influence internationally.

Any recognition of China's economic success must be balanced against a clear-eyed understanding of China's inherent vulnerabilities and interests. China confronts a host of internal political, environmental, and demographic problems that will complicate its transition from a poor to a middle-income country, let alone its pursuit of international economic influence or dominance. Recent protests against official corruption and for labor rights have rocked the sense of stability in China and slowed the continued march toward mass urbanization. The slowing Chinese economy has Chinese leaders worried about the sustainability of its economic model. In December 2011, China's vice finance minister, Zhu Guangyao, publicly claimed that the current economic "crisis" was "grimmer and more challenging than the global financial crisis triggered by the Lehman Brothers bankruptcy in 2008."[9] In the summer of 2012, after China's growth fell to a three-year low of 7.6 percent, observers began to debate the inherent challenges and limitations of the Chinese economic model, with many, including environmentalists, questioning the sustainability of China's industrial and manufacturing-led growth.

China also is beginning to see the reactions to its growing power, as countries search for ways to counter Chinese influence in their respective regions. From Vietnam and Burma to Japan and South Korea, Asian countries are chafing at Chinese attempts to exert power in the South China Sea through their economic influence. Over time, as China accrues power, it will accumulate responsibility for complex geopolitical problems in Iran, Pakistan, Afghanistan, and North Korea, which fester along its borders.

China's success is also predicated in part on the prevailing global economic order, and it has few incentives in the short and medium term to challenge that order. The economic ties between China and the United States bind the two countries and make direct confrontation less likely. Trade between the two economic powers reached $503 billion in 2011, with both sides benefiting.[10] Chinese investment in US Treasuries by 2011 reached $1.15 trillion, 23 percent of the total foreign investment in US government bonds. China's economic ties to the United States—and deep investments in US Treasuries—make it less willing to attack the credibility of the dollar and the US economy.

Nevertheless, China's aggressive, state-led, mercantilist approach challenges US industry, relative power, and global influence. So, too, does it distort the international commercial system, with economically powerful nation-states engaged in commercial investment and economic planning usually reserved for the private sector.[11] This model was further strengthened as Western governments intervened to "bail out" traditionally private industries. As declared by *The Economist* at the time, the state went "back into business."[12]

This new brand of authoritarian capitalism opens the door to a more aggressive blending of economic and political interests. In the Chinese model, economic power and reach is enmeshed directly and intentionally with geopolitical influence and national security strength.[13] As noted by Elizabeth C. Economy, director of Asia Studies at the Council on Foreign Relations, China has realized that "ensuring their supply lines for natural resources requires not only a well-organized trade and development agenda but also an expansive military strategy."[14]

This new model also draws upon the resource pool and investment reach of sovereign wealth funds. Chinese sovereign wealth fund investment was worth $200 billion in 2007, and the Chinese government could add liquidity to the fund at any time and without constraint. Similar investment parastatals (quasi-state entities) have converted national resource wealth into national investment strategies. The Qatar Investment Authority, for example, purchased a 20 percent stake in the London stock exchange in 2007. The power of these funds is such that Wall Street firms, including Merrill Lynch, Morgan Stanley, and Blackstone, were forced to turn to them for over $40 billion in capital infusions during the recent economic crisis.[15] And the size and reach of these government-sponsored entities, or so-called state champions, is growing. Government-owned or -controlled enterprises now make up 20 percent of the global stock market value.[16] From 2004 to the beginning of 2008, over one hundred new state-owned companies joined the Forbes Global 2000 list of the largest companies by "sales, profits, assets and market value."[17]

The appeal of the state champion model is reflected in the fact that Western countries have begun to dip their toes into the deep end of sovereign wealth funds. For example, in November 2008, France established the Fonds Strategique d'Investissement (FSI)—a "strategic investment fund" run by the "armed wing" of the French Treasury, the Caisse des Dépôts et Consignations (Deposits and Consignments Fund)—in order to help French companies navigate the global financial crisis and protect French industry from predatory foreign investments. In 2009, Britain created a strategic investment fund of 750 million pounds to invest in domestic industrial capacities such as low-carbon technologies, high-speed broadband infrastructure, renewable chemicals, and export promotions. More recently, Japan, which has the second largest pool of foreign reserves behind China (approximately $1.2 trillion), has considered establishing a sovereign wealth fund in order to erode the strength of the yen and pull itself out of two decades of economic stagnation. This would involve renovating the publicly funded Japan Bank for International Cooperation to make strategic investments in emerging markets. If Japan made such a move, it would likely diversify its assets by moving out of low-yield US Treasury bonds.

Such investment funds, and the ability of nation-states to control purse strings that are relevant to other nations' assets, raise the specter of new forms of geopolitical influence—tacitly or directly. Consider also the case of government export financing. Whereas the US provides financing for the customers of US companies in foreign markets only in very narrow circumstances (e.g., where it is needed to close an export sale), foreign state capitalists use financing to gain access to natural resources and widespread influence. In so doing, they subvert the semblance of a level playing field by ignoring international transparency standards laid out by the Organisation for Economic Co-operation and Development (OECD). As Fred P. Hochberg, chair of the US Export-Import Bank, recently argued, there "is a vast and growing pool of unregulated government export finance that threatens to undercut US companies around the word. The market increasingly resembles the wild west, where rules are followed loosely, if at all."[18]

Again, China is perhaps the most aggressive player in this game. With an undervalued renminbi, subsidy and investment policies (such as mandatory joint ventures and licensing deals) that benefit Chinese firms, and the transfer of Western technology to Chinese industries, Chinese firms are advantaged not only in China but also in the global marketplace.[19] This advantage is seen in industries from solar panel production and wind turbines to high-speed rail and aircraft manufacturing. In these cases, early partnerships with Western firms have resulted in indigenous manufacturing capabilities that are beginning to compete with Western firms and put Chinese firms at the center of these global markets. The Chinese government imposed a 70 percent local content requirement on both wind turbines and high-speed rail projects, and it limits foreign ownership of new high-speed rail companies to 49 percent.[20] The policies have increasingly marginalized multinational companies while Chinese companies and national champions gained market share. Chinese solar panel companies' share of global production has gone from 9 percent to 48 percent, increasing fiftyfold from 2005 to 2010.[21] China's foreign exchange reserves were $2.85 trillion at the end of 2010.[22] China's Export-Import Bank and Development Bank have used these reserves to lend to the developing world, lending more than $110 billion in long-term loans to other developing countries in 2009 and 2010, thus exceeding World Bank lending for the same period.[23]

China has not only wielded the influence of its markets to advantage its own companies, with stringent investment requirements such as domestic partnership or licensing deals, but has also begun to use a process similar to that of the interagency Committee on Foreign Investment in the United States (CFIUS) to vet investments in certain sensitive industries and areas of the Chinese economy.[24] Finally, analysts have noted that China has begun to use its investment and commercial weight to embed itself in Taiwan and to influence the debate about unification with China.[25] In June 2012, the Bank of China established a bank branch in Taipei, marking the first time a mainland Chinese bank was granted a license for expansion into Taiwan. The governor of the bank estimated that it would be able to lend 220 yuan, approximately $35 billion, to Taiwanese businesses over the course of the next three years.

In contrast to China's aggressive play, on most economic playing fields America too often remains on the sidelines. In the race for resources around the world, especially the developing world, the Chinese have been willing to allow for loss-leading investments to secure necessary resources for their national security.

In Iraq, the United States and its allies have spilled precious blood and spent billions of dollars to topple Saddam Hussein, reconstruct an Iraqi economy and polity, and build a cohesive security infrastructure. Iraq's oil is also a source of investment opportunities and resource wealth for the private sector and global oil markets. US oil companies, however, are not taking advantage of the Iraqi oil market; nor have they profited, as had been predicted by much of the world. On the contrary, most American oil companies—other than ExxonMobil, in concert with Royal Dutch Shell and other partners—are not major players and do not have calls on Iraqi oil.[26]

Chinese oil companies, in contrast, are poised to profit from the US investment in the country. For example, in a highly anticipated auction in 2009 for the rights to pump Iraqi oil—as US military helicopters hovered overhead—the Iraqi oil minister announced winning bids for Russian, Chinese, French, and British firms. None of the eleven contracts went to the United States. Chinese companies are also poised to take advantage of other sectors of the Iraqi economy, such as the construction (especially the cement industry) and infrastructure sectors.[27] On July 17, 2012, a consortium led by LUKOIL—a Russian oil giant—signed a preliminary contract for the rights to explore oil fields in Iraq's southern Block 10.

In Afghanistan, the United States is unprepared to take advantage of nearly $1 trillion in unexplored mineral wealth—including valuable raw materials such as lithium, gold, copper, and cobalt. Beyond short-term profits, mining activity could become the "backbone of the Afghan economy," laying the foundations for a new silk road and thereby tying the economies of the region to exploding markets in South and East Asia as well as Europe.[28] Instead, China is investing heavily in this new industry and is willing to sustain initial losses for the sake of its long-term extraction and economic plan. The result is that Chinese state-owned mining companies are now exploiting copper reserves worth billions of dollars under NATO's protection. As Robert Kaplan, senior fellow at the Center for a New American Security and correspondent for *The Atlantic*, has noted, "China has its eyes on some of the world's last untapped deposits of copper, iron, gold, uranium, and precious gems, and is willing to take big risks in one of the most violent countries to secure them."[29]

Challenges to American Financial Power

Aside from the challenge to American economic predominance, the current environment involves three significant trends that undercut America's use of its financial power. The use of new currencies and technologies outside the formal financial system, through the Internet, and with less and less accountability and transparency undercuts the ability to track money flows with traditional means. At the same time, rogue actors are coalescing around a common goal of circumventing and undermining US financial pressure and using financial weapons themselves. Finally, the US dollar—and its predominance—is a target for competitors and those who bemoan the world's reliance on the dollar as the accepted reserve and trading currency as the central element of US financial power. All of this is happening as the complexity of the global financial system increases, with more financial products and ways of investing and moving money that make tracking and controlling legitimate financial activity more difficult.

The current environment—aided by the cloak of anonymity provided by the Internet and the complexity of a global financial system—allows nefarious actors to collude in their activities— quietly and surreptitiously. Iran, for example, is known to use terrorist and militia proxies, such as Hezbollah and Shia militias in Iraq, to extend its influence. Russian intelligence is understood to have close ties to Russian and Eurasian organized crime. China is alleged to use legions of college-aged students as hackers to help drive the cyber-espionage attacking Western, Asian, and Indian systems.

These actors have new digital tools at their disposal to elude the reach of anti-money-laundering and counter-terrorist-financing efforts. For example, bitcoin (BTC) is a digital currency transferred through peer-to-peer networks on the Internet. The software, an early implementation of the idea of "crypto-currency," uses cryptography rather than central authorities to issue and transfer money. The result is that transactions are cheap, accounts cannot be frozen (unless users keep bitcoins in a separate third-party online wallet service), and there are no prerequisites or arbitrary limits for use. Payments are anonymous, identified only by users' various chosen bitmap addresses. Transactions are irreversible and can be received at any time, even if the user's computer is off. Bitcoin uses open-source software, so anybody can examine the codes of transactions and use the crypto-keys to ensure that no one pays for multiple transactions with the same money. An April 2012 FBI report evaluating bitcoin use and exchange rates (currently about $15 for one bitcoin) identified bitcoins as an increasingly attractive option for cyber-criminals and other illicit groups. The report concluded that criminals will increasingly exploit bitcoins, using malware to steal the digital currency, as well as botnets to generate new currency without preexisting value. The potential for illicit use of bitcoins will only increase as the currency grows in popularity and the exchange rate stabilizes.[30]

Other nontraditional currencies offer criminals and terrorist groups similar opportunities for theft and anonymous movement of money. "Linden" dollars are the virtual currency for the world of Second Life, a digital alternate reality, the first virtual currency to float. They are traded on the LindeX exchange, which is run by the Linden Lab, the creators of Second Life, and can be exchanged for real-world currency. By 2010, user transactions on the LindeX exchange topped $567 million in Linden dollars and users cashed Linden dollars into $55 million in US dollars.

"Ven" is the digital currency of the social networking community Hub Culture, which operates by invite and includes physical "pavilions" where members meet and collaborate. Members from different countries can exchange a wide array of goods and services in ven at a single global price within the pavilion communities as well as online. Although in 2007 the ven was originally given a fixed exchange rate (10 ven to the dollar), it is now a floating currency and was recently tied to carbon futures, making it one of the world's first "green" currencies.

Bartering has also become a more active way of circumventing the classic financial systems used in local or international trade. Barter exchanges facilitate trades between parties by assigning members "trading credits" equal to the values of goods and services. These credits function similarly to money. Members can exchange goods for credits and use the credits in future transactions. ITEX, the country's largest barter network, which is based in Seattle and boasts more than 24,000 members, charges both a subscription fee ($20 per month) and a transaction fee (6 percent for online trades, 7.5 percent for in-person transactions). Its trading credits are called "ITEX dollars." The country's five hundred bartering exchanges have become enormously popular in the wake of the financial crisis, which both limited access to cash and eroded trust in banks for many people. The International Reciprocal Trade Association estimates the annual US bartering market at around $12 billion. Many participants prefer bartering because it encourages local purchases, links businesses with customers they would not otherwise have found, and increases their ability to sell surplus goods or services. Many communities now use local currencies and Local Exchange Trading Systems (LETS), community-specific systems based on mutual credit. A Community Exchange System (CES) offers a global alternative to LETS, setting up a much larger currency and trading marketplace that operates in a similar fashion.

Just as nonstate actors are willing to leverage new digital technologies, states are increasingly willing to leverage nonstate actors for nefarious purposes. Journalist Moisés Naím has written about the rise and threat of Mafia states—countries that look and act like criminal organizations. The increasing convergence of financial interests between criminal networks and certain nation-states represents an alliance of financial rogues that threatens the international system. States are able to leverage the resources and reach of networked organizations while claiming an arm's-length distance from their nefarious activities. If coordinated, those alliances could target the economic vulnerabilities of the United States.[31]

Directed Threats and Alliances of Financial Rogues

Nonstate actors have been quick to recognize and prepare for the coming age of economic and financial warfare. The treasure trove of documents found in Osama bin Laden's Abbottabad compound spoke of a strategic strike at the economy of the United States by hitting oil tankers and critical energy infrastructure. Indeed, Al Qaeda and its associated movements have focused their rhetoric and strategy more and more on bleeding and bankrupting America.[32] Part of this strategy involves killing the United States with a thousand cuts by baiting US overreaction and overspending. Al Qaeda in the

Arabian Peninsula (AQAP) has labeled this "Operation Hemor-rhage." Another part of this strategy involves hitting key targets and vulnerabilities at a time when the US and global economy is weak-ened, so as to prolong and exacerbate economic malaise. Energy nodes, transportation chokepoints, and ports around the world pro-vide terrorists and nefarious actors with ample opportunity to shock the interconnected international commercial system. Al Qaeda attempted to do just this in 2006, with the failed attack on the enor-mous Saudi oil facility at Abqaiq, as well as in 2002, with an attack on the French oil tanker *MV Limburg* off the coast of Yemen.

International organized crime syndicates have expanded the money-laundering operations that have helped fuel their growth and global financial reach, making them more layered and more varied in their use of investment vehicles.[33] Such groups not only understand how to profit from the international system but also recognize that certain types of investments and influence can shield their activities and leadership from law enforcement and political pressure. Translated into a more aggressive posture, such groups and potential terrorist allies could see opportunities in controlling certain businesses or wielding influence over particular markets and states, distorting the political frameworks in which they operate through corruption, intimidation, and deepening influence.

As these criminal groups grow more interconnected in ways that transcend national boundaries, such networks are gaining influence in strategically vital markets that could impact the accessibility to and stability of these markets. In addition, the ability of such groups to provide their infrastructure and expertise to others (including terrorists)—whether through access to fraudulent travel documents or access to nuclear material—raises the specter of alliances of con-venience and profit aligned dangerously against the United States.[34]

These unholy alliances already exist in some cases. For example, drug trade and human trafficking provided most of the finances for the Mumbai attack.[35] The Treasury continues to identify and desig-nate entities in certain jurisdictions—such as Belarus—that are pro-

viding weapons and financial facilitation to sanctioned countries—
such as Syria.

Attack on the Dollar?

Attendant to this crisis of fiscal legitimacy are increasing challenges
to the primacy of the US dollar. The standing of the dollar allows
the United States to shape the global economic and political system
and offers it greater influence abroad, greater flexibility at home,
and greater insulation from international crises.[36] For those who
would downplay the benefits of dollar dominance, the British experience is instructive. Prior to World War II, the British pound sterling was the primary international currency, thereby allowing
Britain to finance military expenditures and manage its wartime
debt. Once the sterling was eclipsed by the dollar in the postwar
years, Britain was no longer able to finance its war debt, a problem
that contributed to its economic decline and exacerbated persistent
financial crises during the 1960s.[37]

The sustainability of the dollar as the leading global reserve currency has been a near constant concern since the 1960s. During this
time, foreign dollar reserves began to outgrow US gold reserves, and
many international actors began to question the United States' ability to convert dollars to gold at the fixed official rate specified by
Bretton Woods. As this confidence declined, speculative attacks
against the dollar abounded. The United States eventually aban-
doned the gold standard, but the dollar has retained its dominance
ever since. Thus, anyone decrying the dollar's current strength risks
crying wolf.

Nevertheless, in the wake of the Great Recession, there are convincing signs that we are headed for a restructuring of the international monetary system as faith in the dollar faltered. The reality is
that countries are now questioning the wisdom of carrying debt
obligations solely in dollars, and they are moving toward baskets of
currencies and alternate trading conventions and currencies to

reduce their reliance on the dollar. The portion of global reserves in dollars declined from approximately 72 percent in 2000 to 62 percent in 2012 as the rest of the world attempted to decouple itself from the US economy.

The Chinese have begun to use their own currency, the renminbi, and reserves in certain trading situations and with some partners with more frequency. China recently completed a $1.08 billion currency swap deal with Kazakhstan and has similar arrangements with Argentina, Belarus, Hong Kong, Indonesia, Malaysia, South Korea, Ireland, Argentina, and Iceland. China has also reached agreements with Russia and Brazil to gradually eliminate the dollar from bilateral trade.[38] All five of the BRICS (Brazil, Russia, India, China, and South Africa, all of which have large, rapidly growing economies) have taken significant steps toward trading in their own currencies, diversifying their foreign exchange reserves, and hedging their bets against the growing instability of the dollar and the euro.

Prior to the G8 summit of 2009, China, Russia, and India explicitly called for an end to dollar dominance. On January 7, 2011, the International Monetary Fund (IMF) produced a paper outlining a plan for replacing the dollar with Special Drawing Rights (SDRs)—IMF-issued currency defined in terms of the weighted average of the dollar, euro, yen, and pound. The plan would create a liquid bond market for SDRs and thereby elevate the IMF to the de facto role of the world central bank.

This portends a world of multiple reserve currencies, one in which the dollar serves as the primary rudder, steering a steady course to prevent erratic devaluations, but in which the currents are more volatile than they have been for decades. In this scenario, the euro, the British pound, the Swiss franc, and the renminbi would play enhanced roles as regional currencies for Europe and Asia, thereby limiting US influence in these areas.

A more dangerous scenario is an intensification of what James Rickards has termed "Currency War III." According to Rickards, this war began in 2010 and involved competitive devaluations of the yuan, dollar, and euro. These concerns were echoed publicly in 2013 by finance ministries and central banks. It is important to note that the biggest threat is not that yuan devaluation directly damages the US economy. The true threat is systemic. The current China-US monetary relationship is unsustainable and brings the fragility of the entire international monetary system into sharp relief. As Rickards contended, by 2011 both countries were "locked in a trillion-dollar financial embrace, essentially a monetary powder keg that could be detonated by either side if the currency wars spiraled out of control."[39] Economic historian Niall Ferguson has dubbed this presently symbiotic yet ultimately dysfunctional relationship "Chimerica." In order to maintain employment for its massive population, China must keep its exports attractive to American consumers and keep the yuan tied to the dollar. As such, China must continue to buy dollar assets and increase its account surpluses. It is caught in a "dollar trap." China's current exchange-rate policy thus ironically helps to preserve dollar dominance.[40] Chimerica is, for Ferguson, highly unstable. A sudden deterioration in political relations, perhaps stemming from a clash over natural resources or Taiwan, could trigger a major war and a corresponding collapse of the international financial system.[41]

Currently, China is the most competitive player in the so-called currency wars. Yet all major powers are attempting to influence the relative value of their currencies, a ruthless competition that places the entire global monetary system at risk. The currency war need not devolve into actual war for it to prove disastrous. A small but systemically critical event—such as the collapse of the Spanish bond market—could ignite a widespread loss of confidence in paper currencies and a massive transition to hard assets (gold) led by a shrewd and forward-leaning competitor state such as Russia or China.[42]

Even if one doubts the likelihood of such a crisis, China is nonetheless taking steps to internationalize the renminbi and thereby enhance its power relative to the dollar. This is happening in two ways. First, by purchasing sovereign debt of other Asian countries, China pushes up the value of these regional currencies and incentivizes its neighbors to reciprocate by buying Chinese debt in order to devalue their currencies against the yuan. The net result is a greater international role for the renminbi. Second, the Chinese government is finalizing programs that would allow select foreign financial institutions to invest their renminbi deposits in Chinese equity and bond markets. With increased stakes in renminbi-based businesses, these foreign firms will have more reasons to promote the renminbi so that they can reap the benefits of renminbi internationalization.[43]

Though the dollar remains predominant for now and seems to be the currency of choice amid economic turmoil in Europe, it—along with American financial predominance—is coming under direct assault.

Growing US Systemic Vulnerabilities

Perhaps most troubling, the United States faces unique systemic vulnerabilities and internal weaknesses that adversaries in the coming financial wars could exploit. The United States has been the driver of a globalized financial and commercial order, but it is also more dependent than other countries upon the economic and digital systems for trade, financing, and information on which that order has been built.[44] As such, although the United States is well equipped to fight kinetic wars, it remains uniquely vulnerable to financial warfare.

Consider first that the United States finds itself increasingly vulnerable to dependency on foreign sources of funding for its fiscal survival. Foreign investors hold more than 50 percent of the publicly held and traded US securities.[45] With the Chinese and Japanese owning 45 percent of US debt, and increasing doubts about American resolve to solve its fiscal and debt crises, the opinions and investment decisions of foreign governments—particularly China—become central to our national survival.[46] The Chinese senior leadership has articulated these concerns in recent statements. Standard & Poor's decision to downgrade the credit rating for the United States was another manifestation of these worries. But China—as both the United States' primary foreign creditor and its greatest geopolitical competitor—is beginning to carry greater economic and political weight directly with the United States. China's economic power derives from the size of its market and its potential, the US debt it holds, and Chinese willingness and ability to penetrate developing markets with massive private and public investments. Taken to the extreme, this accumulating economic power could be leveraged to weaken or limit US influence and reach.

These dependencies move well beyond the world of global debt, finance, and macroeconomics. American dependence on the global trading system has grown over time, with oil, food, crucial minerals, and manufactured goods streaming into the United States from around the world—and a diminished US manufacturing base to make the goods US companies and customers need. America's crippling dependence on foreign sources of oil in recent decades is well known—the United States imported approximately 45 percent of its oil from a world market where unfriendly countries and competitors played a major role in 2011.[47] Iran, Venezuela, Russia, Qatar, and other countries whose interests may not align with those of the United States maintain an ability to disrupt supplies or affect price fluctuations in ways that impact the US economy. Three-quarters of crude-oil reserves are controlled by state-owned or -controlled companies such as Gazprom in Russia, CNPC in China, NIOC in Iran, and PDVSA in Venezuela, and the Organization of the Petroleum Exporting Countries (OPEC) controls 78 percent of the world's conventional reserves. Large multinational companies—including ExxonMobil, BP, and Chevron—produce only 10 percent of the world's oil and gas.[48] The result is that the United States borrows $1 billion per day in order to import oil. The energy landscape—and

America's dependence on foreign oil—however, are changing dramatically with the revolution in shale gas exploration and America's abundant natural gas resources. This development portends a historic geo-economic opportunity for the United States, which can take advantage of the shift toward energy independence and the ability to leverage oil and gas exports to stabilize markets and assist allies.

Less understood is the concentration of sophisticated manufacturing capabilities in sectors such as electronics, aerospace, biotechnology, and energy-specific products in foreign sources. Richard Elkus Jr., founder and CEO of several technology companies, sees this as a fundamental economic vulnerability for America's future. He has argued that the loss of a manufacturing base in such sectors has not only made us more dependent on overseas nodes of manufacturing (namely Japan, South Korea, and China) but also less able to innovate in design and manufacturing in a wide range of new technologies for the long term.[49] With even more concentration of specialized manufacturing, these single points of failure represent potential vulnerabilities for the international system that could be exploited.[50] For example, in 2002, an eleven-day shutdown of US ports on the West Coast—which handle 60 percent of US maritime imports and exports by value—due to a labor dispute was estimated as costing at least half a billion dollars, with one estimate suggesting losses of almost $20 billion.[51]

The devastating earthquake and tsunami in Japan in March 2011 closed 130 assembly plants and disrupted electricity supplies. Japan's economy—which produces 60 percent of the world's silicon wafers, 57 percent of the imager sensors, and 70 percent of the binding for lithium ion batteries—struggled to produce components used in electronics, batteries, cars, and computer systems around the world. Chairman of the Federal Reserve Bank Ben Bernanke commented that the earthquake disrupted supply chains enough to force some automobile companies to restrain production for a time.[52] The effect was moderate and temporary, yet nevertheless a reminder of the single points of systemic failure that are the by-product of the increasing commercial entanglement of the world's economies.

Such supplier and supply-chain dependencies translate directly into the military and defense realm. For example, the US military remains highly dependent on Global Positioning System (GPS) and other satellite-based platforms at a time when its space power is increasingly contested. Moreover, the United States imports 100 percent of its gallium, an element used in solar cells and semiconductor chips and an important component of satellites and radar.[53] The bid of a Chinese state-controlled company to produce the next presidential helicopter prompted the Committee on Foreign Investment in the United States to produce new legislation restricting Chinese companies from bidding on US defense contracts.[54] More recently, President Obama, acting on CFIUS's recommendation, prohibited the Chinese-owned Ralls Corporation from acquiring four wind-farm project companies located in the vicinity of restricted air space at Naval Weapons Systems Training Facility Boardman in Oregon.[55] These concerns led the Obama administration to issue a national strategy to secure global supply-chain security in January 2012.

Perhaps the biggest source of US vulnerability is not in terms of physical resources but rather in virtual systems. As former director of national intelligence Mike McConnell noted before the Senate, "If we were in a cyberwar today, the United States would lose. This is not because we do not have talented people or cutting-edge technology; it is because we are simply the most dependent and the most vulnerable."[56] The Internet contributed an estimated 15 percent to the US GDP between 2004 and 2009, and US companies captured 35 percent of total Internet revenues earned by the top 250 Internet-related companies in the world.[57] In a recent speech, General Keith Alexander, the head of the National Security Agency and Cyber Command, pointing to a seventeen-fold increase in attacks against US infrastructure between 2009 and 2011, graded US preparedness to withstand a cyber-attack against its critical network infrastructure as "around a 3" on a 10-point scale.[58]

The cyber-domain is the newest "final" frontier of geopolitical competition. The low-grade cyber-battle in which Google and China have engaged, with Google fighting off mass penetrations and theft of its data (including proprietary information as well as information tied to the identities of Chinese dissidents), shows that this is a realm in which state and nonstate actors can intermingle and do battle anonymously or via proxy. In addition, the cyber-realm is one in which infrastructure can be disrupted remotely. The globalized cyber supply chain can be easily manipulated. Since hard drives, chips, and the backbone of the cyber-infrastructure (including the increasing reliance on cloud computing) come from overseas, especially from East Asia, this is a particular concern for the United States.

Given the criminal opportunities that abound in this world, it is no surprise that cyber-intrusions and attacks are increasing at a devastating rate—with billions of dollars' worth of intellectual property and value stolen digitally every year. It is estimated that the cost of cyber-crime to the global economy could be more than $1 trillion annually.[59] Over the past few years, economic cyber-intrusions and targeted searches and attacks have hit the International Monetary Fund, Lockheed Martin's information systems (via stolen SecureID data), Google's mainframes, Sony's Playstation data, Bank of America, and Citibank. On August 3, 2011, the computer security firm McAfee issued a report revealing the largest "cyber-attack to date," which had targeted the data and systems of seventy-two organizations and companies around the world for over five years—enabled by an unidentified state actor presumed to be China. According to McAfee's vice president of threat research, Dmitri Alperovitch, "what is happening to all this data is still largely an open question. However, if even a fraction of it is used to build better competing products or beat a competitor at a key negotiation (due to having stolen the other team's playbook), the loss represents a massive economic threat."[60]

This McAfee report was preceded by a February 8, 2011, report, also by McAfee, detailing the hacking of several US oil companies from 2008 to 2010—with the cyber-intruders likely coming from China and having found their way into sensitive research and development files. This was the first time that such a massive intrusion and economic espionage operation had been reportedly directed at US oil company computers. US state secrets were not at risk, but valuable economic and oil resource research was. This research was vital to bidding by US oil companies on oil-field rights in Iraq, Sudan, Ghana, and other lucrative sites around the world.[61] In the words of General Keith Alexander, cyber-attacks on the United States are resulting in the "greatest transfer of wealth in history."[62]

The Coming Cyber Financial Wars

The blending of financial and cyber warfare represents the new frontier. Evidence suggests that state-sponsored cyber warfare is intensifying as part of a growing "cyber arms race."[63] The most prominent cyber-battle to date was the use of the Stuxnet virus— believed to have been jointly developed by the United States and Israel—to sabotage Iranian nuclear facilities, and its subsequent "escape" on the Internet.[64] But interestingly, the cyber-battles of today are beginning to meld with the strategies and tactics of financial warfare. This is also a theater of battle in which multiple actors can align for a common purpose—combining state and nonstate proxies in the cyber-domain. A recently deployed cyber-weapon clearly illustrates the players, payoffs, and perils of cyber-espionage and warfare through economic and digital means.

On August 9, 2012, the Moscow-based security firm Kaspersky Lab announced that it had discovered a new "Gauss" virus (named after a file name in its codebase). Kaspersky Lab has historical connections to Russian intelligence and has made a practice of outing and analyzing computer viruses—often using crowdsourcing to help break codes. The Gauss virus had infected approximately 2,500 computers, the majority of which—1,660, to be exact, including 483 in Israel and 261 in the Palestinian territories—are tied to Lebanese banks, with the first attacks going back to at least September 2011. Once the infection took hold, Gauss was capable of capturing and transmitting detailed records of information, such as browser histories, cookies, profiles, and system configurations. Once the virus was discovered, its communications were shut down, but not disabled. Apparently, they are still lying dormant, awaiting activation by an unknown controlling source.

Gauss's complexity and sophistication have led Kaspersky's experts to conclude that the virus is a state-sponsored descendant of Stuxnet, coming from the same "factory." It is able to track flows of money and tap into infected computers. But it also carries an encrypted "payload" that targets specific systems, much like the Stuxnet virus. Perhaps most revealing is that Gauss shares critical coding and platform features with the Flame virus, another data-mining virus and Stuxnet family member capable of extensive surveillance of infected computers that was discovered on Iranian computers in May 2012. But whereas Flame, which infected only seven hundred computers, cast a wide net toward all types of data, Gauss's focus is more attenuated, capturing primarily transaction data from a handful of specific Lebanese banks.[65] Indeed, unlike typical nonstate cyber-criminal malware, which tends to target a large number of small banks, Gauss targets a small number of large banks.

Gauss is so complex that Kaspersky has not been able to determine the function of its payload (what it has designated "resource 100"), though the firm suspects that it could trigger the destruction of critical infrastructure or some other high-profile target. For more details, Kaspersky has crowd-sourced the solution, asking freelance hackers to crack the payload encryption and publishing the first 32 bytes of each encrypted section in Gauss to facilitate the process. Previously, Kaspersky successfully used crowd-sourcing to identify the programming language used in the state-sponsored DuQu malware.[66]

In light of the target, the claim of state sponsorship makes sense. Lebanon is "something like the Switzerland of the modern Middle East," wrote Katherine Maher, a digital rights security expert, in *The Atlantic.* "More than 60 banks manage nearly $120 billion in private deposits in a country of 4.3 million people, and account for roughly 35 percent of the country's economic activity." Lebanese banks are among the most secretive in the world, and their opacity has long been a concern for US financial regulators seeking to disrupt money launderers and terrorist financiers. The Lebanese banking system has come under direct fire as a financial way station for Iran, Syria, Hezbollah, and illicit financial flows.[67]

With Stuxnet and Flame, the target was a rogue regime's nuclear program. With Gauss, the target seems to be the banks of an important financial center in the Middle East, where rogue elements leverage the banking facilities. Western states' interest in Lebanon's private sector has traditionally focused on "know your customer" and transaction data rules. Gauss now ups the ante with aggressive information collection and destructive payload delivery.[68] All of this suggests that states are willing to use cyber-weapons to impact the banking system and to engage in open cyber financial warfare. If Stuxnet and Flame represent the more "conventional" forms of cyber warfare, then Gauss is akin to financial counterinsurgency: long-term, low-grade, persistent conflict rather than quick, high-profile battles with decisive results. This is a messy process, one with no clear line between enemies and friends or between private and public interests. The process also raises a host of questions about the ethics of cyber warfare and about the overall stability of the global financial system. How does such a financial system go about its business in the shadow of an indecipherable payload that could potentially sabotage the system's entire infrastructure? Perhaps the very existence and broader awareness of the virus is good enough—with the intended goal simply to engender a loss of faith and confidence in the Beirut financial system. Without trust, no financial center can last.

Gauss seems to represent the leading edge of cyber financial warfare. This is a type of conflict in which there are no ceasefires, no clear rules, and no uniforms to identify the combatants. What is more, despite the fact that the United States starts with an enormous technological advantage, its size, relative transparency, and legal constraints may place it at a disadvantage on the cyber-battlefield. Indeed, this is a battlefield defined by potential asymmetric power disparities. An individual hacker can emerge as a cyber-power, one whose relative isolation, anonymity, and small footprint is a source of strength.

The Iranian government has entered the fray in response to the financial assault on its economy and currency. In September 2012, a Middle Eastern hacker group identifying itself as Izz ad-Din al-Qassam Cyber Fighters conducted a massive denial-of-service attack against the electronic banking operations of JP Morgan Chase, Citigroup, PNC Bank, Wells Fargo, US Bancorp, and Bank of America. By increasing fake demands on the banks' sites at a rate some ten to twenty times higher than average denial-of-service attacks, the new group was able temporarily to suspend access to checking accounts, mortgages, and other bank services. Perhaps more troubling is that the mysterious group warned these financial institutions that an attack was imminent, but the banks proved unable to stop it. Though Izz ad-Din al-Qassam is also the name of the military wing of Hamas, Senator Joseph Lieberman, then chairman of the Homeland Security Committee, argued that the attacks were connected to the Iranian Islamic Revolutionary Guard Corps–Qods Force.[69] Major banks, including non-US banks, continue to be attacked by intense denial-of-service operations.

At the same time, hackers calling themselves the "Cutting Sword of Justice" attacked the computers and control systems of Saudi Arabia's national oil company, Aramco—which produces a tenth of the world's oil supply—for weeks. In December 2012, the Saudi government admitted that the virus, dubbed "Shamoon," had destroyed 30,000 computers and wiped out hard drives, but did not succeed in disrupting production or operations.

We can expect viruses far more advanced than Gauss or Shamoon to emerge shortly—the methods of cyber-war will continue to evolve rapidly in sophistication. We can also expect the pace of cyber-attacks to pick up. The technology of cyber warfare is evolving at an exponential rate. Also, unlike traditional combat, cyber warfare has few normative restraints to limit its escalation and few controls to counter its proliferation to nonstate actors.

The Gauss incident highlights the vulnerability that is found in fragile financial markets. Regulators cannot keep up with the pace of growth taking place in the speed, level of anonymity, and volume of trading. In what is described as a "race to zero," trading is moving faster and faster—and further away from the gaze and capacity of national regulators. According to trade negotiator Harald Malmgren and Mark Stys, it has gone "from trading in milliseconds (thousandths of a second) a couple of years ago to trading in microseconds (millionths of a second) now, and for cutting edge traders, pursuit in trading in picoseconds (trillionths of a second)."[70] High-frequency trading firms "represent approximately 2% of the 20,000 or so trading firms operating in the U.S. markets . . . [but] account for 73% of all U.S. equity trading volume," according to one trading technology consultant.[71] During the "Flash Crash" episode of 2010, a trading algorithm dumped 75,000 futures contracts valued at $4.1 billion on the market in a twenty-minute period. The losses were staggering, causing a 600-point fall in the Dow and erasing $862 billion from the value of equities before an automatic circuit breaker paused trading.[72]

Though the mass volume of such trading provides a buffer against manipulation, the sheer speed and anonymity of the cross-border trading across asset classes increase the risks and the potential for markets to be manipulated and cornered by savvy criminal and nefarious actors—for profit or other purposes.[73] The World Economic Forum's Global Risks 2008 report highlighted the paradox that inheres in the international financial system: "While the financial system has been made more efficient and stable in normal times, it is now also more prone to excessive instability in really bad times," the report said. "But changes in the financial markets, while providing many benefits, have also created new and unforeseen risks which may be more susceptible to exogenous shocks (such as geopolitical risk) or internal factors (such as speculative bubbles)."[74]

Such manipulation or shaping of markets could be amplified by the flows of information so readily available via the Internet and twenty-four-hour business channels around the world. The anonymity and speed of trade, combined with lax US laws and regulatory oversight on beneficial ownership of companies and controlling interests of offshore investment funds, adds to the potential that criminals and nefarious actors could use the US financial system not only to launder proceeds but to manipulate, corner, or extort via market control or penetration. The estimated amount of laundered funds that make their way through US banks ranges conservatively between $250 billion and $500 billion a year.[75] Some estimates suggest that the numbers are even higher, reaching into the trillion-dollar range. Thus, strategies to manipulate markets could focus principally on shaping the perception of the markets and then leveraging the market swings to profit or destroy value. It is in part for this reason that the Securities and Exchange Commission (SEC) put new regulations in place to prevent uncovered short selling such as that seen during the financial crisis of 2008.[76]

The coming financial battles may find their most serious theater and articulation in cyberspace, with the vulnerability of the financial sector and the international system of trading and commerce potentially at risk.

Preparing for the Coming Financial Wars

The United States faces direct challenges to its economic predominance and financial influence, and it is unprepared to defend itself from the looming external threats and internal vulnerabilities. Yet it should not imitate state authoritarian models in its structures and systems, nor should it seek to retreat from the world or globalization for fear of deepening dependencies. Instead, the United States must recognize this new global ecosystem and take full advantage of the opportunities that abound.

The United States can strengthen its security by reconceptualizing and defending its economic health and power. Though ensuring that America's fiscal house is in order will be important—as Admiral Mike Mullen, former chairman of the Joint Chiefs of Staff, has stated, "the most significant threat to our national security is our debt"[77]—that is not all that needs to be done. And economic health means more than ensuring that American companies (especially in key manufacturing sectors) and workers can be competitive in the global marketplace—though that is also imperative. What is needed is a strategic framework that accounts for the emerging economic security environment of the twenty-first century. The United States needs to redesign how it thinks about, treats, and addresses national economic security to prepare for the coming financial wars.

Redefining National Economic Security

The first task is to define national economic security—tying economic vulnerabilities and opportunities together to account for new geopolitical realities. Past definitions describe the obvious reality that a country's economic strength and influence form a fundamental part of the nation's geopolitical standing and power. These definitions have also focused on more specific threats and risks the United States faces to its economy and the dollar from competitor states and nefarious networks.[78] Yet in light of the growing overlap between classic national security vulnerabilities and economic and commercial interests and influence, past definitions are insufficient. A working definition might be as follows:

National economic security in the twenty-first century is the ability of the United States to project its power and influence through economic, financial, and commercial means and defend against systemic and specific risks and threats derived from America's economic vulnerabilities.

This holistic articulation of national economic security requires a recognition that in an age of globalization, free flow of information, and digital dependencies, the economic and national security spheres overlap more than ever before. National economic security must encompass a wide spectrum of activities and policies, ranging from macrolevel factors, such as national debt and GDP, to specific threats with economic repercussions, such as terrorist attacks on Wall Street or against US ports. It entails obvious defense-related and economic risks, including cyber-defense and supply-chain vulnerabilities, but also includes systemic threats to the financial system, market manipulation, long-term cyber-espionage and cyber-attacks, and resource access and investment reach in critical markets.

An encompassing definition must acknowledge that in the twenty-first century, our potential enemies are not easily categorized, but they could easily array against US interests by using the economic, digital, and global systems for their purposes. The nature of economic warfare now involves an environment where a single strategic act—enabled with low barriers to entry, digital connectivity, and the promise of relative anonymity—can have enormous global ripple effects. This danger may require the US government and US companies to operate differently. We must recognize that US economic interests—both public and private—are missing long-term opportunities, while international competitors are playing a different economic game entirely.

To date, such threats and risks have not been wholly ignored, but neither have they been viewed systemically or holistically as part of a new national economic security ecosystem that may require the US government and US companies to change the way they do business. The rhetoric of paying attention to our core economic strengths must be matched with a strategy that sees economic and financial power as central to national security and a concerted effort to apply that strategy. We must redefine financial intelligence and public-private collaboration and must refocus our international systems, alliances, and doctrines.

Reaffirming Core US Principles

This new national economic security framework requires a recommitment to the core economic principles that the framework is designed to protect.

The United States should eschew protectionism and retrenchment, remaining the vanguard of the global capitalist system and global trade rules and practices that reinforce trade liberalization.[79] The United States is neither China nor Russia, and it should not seek to emulate their practices. This forces the United States to continue to respect the divide between the public and private sectors while finding creative ways of aligning those interests for the promotion of American economic influence and power.

The United States should also continue to promote and enforce its standards abroad in the economic sphere. Mercantilist threats cannot be countered via mercantilism. But they do demand a muscular, activist strategy that protects the US financial industry and the liberal economic order. This includes enforcement of free trade rules, reciprocal investment opportunities, and anti-money-laundering and sanctions policies. Nowhere is this more significant than in the anti-corruption field, where Chinese and Russian investments with no strings attached can promote corruption in fragile and developing states. This point is particularly important when dealing with economies that rely on extractive industries and the energy sector— where flows of capital can convert societies into kleptocracies.

Setting this new approach into motion then requires a set of policies that recognizes the vulnerabilities and opportunities in this new environment, that takes into account the range of actors and tools that could be leveled against the United States, and that leverages the strategic opportunities therein. Confronting these new realities requires innovative policy, new institutions and doctrines,

new modes of public-private collaboration and international cooperation, and new tools to account for the changes in the geo-
economic ecosystem.

Viewing and Treating the Geo-Economic Landscape Holistically

The US intelligence community should reframe how it treats economic security matters by creating a new national economic security discipline. This would require institutionalizing private outreach
and eliminating current stovepipes between economic, financial,
and commercial expertise and the national security community.

This broadened intelligence view should be matched by a corresponding policy focus on national economic security within the
White House. Though there has always been a connection between
the national security community and international economic issues
like trade and macrolevel policies within the National Security and
Economic Council structures, there is no corresponding policy focus
on national economic security as defined above. Former Deputy
Treasury Secretary Robert Kimmitt and others have argued for making the treasury secretary a statutory member of the National Security
Council to reflect the growing salience of the economic and financial
aspects of national security policy.[80] This policy step would formalize
what has already occurred in practice and is not a sufficient step to
integrate geo-economics into core national security strategies and
deliberations. Other government agencies and the private sector need
a seat at the policymaking table, especially when the United States is
competing abroad for resources and market access.

The growing focus on interrelated systemic risks—to critical
infrastructure and national security systems—should become the
primary focus of the Department of Homeland Security. With its
unique authorities, information, and personnel, already charged
with protecting critical infrastructure and the borders and ports of
entry, the department could forge a post-9/11 view of itself that is
not defined by Al Qaeda or terrorism but instead is focused on pro-

tecting the systems that are critical to the functioning of the nation. This includes the cyber-domain along with the energy, maritime, financial, transport, and other systems that allow the American economy to run. DHS could then begin to shape the way in which the US government addresses these issues, serving as a lead federal agency in concert with the private sector in defending against threats and ensuring systemic redundancy domestically and internationally.

This broader focus on national economic security may require new legislation to create transparency and accountability in the economic and investment space. The broad intent would be to reduce the danger of the United States being blindsided by unseen economic vulnerabilities or nefarious actors using legitimate financial and commercial systems to undermine US interests. An equally important purpose would be to ensure that the United States and the private sector could take full advantage of emergent opportunities. For example, Senator Carl Levin, a Michigan Democrat, has proposed legislation that would require revelation of beneficial ownership of corporate entities formed or operating in the United States. Such legislation would build on existing anti-money-laundering "know your customer" principles and requirements, giving US regulators and law-enforcement agencies better tools for identifying suspicious actors who were controlling companies, supplies, and financial networks operating in or through the United States.

New Means of Public-Private Collaboration

A new economic security approach requires a new paradigm of US public-private engagement and collaboration. This involves an evolution from classic, state-based national security actions toward deeper involvement of the private sector in arenas previously confined to the halls of government, with a commensurate and widening appreciation within governments of the power of markets and the private sector to influence international security. In arenas such as financial sanctions and anti-money-laundering and counter-terrorist-financing programs, the United States has already moved in this direction, relying on the private sector and the ability of financial institutions to act as protective gatekeepers to the financial system by identifying, reporting, and preventing the use of financial facilities by transnational actors and criminals of concern.

The utility of this approach is that it is not based on private-sector altruism or civic duty, but on the self-interest of legitimate financial institutions that want to minimize the risk of facilitating illicit transactions that could bring high regulatory and reputational costs if uncovered. In other economic arenas, this symbiosis takes hold only with great effort, particularly given the private-sector aversion to increased regulatory burdens and associated costs. This means that governments need to check their regulatory practices and work closely to build consistent requirements and regimes across borders to help international financial institutions to operate effectively and efficiently. This challenge will be exacerbated as governments create new regulatory structures and requirements in the wake of the recent financial crisis.

The innovation in public-private coordination is already occurring by necessity in the cyber-domain, with approximately 80 percent of the cyber-infrastructure in private-sector hands. After the attacks on Google servers by Chinese hackers, Google and the National Security Agency began to work together in 2010 to help Google defend against future attacks. In the wake of the massive attacks on US banks in 2012 and continuing into 2013, the National Security Agency has begun a pilot project with the banks to try to track and prevent cyber-attacks. This kind of collaboration opens the door for more creative and widespread public-private cooperation to tackle cyber-threats and serves as a testing ground for such collaboration on broader issues of national economic security.

New Doctrines, International Systems, and Alliances

The United States needs to consider new doctrines that will drive its engagement on these issues and frame new systems and alliances in this intertwined geo-economic landscape. This includes accounting for those who would openly use economic warfare to destroy a country's infrastructure or economy, the growing problem of anonymity and use of proxies via the Internet, and the common dependencies of multinational companies around the world on supply chains and digital and electronic infrastructure.

For instance, if intertwined economies and global systems create vulnerabilities, they may also create barriers for the use of economic weaponry and leverage against US interests. China's deep investment in US Treasuries gives it enormous potential leverage in a confrontation with the United States, yet it has restrained itself from doing anything to undermine the value of the dollar or confidence in the US economic system. Interdependence blunts China's so-called dollar weapon. This suggests that by pursuing a strategy of quasi-bandwagoning with China—embracing interdependence and investing heavily in Chinese industry—the United States can also develop a new doctrine of deterrence by entanglement. With such a doctrine, the United States might set out to convince, cajole, and perhaps even force potential competitor and rival states to adopt a free trade model and practices more consistent with our own.[81]

Importantly, the United States would need to view its relationships —with government and private-sector partners alike—as a vehicle to address some of the more complicated elements of national economic security. Creating alliances and arrangements based not just on trade opportunities or pure security arrangements, but also on shared economic vulnerabilities and strategies, might mitigate some of the risks in the international supply chain and concentrated resource and manufacturing systems.

Such alliances could help shape new international modes of interaction in the global commons. In the context of cyber-security, the Obama administration has set forth a framework for international

cooperation that could serve as the start for such new arrangements—leading to tactical cooperation such as joint international
cyber-forensic teams and to agreements of nonaggression in cyberspace.[82] This could lead to principles of engagement in cyberspace,
rules for addressing anonymous attacks, and new preventive cooperative models, such as the concept of Mutually Assured Support.[83] It
could also enhance current efforts to isolate rogue actors in the international geo-economic system, such as money launderers and terrorist financiers—with countries further unified around labeling and
isolating those who pose threats to the integrity and safety of the
international financial and commercial systems.

Conclusion

In many ways, the United States has taught the world how to use
financial power in the twenty-first century. The United States has
deliberately leveraged US capital markets, the centrality of the dollar, and American ability to set global standards and mores to drive
national security goals. The power of this paradigm is derived from
the centrality and stability of New York as a global financial center,
the importance of dollar-clearing transactions, and the demonstration effects of any regulatory or other steps taken by the United
States or major US financial institutions in the broader international
system. Our competitors have learned from our use of power, and
our enemies have witnessed our vulnerabilities.

Countries such as Russia and China will continue to challenge
the predominance of the US-led international system and the dollar
itself. If such attacks succeed fundamentally, they could potentially
weaken the ability of the United States to affect or move private-
sector decision making in line with national security interests,
regardless of what other governments do. The advent of nuclear
weapons forced scholars and policymakers to rethink their models
and methods for advancing US national security. In a similar way,
the coming financial wars will force the United States to adapt amid

a new geo-economic order defined by globalization and the speed and ease of communication and transnational commerce. In the age of nuclear competition, the United States drew strength from its scientific and technological advantage. But it is becoming increasingly clear that America is losing its competitive edge in the era of economic security. This is particularly troubling in light of the unique advantages it possesses as the vanguard of the international trading and financial system and a hub of innovation and collaboration.

The domain of financial warfare will no longer remain the sole province of American power. A wide array of state and nonstate actors may step up to wield economic power and influence in the twenty-first century. Confronting challenges, seizing opportunities, and minimizing systemic vulnerabilities must therefore proceed as part of a coordinated effort. The United States must begin to play a new and distinctly financial game of geopolitical competition to ensure its security and to seize emerging opportunities. Just as the mistakes leading to 9/11 were deemed a failure of imagination, the inability of the US government to recognize the changed landscape could be considered a collective failure of comprehension.

The financial wars are coming. It is time to redesign a national economic security model to prepare for them. If we fail to do so, the United States risks being left vulnerable and left behind as other competitors race toward the future.

Epilogue: Lessons from the Use of Financial Power

The use of financial power and influence has become an accepted and central tool for protecting and projecting the national security interests of the United States. Just about every day, the US government employs some form of financial pressure—sanctions, financial and diplomatic suasion, regulatory pressure, or prosecution—to address issues in every corner of the globe—from terrorism in the Middle East to the drug wars in Mexico or human smuggling in Asia. The use of financial isolation as a core national security tool has now become deeply embedded in the practices of Western governments. These tools and strategies will not remain the sole province of the West for much longer. As the world changes, we must heed a number of key lessons from the use of these powers.

Tending the Financial Ecosystem

The financial techniques that the US Treasury Department has cultivated over the past decade must be tended carefully if they are to retain their power. Their effectiveness ultimately relies on a global financial, regulatory, and diplomatic ecosystem that rejects rogue financial behavior. That environment must clearly define legitimate financial activity and rules of the road—with rewards for participation and compliance in the legitimate order and guaranteed punishment and isolation for collusion with international rogues.

What's more, illegal or suspect conduct must remain the primary driver for attention and isolation. Though financial suasion may appear to be a tantalizing and powerful tool to achieve political or diplomatic motives, its efficacy will be drastically diminished if diplomatic goals take precedence over conduct-based drivers. Nor should the financial tools be overused. This particular form of financial power is not a silver bullet for each and every national security problem the United States faces, and it should not become the reflexive policy of choice in its maximalist form absent other solutions. It should be viewed as an essential element of creating leverage and shaping the environment, but used in concert with other forms of pressure and influence.

This power relies on continued US leadership, the centrality of the United States as a financial center, and maintenance of the dollar as the world's preferred reserve currency. At the same time, it is a power wielded best when used in conjunction with other tools. It relies principally on the risk aversion and business calculus of the legitimate private sector and the credibility of the financial suasion wielded by the US Treasury and other relevant authorities.

The ecosystem that allows for this form of financial warfare and isolation is resilient but fragile. The forced isolation of more and more actors—and the tendency of the private sector to decline doing business in at-risk sectors and jurisdictions and with suspect actors—raises the possibility of reaching a tipping point where the effectiveness of these tools begins to diminish. This is especially the case when the use of financial sanctions and regulations is used to address a diverse range of diplomatic and political ills and concerns—such as human smuggling, child labor, and human rights abuses. With the threat of financial sanctions, public opprobrium, and an erosion of reputation for doing business with suspect actors, legitimate financial actors—like major international banks—are exiting from problematic markets, "derisking" their operations. This raises concerns that less credible or scrupulous financial actors will step in to fill the vacuum. For authorities, this would entail a potential loss of visibility as certain types of financial activity become murkier and more difficult to detect; for the banks, it would mean even greater pressure to abandon certain segments of the population or regions of the world. We have seen this happening already. Banks that have been stung by enforcement actions and painful, public settlements are beginning to exit markets and business lines wholesale; some of the money-service businesses in North America are struggling to find banking relationships with major banks; and there are embassies that continue to struggle to maintain bank accounts in places like the United States and Switzerland.

An inherent and dynamic tension has emerged between the isolation of suspect behavior from the formal financial system and the incorporation of more of the world into the formal financial system. Going forward, the core principle of isolating and exiling actors from the legitimate financial system needs to be balanced with the need to ensure that rogue actors can be captured and affected by the legitimate financial system.

New technologies and innovative methods of adapting to or evading sanctions will also bedevil US efforts to apply the classic tools of financial suasion. In particular, those financial rogues with enough influence and resources to do so will continue to buy access to global transactions and develop alternative means of engagement. And some financial institutions will take unwarranted risks, opening the gates of the international financial system to suspect actors, and pay the price.

In this regard, the financial warfare of the past decade needs to evolve to include an explicitly inclusionary policy and strategy. An inclusionary strategy would work toward a number of positive ends, ensuring that underdeveloped regions of the world and regions in conflict were banked by legitimate financial actors; that banking centers in developing areas were included in the relevant anti-money-laundering and anti-corruption financial systems that already exist; that, by expanding the "buddy bank" and private-sector dialogue concept, existing banks would help to foster the transparency and accountability of indigenous institutions; that charitable services and backfill could reach the needy around the world—without interference from the coercion and corruption of terrorist and militant organizations; and that compliant and legitimate banks and actors are rewarded with more business, not less. Exclusion and inclusion into the financial system thus represent two sides of the same coin for the future of financial warfare. The underlying goal would be to define clearly and consistently the lines of legitimacy for financial and commercial conduct in the international system.

Revelations in the Use of Financial Power

The use of this type of financial power—and, in particular, its focus on flows of dirty money—has revealed some fundamental policy issues and paved the way for new ways of thinking about national security.

The use of financial intelligence continues to reveal links and associations between America's enemies that tend to remain unseen when these enemies are viewed individually through the lens of conventional intelligence. The "follow the money" doctrine and financial network analysis put both emerging threats and enemy vulnerabilities into sharp relief.

Treasury's designation process—with its public "name and shame" component and mechanics to ensure international financial isolation—has raised difficult and fundamental questions of national security import. As noted in Chapter 3, the question of how to deal with Saudi support to certain suspect Wahhabi causes and organizations, and the historical links of those organizations to the Arab mujahideen, came through the designation process. In addition, new debates emerged and continue to be relevant, including how to

treat organizations that raise money for and advocate the use of suicide bombers, such as the Muslim Brotherhood.

Soon after 9/11, a question arose as to whether to designate the
charismatic Muslim Brotherhood cleric and fundraiser Sheikh Yusuf
al-Qaradawi. Qaradawi was a senior Brotherhood leader and cleric
exiled from Egypt by longtime Egyptian strongman Hosni Mubarak.
Qaradawi had established himself in Qatar as the leading global
voice for Islamist agendas. With his popular show on Al Jazeera and
deep Islamic credentials and political sway, he was known by some
within the US government as the "Larry King" and the "Billy Graham" of the Arab airwaves. When Egyptian President Mubarak fell
from power in 2011, Qaradawi returned to Cairo triumphantly to a
reception and rally in front of hundreds of thousands of followers.
His return portended the coming of the Muslim Brotherhood to
power and rule now seen in Egypt.

This designation debate quickly became a proxy for the broader,
more fundamental question of how to view and treat the Brotherhood. Was the Brotherhood a terrorist organization? Were its
senior-most leaders hiding a secret agenda and providing financial
support to multiple terrorist organizations in opposition to US interests? Could the Brotherhood really be nonviolent and moderate—
and negotiated with or co-opted to work with the West against Al
Qaeda? These remain serious questions about the nature and ambitions of this movement, especially in the wake of the Arab revolutions. The very same debates about the Brotherhood took place in
the immediate wake of 9/11, in the context of Qaradawi's designation, and we went on to designate other Muslim Brotherhood leaders who were supporting Al Qaeda. Questions about how to treat
financial facilitation should continue to emerge. These are difficult
policy questions.

The targeting of financial facilitators also provided novel insights
for a new type of deterrence. Though it may not be possible to deter
a terrorist trigger-puller in the last instant of an attack, others in the
network and business cycle—such as bankers and financiers—could

be deterred if they recognized that their resources and legitimacy were at risk. Such deterrence—whether produced by public attention or quiet regulatory efforts—could affect the availability of capital and the ability of networks to execute significant plots and expand globally. This insight also allowed us to think differently about how to stop terrorist networks from being able to access or use weapons of mass destruction. By looking at the threat as a business cycle—which originates with the source of nuclear material and proceeds with the smugglers, facilitators, and end users—we can find multiple points at which to influence and interrupt the supply chain. Deterrence then was not just something to be aimed at suicide attackers but instead could be aimed at all of the actors in the cycle, with each category of actors reacting to different types of influence. The focus on financial support to America's enemies will continue to present new opportunities to influence their activities.

In addition, it is in the context of financial warfare that the United States has experienced its most consistent questions and tradeoffs about the use of cyber-weapons to disrupt the enemy's financial resources. Concern over the effects of cyber warfare on the financial system, and confidence in the United States as the keeper of the modern capitalist system, has constrained the use of such weapons. With this issue squarely in mind, Treasury Secretary Paulson has often spoken of the need to protect the "magnificent glass house" of the international financial system. Ironically, this is the arena in which the US financial system now faces its greatest vulnerability.

Finally, the financial pressure campaigns revealed the opportunities of financial diplomacy. Countries and the private sector often did not find it difficult to cooperate against terrorist financing or illicit funding flows because it presented a softer and more manageable form of combating transnational threats than other methods. For many countries, freezing bank accounts or seizing cash at borders was a more palatable way of fighting terrorism than sending troops to war zones. Financial diplomacy also revealed new communities of actors—from finance ministries and banks to anti-money-laundering experts and compliance officers—that, if leveraged properly, could affect international security.

From Financial to Strategic Suasion

Perhaps the most important lesson from the use of this type of financial power is what it tells us about leveraging power in the twenty-first century. What made this type of financial warfare different from and more effective than traditional sanctions was that we harnessed the private sector's own interests and calculus to isolate rogue financial actors. The banking community was not an ancillary part of American power, but a seminal and central part of it. The trick, then, was in aligning the concerns of private-sector actors over reputational risk and their bottom line with American national security imperatives. This is why meetings with bank CEOs and compliance officers often became more important than meetings with government officials. Our key insight was in recognizing that financial institutions could be prompted to lock the gates of the financial system.

In an increasingly interconnected world—where trade, financing, travel, and communications are fundamentally intertwined—nonstate, networked actors and systems—from corporations to influential Twitterati—often hold the keys to power and influence globally. The lament of the loss of American power and influence, and our inability to conduct "streetcraft" in addition to "statecraft," especially in the wake of the Arab revolutions, reflects a belief system dependent primarily on the projection of power through classic state institutions.

Power and influence now often lie outside the classic state structures and Westphalian models that have defined the post–World War II era. The state remains relevant, but more than ever before, the global power landscape is shared with other actors and networks. It's not enough to say that power has shifted—we need to

recognize that state-based power may no longer be central to exert-
ing influence in this new environment. White House talking points,
US Agency for International Development relief and programs, and
the might of the US military may not be enough in this new world.

Like the international financial system, this new global landscape offers not just transnational threats to be countered but
advantages and potential new allies as well. The national security
focus since 9/11 has largely centered on the threats brought to us by
globalization and the shifting nature of power. The shock of 9/11
was not just the horrors of a devastating attack against civilians on
American soil, but the fact that it was perpetrated by a small network of dedicated individuals who rejected modernity but were able
to leverage key elements of globalization to strike the sole remaining superpower from the hinterlands of Afghanistan.

We have spent much of the past decade concerned with nefarious
actors and networks—from Al Qaeda to Russian organized crime—
that have drawn strength from globalization and increased access to
information and new technologies. But we have consistently failed
to look at the other side of the ledger—for allies and the networks of
actors and institutions whose interests align with our own.

Just as David Headley, the American recruited by Lashkar-e-
Taiba, was able to use Google Maps to help plot the Mumbai attacks
in 2008, Oscar Morales, an unemployed Colombian engineer, used
Facebook in 2007 to mobilize 11 million people around the world to
march against the FARC and give voice to the anti-kidnapping
movement. In a society in which information moves at the speed of
Twitter, individuals like Julian Assange of WikiLeaks can wantonly
disseminate state secrets, straining diplomatic relations and putting
lives at risk. Yet, the very interconnectedness upon which he preyed
also empowers companies such as Amazon, MasterCard, and PayPal
to shut down his funding sources in ways that are swifter and perhaps more effective than government-led legal action.

Similarly, the US government has worried about groups of
Somali American youth in Minneapolis, Seattle, and Columbus

traveling to Somalia to train and fight (often engaging in suicide attacks) with the Al Qaeda affiliate Al Shabaab. But it has done far less to support the Somali American business elite, including those who have returned to serve in and lead Somalia's Transitional Federal Government (TFG) to establish a new government and a semblance of stability. Although terrorist groups have forged dangerous alliances and networks through shared training camps, tens of thousands of international military and police personnel train in the United States annually—often studying at American universities. They remain an untapped resource for formal and informal global security coordination and cooperation. And though we kill Al Qaeda core leaders in Pakistan's western frontier and strain to maintain diplomatic relations with Islamabad, we spend comparably little time supporting the investments of Pakistani American men and women doing business in and along those borders.

In the twenty-first century, the nation that galvanizes the majority of these new global voices will enjoy more power and exert more influence than has ever before been possible. More than any other state and culture, America—enabled and accelerated by globalization and new technologies—still enjoys a comparative advantage in leveraging power and influence in ways that are commensurate with our enduring strategic security heritage and our prosperity. This opportunity stems from the active employment of our unrivaled strategic suasion. Strategic suasion is the directed use of American power and influence to align influential state and nonstate actors and networks with American interests.

The empowerment of private-sector and nonstate actors does not threaten our interests. Indeed, as the rising power centers, credible voices, and key shapers of environments, these actors are our natural allies in the twenty-first century. Our interaction with them, however, can no longer be passive or ad hoc. We need to develop new structures and doctrines that enable our government and these actors to work in concert and in parallel to realize and achieve common goals and interests.

Though classic state power still matters, we must take a new national security model into account. Two themes are central to this new model: the idea of strategic suasion, and the role of nonstate, networked actors, working alongside classic state power, to influence the world for good. National security policy should be geared toward aligning those nonstate interests with American interests and values. The goal of our national security should not be just the defense and promotion of our interests, but the creation of conditions globally that are commensurate with American interests and values. The rule of law, freedom of expression, freedom of the press, the flow of information, respect for human rights, protection of minorities, the empowerment of women, free trade, systems that empower entrepreneurs and individual expression, the accountability of governments, and transparent civil institutions are all goals that the United States and American society should be promoting. These goals are neither solely the province of the US government nor achievable only by the work of government.

This may be the ultimate lesson of the use of financial power in this era. Nonstate actors can be leveraged when their interests align with those of the United States. American power is more than what the government controls; it also encompasses those activities that shape local and geopolitical environments in line with American interests. The US Treasury leveraged the self-interest of the private sector to promote broader values and interests in service of America's national security. Financial legitimacy and reputation became the coins of the realm. This is not just a new way of viewing financial warfare, but a novel view for the projection and use of power more broadly in the twenty-first century.

ACKNOWLEDGMENTS

This book would not have been possible without the assistance and support of others. I would like to thank all of them for sharing their insights, their support, and their expertise.

I wrote this story to provide a glimpse into the heretofore unseen world of financial warfare, which is being executed every day in both subtle and dramatic ways by dedicated public servants. A small community of actors within the US government and in the private sector has dedicated itself since 9/11 to dismantling the financial underpinnings of America's enemies in novel and aggressive ways. This was an unusually unified group of colleagues and professionals—who often were close friends of mine. Like a family, we fought internally—often fiercely—but we all had the same goal in mind: the protection of US interests and the decimation of America's enemies.

Many of these professionals are mentioned in this book; others are not. But they are all a part of the history of this period. Although there are too many people who made contributions for me to thank each individually in these pages, I will always remain grateful for their friendship, support, and service. I am most grateful to the small group of Treasury colleagues who worked with me to resurrect the organization at a time of great challenge—especially Danny Glaser, Chip Poncy, Jeff Ross, Traci Sanders, Anne Wallwork, Paul DerGarabedian, Nan Donnells, Janice Gardner, Charlie Ott, Ryan Wallerstein, Amit Sharma, and Linda Johnson. Whenever I refer to "we" in this story, it is often this group of colleagues and friends from the Treasury Department that I have in mind.

I must always thank Jimmy Gurulé and Mark Bonner, who brought me into the Treasury Department to help in their enforcement work before 9/11 and gave me enormous responsibility after the attacks. Others at the Treasury who have afforded me their trust and confidence include secretaries Paul O'Neill and John Snow, deputy secretaries Kenneth Dam and Sam Bodman, Undersecretary John Taylor, general counsels David Aufhauser and Arnie Havens, and Tim Adams, Chris Smith, Bill Fox, Bob Werner, Bill Murden, William Langford, Robert Nichols, Adnan Kifayat, Jody Myers, Larry McDonald, Julie Myers, Michael Russell, Michael Dawson, Tim Skud, Pat O'Brien, Eric Hampl, and Jeff Kupfer. Later, Undersecretary Stuart Levey provided leadership, support, and friendship—on which I rely to this day. It was with great pride that I called myself a "US Treasury official," and I thank them all for this privilege.

I would also like to thank my colleagues and friends at the Department of Justice, people like George Toscas, Jack Purcell, John Lancaster, and Bruce Swartz, who trained and supported me—and saw me as a promising prosecutor and policymaker.

I must thank Stephen Hadley and Frances Fragos Townsend for the opportunity to work for them and serve them and President George W. Bush at the White House. They afforded me their trust and confidence as we grappled with some of the most difficult issues facing the country in the second term of the Bush administration. They are two of the great national security professionals from whom I have learned much, and I can never repay them for the honor of having served as deputy national security adviser. I thank them for their leadership, dedication, and patience with me. Others at the National Security Council, including Ambassadors Jim Jeffrey and J. D. Crouch, were unfailing in their support and camaraderie, often under the most difficult of circumstances, and always with utter professionalism.

Ultimately, I need to thank President Bush. His leadership and vision in this period allowed this new era of financial warfare to unfold. The president afforded me the opportunity to serve him, his administration, and the country at a critical time in its history. I will always be grateful for his trust and confidence in me when I arrived at the White House in 2005, and throughout his tenure, until the end of his administration in 2009. It remains a point of pride for me that the Cuban government once called me "Bush's mercenary." History will show that this label was and remains a badge of honor.

Many other people and organizations provided invaluable assistance in the crafting of this book.

I would like to thank my research assistants, Zack Cooper and Matthew Irvine, for their help in shaping and developing this book over the arduous course of many months. Their judgments, insights, and research allowed me to draft this text. These are superb young men who are important thinkers in their own right and will become future policy leaders. I am grateful to have worked with them.

Others who contributed directly to the ideas and research contained in the book include David Gordon, Zack Fellman, and Jonathan Greenstein, who served as critical sounding boards throughout the process. Elizabeth Dennison and Michael Gallagher helped me to craft Chapter 16 and inspired some of my thinking about the future implications of financial warfare. Muhammad Kirdar influenced my thinking about many issues, especially the strategic implications of financial suasion, which is reflected in the Epilogue. I also thank Todd Hinnen and Chip Poncy for their help in honing the book in its final stages and for their constant and critical friendship. I am grateful to Christine Delargy for her help in compiling the photographs for the book.

To write this book I conducted dozens of interviews—many more than I anticipated. Although I interviewed too many people to mention individually, each provided me with insights and stories that added to the richness of this history. To those who were willing to spend time being interviewed and queried—from bankers and academics to former and current US officials—I offer you my thanks.

The book also received financial and material support from the start. I want to thank the Smith Richardson Foundation—and, in particular, Nadia Schadlow—for their enthusiastic support and faith in this project and in me. I am also indebted to the Stavros Niarchos Foundation, which contributed to the elements of the book that look to the future of financial warfare. I am grateful for their financial support and patience.

My colleagues at the Center for Strategic and International Studies (CSIS) have supported me from the time I left government. Because of the leadership and scholarship of Dr. John Hamre, and legends like Arnaud de Borchgrave, CSIS remains one of the preeminent think tanks in the world. I benefit and learn from my CSIS colleagues every day. I would like to thank Tom Sanderson, Ozzie Nelson, Andrew Schwartz, Jon Alterman, Jim Lewis, Craig Cohen, Reuben Jeffrey, John Heyl, Fariborz Ghadar, John MacGaffin, Dick O'Neill, and Jonathan Winer, in particular for their support to me in all phases of my research and writing—on this and other projects.

To John Brockman and Max Brockman, my literary agents, thank you for your faith and confidence in me and this story from the moment we spoke and met in your New York office. Your confidence and aggressive encouragement convinced me that I had to write this book and gave me faith that I could actually do it. Your diligence also allowed us to find Clive Priddle and a home for the book at PublicAffairs.

I could not have written and published a credible book without Clive Priddle and the professionals at PublicAffairs. Clive and Brandon Proia took a scalpel to my original manuscript and prodded and pushed me to make this a more readable, accurate, and interesting text. Melissa Raymond, the managing editor, and Robert Kimzey, my production editor, calmly helped me to navigate the production and editing process, while Katherine Streckfus, my copy editor, helped get the book into solid shape for publication. The marketing team has helped to ensure that this story gets the attention it deserves. I also would like to thank Pete Garceau for the wonderful, evocative cover. If the book is entertaining and educational, it is largely due to the work of the professionals at PublicAffairs. Any mistakes or material omissions are solely my responsibility.

Finally, I must thank my family for their lifelong support and confidence in me. My father and mother came to this country believing in the American dream, and they lived that dream. In so doing, they gave me and my siblings the gift of faith in an America that is the promised land of opportunity for all who are willing to take the risk and work for it—regardless of race, color, or creed. They also imparted to us a solid belief in an America that is a force for good in the world. Without America, the world would be a much darker and deadlier place.

My brothers, sister, nana, and extended family have always been a bastion of support, and I thank them for all they have given me. Most importantly, I want to thank my wife, Cindy, and my children, who endured the many months of this joyful slog and supported me when I needed to write or travel for research. This book was not written during a sabbatical or in a halcyon hideaway. It was written amid everyday family life, which put enormous pressure on my wife, who has a full-time career of her own. As always, Cindy endured with great energy and was unwavering in her faith that this book would be written—for which I am eternally grateful. I love them very much and thank them for everything they have given me.

I have been blessed—both with opportunities to serve at a unique time in our country's history and with family, friends, and colleagues who have always had faith in me. It is fair to say that without all of the people I've mentioned and others left unmentioned, this book would not have been written and published. Thank you to all. I hope the reader finds the book worthy of the time and effort put into it.

Notes

Prologue: "The Hidden War"

1. "Ahmadinejad: Hidden War on Global Scale Waged Against Iran's Oil Sector," *Iran Daily Brief*, October 8, 2012, www.irandailybrief.com/2012/10/08/ahmadinejad-hidden-war-on-global-scale-waged-against-irans-oil-sector/.

2. Ayman al-Zawahiri to Abu Mus'ab al-Zarqawi, July 9, 2005, Federation of American Scientists, Intelligence Resource Program, www.fas.org/irp/news/2005/10/letter_in_english.pdf.

3. "Friday News Roundup," *The Diane Rehm Show*, National Public Radio, October 5, 2012, http://thedianerehmshow.org/audio-player?nid=16725.

Introduction: The Modern Megarian Decree

1. "Criminal Investigations," n.d., United States Secret Service, www.secretservice.gov/criminal.shtml.

2. President Lincoln signed the order to create the Secret Service on April 14, 1865, the same day he was assassinated.

3. Paul D. Taylor, "Economic Coercion in the Service of National Security," June 16, 1998, Current Strategy Forum, www.au.af.mil/au/awc/awcgate/navy/economic_coercion.htm.

4. The best work on this subject is Diane B. Kunz, *The Economic Diplomacy of the Suez Crisis* (Chapel Hill: University of North Carolina Press, 1991).

5. Also see Rose McDermott, *Risk-Taking in International Politics* (Ann Arbor: University of Michigan Press, 1998), Chapter 6, "The 1956 Suez Crisis," online at www.press.umich.edu/pdf/0472108670–06.pdf.

6. Office of Foreign Assets Control (OFAC), *Cuba: What You Need to Know About U.S. Sanctions Against Cuba*, updated January 24, 2012, www.treasury.gov/resource-center/sanctions/Programs/Documents/cuba.pdf.

Chapter 1: A New Kind of War

1. Administration of President George W. Bush, *Highlights of Accomplishments and Results*, December 2008, http://georgewbush-whitehouse.archives.gov/infocus/bushrecord/documents/legacybooklet.pdf, 6.

2. "Appendix A: The Financing of the 9/11 Plot," in National Commission on Terrorist Attacks upon the United States, *The 9/11 Commission Report* (Washington, DC: US Government Printing Office, 2004), http://govinfo.library.unt.edu/911/report/index.htm, 132.

3. Ibid., 140.

4. Jimmy Gurulé, *Unfunding Terror: The Legal Response to the Financing of Global Terrorism* (Northampton, UK: Edward Elgar Publishing, 2008), 202. Under US criminal law, Title 18 USC 1956, money laundering can also be defined as the use of funds with criminal intent, regardless of the source. Thus, the use of the term "reverse money laundering" to describe terrorist financing is technically inaccurate, since the definition of money laundering used by the United States contemplates the use of legitimate funds for illegal purposes.

5. "Terrorist financing" is not defined as such under US law. Instead, pursuant to Title 18 USC 2339A and 2339B, the provision of material support, which includes financial resources or facilitation, to a terrorist or a designated Foreign Terrorist Organization is a criminal act. For purposes of asset freezing under Executive Order 13224, those who provide any manner of support or facilitation to a designated person, or who are controlled by or are acting for or on behalf of such a person, either directly or indirectly, are subject to the asset-freezing provisions of that order. Under international law, the clearest definition of "terrorist financing" comes from Article 2(1) of the International Convention for the Suppression of the Financing of Terrorism: "Any person commits an offence within the meaning of this Convention if that person by any means, directly or indirectly, unlawfully and willfully, provides or collects funds with the intention that they should be used or in the knowledge that they are to be used, in full or in part, in order to carry out: (a) An act which constitutes an offence within the scope of and as defined in one of the treaties listed in the annex, or (b) Any other act intended to cause death or serious bodily injury to a civilian, or to any other person not taking an active part in the hostilities in a situation of armed conflict, when the purpose of such act, by its nature or context, is to intimidate a population, or to compel a government or an international organization to do or to abstain from doing any act."

6. "Terrorist financing, therefore, is different than classic money laundering. In cases of money laundering, the proceeds of illicit activity are laundered or layered in ways to make the proceeds appear legitimate, and the ultimate goal is usually the attainment of more money. With terrorist financing, the source of funding or financing is often legitimate—as in the case of charitable donations or profits from store-front businesses—and the ultimate goal is not necessarily the attainment of more funds. The ultimate goal of terrorist financing is destruction. Uncovering the sources and methods of terrorist financing is a complex endeavor. The complexity stems in part from the sophistication of the individuals attempting to hide their activities. It is also difficult to attribute certain types of activities or movement of money directly to terrorism." "Testimony of Juan C. Zarate, Deputy Assistant Secretary for Terrorism and Violent Crime, U.S. Department of the Treasury, House Financial Subcommittee, Oversight and Investigations," Washington, DC, February 12, 2002. For a complete copy of the testimony, see www.treas.gov/press/releases/po1009.htm.

Hawala is an international alternative remittance system consisting of a global network of financial brokers and money houses that establish lines of credit for individuals or organizations and allow for the deposit and withdrawal of funds from any of the network's brokers. See Patrick Jost and Harjit Singh Sandhu, "The Hawala Alternative Remittance System and Its Role in Money Laundering," Interpol General Secretariat, January 2000.

7. US Government, 2002 National Money Laundering Goal 2, July 2002, 15.

8. The Department of State has named seven states as "Sponsors of Terrorism": Iran, Iraq, Syria, Cuba, North Korea, Sudan, and Libya. It is well known that Iran and Syria provide direct support to Hezbollah.

9. Kimberley L. Thachuk, "Terrorism's Financial Lifeline: Can It Be Severed?" *Strategic Forum*, Institute for National Strategic Studies, National Defense University, no. 191, May 2002.

10. US Department of Treasury, "Frequently Asked Questions," May 2, 2006, www.treasury.gov/resource-center/faqs/Sanctions/Pages/answer.aspx#2.

11. President Jimmy Carter, Executive Order 12170, "Blocking Iranian Government Property," November 14, 1979.

12. "Bush: 'We Will Starve the Terrorists,'" CNN, September 24, 2001, http://edition.cnn.com/2001/US/09/24/ret.bush.transcript/index.html.

13. Scott Shane, "Behind Bush's Fury, a Vow Made in 2001," *New York Times*, June 29, 2006, www.nytimes.com/2006/06/29/washington/29intel.html.

14. See Jimmy Gurulé, "The Global Fight Against the Financing of Terror: Prevention—A New Paradigm," speech delivered to the Heritage Foundation, Washington, DC, June 26, 2002.

15. United Nations Security Council Resolution 1373, September 28, 2001, Section 1.

16. US Customs Service, "Press Release: U.S. Customs Service Launches 'Operation Green Quest,'" October 25, 2001, www.cbp.gov/hot-new/pressrel/2001/1025–03.htm.

17. Douglas Farah, "The Role of Conflict Diamonds and Failed States in the Terrorist Financial Structure," October 24, 2003, Watson Institute, www.douglasfarah.com/articles/conflict-diamonds.php.

18. Naftali Bendavid, "Money War Intensifies: U.S. Raids Two Global Banking Networks," *Chicago Tribune*, November 8, 2001.

19. Paul O'Neill, "Remarks by Treasury Secretary Paul O'Neill on New U.S.–Saudi Arabia Terrorist Financing Designations," US Treasury Department, March 11, 2002, www.treasury.gov/press-center/press-releases/Pages/po1086.aspx.

20. See "Treasury Targets al Qaeda Finance Official," Reuters, August 24, 2010, www.reuters.com/article/2010/08/24/us-usa-qaeda-financing-idUSTRE67N5CP20100824.

21. Stuart Levey, "Loss of Moneyman a Big Blow to al Qaeda," *Washington Post*, June 6, 2010, www.washingtonpost.com/wp-dyn/content/article/2010/06/04/AR2010060404271.html.

Chapter 2: Financial Footprints

1. Jean-Louis Bruguiere, "Second Report on the Processing of EU-Originating Personal Data by the United States Treasury Department for Counter Terrorism Purposes: Terrorist Finance Tracking Programme," January 2010, Statewatch, www.statewatch.org/news/2010/aug/eu-usa-swift-2nd-bruguiere-report.pdf.

2. Anthony Cordesman and Khalid Al-Rodhan, "Iranian Nuclear Weapons? The Uncertain Nature of Iran's Nuclear Programs," Center for Strategic and International Studies, April 12, 2006, 28.

3. Eric Lichtblau, "Homeland Security Department Experiments with New Tool to Track Financial Crime," *New York Times*, December 12, 2004, http://query.nytimes.com/gst/fullpage.html?res=9B04E0D61E31F931A25751C 1A9629C8B63.

4. See Matthew Levitt, "Follow the Money: Leveraging Financial Intelligence to Combat Transnational Threats," *Georgetown Journal of International Affairs*, Winter/Spring 2011, http://journal.georgetown.edu/wp-content/ uploads/34–43-FORUM-Levitt.pdf, originally in Elizabeth Kelleher, "U.S. Defends Use of Bank Messaging System to Track Terrorists," The Washington File, Bureau of International Information Programs, US Department of State, June 23, 2006.

Chapter 3: Nose Under the Tent

1. "Terrorist Finance: The Iceberg Beneath the Charity," *The Economist*, March 13, 2003.

2. Laurie Goodstein, "U.S. Muslims Taken Aback by Charity's Conviction," *New York Times*, November 26, 2008.

3. Stephen Ulph, "Jihadists Respond to Earthquake Victims in Pakistan," October 31, 2005, www.jamestown.org/programs/gta/single/?tx_ttnews% 5Btt_news%5D=595&tx_ttnews%5BbackPid%5D=238&no_cache=1.

4. John Roth, Douglas Greenburg, and Serena White, *National Commission on Terrorist Attacks upon the United States: Monograph on Terrorist Financing. Staff Report to the Commission*, Chapter 7, "Al Haramain Case Study," http://govinfo. library.unt.edu/911/staff_statements/911_TerrFin_Monograph.pdf, 119.

5. US Department of the Treasury, "Treasury Designates Benevolence International Foundation and Related Entities Financiers of Terrorism," November 19, 2002, www.treasury.gov/press-center/press-releases/Pages/po3632.aspx.

6. For more on the Golden Chain, see "Written Testimony of Jean-Charles Brisard, International Expert on Terrorism Financing, Before the Committee on Banking, Housing and Urban Affairs, United States Senate," October 22, 2003, http://banking.senate.gov/public/index.cfm?FuseAction=Files.View&File-Store_id=c9b0cf41-cb29–4370–9666–6281e97f5170, 3.

7. Victor Comras, "It's Time to Put Yasin al Kadi Out of Business!" Counterterrorism Blog, September 20, 2005, http://counterterrorismblog.org/2005/ 09/its_time_to_put_yasin_al_kadi.php.

8. See "Yassin Abdullah Kadi and Al Barakaat International Foundation," European Court of Justice, September 3, 2008, www.tamilnet.com/img/publish/2008/09/ecj-judgment0904.pdf.

9. US Department of the Treasury, "Treasury Targets Key al-Qa'ida Funding and Support Network Using Iran as a Critical Transit Point," July 28, 2011, www.treasury.gov/press-center/press-releases/Pages/tg1261.aspx.

10. Robert Lenzner and Nathan Vardi, "Terror Inc.," *Forbes*, October 18, 2004, www.forbes.com/global/2004/1018/016.html; Christopher M. Blanchard and Alfred B. Prados, "Saudi Arabia: Terrorist Financing Issues," Congressional Research Service, updated September 14, 2007, www.fas.org/sgp/crs/terror/RL32499.pdf. The edict creating Account 98 was Royal Decree 8636.

11. Timothy O'Brien, "US Presses Saudis to Police Accounts Used to Aid Palestinians," *New York Times*, June 24, 2003, www.nytimes.com/2003/06/24/world/us-presses-saudis-to-police-accounts-used-to-aid-palestinians.html.

12. Steven Stalinsky, "Saudi Royal Family's Financial Support to the Palestinians 1998–2003: More Than 15 million Riyals ($2 Billion US) Given to 'Mujahideen Fighters' and 'Families of Martyrs,'" Middle East Media Research Institute, Special Report No. 17, July 3, 2003, www.memri.org/report/en/0/0/0/0/0/0/902.htm.

13. Ibid.

14. Lenzner and Vardi, "Terror Inc."

15. Ibid.

16. Blanchard and Prados, "Saudi Arabia: Terrorist Financing Issues," 12.

17. O'Brien, "US Presses Saudis." One Saudi spokesman commented, "It's a cheap shot to say our money goes to fund terrorists."

18. Ibid.

19. Marc Perelman, "Banks Eyed in Lawsuits on Funding for Terror: Saudi Accounts at Issue," *Forward*, October 15, 2004, http://forward.com/articles/4323/banks-eyed-in-lawsuits-on-funding-for-terror/.

20. Lenzner and Vardi, "Terror Inc."

21. Ibid.

Chapter 4: Financial Chokepoints

1. Samuel Munzele Maimbo, "The Money Exchange Dealers of Kabul: A Study of the Hawala System in Afghanistan," World Bank, Finance and Private Sector Unit, South Asia Region, June 2003, www.ifc.org/ifcext/gfm.nsf/AttachmentsByTitle/Tool6.13.WorldBankReport-HawalaSystem/$FILE/Tool+6.13.+World+Bank+Report+-+Hawala+System.pdf.

2. Patrick M. Jost and Harjit Singh Sandhu, "The Hawala Alternative Remittance System and Its Role in Money Laundering," 1999, Financial Crimes Enforcement Network, US Department of the Treasury, in cooperation with INTERPOL/FOPAC, www.treasury.gov/resource-center/terrorist-illicit-finance/Documents/FinCEN-Hawala-rpt.pdf.

3. See Financial Action Task Force (FATF)–Groupe d'Action Financière (GAFI), "FATF Recommendations: IX Special Recommendations, VI: Alternative

Remittance," October 2001, www.fatf-gafi.org/topics/fatfrecommendations/doc uments/ixspecialrecommendations.html#VI.

4. Abu Dhabi Declaration on Hawala, May 16, 2002, www.hsdl.org/?view &did=455469.

5. Financial Action Task Force (FATF)–Groupe d'Action Financière (GAFI), "International Best Practices: Detecting and Preventing the Cross-Border Transportation of Cash by Terrorists and Other Criminals," February 12, 2005, www.fatfgafi.org/media/fatf/documents/recommendations/International%20B PP%20Detecting%20and%20Preventing%20illicit%20cross-border%20trans portation%20SR%20IX%20%20COVER%202012.pdf.

6. Brett Gentrup, US Immigration and Customs Enforcement, *United States of America v. Abdurahman Muhammad Alamoudi: Criminal Complaint*, 2003, news.findlaw.com/wp/docs/terrorism/usalamoudi93003cmp.pdf, 8–9.

7. Brett Gentrup, US Immigration and Customs Enforcement, *United States of America v. Abdurahman Muhammad Alamoudi: Supplemental Declaration in Support of Detention*, news.findlaw.com/cnn/docs/terrorism/usalamoudi102203sdec. pdf, 4.

8. Ibid., 17–18.

9. Ibid., 25–26.

10. Gentrup, *Criminal Complaint*, 12–15.

11. Ibid., 23, 27–28.

12. Gentrup, *Supplemental Declaration*, 23.

13. Ibid., 14–23.

14. US Department of Justice, "Abdurahman Alamoudi Sentenced to Jail in Terrorist Financing Case," October 15, 2004, www.justice.gov/opa/pr/2004/ October/04_crm_698.htm.

15. Gentrup, *Criminal Complaint*, 2, 7–8.

16. Ibid., 10–12.

17. National Corruption Index, "Profile: Abdurahman Alamoudi," January 12, 2009, www.nationalcorruptionindex.org/pages/profile.php? profile_id=4.

18. Steve Emerson, "Testimony of Steven Emerson Before the United States House of Representatives Committee on Foreign Affairs, Subcommittee on Terrorism, Nonproliferation, and Trade," July 2008, http://foreignaffairs.house. gov/110/eme073108.pdf, 8.

19. Gentrup, *Criminal Complaint*, 10–11.

20. National Corruption Index, "Profile: Abdurahman Alamoudi."

21. US Department of Justice, "Abdurahman Alamoudi Sentenced."

22. Craig Whitlock, "The CIA and the Militant That Eluded It in Norway," *Washington Post*, December 4, 2006.

23. "Judge Sentences Mullah Krekar to Five Years in Prison for Making Threats," March 26, 2012, News In English, www.newsinenglish.no/2012/03/ 26/judge-sentences-mullah-krekar-to-five-years-in-prison/.

24. Nicholas Schmidle, "Disarming Viktor Bout," *New Yorker*, March 5, 2012.

25. Douglas Farah and Stephen Braun, *Merchant of Death: Money, Guns, Planes and the Man Who Makes War Possible* (New York: Wiley, 2007).

26. Ariel Zirulnick, "Arms Dealer Viktor Bout, Blamed for Arming Al Qaeda, Receives 25 Years in Prison," *Christian Science Monitor*, April 6, 2012, www.csmonitor.com/World/terrorism-security/2012/0406/Arms-dealer-Viktor-Bout-blamed-for-arming-Al-Qaeda-receives-25-years-in-prison-video.

Chapter 6: Bad Banks

1. Glenn Kessler, "President Imposes Sanctions on Syria," *Washington Post*, May 12, 2004, www.washingtonpost.com/wp-dyn/articles/A19087–2004 May11.html.

2. "Syrian Minister Admits US Sanctions Will Hurt," Agence France-Presse, May 29, 2004.

3. Note that the Section 311 regulatory actions were eventually rescinded for the Ukraine, Nauru, Asia Wealth Bank, Myanmar Mayflower Bank, First Merchant Bank, Multibanka, and VEF Banka. For updates on status of Section 311 actions and rules, see www.fincen.gov/statutes_regs/patriot/section 311.html.

Chapter 7: "The Mother of All Financial Investigations"

1. "A Fridge Full of Dollars," *The Bulletin*, March 21, 2006, www.ericellis.com/archive/moosa.htm.

2. John Taylor, "Reconstruction in Iraq: Economic and Financial Issues," US Department of the Treasury, June 4, 2003, www.treasury.gov/press-center/press-releases/Pages/js452.aspx.

3. United Nations Security Council, Resolution 986, April 14, 1995, http://usiraq.procon.org/sourcefiles/UNSCR986.pdf.

4. United Nations, "Observations on the Oil for Food Program: Statement of Joseph A. Christoff, Director, International Affairs and Trade," GAO-04–651T, April 7, 2004, www.gao.gov/new.items/d04651t.pdf.

5. US Department of State, "Saddam Hussein's Iraq," September 1999, www.gwu.edu/~nsarchiv/NSAEBB/NSAEBB167/13.pdf.

6. "Comprehensive Report of the Special Advisor to the DCI on Iraq's WMD, with Addendums (Duelfer Report)", September 30, 2004, http://permanent.access.gpo.gov/lps60059/Volume_1.pdf.

7. Edward Iwata, "Posse Tracks Billions of Saddam's 'Blood Money,'" *USA Today*, / May 14, 2003, http://usatoday30.usatoday.com/money/world/iraq/2003-05-14-bloodmoney_x.htm.

8. Juan C. Zarate, Testimony Before the Senate Permanent Subcommittee on Investigations, November 15, 2004.

9. George W. Bush, "President's Statement on Kleptocracy," White House Archives, August 10, 2006, http://georgewbush-whitehouse.archives.gov/news/releases/2006/08/20060810.html.

Chapter 8: Resurrection

1. For more information about the new organizational structure, see US Department of the Treasury, "Terrorism and Financial Intelligence," n.d., www.treasury.gov/about/organizational-structure/offices/Pages/Office-of-Terrorism-and-Financial-Intelligence.aspx.

2. Public Law 108–447, Division H, Title II, Section 222, December 8, 2004, 31 USC § 313.

3. William J. Broad and David E. Sanger, "C.I.A. Secrets Could Surface in Swiss Nuclear Case," *New York Times*, December 23, 2010, www.nytimes.com/2010/12/24/world/europe/24nukes.html?pagewanted=all.

4. The Federal Authorities of the Swiss Confederation, "Charges Filed in the Tinner Case," 2011, www.parlament.ch/e/organe-mitglieder/delegationen/geschaeftspruefungsdelegation/fall-tinner/Documents/fall-tinner-anklage-2011–12–13-e.pdf, 1–2.

5. "Chronology: A.Q. Khan," *New York Times*, April 16, 2006, www.nytimes.com/2006/04/16/world/asia/16chron-khan.html?pagewanted=all.

6. *World at Risk: The Report of the Commission on the Prevention of WMD Proliferation and Terrorism*, Bob Graham and Jim Talent, co-chairs (New York: Vintage Books, 2008).

Chapter 9: "Killing the Chicken to Scare the Monkey"

1. Peter Prahar, Testimony Before the US Senate Committee on Homeland Security and Governmental Affairs, "North Korea: Illicit Activity Funding the Regime," April 25, 2006, 5.

2. David L. Asher, Victor D. Comras, and Patrick M. Cronin, *Pressure: Coercive Economic Statecraft and U.S. National Security* (Washington, DC: Center for a New American Security, 2011), 32; also see David Rose, "North Korea's Dollar Store," *Vanity Fair*, August 5, 2009.

3. Bill Gertz, "North Korean General Tied to Forged $100 Bills," *Washington Times*, June 2, 2009.

4. Dick K. Nanto, "North Korean Counterfeiting of U.S. Currency," Congressional Research Service, June 12, 2009, www.fas.org/sgp/crs/row/RL333 24.pdf, 4.

5. "Counterfeiting: Notes on a Scandal," *The Independent*, August 24, 2009.

6. George W. Bush, *Decision Points* (New York: Crown, 2010), 420–422.

7. Financial Crimes Enforcement Network, US Department of the Treasury, Notice of Finding, "Finding That Banco Delta Asia SARL Is a Financial Institution of Primary Money-Laundering Concern," www.fincen.gov/statutes_regs/patriot/pdf/noticeoffinding.pdf.

8. "Macau's Gambling Industry: A Window on China," *The Economist*, December 10, 2011.

9. Asher et al., *Pressure*, 30–31.

Chapter 10: The Awakening

1. Financial Crimes Enforcement Network, US Department of the Treasury, Notice of Finding, "Finding That Banco Delta Asia SARL Is a Financial Institution of Primary Money-Laundering Concern," www.fincen.gov/statutes_regs/patriot/pdf/noticeoffinding.pdf.

2. "World Watch," *Wall Street Journal* (Eastern edition), October 4, 2005, A15.

3. Henry Paulson, "Remarks by Treasury Secretary Paulson on Targeted Financial Measures to Protect Our National Security," June 14, 2007, US Department of the Treasury, www.treasury.gov/press-center/press-releases/Pages/hp457.aspx.

4. Victor Cha, *The Impossible State* (2012), 266.

5. Author interview with Victor Cha, Washington, DC, December 13, 2011.

Chapter 11: Putting the Genie Back in the Bottle

1. See Jayshree Bajoria, "The Six Party Talks on North Korea's Nuclear Program," February 29, 2012, Council on Foreign Relations, www.cfr.org/proliferation/six-party-talks-north-koreas-nuclear-program/p13593.

2. "North Korea Missile Launches," July 4, 2006, Office of the Press Secretary, White House Press Release, US Department of State Archive, http://2001–2009.state.gov/p/eap/rls/prs/68546.htm; see also Federation of American Scientists, "North Korea's Taepodong and Unha Missiles," 2011, www.fas.org/programs/ssp/nukes/nuclearweapons/Taepodong.html.

3. "Statement by the President on North Korea," October 9, 2006, US Department of State Archive, http://2001–2009.state.gov/p/eap/rls/ot/73741.htm.

4. Choe Sang-Hun and John O'Neil, "N. Korea Expects Talks to End Sanctions," *New York Times*, November 1, 2006, www.nytimes.com/2006/11/01/world/asia/01cnd-korea.html?pagewanted=print&_r=0.

5. "Statement by DAS Glaser on the Disposition of DPRK-Related Funds Frozen at Banco Delta Asia," March 19, 2007, US Department of the Treasury, www.treasury.gov/press-center/press-releases/Pages/hp322.aspx.

6. Steven Weisman, "The Ripples of Punishing One Bank," *New York Times*, July 3, 2007.

Chapter 12: Revelation

1. Glenn R. Simpson, "U.S. Treasury Tracks Financial Data in Secret Program," *Wall Street Journal*, June 22, 2006; Josh Meyer and Greg Miller, "Secret U.S. Program Tracks Global Bank Transfers," *Los Angeles Times*, June 22, 2006; Barton Gellman, Paul Blustein, and Dafna Linzer, "Bank Records Secretly Tapped," *Washington Post*, June 23, 2006.

2. "John W. Snow: Treasury Dept.'s View of the Bank Data," Letter to the Editor, *New York Times*, June 29, 2006, www.nytimes.com/2006/06/29/opinion/l29terror.html.

3. "Testimony of Stuart Levey, Under Secretary Terrorism and Financial Intelligence, U.S. Department of the Treasury, Before the House Financial Services Subcommittee on Oversight and Investigations," July 11, 2006, US Department of the Treasury, www.treasury.gov/press-center/press-releases/Pages/hp05.aspx ("Testimony of Stuart Levey" hereafter).

4. "Update and Q&A to SWIFT's 23 June 2006 Statement on Compliance," August 25, 2006, SWIFT, www.swift.com/about_swift/legal/compliance/statements_on_compliance/update_and_q_and_a_to_swift_s_23_june_2006_statement_on_compliance/index.page?.

5. "SWIFT Statement on Compliance Policy," June 23, 2006, SWIFT, www.swift.com/about_swift/legal/compliance/statements_on_compliance/swift_statement_on_compliance_policy/index.page?.

6. Byron Calame, "Secrecy, Security, the President and the Press," *New York Times*, July 2, 2006, www.nytimes.com/2006/07/02/opinion/02pub-ed.html?pagewanted=1.

7. Byron Calame, "Banking Data: A Mea Culpa," *New York Times*, October 22, 2006, www.nytimes.com/2006/10/22/opinion/22pubed.html?pagewanted=2&_r=2.

8. "Testimony of Stuart Levey."

9. "Processing of EU Originating Personal Data by United States Treasury Department for Counter Terrorism Purposes—'SWIFT,'" *Official Journal of the European Union* 100, no. 166 (2007): 3–8, http://eur-lex.europa.eu/LexUriServ/site/en/oj/2007/c_166/c_16620070720en00180025.pdf.

10. Stuart Levey, "Letter from the United States Department of the Treasury Regarding SWIFT / Terrorist Finance Tracking Programme," *Official Journal of the European Union* 100, no. 166 (2007), http://eur-lex.europa.eu/LexUriServ/site/en/oj/2007/c_166/c_16620070720en00170017.pdf.

11. Council of the European Union, "EU-US Agreement on the Transfer of Financial Messaging Data for Purposes of the Terrorist Finance Tracking Programme," February 9, 2010, www.consilium.europa.eu/uedocs/cms_data/docs/pressdata/en/jha/112850.pdf, 1.

12. European Parliament, "European Parliament Resolution of 17 September 2009 on the Envisaged International Agreement to Make Available to the United States Treasury Department Financial Payment Messaging Data to Prevent and Combat Terrorism and Terrorist Financing," September 17, 2009, www.europarl.europa.eu/sides/getDoc.do?type=TA&reference=P7-TA-2009–0016&language=EN.

13. Council of the European Union, "EU-US Agreement," 1. See also Europa, "Cecilia Malmstrom Member of the European Commission Responsible for Home Affairs Terrorist Finance Tracking Programme (TFTP), European Parliament Debate on SWIFT, Strasbourg, 10 February 2010," http://europa.eu/rapid/pressReleasesAction.do?reference=SPEECH/10/24&format=HTML&aged=1&language=EN&guiLanguage=en.

14. European Parliament, "SWIFT: European Parliament Votes Down Agreement with the US," February 11, 2010, www.europarl.europa.eu/sides/getDoc.do?pubRef=-//EP//TEXT+IM-PRESS+

20100209IPR68674+0+DOC+XML+V0//EN. European Parliament President Jerzy Buzek said, "The majority view in the European Parliament is that the correct balance between security, on the one hand, and the protection of civil liberties and fundamental rights, on the other, has not been achieved in the text put to us by the Council." Europa, "EP President Jerzy Buzek on the Rejection of the SWIFT Agreement by the European Parliament," February 11, 2010, www.europarl.europa.eu/sides/getDoc.do?type=IM-PRESS&reference=20100211IPR68856&language=EN.

15. Mark Hallam, "Finance, Security and Privacy Collide in SWIFT Controversy," DW, n.d., www.dw.de/finance-security-and-privacy-collide-in-swift-controversy/a-14987543.

16. US Department of the Treasury, "Terrorist Finance Tracking Program: Questions and Answers," www.treasury.gov/resource-center/terrorist-illicit-finance/Terrorist-Finance-Tracking/Documents/Final%20Updated TFTP%20 Brochure%20(8-5-11).pdf, 1–2.

17. "Agreement Between the United States of America and the European Union on the Processing and Transfer of Financial Messaging Data from the European Union to the United States for the Purposes of the Terrorist Finance Tracking Program," June 28, 2010, US Department of the Treasury, www.treasury.gov/resource-center/terrorist-illicit-finance/Terrorist-Finance-Tracking/Documents/Final-TFTP-Agreement-Signed.pdf, 10, 14, 15–18, 20–21, 27.

18. Eric Lichtblau, "Controls on Bank-Data Spying Impress Civil Liberties Board," *New York Times*, November 29, 2006, www.nytimes.com/2006/11/29/washington/29nsa.html.

Chapter 13: The Constriction Campaign

1. Frederic Wehrey, Jerrold D. Green, Brian Nichiporuk, Alireza Nader, Lydia Hansell, Rasool Nafisi, and S. R. Bohandy, *The Rise of the Pasdaran: Assessing the Domestic Roles of Iran's Islamic Revolutionary Guards Corps* (Washington, DC: RAND Corporation, 2009).

2. Emanuele Ottolenghi, *The Pasdaran: Inside Iran's Islamic Revolutionary Guard Corps* (Washington, DC: Foundation for Defense of Democracies, 2011), 44–45.

3. Ibid., 43.

4. Matthew Levitt, "Financial Sanctions," in *Iran Primer* (Washington, DC: United States Institute of Peace Press, 2010), http://iranprimer.usip.org/sites/iranprimer.usip.org/files/Financial%20Sanctions.pdf.

5. US Department of State, "Designation of the Islamic Republic of Iran Shipping Lines (IRISL) and Subsidiaries for Proliferation Activities," September 11, 2008, http://2001–2009.state.gov/r/pa/prs/ps/2008/sept/109485.htm.

6. US Department of State, "Iran's Defense Industries Organization Designated by State," March 30, 2007, http://2001–2009.state.gov/r/pa/prs/ps/2007/mar/82487.htm.

7. US Department of State, "Designation of Iranian Entities and Individuals

for Proliferation Activities and Support for Terrorism," October 25, 2007, http://2001–2009.state.gov/r/pa/prs/ps/2007/oct/94193.htm.

8. Vikas Bajaj and John Eligon, "Iran Moved Billions via U.S. Banks," *New York Times*, January 9, 2009, www.nytimes.com/2009/01/10/business/world business/10bank.html.

9. Robert M. Morgenthau and Adam S. Kaufmann, Testimony Before the US Senate Committee on Foreign Relations, May 6, 2009, www.iranwatch.org/government/US/Congress/Hearings/sfrc-050609/documents/us-sfrc-morgenth aukaufmanntestimony-050609.pdf.

10. Robert Morgenthau, "The Emerging Axis of Iran and Venezuela," *Wall Street Journal*, September 8, 2009.

11. Clearstream, "About Us," www.clearstream.com/ci/dispatch/en/kir/ci_nav/about_us; Clearstream, "Clearstream Snapshot 2011/2012," December 2011, www.clearstream.com/ci/dispatch/en/binary/ci_content_pool/attache ments/001_about_us/clearstream_snapshot.pdf.

12. *Peterson v. Clearstream Banking, S.A., Citibank et al.*, https://materials.prox-yvote.com/Approved/629491/20110509/NPS_91360/PDF/nyse_euronext-smproxy2011_0255.pdf.

13. "Rafsanjani Urges Iran Not to Dismiss Sanctions as 'Jokes,'" Agence France-Presse, September 14, 2010.

Chapter 14: Dusting Off the Playbook

1. Timothy Geithner, "Finance Committee Questions for the Record," US Senate Committee on Finance, January 21, 2009, 66.

2. For more information on the Center for Strategic and International Studies' "Smart Power Initiative," see http://csis.org/program/smart-power-initiative.

3. David L. Asher, Victor D. Comras, and Patrick M. Cronin, *Pressure: Coercive Economic Statecraft and U.S. National Security* (Washington, DC: Center for a New American Security, 2011), 5–6, 23.

4. For a detailed chronology of events, see "Chronology of U.S.–North Korean Nuclear and Missile Diplomacy," April 2012, Arms Control Association, www.armscontrol.org/factsheets/dprkchron.

5. David Ignatius, "Obama's Signal to Iran," *Washington Post*, April 5, 2012.

6. For background on EU sanctions and designations of Iran in 2007–2008, see Council of the European Union, "Fact Sheet: The European Union and Iran," April 23, 2012, www.consilium.europa.eu/uedocs/cms_data/docs/pressdata/EN/foraff/127511.pdf.

7. The arguments in this paragraph were first featured in Juan Zarate, "Beyond Sanctions," *National Review*, October 4, 2010.

8. "Senior US Senator Calls on Ending Appeasement Policy vis-à-vis Mullahs in Iran," February 14, 2012, CNN, http://ireport.cnn.com/docs/DOC-748676.

9. Karen DeYoung and Michael Shear, "U.S., Allies Say Iran Has Secret Nuclear Facility," *Washington Post*, September 26, 2009.

10. Stuart Levey, "Comments During Panel on Terrorist Financing," Aspen Institute, July 2011, cited in "Zarate Blasts Obama's Iran Sanctions Pause," *Money Jihad*, October 7, 2011, http://moneyjihad.wordpress.com/2011/10/07/zarate-blasts-obamas-iran-sanctions-pause/.

11. Hillary Rodham Clinton and Timothy Geithner, "Measures to Increase Pressure on Iran," US Department of State, November 21, 2011, www.state.gov/secretary/rm/2011/11/177610.htm.

12. Stuart Levey, "Iran's New Deceptions at Sea Must Be Punished," *Financial Times*, August 15, 2010.

13. "Levey Lauds Iran Sanctions," *Money Jihad*, June 29, 2010, http://moneyjihad.wordpress.com/2010/page/16/.

14. "Comprehensive Iran Sanctions, Accountability, and Divestment Act of 2010," Public Law 111–195, July 1, 2010.

15. US Department of the Treasury, "Amendment to the Iranian Financial Sanctions Regulations," February 27, 2012, www.treasury.gov/resource-center/sanctions/OFAC-Enforcement/Pages/20120227.aspx.

16. Flavia Krause-Jackson "Sanctions Cost Iran $60 Billion in Oil Investments, Burns Says," *Bloomberg*, December 1, 2010, http://www.bloomberg.com/news/2010–12–01/sanctions-cost-iran-60-billion-in-oil-investments-burns-says.html.

17. See Juan C. Zarate, "Beyond Sanctions," *National Review*.

18. Benjamin Netanyahu, "Address to the American Israel Public Affairs Committee," Washington, DC, March 5, 2012.

19. "Japan's Crude Imports from Iran Drop as Sanctions Bite," Reuters, April 26, 2012, www.reuters.com/article/2012/04/26/us-crude-japan-iran-idUSBRE83P0DV20120426.

20. "Iran Exchange to Start Fuel-Oil Trading in April, Official Says," Reuters, April 1, 2011, www.bloomberg.com/news/2011–04–01/iran-exchange-to-start-fuel-oil-trading-in-april-official-says.html.

21. Kenneth Katzman, "Iran Sanctions," Congressional Research Service, December 7, 2012, 19.

22. Kenneth Katzman, "Iran Sanctions," Congressional Research Service, February 3, 2011, 51.

23. "Sanctions Felt," *Times Daily*, October 4, 2012, http://timesdaily.com/stories/Sanctions-felt,196708.

24. Katzman, "Iran Sanctions," Congressional Research Service, February 3, 2011, 49.

25. "Iran's Rial Hits an All-Time Low Against the U.S. Dollar," BBC News, October 1, 2012, www.bbc.co.uk/news/business-19786662.

26. Katzman, "Iran Sanctions," Congressional Research Service, February 3, 2011, 50.

27. "Sanctions on Iran Effect [*sic*] Ordinary Iranians Psyche," National Public Radio, January 6, 2012, www.npr.org/2012/01/06/144772880/sanctions-on-iran-effect-ordinary-iranians-psyche.

28. Hiedeh Farmani, "Ahmadinejad Says Iran Open to More Nuclear Talks," Iran Focus, January 23, 2011, www.iranfocus.com/en/index.php?option=com_

content&view=article&id=22654:ahmadinejad-says-iran-open-to-more-nuclear
-talks&catid=8:nuclear&Itemid=45.

29. Hashem Kalantari, "Iran New Year Marred by Mideast Unrest—
Khamenei," Reuters, March 20, 2011, www.reuters.com/article/2011/03/21/
iran-khamenei-idAFLDE72K00320110321.

30. "Iran Downplays Report India Paying for Oil via Russia," Reuters, October 29, 2011, www.reuters.com/article/2011/10/29/iran-india-oil-idUSL5E7LT
06U20111029.

31. "U.N.: Iran Seeks to Skirt Nuke Sanctions," United Press International,
May 12, 2011, www.upi.com/Top_News/US/2011/05/12/UN-Iran-seeks-to-
skirt-nuke-sanctions/UPI-77751305218161/.

32. "'Sanctions Have Had No Impact,'" February 16, 2011, PressTV,
www.presstv.ir/detail/165434.html.

33. Thomas Erdbrink, "Ahmadinejad Admits Impact of Sanctions on Iran,"
Washington Post, November 1, 2011, www.washingtonpost.com/world/
middle_east/ahmadinejad-admits-impact-of-sanctions-on-iran/2011/11/01/
gIQAvBIacM_story.html.

34. Caren Bohan and Glenn Somerville, "Key Obama Aide on Iran Sanctions Steps Down," Reuters, January 24, 2011, www.reuters.com/article/2011/
01/24/us-iran-usa-sanctions-idUSTRE70N5PK20110124.

35. "Official: US, EU Economic Institutions Opposed to Sanctions Against
Iran," Fars News Agency, January 26, 2011, http://english.farsnews.com/
newstext.php?nn=8911060616.

36. Robert O'Harrow Jr., James V. Grimaldi, and Bradley Dennis, "Sanctions in 72 Hours: How the U.S. Pulled Off a Major Freeze of Libyan Assets,"
Washington Post, March 23, 2011, www.washingtonpost.com/investigations/
sanctions-in-72-hours-how-the-us-pulled-off-a-major-freeze-of-libyan-
assets/2011/03/11/ABBckxJB_story.html.

37. "Standard Chartered Bank in '$250bn Scheme with Iran,'" BBC News,
August 6, 2012, www.bbc.co.uk/news/business-19155577.

38. Ivanka Barzashka, "Using Enrichment Capacity to Estimate Iran's
Breakout Potential," January 21, 2011, Federation of American Scientists,
www.fas.org/pubs/_docs/IssueBrief_Jan2011_Iran.pdf.

39. James R. Clapper, "Statement for the Record on the Worldwide Threat
Assessment of the U.S. Intelligence Community for the Senate Select Commit-
tee on Intelligence," February 16, 2011, Office of the Director of National
Intelligence, http://intelligence.senate.gov/110216/dni.pdf.

40. International Atomic Energy Agency Board of Governors, "Implementation of the NPT Safeguards Agreement and Relevant Positions of Security
Council Resolutions in the Islamic Republic of Iran," May 25, 2012.

Chapter 15: Learning Curve

1. US Department of the Treasury, "Treasury Targets Major Money Laundering Network Linked to Drug Trafficker Ayman Joumaa and a Key Hizballah
Supporter in South America," June 27, 2012, www.treasury.gov/press-

center/press-releases/Pages/tg1624.aspx; also see US Department of the Treasury, "Treasury Identifies Lebanese Canadian Bank Sal as a 'Primary Money Laundering Concern,'" February 10, 2011, www.treasury.gov/press-center/press-releases/pages/tg1057.aspx; Jo Becker, "Beirut Bank Seen as a Hub of Hezbollah's Financing," *New York Times*, December 13, 2011.

2. Samuel Rubenfeld, "Treasury Targets Drug-Money Laundering Network, Hezbollah Fundraiser," *Wall Street Journal*, June 27, 2012.

3. David Cohen, "Treasury's Role in National Security," Interview by Juan Zarate, Washington, DC, May 10, 2012, http://csis.org/files/attachments/051412_TreasuryRoleInNatSec_Transcript.pdf.

4. Michael Jacobson and Matthew Levitt, "Staying Solvent: Assessing Al-Qaeda's Financial Portfolio," November 2009, Washington Institute for Near East Policy, www.washingtoninstitute.org/uploads/Documents/opeds/4b28f9a9e2216.pdf.

5. Daniel Benjamin, Testimony Before the House Foreign Affairs Committee, "LRA, Boko Haram, Al-Shabaab, AQIM, and Other Sources of Instability in Africa," April 25, 2012.

6. United Nations Security Council, "Letter from the Chairman of the Security Council Committee Pursuant to Resolutions 751 (1992) and 1907 (2009) Concerning Somalia and Eritrea, Addressed to the President of the Security Council," July 18, 2011, www.un.org/ga/search/view_doc.asp?symbol=S/2011/433&referer=http://www.un.org/sc/committees/751/mongroup.shtml&Lang=E.

7. Ibid., 28.

8. Ibid., 28, 30.

9. Ibid., 182–186.

10. Greg Bruno, "Backgrounder: Al-Qaeda's Financial Pressures," February 1, 2010, Council on Foreign Relations, www.cfr.org/terrorist-organizations/al-qaedas-financial-pressures/p21347.

11. "Nigeria: Boko Haram, al Shabaab, AQAP Sharing Funds—U.S. General," *Stratfor*, June 25, 2012, http://stratfor.us4.list-manage1.com/track/click?u=74786417f9554984d314d06bd&id=392762032c&e=827da1dca2.

12. US Department of the Treasury, "Treasury Targets Key Al-Qa'ida Funding and Support Network Using Iran as a Critical Transit Point," June 28, 2011, www.treasury.gov/press-center/press-releases/Pages/tg1261.aspx.

13. Whitney Eulich, "Developing Countries Lead the Way in Deploying Mobile Technology," *Christian Science Monitor*, July 28, 2012, www.csmonitor.com/World/Global-Issues/2012/0728/Developing-countries-lead-the-way-in-deploying-mobile-technology.

14. Steve Ragan, "Four Arrested for Hacking Phone Systems to Fund Terrorism," *Security Week*, November 28, 2011, www.securityweek.com/four-arrested-hacking-phone-systems-fund-terrorism.

15. Mike Braun, Testimony Before the House Foreign Affairs Committee, "Ahmadinejad's Tour of Tyrants and Iran's Agenda in the Western Hemisphere," February 2, 2012, http://foreignaffairs.house.gov/112/HHRG-112-FA-WState-MBraun-20120202.pdf.

16. Ibid.

17. White House, "Release of Strategy to Combat Transnational Organized Crime," July 25, 2011, http://iipdigital.usembassy.gov/st/english/texttrans/2011/07/20110725153733su0.5098492.html#axzz1gMFUYLxA.

18. Colleen Cook, "Mexico's Drug Cartels," Congressional Research Service, February 25, 2008, www.statealliancepartnership.org/Resources/CRS%20Report%20to%20Congress%20-%20Mexico%27s%20Drug%20Cartels.pdf.

19. Stephanie Hanson, "FARC, ELN: Colombia's Left-Wing Guerillas," August 19, 2009, Council on Foreign Relations, www.cfr.org/colombia/farc-eln-colombias-left-wing-guerrillas/p9272.

20. Eric Schmitt, "Many Sources Feed Taliban War Chest," *New York Times*, October 18, 2009, www.nytimes.com/2009/10/19/world/asia/19taliban.html.

21. Gretchen Peters, "How Opium Profits the Taliban," August 2009, United States Institute of Peace, www.usip.org/files/resources/taliban_opium_1.pdf.

22. Braun, "Ahmadinejad's Tour of Tyrants."

23. "Kurds and Pay: Examining PKK Financing," *Jane's Intelligence Review*, March 13, 2008, www.silkroadstudies.org/new/docs/publications/2007/0803 JIR-PKK.pdf.

24. United Nations Office on Drugs and Crime, "Estimating Illicit Financial Flows Resulting from Drug Trafficking and Other Transnational Crimes: Research Report," October 2011, www.unodc.org/documents/data-and-analysis/Studies/Illicit_financial_flows_2011_web.pdf.

25. Matthew Greene, "Afghanistan Acts to Curb Flight of Capital," *Financial Times*, March 18, 2012, www.ft.com/cms/s/0/a888d1fc-6f12–11e1-afb8–00144feab49a.html#axzz258fZB86J.

26. James Risen and Duraid Adnan, "U.S. Says Iraqis Are Helping Iran Skirt Sanctions," *New York Times*, August 18, 2012.

27. Mark Dubowitz, "So You Want to Be a Sanctions Buster," *Foreign Policy*, August 10, 2012, www.foreignpolicy.com/articles/2012/08/10/so_you_want_to_be_a_sanctions_buster.

28. Edith Lederer, "Diplomats: UN Experts Say North Korea Violates Sanction," *The Guardian*, May 18, 2012.

29. United Nations, "Report of the Panel of Experts Established Pursuant to Resolution 1874," 2009.

30. Dick Nanto and Mark Manyin, "China–North Korea Relations," Congressional Research Service, December 28, 2010, 12.

31. Ibid., 19.

32. John S. Park, "North Korea, Inc.," April 22, 2009, United States Institute of Peace Working Paper, www.usip.org/files/resources/North%20Korea,%20Inc.PDF, 12; Drew Thompson, "Silent Partners: Chinese Joint Ventures in North Korea—Executive Summary," February 2011, US-Korea Institute at SAIS, http://uskoreainstitute.org/wp-content/uploads/2011/02/USKI_Report_SilentPartners_DrewThompson_ExecSum3.pdf.

33. Jayshree Bajoria, "The China-North Korea Relationship,"October 7, 2010, Council on Foreign Relations, www.cfr.org/china/china-north-korea-relationship/p11097.

34. Ibid.

35. Nanto and Manyin, "China–North Korea Relations," 17.

36. Ibid.

37. Asia Society Center on US-China Relations and University of California Institute on Global Conflict and Cooperation, "North Korea Inside Out: The Case for Economic Engagement," December 2009, http://asiasociety.org/files/pdf/North_Korea_Inside_Out.pdf, 12; Scott Snyder, "China Embraces North and South, But Differently," January 2010, Asia Foundation / Pacific Forum CSIS, http://asiafoundation.org/resources/pdfs/SnyderByunChina Korea.pdf.

38. "Otto Reich: Hugo Chavez Helps Assad Slaughter Syrian Civilians," June 19, 2012, Americas Forum, www.americas-forum.com/otto-reich-hugo-chavez-helps-assad-slaughter-syrian-civilians/.

39. Roger Noriega, Testimony Before the Senate Foreign Relations Committee, Subcommittee on the Western Hemisphere, Peace Corps, and Global Narcotics Affairs, "Iran's Influence and Activity in Latin America," February 16, 2012, www.foreign.senate.gov/imo/media/doc/Roger_Noriega_Testimony1.pdf.

40. Ibid., 28; see also Jerome Bjelopera and Kristin Finklea, "Organized Crime: An Evolving Challenge for U.S. Law Enforcement," Congressional Research Service, January 6, 2012, www.fas.org/sgp/crs/misc/R41547.pdf.

41. United Nations Office on Drugs and Crime, *The Globalization of Crime: A Transnational Organized Crime Threat Assessment*, 2010, www.unodc.org/docu ments/data-and-analysis/tocta/TOCTA_Report_2010_low_res.pdf?bcsi_scan_ E6B5D3DA0AAC65B7=0&bcsi_scan_filename=TOCTA_Report_2010_low_res. pdf; United Nations Office on Drugs and Crime, "United Nations Convention Against Transnational Organized Crime and the Protocols Thereto," November 15, 2000, www.unodc.org/unodc/en/treaties/CTOC/.

42. Rolf Mowatt-Larssen, "Al Qaeda Weapons of Mass Destruction: Hype or Reality?" January 2010, Belfer Center for Science and International Affairs, http://belfercenter.ksg.harvard.edu/publication/19852/al_qaeda_weapons_of_ mass_destruction_threat.html.

43. Remarks by Under Secretary of the Treasury David S. Cohen on the Presidential Strategy to Combat Transnational Organized Crime, July 25, 2011, www.treasury.gov/press-center/press-releases/Pages/tg1256.aspx.

44. Kristin M. Finklea, "Organized Crime in the United States: Trends and Issues for Congress," Congressional Research Service, January 27, 2010.

45. Michael Mukasey, "Combating the Growing Threat of International Organized Crime," Remarks at the Center for Strategic and International Studies, April 23, 2008, http://csis.org/files/media/csis/events/080423_mukasey.pdf.

46. Richard Shultz, Roy Godson, Querine Hanlon, and Samantha Ravich, "The Sources of Instability in the Twenty-First Century," *Strategic Studies Quarterly*, Summer 2011; Douglas Farah, "Terrorist-Criminal Pipelines and Criminalized States: Emerging Alliances," *Prism* 2, no. 3 (2011), www.ndu.edu/press/emerging-alliances.html.

47. Raymond Bonner, "Russian Gangsters Exploit Capitalism to Increase Profits," *New York Times*, July 25, 1999, www.nytimes.com/1999/07/25/world/

russian-gangsters-exploit-capitalism-to-increase-profits.html?pagewanted=
print&src=pm.

48. Robert S. Mueller III, "Remarks at the 10th Anniversary of ILEA
Budapest," May 12, 2005, www.fbi.gov/news/speeches/moving-beyond-the-
walls-global-partnerships-in-a-global-age.

49. White House, "Strategy to Combat Transnational Organized Crime,"
July 2011, www.whitehouse.gov/sites/default/files/Strategy_to_Combat_
Transnational_Organized_Crime_July_2011.pdf.

50. White House, "Fact Sheet: Strategy to Combat Transnational Organized
Crime," July 25, 2011, www.whitehouse.gov/the-press-office/2011/07/25/fact-
sheet-strategy-combat-transnational-organized-crime.

Chapter 16: The Coming Financial Wars

1. See Henry M. Paulson Jr., *On the Brink: Inside the Race to Stop the Collapse of
the Global Financial System* (New York: Business Plus, 2010).

2. See Gideon Rachman, "Why 9/15 Changed More Than 9/11," *Financial
Times*, September 13, 2010. Rachman wrote, "[In 2008] America's economic
prowess still seemed to provide a reliable basis for the country's global political
position. The financial crisis has changed that assumption, almost certainly forever. In its aftermath, the US is much more conscious of the limits to its own
power."

3. Jason Dean, Andrew Browne, and Shai Oster, "China's 'State Capitalism'
Sparks a Global Backlash," *Wall Street Journal*, November 16, 2010.

4. Liane Hansen, Host, "Sanctions Turn Tables in U.S.–China Relations,"
National Public Radio, Weekend Edition, February 7, 2010, www.npr.org/
templates/story/story.php?storyId=123463748.

5. Emma Simpson, "Russia Wields the Energy Weapon," BBC News, February 14, 2006, http://news.bbc.co.uk/2/hi/4708256.stm. See also "Russia
Blamed for 'Gas Sabotage,'" BBC News, January 22, 2006, http://news.bbc.
co.uk/2/hi/europe/4637034.stm.

6. Peter Guest, "Is the Greek Crisis a Boon for Russia's Gazprom?" CNBC,
June 29, 2011, www.cnbc.com/id/43561012.

7. "Spy Agency Told to Help Companies," *St. Petersburgh Times*, October 23,
2007.

8. Hillary Rodham Clinton, "Remarks at the 2011 U.S. Global Leadership
Coalition (USGLC) Conference," July 12, 2011, www.state.gov/secretary/rm/
2011/07/168061.htm.

9. Damian Grammaticas, "Are China's Leaders Worried?" BBC News,
December 2, 2011, www.bbc.co.uk/news/world-asia-16003625.

10. Wayne M. Morrison, "China-U.S. Trade Issues," Congressional Research
Service, May 21, 2012, www.fas.org/sgp/crs/row/RL33536.pdf.

11. See Ian Bremmer, *The End of the Free Market: Who Wins the War Between
States and Corporations?* (New York: Penguin, 2010). Bremmer wrote: "Corporate leaders and investors must recognize that globalization is no longer the
unchallenged international economic paradigm—and that politics will have a

profound impact on the performance of markets for many years to come."

12. "Leviathan Inc: The State Goes Back into Business," *The Economist*, August 5, 2011, www.economist.com/node/16743343; Niall Ferguson, "In China's Orbit," *Wall Street Journal*, November 18, 2010; "China Buys Up the World," *The Economist*, November 11, 2011, www.economist.com/node/17463473/.

13. Bremmer, *The End of the Free Market*.

14. Elizabeth Economy, "The Game Changer: Coping with China's Foreign Policy Revolution," *Foreign Affairs*, November/December 2010, www.foreign affairs.com/articles/66865/elizabeth-c-economy/the-game-changer.

15. "Sovereign-Wealth Funds: Asset Backed Insecurity," *The Economist*, January 17, 2008, www.economist.com/node/10533428.

16. "China Buys Up the World."

17. Bremmer, *The End of the Free Market*.

18. Fred P. Hochberg, "State Capitalists Map Out a New Wild West," *Financial Times*, July 11, 2012.

19. US Census Bureau, "Trade in Goods with China," 2010, www.census. gov/foreign-trade/balance/c5700.html; Robert J. Samuelson, "China's New World Order Demands Stronger U.S. Response," *Washington Post*, January 24, 2011, www.washingtonpost.com/wp-dyn/content/article/2011/01/23/AR2011 012302895.html.

20. Thomas M. Hout and Pankaj Ghemawat, "China vs the World: Whose Technology Is It?" *Harvard Business Review*, December 2010.

21. Samuelson, "China's New World Order."

22. Keith Bradsher, "Chinese Foreign Currency Reserves Swell by Record Amount," *New York Times*, January 11, 2011, www.nytimes.com/2011/ 01/12/business/global/12yuan.html?_r=0.

23. Geoff Dyer and Jamil Anderlini, "China's Lending Hits New Heights," *Financial Times*, January 17, 2011, www.ft.com/intl/cms/s/0/488c60f4– 2281–11e0-b6a2–00144feab49a.html#axzz1BEtk4jFy.

24. Gary Locke, "Commerce Secretary on Chinese Foreign Investment in the U.S.," International Information Programs, May 4, 2011, http://iipdigital. usembassy.gov/st/english/texttrans/2011/05/20110505183643su0.5584615.ht ml#ixzz1QYywXPwG. China has also recently announced a new review system to vet foreign investments based on vague national security parameters. Again, while we must wait for implementation, these measures are very broad and provide another unnecessary hoop to jump through for US companies. Even more troubling, the review system allows for competitors and others outside of the Chinese government to influence the process by proposing to the Chinese authorities that a particular transaction be reviewed.

25. Rob Gifford, "China's Rise: Inward-Looking or Expansionist?," NPR, June 30, 2011, www.npr.org/2011/06/30/137460232/chinas-rise-inward-look-ing-or-expansionist. Some have argued that China may be engaged in a deliberate game of forcing the United States to overextend itself and thereby go bankrupt trying to meet all the perceived challenges from China. See Brad Glosserman, "Is China Trying to Bankrupt US?" *The Diplomat*, June 9, 2011.

26. Andrew E. Kramer, "U.S. Companies Get Slice of Iraq Pie," *New York Times*, June 14, 2011, www.nytimes.com/2011/06/15/business/energy-environment/15iht-srerussia15.html?_r=1&scp=1&sq=Iraq%20U.S.%20companies %20oil&st=cse; Vivienne Walt, "U.S. Companies Shut Out as Iraq Auctions Its Oil Fields," *Time*, December 19, 2009, www.time.com/time/world/article/0,85 99,1948787,00.html.

27. Leila Fadel and Ernesto Londoño, "Risk-Tolerant China Investing Heavily in Iraq as U.S. Companies Hold Back," *Washington Post*, July 2, 2010, www.washingtonpost.com/wp-dyn/content/article/2010/07/01/AR20100 70103406.html. Since the 2003 invasion of Iraq, China has aggressively sought to secure oil resources for its growing economy. With their once lucrative oil contracts voided by the overthrow of Saddam Hussein, the Chinese have used lower oil prices during this global recession to embark on a resource grab of epic proportions. Maximizing the collective strength of China's banking institutions and the diplomatic resources of the Chinese government, China's state-owned oil companies are positioning themselves to control a substantial amount of the oil produced in Africa, Asia, and South America. Whether this is through preferential bank loans to ailing countries or major investments in international oil companies on the open market, one thing has become clear: the Chinese are making sure that they have the oil they need in this limited resource market.

28. Jalil Jumriany, an adviser to the Afghan minister of mines, as quoted in James Risen, "U.S. Identifies Vast Mineral Riches in Afghanistan," *New York Times*, July 13, 2010, www.nytimes.com/2010/06/14/world/asia/14minerals. html.

29. Robert D. Kaplan, "Beijing's Afghan Gamble," *New York Times*, October 6, 2009, www.nytimes.com/2009/10/07/opinion/07kaplan.html.

30. US Federal Bureau of Investigation, "Bitcoin Virtual Currency: Unique Features Present Distinct Challenges for Deterring Illicit Activity," April 24, 2012, http://cryptome.org/2012/05/fbi-bitcoin.pdf.

31. Moisés Naím, "Mafia States," *Foreign Affairs*, April 20, 2012, www.foreignaffairs.com/articles/137529/moises-naim/mafia-states.

32. "Bin Laden: Goal Is to Bankrupt U.S.," CNN, November 1, 2004, http://articles.cnn.com/2004–11–01/world/binladen.tape_1_al-jazeera-qaeda-bin?_s=PM:WORLD.

33. Kristin M. Finklea, "Organized Crime in the United States: Trends and Issues for Congress," Congressional Research Service, January 27, 2010.

34. Richard Shultz, Roy Godson, Querine Hanlon, and Samantha Ravich, "The Sources of Instability in the Twenty-First Century," *Strategic Studies Quarterly*, Summer 2011; Douglas Farah, "Terrorist-Criminal Pipelines and Criminalized States: Emerging Alliances," *Prism* 2, no. 3 (2011), www.ndu.edu/press/emerging-alliances.html.

35. US Senate Permanent Subcommittee on Investigations, "U.S. Vulnerabilities to Money Laundering, Drugs, and Terrorist Financing: HSBC Case History," July 17, 2012, http://www.gpo.gov/fdsys/pkg/CHRG-112shrg76061/html/CHRG-112shrg76061.htm.

36. Benjamin J. Cohen, *The Geography of Money* (Ithaca, NY: Cornell University Press, 1998), 128.

37. Hyoung-Kyu Chey, "Theories of International Currencies and the Future of the World Monetary Order," *International Studies Review* 14, no. 1 (2012): 51–77; Barry Eichengreen, *Globalizing Capital: A History of the International Monetary System*, 2nd ed. (Princeton, NJ: Princeton University Press, 1996), 103; Barry Eichengreen, *Exorbitant Privilege: The Rise and Fall of the Dollar and the Future of the International Monetary System* (Oxford: Oxford University Press, 2011), 40–42; Jonathan Kirshner, "Dollar Primacy and American World Power: What's at Stake?" *Review of International Political Economy* 15, no. 3 (2008): 418–438.

38. "Brazil-China Bilateral Trade in Real and Yuan Instead of US Dollar," *MercoPress*, June 30, 2009, http://en.mercopress.com/2009/06/29/brazil-china-bilateral-trade-in-real-and-yuan-instead-of-us-dollar; Toni Vorobyova, "Russia, China to Boost Rouble, Yuan Use in Trade," Reuters, June 17, 2009, www.reuters.com/article/2009/06/17/russia-china-currency-idUSLH721678 20090617.

39. James Rickards, *Currency Wars: The Making of the Next Global Crisis* (New York: Penguin, 2011), 107.

40. Niall Ferguson, *The Ascent of Money: A Financial History of the World* (New York: Penguin, 2008), 336–337. In Ferguson's view, "Chimerica" was "the underlying cause of the surge in bank lending, bond issuance and new derivative contracts . . . the underlying cause of the hedge fund population explosion . . . the underlying reason why private equity partnerships were able to borrow money left, right, and center to finance leveraged buyouts . . . the underlying reasons why the US mortgage market was so awash with cash in 2006 that you could get a 100 per cent mortgage with no income, no job or assets." Ferguson has further argued that the United States' loose monetary policy is its own form of currency manipulation, causing the dollar to depreciate approximately 25 percent against the currencies of its major trading partners in recent years (9 percent against the renminbi).

41. Ferguson wrote: "One important lesson of history is that major wars can arise even when economic globalization is very far advanced and the hegemonic position of an English-speaking empire seems fairly secure." Ferguson, *The Ascent of Money*, 339–340.

42. Rickards concluded: "The path of the dollar is unsustainable and therefore the dollar will not be sustained. In time, the dollar will join a crowd of multiple reserve currencies, be subordinated to SDRs, be rejuvenated by gold or descend into chaos with both redemptive and terminal possibilities." Rickards, *Currency Wars*, 255.

43. Chey wrote: "And in fact, a group of prominent international banks, among them HSBC, Standard Chartered, Citigroup, and JPMorgan[,] have recently been holding international roadshows to promote use of the renminbi by their corporate customers for trade deals with China, instead of the dollar. Some of them have moreover offered financial incentives, such as discounted transaction fees, to firms opting to settle their trades in renminbi." Chey,

"Theories of International Currencies," 71. See also Robert Cookson, "Banks Back Switch to Renminbi for Trade," *Financial Times*, August 26, 2010.

44. Testimony of Michael McConnell Before the Senate Committee on Commerce, Science, and Transportation, "Seizing Opportunity While Managing Risk in the Digital Age," February 23, 2010, http://commerce.senate.gov/public/?a=Files.Serve&File_id=52507485-dfbe-4873–8089–82dd24f7beaa.

45. James K. Jackson, "Foreign Direct Investment in the United States: An Economic Analysis," Congressional Research Service, February 1, 2011, www.fas.org/sgp/crs/misc/RS21857.pdf.

46. US Department of the Treasury, "Major Foreign Holders of Treasury Securities," www.treasury.gov/resource-center/data-chart-center/tic/Documents/mfh.txt.

47. US Energy Information Administration (EIA), "Frequently Asked Questions," www.eia.gov/tools/faqs/faq.cfm?id=32&t=6; Neelesh Nerurkar, "U.S. Oil Imports: Context and Considerations," Congressional Research Service, April 1, 2011, www.fas.org/sgp/crs/misc/R41765.pdf.

48. Bremmer, *The End of the Free Market*.

49. Richard J. Elkus Jr., *Winner Take All: How Competitiveness Shapes the Fate of Nations* (New York: Basic Books, 2008).

50. Mark Clayton, "WikiLeaks List of 'Critical' Sites: Is It a 'Menu for Terrorists'?" Christian Science Monitor, December 6, 2010, www.csmonitor.com/USA/Foreign-Policy/2010/1206/WikiLeaks-list-of-critical-sites-Is-it-a-menu-for-terrorists.

51. Directorate for Science, Technology and Industry, Maritime Transport Committee, "Security in Maritime Transport: Risk Factors and Economic Impact," July 2003, Organisation for Economic Co-operation and Development, www.oecd.org/dataoecd/19/61/18521672.pdf, 18–19.

52. "Highlights: Bernanke's Press Conference on Fed Policy," Reuters, April 27, 2011, http://uk.reuters.com/article/2011/04/27/us-usa-fed-bernanke-highlights-idUKTRE73Q6ZU20110427.

53. Christine Parthemore, "Elements of Security: Mitigating the Risks of U.S. Dependence on Critical Minerals," June 12, 2011, www.cnas.org/files/documents/publications/CNAS_Minerals_Parthemore_1.pdf.

54. See "DeLauro, Wolf to Protect American Defense Interests," May 25, 2011, http://delauro.house.gov/index.php?option=com_content&view=article&id=536:delauro-wolf-work-to-protect-american-defense-interests&catid=7:2011-press-releases&Itemid=23. Congresswoman DeLauro, a sponsor of the amendment to the defense bill, stated: "With China making significant progress in the defense and aerospace industries, including a Chinese state-controlled company considering a bid for the next presidential helicopter, it is critical that we ensure U.S. national security is protected and that the highly skilled jobs and associated technologies in these industries are not outsourced overseas."

55. US Department of the Treasury, "Statement from the Treasury Department on the President's Decision Regarding Ralls Corporation," September 29, 2012, www.treasury.gov/press-center/press-releases/Pages/tg1724.aspx.

56. Testimony of Michael McConnell Before the Senate Committee on Commerce, Science, and Transportation, "Seizing Opportunity While Manag-

ing Risk in the Digital Age," February 23, 2010, http://commerce.senate.gov/public/?a=Files.Serve&File_id=52507485-dfbe-4873–8089–82dd24f7beaa.

57. "Internet Matters: The Net's Sweeping Impact on Growth, Jobs, and Prosperity," May 2011, McKinsey Global Institute, www.mckinsey.com/mgi/publications/internet_matters/pdfs/MGI_internet_matters_full_report.pdf.

58. Keith Alexander, "Cybersecurity," speech at the Aspen Security Forum, July 26, 2012, www.aspeninstitute.org/about/blog/general-keith-alexander-protecting-homeland-cyber-attacks.

59. McAfee and Science Applications International Corporation (SAIC), Underground Economies, 2011, McAfee, Inc., www.mcafee.com/us/resources/reports/rp-underground-economies.pdf. Note that McAfee has extrapolated the figure $1 trillion in economic loss from its study and estimates of value of intellectual property and expenses paid by companies affected by cyber-attacks and espionage.

60. Dmitri Alperovitch, "Revealed: Operation Shady RAT," Threat Research, McAfee, Inc., August 3, 2011, www.mcafee.com/us/resources/white-papers/wp-operation-shady-rat.pdf.

61. Joseph Menn, "Chinese Hackers Hit Energy Groups," *Financial Times*, February 10, 2011, www.ft.com/cms/s/0/8a4b497a-34b4–11e0–9ebc-00144feabdc0.html#axzz1R3BKyVFS.

62. Keith Alexander, "Cybersecurity and American Power," July 9, 2012, American Enterprise Institute, www.aei.org/events/2012/07/09/cybersecurity-and-american-power/.

63. "Code Wars," editorial, *Washington Post*, June 3, 2012, www.washingtonpost.com/opinions/code-wars/2012/06/03/gJQAlUM1BV_story.html.

64. Nicole Perlroth, "Virus Seeking Bank Data Is Tied to Attack on Iran," *New York Times*, August 9, 2012.

65. Katherine Maher, "Did the Bounds of Cyber War Just Expand to Banks and Neutral States?" *The Atlantic*, August 17, 2012.

66. Kim Zetter, "Researchers Seek Help Cracking Gauss Mystery Payload," *Wired*, August 14, 2012, www.wired.com/threatlevel/2012/08/gauss-mystery-payload/.

67. Ibid.

68. David Nordell, "Is the New 'Gauss' Malware a Counter-Terror Finance Intelligence Tool?" August 12, 2012, Terror-Finance Blog, www.terrorfinance.org/the_terror_finance_blog/2012/08/is-the-new-gauss-malware-a-counter-terror-finance-intelligence-tool.html?utm_source=feedburner&utm_medium=email&utm_campaign=Feed%3A+TerrorFinanceBlog+%28The+Terror+Finance+Blog%29.

69. E. Scott Reckard, Andrew Tangel, and Jim Puzzanghera, "Banks Fail to Repel Cyber Threat," *Los Angeles Times*, September 27, 2012; see also Kaspersky Labs, "Kaspersky Lab Discovers 'Gauss'—A New Complex Cyber-Threat Designed to Monitor Online Banking Accounts," Kaspersky Labs Virus News, August 9, 2012, www.kaspersky.com/about/news/virus/2012/Kaspersky_Lab_and_ITU_Discover_Gauss_A_New_Complex_Cyber_Threat_Designed_to_Monitor_Online_Banking_Accounts.

70. Harald Malmgren and Mark Stys, "Computerized Global Trading 24/6: A Roller Coaster Ride Ahead?" *The International Economy*, Spring 2011, 32.

71. Rob Iati, "The Real Story of Software Trading Espionage," *Advanced Trading*, July 10, 2009.

72. "Findings Regarding the Market Events of May 6, 2010," Report of the Staffs of the CFTC and SEC to the Joint Advisory Committee on Emerging Regulatory Issues, September 30, 2011, www.sec.gov/news/studies/2010/market events-report.pdf.

73. Ibid., 62.

74. World Economic Forum, "Global Risks 2008: A Global Risk Network Report," January 2008, https://members.weforum.org/pdf/globalrisk/report 2008.pdf, 10–11.

75. In Eric Doll, "The Price of Globalization: Economic Growth Requires Corporate Responsibility," September 2009, JP Morgan, www.jpmorgan.com/cm/ContentServer?cid=1159398714398&pagename=jpmorgan%2Fts%2FTS_Content%2FGeneral&c=TS_Content. Senator Carl Levin is quoted as saying, "Estimates are that $500 billion to $1 trillion of international criminal proceeds are moved internationally and deposited into bank accounts annually. It is estimated that half of that money comes to the United States."

76. Rule 204T was adopted in 2008 in response to continuing concerns regarding "fails to deliver" and potentially abusive "naked" short selling. In particular, Rule 204T(a) makes it a violation of Regulation SHO if a broker-dealer does not close out a fail resulting from a short sale in any equity security by no later than the beginning of trading on the day after the scheduled settlement of the trade. Under Rule 204T(a), a broker-dealer that is a participant of a registered clearing agency (a "participant") must deliver securities to a registered clearing agency for clearance and settlement on a long or short sale in any equity security by the settlement date. If a participant has a fail position at a registered clearing agency resulting from a short sale, the participant is required, by no later than the beginning of regular trading hours on the settlement day following the settlement date (i.e., T+4), to immediately close out the fail by borrowing or purchasing securities of like kind and quantity. See "SEC Issues New Rules to Protect Investors Against Naked Short Selling Abuses," September 17, 2008, www.sec.gov/news/press/2008/2008–204.htm.

77. "Mullen: Debt Is Top National Security Threat," CNN, August 27, 2010, http://articles.cnn.com/2010–08–27/us/debt.security.mullen_1_pentagon-budget-national-debt-michael-mullen?_s=PM:US.

78. James G. Rickards, "Economic Security and National Security: Interaction and Synthesis," *Strategic Studies Quarterly*, Fall 2009, www.au.af.mil/au/ssq/2009/Fall/rickards.pdf; Vincent Cable, "What Is International Economic Security?" *International Affairs* 71, no. 2 (1995): 305–324.

79. Robert M. Kimmitt, "Public Footprints in Private Markets: Sovereign Wealth Funds and the World Economy," *Foreign Affairs*, January/February 2008, www.foreignaffairs.com/articles/63053/robert-m-kimmitt/public-footprints-in-private-markets.

80. Robert M. Kimmitt, "Give Treasury Its Proper Role on the National Security Council," *New York Times*, July 23, 2012, www.nytimes.com/2012/07

/24/opinion/give-treasury-its-proper-role-on-the-national-security-council.html.

81. Chi Lo, "Going Global: The Risks and Rewards of China's New International Expansion," *The International Economy*, Spring 2011, 55. Chi Lo wrote, "New times need new policies. A plausible way to make China play by the international rules would be to weave a web of multilateral arrangements into which China could fit and by which China would be bound."

82. White House, "Cyberspace Policy Review: Assuring a Trusted and Resilient Information and Communications Infrastructure," May 2009, www.whitehouse.gov/assets/documents/Cyberspace_Policy_Review_final.pdf.

83. Baruch Fischhoff, Scott Atran, and Marc Sageman, "Mutually Assured Support: A Security Doctrine for Terrorist Nuclear Weapon Threats," *Annals of the American Academy of Political and Social Science* 618, no. 1 (2008): 160–167.

Selected Bibliography

Books

Bremmer, Ian. *The End of the Free Market: Who Wins the War Between States and Corporations?* New York: Penguin, 2011.

Bush, George W. *Decision Points*. New York: Crown, 2010.

Cassara, John, and Avi Jorisch. *On the Trail of Terror Finance: What Law Enforcement and Intelligence Officers Need to Know*. Arlington, VA: Red Cell Intelligence Group, 2010.

Cha, Victor. *The Impossible State: North Korea, Past and Future*. New York: Ecco, 2012.

Chinoy, Mike. *Meltdown: The Inside Story of the North Korean Nuclear Crisis*. New York: St. Martin's Griffin, 2009.

Cohen, Benjamin J. *The Geography of Money*. Ithaca, NY: Cornell University Press, 2000.

Cortright, David, and George Lopez, eds. *Smart Sanctions: Targeting Economic Statecraft*. New York: Rowan and Littlefield, 2002.

Cronin, Audrey Kurth. *How Terrorism Ends: Understanding the Decline and Demise of Terrorist Organizations*. Princeton, NJ: Princeton University Press, 2011.

Crumpton, Henry. *The Art of Intelligence: Lessons from a Life in the CIA's Clandestine Service*. New York: Penguin, 2012.

Drezner, Daniel. *The Sanctions Paradox: Economic Statecraft and International Relations*. Cambridge: Cambridge University Press, 1999.

D'Souza, Jayesh. *Terrorist Financing, Money Laundering, and Tax Evasion: Examining the Performance of Financial Intelligence Units*. Boca Raton, FL: CRC Press, 2011.

Eberstadt, Nicholas. *The North Korean Economy: Between Crisis and Catastrophe*. Edison, NJ: Transaction, 2009.

Elkus, Richard J., Jr. *Winner Take All: How Competitiveness Shapes the Fate of Nations*. New York: Basic Books, 2008.

Farah, Douglas, and Stephen Braun. *Merchant of Death: Money, Guns, Planes and the Man Who Makes War Possible*. New York: Wiley, 2008.

Ferguson, Niall. *The Ascent of Money: A Financial History of the World*. New York: Penguin, 2008.

Glenny, Misha. *McMafia: A Journey Through the Global Criminal Underworld*. New York: Vintage, 2009.

Godson, Roy. *Dirty Tricks or Trump Cards: U.S. Covert Action and Counterintelligence*. Edison, NJ: Transaction, 2000.

Gurulé, Jimmy. *Unfunding Terror: The Legal Response to the Financing of Global Terrorism*. Northampton, MA: Edward Elgar, 2009.

Haass, Richard. *Economic Sanctions and American Diplomacy*. New York: Council on Foreign Relations Press, 1998.

Kunz, Diane B. *The Economic Diplomacy of the Suez Crisis*. Chapel Hill: University of North Carolina Press, 1991.

Levitt, Matthew. "Financial Sanctions." In *The Iran Primer*. Washington, DC: United States Institute of Peace, 2010.

———. *Hamas: Politics, Charity and Terrorism in the Service of Jihad*. New Haven, CT: Yale University Press, 2007.

Mazur, Robert. *The Infiltrator: My Secret Life Inside the Dirty Banks Behind Pablo Excobar's Medellin Cartel*. New York: Little, Brown, 2009.

McDermott, Rose. *Risk-Taking in International Politics: Prospect Theory in American Foreign Policy*. Ann Arbor: University of Michigan Press, 2001.

Naím, Moisés. *Illicit: How Smugglers, Traffickers and Copycats Are Hijacking the Global Economy*. New York: Anchor, 2006.

National Commission on Terrorist Attacks upon the United States. *The 9/11 Commission Report*. Washington, DC: US Government Printing Office, 2004. Available at http://govinfo.library.unt.edu/911/report/index.htm.

O'Sullivan, Meghan. *Shrewd Sanctions: Statecraft and State Sponsors of Terrorism* (Brookings Institution Press, 2003).

Ottolenghi, Emanuele. *The Pasadran: Inside Iran's Islamic Revolutionary Guard Corps*. Washington, DC: Foundation for Defense of Democracies, 2011.

Parsi, Trita. *A Single Roll of the Dice: Obama's Diplomacy with Iran*. New Haven, CT: Yale University Press, 2012.

Paulson, Henry M., Jr. *On the Brink: Inside the Race to Stop the Collapse of the Global Financial System*. New York: Business Plus, 2010.

Peters, Gretchen. *Seeds of Terror: How Drugs, Thugs and Crime Are Reshaping the Afghan War*. New York: Picador, 2010.

Rickards, James. *Currency Wars: The Making of the Next Global Crisis*. New York: Penguin, 2012.

Schmitt, Eric, and Thom Shanker. *Counterstrike: The Untold Story of America's Secret Campaign Against Al Qaeda*. New York: Holt, 2011.

Taylor, Brendan. *Sanctions as Grand Strategy*. New York: Routledge, 2010.

Taylor, John. *Financial Warriors: The Untold Story of International Finance in the Post-9/11 World*. New York: W. W. Norton, 2008.

Trinkunas, Harold, and Jeanne Giraldo, eds. *Terrorism Financing and State Responses: A Comparative Perspective*. Palo Alto, CA: Stanford University Press, 2007.

Wehrey, Frederic, Jerrold D. Green, Brian Nichiporuk, and Alireza Nader. *The Rise of the Pasadran: Assessing the Domestic Roles of Iran's Islamic Revolutionary Guards Corps*. Washington, DC: RAND, 2009.

World at Risk: The Report of the Commission on the Prevention of WMD Proliferation and Terrorism. Bob Graham and Jim Talent, cochairs. New York: Vintage Books, 2008.

Reports, Articles, and Testimonies

Allbritton, Chris, and Mark Hosenball, "Special Report: Why the U.S. Mistrusts Pakistan's Spies." Reuters, May 5, 2011.

Asher, David, Victor Comras, and Patrick Cronin. "Pressure: Coercive Economic Statecraft and U.S. National Security." Center for a New American Security, January 2011.

Bahney, Benjamin, Howard Shatz, et al. "An Economic Analysis of the Financial Records of al-Qa'ida in Iraq." RAND, 2010.

Bajoria, Jayshree. "The Six Party Talks on North Korea's Nuclear Program." Council on Foreign Relations, February 29, 2012.

Baker, Peter. "U.S. Sets New Sanctions Against Technology for Syria and Iran." *New York Times*, April 23, 2012.

Becker, Jo. "Beirut Bank Seen as a Hub of Hezbollah's Financing." *New York Times*, December 13, 2011.

———. "U.S. Approved Business with Blacklisted Nations." *New York Times*, December 23, 2010.

———. "Web of Shell Companies Veils Trade by Iranian Ships." *New York Times*, June 7, 2010.

Benjamin, Daniel. Testimony Before the House Foreign Affairs Committee, "LRA, Boko Haram, Al-Shabaab, AQIM, and Other Sources of Instability in Africa," April 25, 2012.

Bjelopera, Jerome, and Kristin Finklea. "Organized Crime: An Evolving Challenge for U.S. Law Enforcement." Congressional Research Service, January 6, 2012.

Blanchard, Christopher M., and Alfred B. Prados. "Saudi Arabia: Terrorist Financing Issues." Congressional Research Service, updated September 14, 2007.

Braun, Mike. Testimony Before the House Foreign Affairs Committee, "Ahmadinejad's Tour of Tyrants and Iran's Agenda in the Western Hemisphere," February 2, 2012.

Brennan, John. "Ensuring al-Qa'ida's Demise." Speech at Paul H. Nitze School of Advanced International Studies, June 29, 2011.

Brisard, Jean-Charles. "Written Testimony of Jean-Charles Brisard, International Expert on Terrorism Financing, Before the Committee on Banking, Housing and Urban Affairs, United States Senate," October 22, 2003.

Brugière, Jean-Louis. "Second Report on the Processing of EU-Originating Personal Data by the United States Treasury Department for Counterterrorism Purposes," January 2010.

Bruno, Greg. "Backgrounder: Al-Qaeda's Financial Pressures." Council on Foreign Relations, February 1, 2010.

Burns, John, and Kirk Semple. "U.S. Finds Insurgency Has Funds to Sustain Itself." *New York Times*, November 26, 2006.

Carter, Jimmy. Executive Order 12170, "Blocking Iranian Government Property," November 14, 1979.

Caryl, Christian. "Bank Shot." *Foreign Policy*, June 21, 2010.

Choi Kung-soo. "The Mining Industry of North Korea." Nautilus Institute for Security and Sustainability, August 4, 2011.

Christoff, Joseph A. Testimony Before the Committee on Foreign Relations, "Observations on the Oil for Food Program," US Senate, April 7, 2004.

Clinton, Hillary. "Remarks at the 2011 U.S. Global Leadership Coalition (USGLC) Conference," July 12, 2011.

Cohen, David. "Enhancing International Cooperation Against Terrorism Financing." Speech to Washington Institute for Near East Policy, April 7, 2010.

Cook, Colleen. "Mexico's Drug Cartels." Congressional Research Service, February 25, 2008.

Cordesman, Anthony, and Khalid al-Rodhan. "Iranian Nuclear Weapons? The Uncertain Nature of Iran's Nuclear Programs." Center for Strategic and International Studies, April 12, 2006.

Dubowitz, Mark. "So You Want to Be a Sanctions Buster." *Foreign Policy*, August 10, 2012.

Duelfer, Charles. "Comprehensive Report of the Special Advisor to the DCI on Iraq's WMD." Central Intelligence Agency, September 30, 2004.

Economy, Elizabeth. "The Game Changer: Coping with China's Foreign Policy Revolution." *Foreign Affairs*, November/December 2010.

Emerson, Steven. Testimony Before the United States House of Representatives Committee on Foreign Affairs, Subcommittee on Terrorism, Nonproliferation and Trade, July 31, 2008.

Farah, Douglas. "The Role of Conflict Diamonds and Failed States in the Terrorist Financial Structure." The Watson Institute, October 24, 2003.

———. "Terrorist-Criminal Pipelines and Criminalized States: Emerging Alliances." *Prism* 2, no. 3 (2011).

Financial Action Task Force (FATF). "International Best Practices: Detecting and Preventing the Cross-Border Transportation of Cash by Terrorists and Other Criminals," February 12, 2005.

Financial Action Task Force (FATF). "Global Money Laundering and Terrorist Financing Threat Assessment," July 2010. Available at www.fatf-gafi.org/topics/methodsandtrends/documents/globalmoneylaunderingterroristfinancingthreatassessment.html.

Finklea, Kristin M. "Organized Crime in the United States: Trends and Issues for Congress." Congressional Research Service, January 27, 2010.

Fischhoff, Baruch, Scott Atran, and Marc Sageman. "Mutually Assured Support: A Security Doctrine for Terrorist Nuclear Weapon Threats." *The Annals of the American Academy of Political and Social Science* 618, no. 1 (2008): 160–167.

Gurulé, Jimmy. "The Global Fight Against the Financing of Terror: Prevention—A New Paradigm." US Department of the Treasury, June 26, 2002.

Hosenball, Mark. "A Swiss Connection to a Pakistani Bomb Racket?" *Newsweek*, March 1, 2004.

Hosenball, Mark, Kevin Peraino, and Catherine Skipp. "Terror's Cash Flow." *Newsweek*, March 25, 2002.

Hout, Thomas M., and Pankaj Ghemawat. "China vs the World: Whose Technology Is It?" *Harvard Business Review*, December 2010.

Jacobson, Michael. "Terrorist Financing and the Internet." *Studies in Conflict and*

Terrorism, March 9, 2010.

Jost, Patrick M. "The Hawala Alternative Remittance System and Its Role in Money Laundering." US Department of the Treasury, 1999.

Jost, Patrick, and Harjit Singh Sandhu. "The Hawala Alternative Remittance System and Its Role in Money Laundering." Interpol General Secretariat, January 2000.

Katzmann, Kenneth. "Iran Sanctions." Congressional Research Service, December 7, 2012.

Kimmitt, Robert M. "Public Footprints in Private Markets: Sovereign Wealth Funds and the World Economy." *Foreign Affairs*, January/February 2008.

"Kurds and Pay: Examining PKK Financing." *Jane's Intelligence Review*, March 13, 2008.

Leiter, Mike. Testimony Before the Senate Homeland Security and Government Affairs Committee, "Eight Years After 9/11: Confronting the Terrorist Threat to the Homeland," September 30, 2009.

Lenzner, Robert, and Nathan Vardi. "Terror Inc." *Forbes*, October 18, 2004.

Levey, Stuart. "Fighting Corruption After the Arab Spring." *Foreign Affairs*, June 2011.

Levey, Stuart. "Letter from the United States Department of the Treasury Regarding SWIFT/Terrorist Finance Tracking Programme." *Official Journal of the European Union* 100, no. 166 (2007).

———. "Loss of Moneyman a Big Blow to al Qaeda." *Washington Post*, June 6, 2010.

Levey, Stuart, and Christy Clark. "Follow the Money." *Foreign Policy*, October 3, 2011.

Levitt, Matthew. "Checkbook Jihad." *Foreign Policy*, May 11, 2011.

———. "Following the Money: Leveraging Financial Intelligence to Combat Transnational Threats." *Georgetown Journal of International Affairs*, Winter/Spring 2011.

Lichtblau, Eric. "Controls on Bank-Data Spying Impress Civil Liberties Board." *New York Times*, November 29, 2006.

———. "Homeland Security Department Experiments with New Tool to Track Financial Crime." *New York Times*, December 12, 2004.

———. "White House Challenges Critics on Spying." *New York Times*, August 7, 2007.

Lichtblau, Eric, and James Risen. "Bank Data Is Sifted by U.S. in Secret to Block Terror." *New York Times*, June 23, 2006.

———. "Hoard of Cash Lets Qaddafi Extend Fight Against Rebels." *New York Times*, March 9, 2011.

Lichtblau, Eric, and Eric Schmitt. "Cash Flow to Terrorists Evades U.S. Efforts." *New York Times*, December 5, 2010.

Loeffler, Rachel. "Bank Shots: How the Financial System Can Isolate Rogues." *Foreign Affairs*, March/April 2009.

Maimbo, Samuel Munzele. "The Money Exchange Dealers of Kabul: A Study of the Hawala System in Afghanistan." World Bank, Finance and Private Sector Unit, South Asia Region, June 2003.

McConnell, Michael. Testimony Before the Senate Committee on Commerce,

Science, and Transportation, "Seizing Opportunity While Managing Risk in the Digital Age," February 23, 2010.

Meyer, Josh, and Greg Miller. "U.S. Secretly Tracks Global Bank Data." *Los Angeles Times*, June 23, 2006.

Mowatt-Larssen, Rolf. "Al Qaeda Weapons of Mass Destruction: Hype or Reality?" Belfer Center for Science and International Affairs, January 2010.

Naím, Moisés. "Mafia States." *Foreign Affairs*, April 20, 2012.

Nanto, Dick K. "North Korean Counterfeiting of U.S. Currency." Congressional Research Service, June 12, 2009.

O'Harrow, Robert, Jr., James V. Grimaldi, and Bradley Dennis. "Sanctions in 72 Hours: How the U.S. Pulled Off a Major Freeze of Libyan Assets." *Washington Post*, March 23, 2011.

Osnos, Evan. "The God of Gamblers." *The New Yorker*, April 9, 2012.

Park, John S. "North Korea, Inc." United States Institute of Peace Working Paper, April 22, 2009.

Parthemore, Christine. "Elements of Security: Mitigating the Risks of U.S. Dependence on Critical Minerals." Center for a New American Security, June 12, 2011.

Peters, Gretchen. "How Opium Profits the Taliban." United States Institute of Peace, August 2009.

Pound, Edward. "Following the Old Money Trail." *U.S. News and World Report*, March 27, 2005.

Prahar, Peter. Testimony Before the US Senate Committee on Homeland Security and Governmental Affairs, "North Korea: Illicit Activity Funding the Regime," April 25, 2006.

Reilly, James. "China's Unilateral Sanctions." *Washington Quarterly*, Fall 2012.

Rickards, James G. "Economic Security and National Security: Interaction and Synthesis." *Strategic Studies Quarterly*, Fall 2009.

Rose, David. "North Korea's Dollar Store." *Vanity Fair*, August 5, 2009.

Schmidle, Nicholas. "Disarming Viktor Bout." *The New Yorker*, March 5, 2012.

Shannon, Elaine, Adam Zagorin, and Michael Duffy. "Feds Doubt Allegations of Saudi Terror Funding." *Time*, November 24, 2002.

Shultz, Richard, Roy Godson, Querine Hanlon, and Samantha Ravich. "The Sources of Instability in the Twenty-First Century." *Strategic Studies Quarterly*, Summer 2011.

Simpson, Glen. "Treasury Tracks Financial Data in Secret Program." *Wall Street Journal*, June 23, 2006.

Solomon, Jay. "U.S. Renews Exemptions from Iran Sanctions." *Wall Street Journal*, December 7, 2012.

Solomon, Jay, and Glenn Simpson. "U.S. Turns Up the Heat on Iran." *Wall Street Journal*, October 26, 2007.

Stalinsky, Steven. "Saudi Royal Family's Financial Support to the Palestinians, 1998–2003: More Than 15 Million Riyals ($2 Billion US) Given to 'Mujahideen Fighters' and 'Families of Martyrs.'" Middle East Media Research Institute, Special Report No. 17, July 3, 2003.

Taylor, Paul D. "Economic Coercion in the Service of National Security."

Address to Current Strategy Forum, US Naval War College, June 16, 1998.

Thachuk, Kimberley L. "Terrorism's Financial Lifeline: Can It Be Severed?" Strategic Forum, Institute for National Strategic Studies, National Defense University, no. 191, May 2002.

United Nations, Office on Drugs and Crime. "Estimating Illicit Financial Flows Resulting from Drug Trafficking and Other Transnational Crimes: Research Report," October 2011.

United Nations Security Council. Resolution 986, April 14, 1995.

———. Resolution 1373, September 28, 2001.

US Department of State. "Saddam Hussein's Iraq," September 1999.

US Department of the Treasury, Office of Foreign Assets Control. "Cuba: What You Need to Know About U.S. Sanctions Against Cuba," January 24, 2012.

US Senate Permanent Subcommittee on Investigations. "U.S. Vulnerabilities to Money Laundering, Drugs, and Terrorist Financing: HSBC Case History," July 17, 2012.

White House. "Cyberspace Policy Review: Assuring a Trusted and Resilient Information and Communications Infrastructure," May 2009.

———. "Strategy to Combat Transnational Organized Crime," July 2011.

Zarate, Juan C. Keynote Address to Harper's Bazaar / International Anti-Counterfeiting Coalition Summit, New York, February 1, 2005.

———. "Playing a New Geoeconomic Game." Center for Strategic and International Studies, April 17, 2012.

———. "Prepared Remarks to Florida Bankers Association," February 9, 2005.

———. "Prepared Remarks to Islamic Society of North America's Sixth Annual Education Event," March 25, 2005.

———. "Securing the Financial System Against Rogue Capital." Keynote Address for Investment Company Institute, November 10, 2003.

———. Testimony Before the House Armed Services Committee, "Al-Qa'ida in 2010: How Should the US Respond?" January 27, 2010.

———. Testimony Before the House Financial Services Subcommittee on Oversight and Investigations, February 16, 2005.

———. Testimony Before the House Financial Services Subcommittees on Domestic and International Monetary Policy, Trade and Technology, and Oversight and Investigations, September 30, 2004.

———. Testimony Before the House Foreign Affairs Committee, Subcommittee on Terrorism, Nonproliferation, and Trade, "Financial Hardball: Corralling Terrorists and Proliferators," April 6, 2011.

———. Testimony Before the House International Relations Financial Subcommittee on the Middle East and Central Asia, March 24, 2004.

———. Testimony Before the Senate Caucus on International Narcotics Control, March 4, 2004.

———. Testimony Before the Senate Foreign Relations Committee, March 18, 2003.

———. Testimony Before the Senate Permanent Subcommittee on Investigations, November 15, 2004.

INDEX

Abacha, Sani, 355
Abbottabad (Pakistan), 362, 397
Abdullah, Crown Prince (later King), 67
  attempted assassination of, 107
  on terrorist financing, 73–75, 78
ABN Amro, 302
Abqaiq (Saudi Arabia), 398
Abrams, Elliott, 156, 291
Abu Dhabi Declaration on Hawala, 95–96
Adams, Tim, 16, 134–135, 138
Aden (Yemen), 18
Afghan Threat Finance Cell, 196
Afghanistan, 370, 388, 389
  Al Qaeda in, 17, 70, 113
  bin Laden in, 42
  Finance Ministry of, 97, 100
  and hawalas, 94, 97–101
  mineral wealth of, 394
  and mujahideen financing, 68, 70, 84–85
  Soviet Union in, 17, 68, 84, 120
  Taliban in, 16–17, 79, 116, 197
  and terrorist financing, 15, 81, 116, 304
African Union, 363
Agency for International Development
  (AID), 100, 430
Ahmad, Najmuddin Faraj. See Krekar, Mullah
Ahmadinejad, Mahmoud, 327, 338, 341–342
Alabama, 204
al-'Ajmi, 'Ali Hasan 'Ali, 82–83
Alamoudi, Abdurahman Muhammad, 208
  and Al Qaeda, 108
  and assassination plot, 107
  as cash courier, 105–108
  political views of, 107–108
Albania, 81, 299
al-Aqil, Sheikh Aqeel Abdulaziz, 72, 76
al-Assad, Bashar (and regime of), 86,
  156–157, 354, 366
  assets of, 352–354
  and Iran, 350
  and Lebanon, 191, 193–194
  opposition to, 355
Al Barakaat Foundation, 81
Al Barakaat network, 37–39, 362

al-Dulaimi, Khalaf, 194–195
Alexander, Keith, 405, 407
al-Fadl, Jamal, 80
Algeria, 164
Algiers Accords, 24, 287
al-Hamzi, Nawaf, 20, 85
Al Haramain Foundation, 72–73, 75–76, 77
al-Hassan, Wissam, 194
al-Hawsawi, Mustafa Ahmad, 20
Al Jazeera, 425
al-Jubeir, Adel, 74, 370
al-Kassar, Manzar (aka "Prince of Marbella"),
  368, 378
al-Khawar, Abdallah Ghanim Mafuz Muslim,
  82
al-Kuwari, Salim Hasan Khalifa Rashid, 82
Allianz, 335
Al Manar cable station, 358
al-Mihdhar, Khalid, 20, 85
al-Otari, Muhammad Naji, 157
Alperovitch, Dmitri, 406
al-Qadi, Yasin, 81
Al Qaeda, 116, 197, 207, 288, 348, 430–431
  attacks on Saudi Arabia, 76
  budget of, 2, 362
  and cash couriers, 102, 104, 108
  funding of, 19–20, 36, 37–38, 42–43, 51,
    69–70, 78–80, 86, 90–91, 110–111, 127,
    199
  and Golden Chain list, 80, 82
  and hawalas, 94–95
  in Iran, 364
  in Iraq, 113–114, 194–196, 362, 365
  and Jemaah Islamiyah, 63
  and kidnapping, 363
  and money transfers, 62–63, 71–72
  and Muslim Brotherhood, 427
  and 9/11, 8, 19–20, 362
  in Pakistan, 364–365, 366
  pensions of, 1
  sanctions against, 7, 12
  and SWIFT, 59
  as target of OFAC, 26
  and UN, 33

Al Qaeda and Associated Movements
    (AQAM), 362, 364–365, 367
Al Qaeda in the Arabian Peninsula (AQAP),
    78
  and Operation Hemorrhage, 397–398
Al Qaeda in the Islamic Maghreb (AQIM),
    362–363, 365
al-Qaradawi, Sheikh Yusuf, 427
Al Quds Intifada, 86–87
al-Rahman, Atiyah Abd, 82, 366
al-Rajhi, Suleiman, 80
al-Rifai, Ghassan, 157
al-Saud, Prince Nayef bin Abdulaziz, 74, 77,
    87
Al Shabaab, 363–365, 431
al-Suweidi, Sultan, 95, 96
Al Taqwa network, 40
al-Tikriti, Barzan, 187
Al Wasel & Babel, 186
al-Yazid, Mustafa (aka Sheikh Said), 42–43
al-Zarqawi, Abu Mus'ab, 113, 114
al-Zawahiri, Ayman, 42, 43, 79
  on Islamic charities, 71
  and terrorist financing, 82
Amazon, 430
American Israel Public Affairs Committee
    (AIPAC), 338
American Muslim Council (AMC), 105
American Muslim Foundation (AMF),
    105–106
Amman (Jordan), 182–183, 189
Amsterdam (Netherlands), 311
Angola, 119, 149
Annan, Kofi, 192
Ansar al-Islam (AI), 112
Ansar al-Sunnah (AS). See Ansar al-Islam
Arab Bank PLC, 148
Arab League, 87
  summit meetings of, 107
  and Syria, 354, 355
Arabian Gulf, 36, 65
Aramco, 410
Argentina, 117, 400
Arian Bank, 306
Arizona (US), 276
Armenia, 303
Armitage, Richard, 228, 250
Arms Export Control Act, 306
Asaluyeh (Iran), 334
Ashcroft, John, 31
Asher, David, 228–231, 236, 237, 245
Asia Pacific Economic Cooperation (APEC),
    64
Asia Wealth Bank, 155
Asian Clearing Union (ACU), 339
Assange, Julian, 430
Atlantic, The, 394, 409
AT&T, 367
Aufhauser, David, 26, 135, 143
  and financial intelligence, 46
  and policy coordination committees, 39
  on Saudi Arabia, 83
  and SWIFT, 51–54, 56–58

and white paper on restructuring Treasury,
    201–202, 205
Aum Shinrikyo, 23
Australia, 233
Austria, 233, 241
Aviatrans Anstalt, 188
Azadegan development project (Iran), 337
Aziz Ali, Ali Abdul, 20
Aziz, Tariq, 181

Baasiri, Muhammad, 164
Bad Bank Initiative, 146, 148, 211
  and Iran, 290
  and money-laundering concerns, 153, 159
  and North Korea, 225, 226, 230
  and reputational risk, 147, 150–153
Baghdad (Iraq), 169–170, 350
Baghdad International Airport, 180
Bahamas, 40
Bahrain, 90, 183
  and FATF, 164
  and Iran, 304, 307
Balkans, 79, 177, 236, 387
Banca d'Italia
  and SWIFT, 49
Banco Delta Asia (BDA), 333, 360
  and Bad Bank Initiative, 226–227
  and North Korea, 225–226, 230–232, 235,
    237, 239–240, 242–246, 249, 251–258,
    261–262, 264–265, 267, 291, 299, 323
  See also North Korea and counterfeiting,
    North Korea and Section 311
Banco Internacional de Desarollo, CA, 304
Bandar Abbas (Iran), 334
Bandar Khomeini (Iran), 334
Bandar, Prince, 74,
  and relationship with US, 84–86
Bangkok (Thailand), 122
Bank Kargoshee, 304
Bank Markazi, 290, 313, 315, 371
  and Section 311, 332–333, 335
Bank of America, 406, 410
  and Al Qaeda, 20
Bank of Canada, 49
Bank of China (Macau), 226, 240, 242
Bank of Credit and Commerce (BCCI), 61,
    129, 145–146
Bank of England, 49, 171
Bank of Japan, 49
Bank of Russia, 161, 162
Bank Melli, 289–290, 304, 307
Bank Melli Iran ZAO, 304
Bank Mellat, 289–290, 303, 307
Bank Saderat, 289–290, 291, 303, 307
  and Bad Bank Initiative, 290
  and Executive Order 13224, 303
  and Hezbollah, 358
Bank Secrecy Act (1970), 18, 30
Bank Sepah, 289–290, 303, 332
Bank Sepah International PLC, 303
Bankers Trust, 313

Banque de France, 49
Barakat, Assad Ahmad, 117–119, 358
Barakat Import Export Ltd., 117–118
Bartlett, Dan, 270
Barzashka, Ivanka, 351
Basham, Ralph, 134
Basque terrorists, 23
Baxter, Tom, 167, 232, 264
Beijing (China), 249
  and North Korea, 220, 226, 227, 254, 258,
    260, 262–263, 266, 323
Beirut (Lebanon), 90, 409
  Hezbollah in, 119, 190, 289–290, 361
  and Iran, 289–290, 333, 360
  and Iraq, 174, 181, 182, 189–192
Belarus, 158, 162, 375, 398, 400
Belgium 120
Benevolence International Foundation (BIF),
  79
Benghazi (Libya), 344
Bernanke, Ben, 404
Biden, Joe, 111
bin Abdulaziz, Prince Salman, 87
bin Laden, Osama, 23, 116, 397
  and Bosnia, 79
  death of, 90
  finances of, 36, 37, 42–43, 110, 362, 363
  and Saudi Arabia, 86
  and South America, 118
  in Sudan, 60
bin Mahfouz, Khalid, 80
bin Nayef (MbN), Prince Muhammad
  attempted assassination of, 78
  and counterterrorism, 77–78
bitcoin (BTC), 395–396
Black, Cofer, 40–41
  and bin Laden, 60, 62
Black Market Peso Exchange, 359
Blackstone, 390
Blair, Tony, 111
Bodman, Sam, 143, 234
Boko Haram, 363, 365
Bollywood, 115
Bolten, Josh, 271
Bombay Stock Exchange, 115
Bond, James, 249
Bonner, Rob, 34–35, 134
bonyads (charitable foundations), 293
Bosnia, 72, 76, 87
  and Al Qaeda financing, 79
Bout, Viktor (aka "Merchant of Death"),
  119–123, 368, 378
  and Air Bas, 120
  and Air Cess, 120
Brandbergen Mosque, 113
Braun, Michael "Mike," 122, 197, 368
Brazil, 117, 118, 400
Brennan, John, 380–381
Bretton Woods, 399
Bridgeman, Mike, 184
British Petroleum (BP), 337, 403
Brothers' Circle, 376, 381
Bruelhart, René, 188

Bruguière, Jean-Louis, 278, 279
Brussels (Belgium)
  as SWIFT headquarters, 54, 56, 270, 274,
    279, 284
Buckles, Brad, 134
Budapest (Hungary), 380
Buddy Bank Initiative, 165–167, 426
Bulgaria, 113
Bunning Jim, 276
Bureau of Alcohol, Tobacco, and Firearms
  (ATF), 18, 26
  and Department of Homeland Security,
    128, 130–132
Bureau of Engraving and Printing, 223
Bureau of Intelligence and Research (INR),
  228
Burma (Myanmar), 158, 172, 241, 322, 389
  money laundering in, 155
Burns, R. Nicholas, 296–299
Burns, William, 264
Bush, George W. (and administration of), 216
  and Alamoudi, 107
  and Department of Homeland Security,
    128–131
  and Executive Order 13315, 170, 186
  and Executive Order 13382, 214–215, 305,
    306, 307, 354
  and Iran, 295–296, 305, 313, 316, 330
  on kleptocracy, 198–197
  National Money Laundering Strategy of, 19
  and National Strategy to Internationalize
    Efforts Against Kleptocracy, 198
  on 9/11, 19
  and North Korea, 224, 228, 232, 249, 253,
    262, 264, 266
  and organized crime, 376–380
  and Proliferation Security Initiative (PSI),
    211
  and Russia, 160
  and SWIFT, 275, 277, 281, 285
  and Syrian Accountability Act, 156–157
  and terrorist financing executive order (EO
    13224), 147

Cairo, 427
Cairo University, 105
Caisse des Dépôts et Consignations (Deposits
  and Consignments Fund), 391
Calame, Byron, 278
California (US), 235
Cameron, Art, 204–206
Camorra, 381
Canada, 380
Capone, Al, 34, 118, 176, 376
Caracas (Venezuela), 375
Card, Andrew, 131
Carter, Jimmy (and administration of)
  and Iran sanctions, 24, 287
Casa Apollo, 117–118
cash couriers, 15, 36, 93, 102–105, 365
Caterpillar, 339

Cedel International, 311
Center for a New American Security, 394
Centrafrican Airlines, 120
Central Bank of Iran. *See* Bank Markazi
Central Bank of Iraq, 172, 173, 362
    and asset recovery, 175–176, 178, 180, 185
    looting of, 169–170, 176, 179
    and record keeping, 179
Central Bank of Jordan, 182
Central Bank of Lebanon, 361
Central Command (CENTCOM), 195
Central Intelligence Agency (CIA), 34
    and Alec Station, 62
    and capture of Hambali, 64
    coordination of, 40–42, 83–84
    Counterterrorist Center (CTC) of, 40
    and Khan, AQ, 212
CET Aviation, 120
Cha, Victor, 244, 245, 253, 255
Chang (Mr.), 263
charities (Islamic)
    effects of financial warfare on, 68–71
    See also Al Barakaat Foundation, Al Hara-
        main Foundation, Benevolence Interna-
        tional Foundation, Muwafaq
        Foundation, Revival of the Islamic Her-
        itage Society
Chase Manhattan bank, 50
Chávez, Hugo, 310, 373
Chechnya, 79, 87
Chemical Bank, 313
Cheney, Dick, 63, 111
    and SWIFT, 58, 271
Chertoff, Michael, 35
Chevron, 403
Chicago (US), 79
"Chimerica," 401
China, 159, 162, 165, 356, 395,
    and anti-money-laundering, 163
    and cyber-crime, 395, 406–407
    Development Bank of, 392
    Export-Import Bank of, 392
    financial power of, 386–387, 389–390,
        392–393, 400, 404, 420
    and Iran, 297, 309, 311, 348, 371
    and Iraq, 392–394
    and Japan, 387
    and North Korea, 220–221, 226–227, 232,
        241–242, 254, 258–259, 265, 267, 323,
        372–373
    and SWIFT, 284
    and Syria, 355
    and US debt, 403, 419
    and US financial crisis (2008), 383, 384
China Tonghua Iron and Steel Group,
    374
Citibank and Citigroup, 150, 406
    and Iran, 311–312, 410
    and Saudi Arabia, 86, 87–89
    and SWIFT, 50
Ciudad Juárez, 1
civil liberties
    and SWIFT, 59, 273, 275, 283
Civil War (US), 4

Clapper, James, 351
Clearstream Banking, 311–312
Clinton, Bill (and administration of)
    and Alamoudi, 107
    and "la lista," 7, 25
    sanctions against Al Qaeda, 7
    sanctions against Cuba, 5
    sanctions against Hezbollah, 7
    sanctions against Serbia, 6
Clinton, Hillary, 264, 342, 388
    and Iran, 331, 333, 349
Cohen, David, 333, 348, 360–361
    on organized crime, 377
Colombia, 369, 430
    and organized crime, 120, 122
    sanctions against, 7
Columbia University
    and Graduate School of International Pub-
        lic Affairs, 165
Commercial Bank of Syria (CBS), 155–157,
    183, 185, 353, 354
Commerzbank, 302
Commission on the Intelligence Capabilities
    of the United States Regarding Weapons
    of Mass Destruction (WMD Commis-
    sion), 214
Committee on Foreign Investment in the
    United States (CFIUS), 393, 405
Community Exchange System (CES),
    397
Comprehensive Iran Sanctions, Accountabil-
    ity, and Divestment Act (CISADA),
    336–337
    Section 103 of, 337
Company D, 115–117
Congressional Research Service, 339
Conlon, Pat, 177–178, 180–181
"Control, The," 23–24
Council of the European Union, 281
Council on Foreign Relations, 390
Craig, Daniel, 249
Credit Suisse
    and Iran, 302, 332
Cuba
    blockade of, 5
    sanctions against, 24, 148, 322
currency wars, 399–402
    and "Currency War III," 401
Customs Service, 18
    and Department of Homeland Security,
        128, 130–132
    and terrorist investigations, 34–35
    See also Operation Green Quest
"Cutting Sword of Justice," 410
cyber-crime and cyber-warfare, 385,
    407–412, 428
    and bitcoins, 395
    and China, 395, 406–407
    and Iraq, 170
    and Secret Service, 131–132
    US preparedness against, 405–406
    See also Flame, Gauss, Shamoon, and
        Stuxnet viruses, Google
Cyprus, 158

Daedong Credit Bank, 225, 243
Dam, Kenneth, 51–52
  and SWIFT, 57–58
Damascus (Syria), 156–157, 183–184, 191,
  350, 366, 375
  and cash couriers, 105
Damascus International Airport, 196
Davis, Lanny, 283
Davis, Michele, 74, 270
Dawa (fundraising), 70
Delta Asia Group (Holdings) Ltd., 225
Democratic People's Republic of Korea
  (DPRK). *See* North Korea
Democratic Republic of the Congo, 119
De Nederlandsche Bank, 49
Department of Defense
  coordination of, 41–42
  Special Operations Command of, 197
Department of Homeland Security (DHS),
  174, 178, 416–418
  creation of, 128–131, 201
  effect on Treasury, 131–136, 202–205,
  208–209
Department of Justice, 129, 133, 208, 300, 343
  Terrorism and Violent Crimes Section of, 18
DerGarabedian, Paul, 103, 140–141
  and Burma, 155
  and China, 163
Deutsche Börse Clearing, 311
Deutsche Bundesbank
  and SWIFT, 49
Development Fund of Iraq (DFI), 189
Dibble, Philo, 156
Doha (Qatar)
  and cash couriers, 105
Donilon, Tom, 345, 347
Donnells, Nan, 140
Dow, 411
Dresdner Bank, 20
Drug Enforcement Administration (DEA),
  35, 369
  and Hezbollah, 360
  and organized crime, 121
  Special Operations Division of, 368
  Strategic Operations Division (SOD) of, 197
Dubai (UAE), 90, 212
  and Al Qaeda, 20
  and cash couriers, 104–105
  and Iran, 289, 331, 371
  and Iraq, 174, 181, 186
Dublin (Ireland), 222–223
Duelfer Report, 173
Dujail Massacre (1982), 187
Duncan, John, 205–206
DuQu malware, 409

East Asia Commercial Bank, 243
Economist, The, 390
Economy, Elizabeth C., 390
Edson, Gary, 21, 189
Egmont Group of Financial Intelligence
  Units, 90, 199

Egypt, 164, 427
  and cash couriers, 105, 106
  and Suez Canal, 5
1811s (Treasury agents), 129, 203
80/20 rule, 35–36, 37, 39
Eisenhower administration, 5
Elaf Bank, 371
Elkus, Jr., Richard, 404
Emanuel, Rahm, 320
ENI oil, 337
Equatorial Guinea, 149
Erdogan, Recep Tayyip, 81
Ernst and Young, 339
Espionage Act, 276
Eurasia Group, 162
European Central Bank, 49
European Commission, 281
European Council of Ministers, 281
European Court of Human Rights, 195
European Court of Justice, 81
European-Iranian Trade Bank AG, 332
European Parliament, 280–281
European Union, 81
  and Iran, 288, 298, 308–309, 331,
  337–339, 348
  and SWIFT, 279–281, 284
  and Syria, 354
Europol, 282
Executive Office of Terrorist Financing
  and Financial Crimes (EOTF/FC), 98,
  165
  creation of, 143
  expansion of, 202, 207
Executive Order 12170, 24
Executive Order 13224, 26–28, 35, 303
Export Administration Act, 306–307
Export Development Bank, 304
ExxonMobil, 393, 403

Facebook, 430
Fahd, King, 67, 74, 87
Fannie Mae, 383
Far Eastern Bank, 264
fatwas (religious rulings), 109
Federación Latinoamericano de Bancos
  (FELEBAN), 166
Federal Bureau of Investigation (FBI), 35, 46,
  203
  on bitcoins, 395–396
  coordination of 41–42, 129, 208, 369
  and North Korea, 229, 235
  and Saudi Arabia, 84–85
  See also Terrorist Financing Operations Section.
Federal Law Enforcement Training Center
  (FLETC), 18, 128, 131
Federal Reserve Bank of New York, 25, 232,
  319, 405
  and Buddy Bank system, 167
  and Iraq reconstruction, 170, 185, 189
  and North Korea, 263–264
  and SWIFT, 49

Federal Reserve System, 148
  and SWIFT, 49
Federation of American Scientists, 351
Feingold, Russ, 273
Ferguson, Niall, 401
Filip, Mark, 379
FININT, 46
Financial Action Task Force (FATF), 90,
  139–140, 211, 250
  and anti-money-laundering, 153, 159–163
  and cash couriers, 103
  and China, 163–164
  global reach of, 164
  and hawalas, 95
  and Iran, 310–311, 333
  and kleptocracy, 199
  and Middle East and North Africa (MENA),
    164, 167
  and Private Sector Development (PSD),
    167
  and Russia, 160–163
  and Special Recommendation VI, 95
  and SWIFT, 52, 59
  on terrorist financing, 31
  and WMD, 215
Financial Crimes Enforcement Network (Fin-
    CEN), 47, 133, 148, 157, 214
  expansion of, 202, 204, 206
financial intelligence
  definition of, 46–47
  effectiveness of, 63–65, 89
  history of, 61–62
  and nuclear proliferation, 62
  uses of, 48–49
financial intelligence units (FIUs), 47
financial power and warfare
  and extraterritorially, 302
  and First Amendment concerns, 111,
    113–114
  history of, 3
  management of, 101–102, 150–151,
    351–352, 426–429
  as national security strategy, 9–12, 29,
    45–46, 63, 383–386, 429–432
  and US dollar, 25–26
  See also USA Patriot Act
Financial Review Group (FRG)
  and 9/11 investigations, 34
  See also Terrorist Financing Operations Sec-
    tion
Financial Times, 334
First East Export Bank, 303
First Merchant Bank, 158
Fitzgerald, Patrick, 18
Flame virus, 408–409
Fonds Strategique d'Investissement (FSI),
  391
Forbes Global 2000, 391
Foreign Intelligence Surveillance Act (FISA),
  272
Foreman, Marcy, 35
Fowler, Jennifer, 260
Fox, Bill, 26
  and SWIFT, 56–57

France, 5, 164, 190, 391, 398
  and Iran, 298, 324
  and Iraq, 393–394
Frankfurt
  and cash couriers, 105
  and Iran, 289, 309, 333
Franklin, Ben, 223
Fratto, Tony, 207
  and SWIFT, 269–274
Freddie Mac, 383
full-time equivalents "FTEs," 141
Future Bank, 304, 306

G7 meetings, 31, 32, 384
G8 summits
  in 2007, 264
  in 2009, 400
G20 Meeting of Finance Ministers, 384
  and Iran, 300
  in 2002, 15
Gardner, Janice, 206–207
Garland, Sean, 222
Gates, Robert, 320, 349
"Gauss" virus, 407–410
Gavito, Jen Sublett, 189–190
Gazprom, 387, 403
Geithner, Timothy, 167, 342
  and Iran, 319–321, 323, 333
  and Libya, 345
  and North Korea, 232, 264
General Electric (GE), 339
Geneva, 187
Georgetown University, 244
Georgia, 377, 387
Germany, 5, 113
  and Iran, 288, 296 298, 301, 324, 332
  and North Korea, 234
Ghana, 407
Gibbons, Tom, 259–260
Glaser, Danny, 31, 139, 157, 167, 245, 348
  and Iran 310–311, 333
  and Middle East and North Africa, 164
  and North Korea, 249–251, 253–254,
    257–262, 299
  and Russia, 160–161
Glencore, 337
Global Positioning System (GPS), 405
Golden Chain list, 80, 82
Golden Star Bank, 233, 241, 267
Goldman Sachs, 255, 295, 300
Google, 406, 418, 430
Goss, Porter, 58
Gotti, John, 376
government-sponsored enterprises (GSEs),
  383
Great Britain, 5, 164, 391
  and Iran, 298, 303, 304, 324, 332
  and Iraq, 393–394
Great Recession of 2008, 9, 383–384, 399
Greece
  Ancient, 3–4, 5
  and DEPA, 387

Green, Mike, 224, 228, 241, 253
Greenberg, Ted, 160, 162
Greenspan, Alan, 57, 58
Group of Ten (G10) countries, 49
Guantanamo Bay (Cuba), 64
Guatemala City (Guatamala), 166
Gucci, 374
Gulf Cooperative Council (GCC), 364
Gurulé, Jimmy, 142
  and CIA, 40
  and Department of Homeland Security,
    127, 131–134
  on money laundering, 18–19
  on terrorist financing, 31, 34–35

Hadley, Steve, 379
  and Iran, 295–296, 299
  and North Korea, 231, 246
  and SWIFT, 271
Hagin, Joe, 129
Hajj, 67
  and Islamic charities, 71
Halliburton, 339
Hamas, 107
  and cash couriers, 105
  fundraising of, 70, 71, 81
  and Iran, 2, 303, 304, 410
  Saudi Arabia's support of, 87
Hambali. *See* Isamuddin, Riduan
Hamilton, Alexander, 45, 130
Hamilton, Lee, 273, 321
Hample, Eric, 134
Hannover Re, 335
Hariri, Rafik, 190–193
Hariri, Saad, 193
Harris, Steve, 204
Hassan, Sheikh Dawood. *See* Ibrahim,
  Dawood
Hatch, Orrin, 18
hawala network, 1, 8, 15, 365
  and Abu Dhabi Declaration, 96
  in Afghanistan, 94, 97–99
  extent of, 93–95
  and FATF Special Recommendation VI, 95
  and hawaladars, 21, 32, 36, 46, 99–100
  in India, 96, 97
  in Pakistan, 94
  regulation of, 96–97, 101
  in Somalia, 37, 94
  in Syria, 157
Hayden, Michael, 244, 276–277
Hayworth, J. D., 276
Headley, David, 430
Hezbollah, 108
  and drug trade, 358–359
  fundraising of, 70
  and Iran, 2, 289–291, 303, 304
  and Lebanon, 190, 193–194, 409
  money laundering of, 359–360
  sanctions against, 7
  in South America, 117–119, 358

and Syria, 354
and used cars, 358–359
in West Africa, 357–359
Hill, Chris
  and North Korea, 236–237, 274, 252, 254,
    256, 259–263, 266
Hinnen, Todd, 111, 113
Ho, Stanley, 225–226
Hochberg Fred P., 392
Hong Kong (China), 31, 400
  and cash couriers, 103, 105
  and Iran, 333, 334, 339
  and North Korea, 220, 221, 226, 241
Hong Kong Electronics, 375
House Financial Services Subcommittee on
    Oversight and Investigations, 275, 278
House Homeland Security Committee, 276
HSBC bank, 185
  and Iran, 349, 370, 371
Hub Culture, 396
  See also Ven digital currency
human intelligence (HUMINT), 48
Hungary, 380
Huntsman, 339
Hussein, Qusay, 169, 173–174, 186
Hussein, Uday, 173–174, 186
Hussein, Saddam (and regime of), 6, 158,
    355, 393
  assets of, 175–200
  and emptying of Central Bank of Iraq,
    169–170, 176
  and Oil for Food Program (OFF), 6, 158,
    172–173, 181, 199
  sanctions against, 171, 344
  and WMD, 212

Ibrahim, Dawood (aka Sheikh Dawood Has-
    san), 115–117, 365
Ibrahim, Hikmat, 169
Iguazu Falls, 117
India, 116, 356, 400
  and controls on illicit financing, 15, 165
  and hawalas, 95, 97
  and Iran, 339, 341, 348
  and organized crime, 115
Indonesia, 63, 72, 400
  and attack on Bali, 64
InfoBank, 158
ING, 302
Ingersoll Rand, 339
Inpex, 337
Interagency Policy Committees. *See* National
    Security Council policy coordination
    committees (PCC's) of
Internal Revenue Service (IRS), 108
  Criminal Investigative Division (IRS-CID)
    of, 18, 128, 132, 133, 176–177, 202, 208
  in Iraq, 176–177, 186–187
International Atomic Energy Agency (IAEA),
    252
  and Iran, 306, 307, 311, 350–351

International Economic Emergency Powers
    Act (IEEPA), 107, 170
International Energy Agency, 337
International Islamic Relief Organization
    (IIRO), 69
International Monetary Fund (IMF), 35, 47,
    137, 400, 406
International Reciprocal Trade Association,
    397
International Standards on Combating
    Money Laundering and the Financing of
    Terrorism and Proliferation, 215
Interpol, 31, 121, 233
  Orange Notice of, 234
Inter-Services Intelligence Directorate (ISI),
    116
Iran, 86, 200, 241, 264, 283, 346, 370–371,
    375, 389
  Aerospace Industries Organization (AIO),
    307
  Al Qaeda in, 366
  and Bad Bank Initiative, 290
  and cyber-warfare, 407–410
  Defense Industries Organization (DIO) of,
    306–307
  and designation of, 290–316
  elections in, 327
  Green Movement in, 327–328
  and Hezbollah, 290–291, 358, 395
  hostage crisis in, 287
  and Iraq, 194, 325, 395
  Islamic Revolutionary Guard Corps of,
    293–294
  and Lebanon, 190, 289–290, 409
  and Ministry of Defense and Armed Forces
    Logistics, 307
  and North Korea, 290, 327, 375
  nuclear program of, 62, 211, 212, 214, 215,
    287, 297, 301, 304, 324–325, 328, 338,
    341, 349–352
  oil in, 288–289, 336–337, 403
  and Persian Spring, 328
  and Quds Force, 370
  sanctions against, 12, 24, 148, 287–288,
    297, 322, 324–343, 349
  and Section 311, 167, 290–291, 332–333,
    335
  Shia militias in, 292, 395
  and Straits of Hormuz, 289
  and SWIFT, 283–284, 338–339, 350
  and Syria, 354, 355
  and terrorist financing, 2, 83
  and US Congress, 335–336
  See also Bush, George W., Islamic Revolu-
    tionary Guard Corps, Obama, Barack,
    United Nations
Iran and Syria Nonproliferation Act (ISNA),
    306
Iran Transaction Regulations (ITR), 303
Iranian Assembly of Experts, 314
Iranian Financial Sanctions Regulations, 337
Iraq, 112, 299, 355, 371, 388, 393
  Al Qaeda in, 113–114

  asset recovery of, 169–187, 344
  Baathist resistance in, 170, 183, 195
  economy of, 174, 393–394
  and Iran, 325, 371
  oil in, 393–394, 407
  and Oil for Food Program (OFF), 6, 158,
    172–173, 183
  and organized crime, 119
  sanctions against, 6, 171
  Shia militias in, 194
  Sunnis in, 194
  war in, 169, 213
  See also Development Fund of Iraq, United
    Nations Security Council Resolution
    1483
Iraq Threat Finance Cell, 196–197
Iraqi Intelligence Service, 173, 187, 194–195
Irbis, 120
Ireland, 222, 400
Ireland, Leslie, 207
Irish Republican Army (IRA)
  and North Korea, 222
Isamuddin, Riduan "Hambali," 63–64
Islamabad, 431
Islamabad High Court, 213
Islamic Call Society, 106
Islamic Center of San Diego
  and Al Qaeda, 20
Islamic Republic of Iran Shipping Lines
    (IRISL), 304–305, 334
Islamic Revolutionary Guard Corps (IRGC),
    293–294, 300–301, 304, 307, 331–332,
    351, 354
  Qods Force of, 294, 304, 354, 410
Islamists in Chechnya, 365
Israel, 5, 36
  and cyber-warfare, 407–409
  and Hezbollah, 290, 358
  and Iran, 304, 338, 351
  and Lebanon, 190
  and Syria, 224
Istanbul (Turkey)
  and cash couriers, 105
  and Iran, 341, 350
Italy, 127, 133
Italy-Greece-Turkey Interconnector (IGTI),
    387
ITEX barter network, 396–397
Izz ad-Din al-Qasam Cyber Fighters, 410

Jakarta, 64
Japan, 221, 391, 404–405
  and China, 387, 389
  and Iran, 336, 338
  and North Korea, 252
  sanctions against, 5
  and US debt, 403
Japan Bank for International Cooperation,
    391
Jardini, Nancy, 176–177
Jeddah (Saudi Arabia), 67, 71, 73

Jeffrey, James, 298–299
Jemaah Islamiyah (JI, Islamic Congregation), 63–64, 367
Johnson, Linda, 141
Jordan, 164
    and Iraq, 171–172, 181–183, 187–188
Jordan, Robert, 73
Joumaa, Ayman, 359–360
JP Morgan Chase, 150, 410
JSC CredexBank, 158
Jumale, Ahmed, 37–38, 363

Kabul (Afghanistan), 15–17, 370
    and Afghan Threat Finance Cell, 196–197
    and hawalas, 98–99
    and Hindu Kush Mountains, 16
Kaesong Industrial Complex, 373
Kaiser, Larry, 181–182, 184–185
Kandahar Exchange, 100
Kaplan, Robert, 394
Karachi (Pakistan)
    and cash couriers, 104
    and Ibrahim, Dawood, 116–117
Kashmir (India), 79, 115
Kaspersky Lab, 407–408
Kazakhstan, 162, 400
Kazan, Ali, 117
Kean, Thomas, 273, 321
Keller, Bill, 273, 276–278
Kelly, James A., 228, 236
Kentucky (US), 276
Kenya, 363, 364
Khalden terrorist training camp, 113
Khalifa, Mohammed Jamal, 82
Khalil, Ezedin Abdel Aziz, 82, 366
Khalizaid, Zal, 100
Khamenei, Ayatollah Ali, 293, 324, 341
Khan, Abdul Qadeer (AQ), 62, 211–214
    and North Korea, 224
Kim Jong Il (and regime of), 235, 254
    assets of, 219
    and Obama administration, 322
    survival of dynasty, 220–221
    See also North Korea, Pyongyang
Kimmitt, Robert M., 312–313, 416
King, Peter, 276
Kish Island (Iran), 375
Kismayo (Somalia), 363, 364
kleptocracy, 197–200, 210, 415
Kongra Gel. *See* Kurdish terrorism
Korean Mining and Development Corporation (KOMID), 225
Korean War, 220
    and "The Control," 24
Koryo Asia Ltd., 243
Kozlov, Andrei, 162
KPMG, 339
Kredittrrust, 161
Krekar, Mullah (aka Najmuddin Faraj Ahmad), 112–114
Kris, David, 272

Kroll, Steve, 204
Kunlun Bank, 371
Kupfer, Jeff, 135, 140
Kurdish terrorism, 112
    and PKK, 369
Kuwait, 164, 171, 344
    and terrorist financing, 82
Kyrgyzstan, 162

La Cosa Nostra (Mafia), 234–235
La Familia, 376
Lahoud, Emile, 190, 191
Lancaster, John, 18
Lashkar-e-Taiba (LT), 115, 364, 365, 367, 430
Las Vegas (US), 226
Latif, Mahmoud Abdel, 165
Latvia, 158, 167
League of Nations, 4
Lebanese Canadian Bank (LCB), 119, 359–361
    and Section 311, 361
Lebanon, 164
    as banking center, 408–409
    and cash couriers, 106
    and Hezbollah, 118–119, 289–290, 358–360
    and Iraq, 172, 189–193
    Shia in, 190
    Sunnis in, 190
    See also Hariri, Rafik
Lehman Brothers, 389
Levey, Stuart, 250
    and Iran, 268, 288, 291–292, 295–302, 304, 305, 307, 309, 314, 324, 328–331, 333, 335, 342
    and Libya, 343–348
    and North Korea, 255, 260, 268, 323
    and Obama administration, 319–320
    and SWIFT, 271–276, 278, 280
    and TFI, 208–210, 216
    and WMD, 214
Levin, Carl, 418
Liberia, 119–121
Libya
    and assassination plot, 107
    assets of, 346–348
    and cash couriers, 106–108
    and Iraq, 196
    and Mission to the UN, 106
    nuclear program of, 62, 212, 213
    regime change in, 343–346
    sanctions against, 6, 107, 148, 313, 344–346
Lichtblau, Eric, 270–275
Lieberman, Joseph, 410
Liechtenstein, 40, 89, 90, 188
Lincoln, Abraham, 4
Linden dollars
    and Linden Lab, 396
    and LindeX, 396
Lindt, Anna, 38

Lisbon Treaty, 280–281
Lloyds of London, 305, 334–338
Lloyds TSB Group, 309
Lo, Clarie, 31
Local Exchange Trading Systems (LETS), 397
Lockheed Martin, 406
Logarcheo, 187
London (UK), 81, 95
  and cash couriers, 104–105
  and Iran, 289, 303, 309, 313, 333
Lormel, Dennis, 34
Los Angeles Times, 273–275
Los Zetas, 370, 378, 381
Lukashenko, Alexander, 158
LUKOIL, 337, 394
Luxembourg, 89

Macau (China)
  as gambling center, 225–226
  and North Korea, 219, 220, 221, 232, 235,
    240–241, 244, 258, 264
Macau Monetary Authority, 264
Maersk, 334
Mafia state, 397
  See also North Korea
Mahan Air, 354
Maher, Katherine, 409
Majd, Hooman, 340
Makhlouf, Rami, 353
Malaysia, 63, 212, 303, 374, 400
  and Iran, 334
Mali, 362
Malmgren, Harald, 411
Manama (Bahrain), 164
Manila (Philippines), 140
  and North Korea, 222
Manufacturers Hanover, 313
MasterCard, 367, 430
Mauritania, 82
McAfee, 406–407
McBrien, Bob, 24–25, 121
McChrystal, Stanley A., 197
McConnell, Mike, 379, 405
McDonough, Denis, 346
Megarian Decree, 3–4, 5, 12
Meiners, Molly Millerwise, 207
  and North Korea, 250–251, 260–261, 262
  and SWIFT, 270–271, 274
Mellat Bank SB CJSC, 303
Melli Bank PLC, 304
"Merchant of Death." *See* Bout, Viktor
Merrill Lynch, 390
Mexico, 33, 369–370, 378, 423
Meyer, Josh, 273, 275
Meyers, Jody, 178
MGM, 226
Middle East Media Research Institute, 87
Miers, Harriet, 271
Milan 40, 127
Miliband, David, 342
Miller, Greg, 275

Milosevic, Slobodan, 6
Ministry of Defense and Armed Forces Logis-
    tics (MODAFL), 305
Misrata (Libya), 344
Mogadishu (Somalia), 364
Moghadam, Ismail Ahmadi, 354
Mogilevich, Semion, 380
Mongolia, 300
Montana Management, 187
Morales, Oscar, 430
Morgan Stanley, 390
Morgener, Andreas, 121
Morgenthau, Robert, 309–310
Morocco, 164
  and Iraq, 196
Moscow (Russia), 123, 161–162, 408
Moumou, Mohammed, 112–114
Mubarak, Hosni, 427
Mueller, Bob, 50, 380
  and SWIFT, 58
Muhammadi, Umid, 82
Mukasey, Michael, 378–379
Mullen, Mike, 413
Müller, Andreas, 212
Mumbai (India), 115
  terrorist attacks on, 115–117, 398, 430
Munich Olympics (1972), 24
Munich Re, 335
Murden, Bill, 32–33, 74
Musan Iron Mine, 374
Muslim Brotherhood, 427
Mutually Assured Support, 420
Muwafaq Foundation, 81
MV Limburg, 398
Myanmar. *See* Burma
Myanmar May Flower Bank, 155

Nada, Yousef, 40
Naftiran Intertrade Company Ltd., 308
Naftiran Intertrade Company Sarl, 308
Nahavandian, Mohammad, 342–343
Naím, Moisés, 397
Nasrallah, Sheikh Hassan, 117–118
Nasreddin, Ahmed Idris, 40
Nasser, Gamal Abdel, 5
Natanz (Iran), 351
National Bank of Belgium, 50
National Defense Authorization Act (NDAA),
    339
National Intelligence Estimate, 376
National Intelligence Manager, 207
National Iranian Oil Company, 308, 341
National Money Laundering Strategy (2001),
    19, 31
National Public Radio, 340
National Security Agency (NSA), 46, 275,
    418
National Security Council, 111, 142, 156,
    178, 198, 216, 312, 405, 416
  Deputies Committee of, 291
  and Iran, 291

and Iraq, 189
and North Korea, 227, 231, 241, 244
policy coordination committees (PCC's) of, 39
National Security Division, 272
National Strategy to Internationalize Efforts Against Kleptocracy, 198
Nauru, 153
naval blockades, 4
Naval Weapons Systems Training Facility Boardman, 405
Nazis
counterfeiting by, 224
Negroponte, John, 33
Ness, Eliot, 34, 129
Netanyahu, Benjamin, 338, 351
New Delhi (India), 96–97, 138
Newcomb, Rick, 134
and CIA, 40
and OFAC, 23–26
Newcomb, William, 228–230
New Jersey (US), 235–236
New York (US), 65, 95, 123, 146, 276
and Arab Bank, 148
as financial center, 9, 12, 25, 26, 147, 150–151, 242
and Hezbollah, 361
and Iran, 309–310, 349
and 9/11, 19, 28, 61
and North Korea, 254–255
New York Federal Reserve Bank. *See* Federal Reserve Bank of New York
New York Times, The, 380
and SWIFT, 269–276
and Terrorist Surveillance Program, 269
Nichols, Rob, 16, 207, 270
Nigeria, 355, 363, 365
9/11 attacks, 17–19
as basis for financial warfare, 2–3, 7–9, 11, 21, 288
economic effects of, 20
and financial intelligence, 48
and hijackers, 20, 67
9/11 Commission, 63, 273, 321
Noble, Ron, 31, 233–234
See also Interpol
Noor Islamic Bank, 371
North Atlantic Treaty Organization (NATO), 23
North Korea, 200, 284, 287, 289, 291, 298, 348, 350, 375, 389
and banking, 219–220, 225–227
and "Chosen Soren," 221
and counterfeiting, 1, 221–237, 258, 265, 267
as criminal state, 219
and Iran, 290, 375
missiles of, 253
and narcotics trade, 233
natural resources of, 373–374
nuclear program of, 62, 211, 212, 213–215, 221, 224, 253, 320
and "Office 39," 221, 232

and organized crime, 119, 234-235
and *Pong Su,* 233
sanctions against, 12, 220, 320–321, 371–372
and Section 311, 167, 227, 230–232, 235–237, 239–246, 252–268, 299–300
and six-party talks, 229, 236, 243, 245, 249, 252, 255, 259, 261, 264, 322
and special economic zones, 374
and State Department, 227–229, 256–259, 265, 267, 323
See also Banco Delta Asia, China and North Korea
North Korea Illicit Activity Initiative, 230–231
North Korean Foreign Trade Bank, 264
North Korean Illicit Finance Action Group (NORKAG), 231
Northern Alliance (Afghanistan), 120
Norway, 112–114

Obama, Barack (and administration of), 272
cyber-security of, 419–420
and Executive Order 13572, 353
and Executive Order 13573, 353
and Executive Order 13582, 353
and Executive Order 13606, 353
and Iran, 316, 319–321, 324–329, 354, 371
and Libya, 347
Nobel Peace Price of, 326
and organized crime, 380–381
and SWIFT, 287
and Syria, 352–355
transition into office of, 319–321
O'Brien, Pat, 300
Office of the Comptroller of the Currency (OCC), 148
Office of the Deputy Attorney General, 208
Office of Enforcement, 128, 250
dissolution of, 132, 135–136
Office of Foreign Assets Control (OFAC), 18, 133, 142, 148, 343
and Al Barakaat, 38
and Al Qaeda, 26–27
and Cuba, 24, 148
and Executive Order 13224, 26–28
expansion of, 202, 206
and Iran, 24, 303, 333
and Iraq, 174, 195–196
and Latin America, 7
and Libya, 345, 347
and organized crime, 121
power of, 24–27
and Specially Designated Nationals (SDNs), 7, 25
and US sanctions, 33
and WMD, 214
See also "The Control," Iraq Threat Finance Cell
Office of Intelligence and Analysis (OIA), 205–206

484

INDEX

Office of International Affairs, 32
Office of Management and Budget (OMB), 139
Office of Terrorism and Financial Intelligence (TFI), 320
  creation of, 207–210, 216
Olsen, Eric T., 197
Oman, 164
O'Neill, Paul, 16, 31, 38, 78
  and 80/20 rule, 25–36, 37, 39, 108
  and financial intelligence, 49, 51
  and hawalas, 96–97
  and Saudi Arabia, 67, 73–75, 86
  and SWIFT, 58
  on Treasury role, 35, 45–46, 130, 133, 138–139
  and workplace safety, 134
Operation Green Quest, 35, 106, 208–209
Oregon (US), 72, 405
Organisation for Economic Co-operation and Development (OECD), 392
Organization of the Petroleum Exporting Countries (OPEC), 403
organized crime, 2, 210–211
  designation of, 115–117, 122–123
  as national security threat, 376–382, 398
  and North Korea, 234–235
  in Italy, 127
  undermining of, 29
Ott, Charlie, 141

Palestine, 86, 148
Palestinian Authority, 87
Palestinian Islamic Jihad, 303
Pakistan, 389, 431
  Al Qaeda and Taliban in, 15, 20, 70, 82, 364–365
  bin Laden in, 42
  and hawalas, 94
  and Khan, AQ, 213
  mujahideen in, 85
  nuclear program of, 62
  and organized crime, 115–116, 119
Panama, 187
Paraguay, 117, 118
Paris (France), 31, 215, 298
Passos, Nikos, 96
Paulson, Henry, 243, 249, 313, 379, 383, 428
  and Iran, 295–296, 300, 312
  and North Korea, 256, 260, 262
PayPal, 430
Pearl Harbor (US), 5
Peloponnesian War, 3
Pentagon, 18
People's Bank of China, 241–242, 261–262, 393
Pericles, 3
Persian International Bank PLC, 303
Peru, 222
Peshawar (Pakistan), 20, 82
Petraeus, David, 197

Philippines, 63, 140, 367
PNC Bank, 150, 410
Poland, 387
politically exposed persons (PEPs), 199
Poncy, Chip, 139–140, 167, 215, 348, 382
  and Iran, 310–311
Pong Su, 233
Popular Front for the Liberation of Palestine–General Command, 303
Post Bank of Iran, 332
Potomac River, 17–18
Powell, Colin, 182, 250
Presidential Personnel Office, 209
Price, Dan, 379
PricewaterhouseCoopers, 339
"Prince of Marbella." See al-Kassar, Manzar
Privacy and Civil Liberties Oversight Board (PCLOB), 283
Proliferation Security Initiative (PSI), 211
Pyongyang (North Korea), 219, 220, 236, 239, 241, 243, 252, 288, 322–323
  and counterfeiting, 222–225, 229
  and Section 311, 252, 257–258, 263
Putin, Vladimir (and administration of), 159–160, 162, 388
  and North Korea, 264

Qaddafi, el-, Muammar (and regime of), 106–107, 313,
  overthrow of, 343–348, 354
Qamsari, Mohsen, 341
Qatar, 82, 164, 307, 374, 403, 427
  and cash couriers, 105
  and Syria, 354
  and US financial crisis (2008), 384
Qatar Investment Authority, 390
Qin Gang, 242
Qom nuclear facility (Iran), 328, 338

Radan, Ahmad-Reza, 354
Rafah border crossing, 105
Rafidain Bank, 172, 177
Rafsanjani, Akbar Hashemi, 314
Ralls Corporation, 405
Rasheed Bank, 172, 177
Ravich, Samantha, 111
Reagan National Airport, 17
Red Cross, 87
Reding, Viviane, 281
Reliance, 337
Report of International Transportation of Currency or Monetary Instruments, 103
reputational risk, 10–11, 89, 147, 241, 330, 429
Reserve Bank of India, 339
Reuters, 337
Revival of the Islamic Heritage Society (RIHS), 82
Revolutionary Armed Forces of Colombia (FARC), 33, 122–123, 368–369, 430

Revolutionary United Front (RUF), 121
Rice, Condoleezza, 63, 189, 191, 379
    and Iran, 291, 295–296
    and North Korea, 227, 231, 236, 252, 256,
        259–260, 263, 266
    and SWIFT, 58
Rice, Susan, 330
Rickards, James, 400–401
Ridge, Tom, 129
Riga (Latvia), 167
Riggs Bank, 85, 263
    and fine, 148–150
Risen, James, 271–272, 275
Riyadh (Saudi Arabia), 67, 73, 87
    Al Qaeda attacks in, 76
    and cash couriers, 106
Rome (Italy), 127, 131, 132
Ross, Jeff, 140, 142–143, 157–158
Rotterdam (Netherlands), 334
Royal Australian Air Force, 233
Royal Charm investigation, 235
Royal Dutch Shell, 337, 393
Rumsfeld, Donald, 232
Russia, 44, 68, 119, 165, 223, 374, 403
    and anti-money-laundering, 159–163
    financial power of, 387–388, 400, 420
    and Iran, 297, 304, 309, 311, 348
    and Iraq, 186–187, 393–394
    and North Korea, 220, 264
    and organized crime, 122–123, 393, 430
    and SWIFT, 284
    and Syria, 355
    and US financial crisis (2008), 383–385
Russian Air Force, 119
Russian Military Institute of Foreign Lan-
    guages, 119

SAAR Foundation, 105
Said, Sheikh. *See* al-Yazid, Mustafa
Saif, Abdullah, 164
Saloom, Joseph, 178
San Air General Trading, 120
Sanders, Traci, 141, 155
Santa Cruz Imperial, 120
Sarkozy, Nicolas, 308–309
Saudi Arabia, 164, 4010, 426
    and Account 98, 86–89
    and Al Haramain Foundation, 72–73,
        76–77
    Al Qaeda attacks in, 76, 398
    and the Hajj, 67, 71
    and Iraq, 196
    and Lebanon, 190
    and Mecca and Medina, 69
    and Mubahith, 76, 77
    and mujahideen financing, 68, 84–85
    and 9/11, 67
    and Riggs Banks, 149
    and Syria, 355
    and terrorist financing, 67–68, 72,
        80–91
Saudi American Bank (Samba), 87–88

Saudi Committee for the Relief of the Pales-
    tinian People, 86–87
Saudi Committee for the Support of the
    Intifida Al Quds
    See Saudi Committee for the Relief of the
        Palestinian People
Schick, Alan, 181–182
Schneider, Scott, 177–178, 180–181
Schrank, Leonard "Lenny"
    and SWIFT, 52–54, 57, 58, 274, 277, 283
Scobey, Margaret, 73, 157, 183
Scolinos, Tasia, 18, 127
Scomi Precision Engineering (SCOPE), 212
Second Life, 396
    See also Linden dollars
Secret Service, 208, 233, 250
    and Counter Assault Team (CAT), 16
    and counterfeiting, 4, 129, 221–224, 229,
        234
    and Department of Homeland Security,
        128, 130–132
    investigation of 9/11 hijackers, 34
Securities and Exchange Commission (SEC),
    412
Senate Banking Committee, 204
Senate Foreign Relations Committee, 321,
    335
Senate Homeland Security Committee, 410
Senate Permanent Select Committee on
    Intelligence, 205
Seng Heng Bank, 240
Seoul (South Korea), 323
Shamoon virus, 410
Sharjah Cooperative Society, 367
Sharjah Islamic Bank, 367
Sharma, Amit
    and hawaladars, 97–101, 102
    and North Korea, 260
Shedd, David, 227–228, 231, 245
Sheikh Mohammed, Khalid
    bank accounts of, 20
Shelby, Richard, 204–206
Shell oil, 337
Sierra Leone, 120, 121
signals intelligence (SIGINT), 48
Simon, Steve, 178
Simpson, Glenn, 274
Singapore, 63, 64
    and Iran, 333, 334
    and North Korea, 220, 241
Siniora, Fouad, 192
Sloan, Jim, 134
smart financial power, 321
Smith, Chris, 206
Smoking Dragon investigation, 235
Snow, John, 143, 150
    and Crown Prince Abdullah, 78
    and expansion of Treasury, 205–207,
        215–216
    and Iran, 295
    and Iraq, 170
    and North Korea, 232, 241–242
    and Prince Bandar, 84, 86
    and SWIFT, 271, 273, 275

Society for Worldwide Interbank Financial Telecommunication (SWIFT)
and effectiveness of data, 55–57, 63–65
and expanded Treasury, 201, 203
history and purpose of, 49–50
and Iran, 283–284, 338–339, 374
and Ismuddin, Riduan, 64
public knowledge of, 269–285, 269–285
and "scrutineers," 59
and Treasury subpoenas, 54–55
US access to, 50–54, 56, 57–58, 282
Sodbiznesbank, 161
Somalia, 37, 76, 79, 430–431
Al Qaeda in, 363–364
and hawalas, 94
Transitional Federal Government (TFG) of, 431
See also Al Barakaat network, Al Shabaab
Sony Playstation, 406
Sopranos, The, 235, 236
and Soprano State, 239
South Africa, 6, 212, 400
South Korea, 220, 236, 389, 400, 404
and Iran, 288, 334, 336
and North Korea, 252, 324, 373
and ROKS Cheonan, 322
Soviet Union, 17, 119
Special Drawing Rights (SDRs), 400
Specially Designated Nationals, 25
Spiegel Online, 281
Stafford, Brian, 134
Standard & Poor, 384, 403
Standard Chartered bank, 332, 348–349, 370, 371
Starbucks, 191
Star Wars, 368
State Department, 33, 46, 88, 107, 142, 150, 178, 215
and Iran, 295, 307, 333, 337
and Iraq, 172
and Khan, AQ, 213
See also North Korea and State Department
state-owned enterprises (SOEs), 386
Steinberg, Jim, 323
Straits of Hormuz, 289
Stuxnet virus, 407–409
Stys, Mark, 411
Success Foundation, 106
Sudan, 81, 149, 320, 407
and bin Laden, 42, 60
Suez Canal, 5
Sun Trust Bank, 20
Sunni Wahhabi Islam, 68–69, 424
supernote. See North Korea counterfeiting
Suspicious Activity Reports, 20
Sveriges Riksbank, 49
Swartz, Bruce, 235
Sweden, 38, 112–113
SWIFT. See Society for Worldwide Interbank Financial Telecommunication
Swiss Federal Council, 212–213
Swiss National Bank, 49
Switzerland, 40, 89, 90, 425
and asset recovery, 199

and Iraq, 174, 181, 187, 188, 195
and WMD, 212
and White Money Initiative, 199
Syria, 86, 164, 170, 200, 284, 365–366, 375
and cash couriers, 106
and Hezbollah, 358
and Iraq, 171, 181, 183–185, 195
and North Korea, 224
in Lebanon, 190, 193, 409
and money laundering, 156–158
nuclear program of, 62, 211, 212–214
and Section 311, 353
Syrian Accountability Act, 156–157
Syrian International Islamic Bank (SIIB), 354–355
Syrian Lebanese Commercial Bank, 156–157
Szubin, Adam, 341, 346–348

Taepo Dong 2 missile, 253
Tahir, B.S.A., 212
Taipei (Taiwan), 393
Taiwan
and China, 163, 387, 393, 401
and North Korea, 222
Tajikistan, 162
takfir (apostates), 69
Taliban, 79
and hawalas, 94
and heroin and opium trade, 23, 197, 368, 369
and Islamic charities, 71
and organized crime, 120
and UN, 33
Tamil Tigers, 23
Tanchong Commercial Bank, 225
Taylor, Charles, 120–121
Taylor, John, 74
and Taylor rule, 32
Tehran (Iran), 287, 288, 294, 322, 324, 338, 340, 351, 375
Terrorist Finance Tracking Program, 64, 203, 285
Terrorist Finance Tracking System (TFTS), 282
terrorist financing, 210–211
and comingling of funds, 22
and deep-pocket donors, 19–20, 78, 80–82, 109
designations of, 27–28, 29, 36, 38–41, 70–73, 108–114
and funder intent, 22
as "reverse money laundering," 21
See also cash couriers, charities (Islamic), Golden Chain list, organized crime
Terrorist Financing Operations Section (TFOS)
origin of, 34, 60
Terrorist Surveillance Program (TSP), 269
Thailand, 63, 122–123
Tinner, Friedrich, 212–213
Tinner, Marco, 212–213
Tinner, Urs, 212–213

threat finance cells (TFCs), 196–197
Tokyo
  and Iran, 289
  and North Korea, 323
Toscas, George, 18
Total oil, 335
Townsend, Frances M. Fragos, 83–84
Trafigura, 337
Transavia Travel, 120
Transitional Federal Government (Somalia), 364
transnational organized crime (TOC) strategy, 381
Transparency International, 199
Treasury Executive Office for Asset Forfeiture (TEOAF), 18, 133
  expansion of, 202
Treasury Terrorist Financing Tracking Program ("Turtle"), 54, 64, 285
  See also SWIFT
Tri-Border Area of South America (TBA), 117–119
Tripoli (Libya), 106, 344
Tunisia, 164
Turkey, 81, 299, 369
  and Iran, 288, 348
  and Iraq, 171
  and Syria, 355
  and US financial crisis (2008), 384
Turkish Republic of Northern Cyprus, 158
Twitter, 430

UBS
  and Iran, 302, 371
  penalty against, 148
  and SWIFT, 57
Ukraine, 387
  and Bad Bank Initiative, 153
Unha-2 missile, 320
United Against a Nuclear Iran, 361
United Arab Emirates, 90, 164
  and cash couriers, 105
  and hawalas, 95, 96
  and Iran, 288, 307
  and Libya, 354
  and organized crime, 115, 121
  and Sharjah, 121
  and Syria, 355
United Nations, 32, 87, 192, 195
  and Iran, 296–297, 303, 325–326, 330–331, 341–342
  and 1518 Committee, 186, 187
  and North Korea, 372
  and Oil for Food Program (OFF), 6, 158, 172–173, 199
  and organized crime, 376
  sanctions of, 81, 121, 215
  Security Council of, 38, 171, 215, 325, 341
  Security Council Resolution 1267, 33, 38, 234
  Security Council Resolution 1373, 33
  Security Council Resolution 1483, 175, 178, 188–189, 192
  Security Council Resolution 1540, 215
  Security Council Resolution 1696, 306
  Security Council Resolution 1737, 306
  Security Council Resolution 1803, 306
  Security Council Resolution 1874, 322
  Security Council Resolution 1929, 331
  and Somalia, 364
  and Syria, 355
United Wa State Army, 155
USA PATRIOT Act (2001), 137, 147
  and Section 311, 151–158, 164, 167, 290, 332, 353, 360
  and Title III, 30, 47, 151
US Bancorp, 410
US District Court for the Southern District of New York, 123, 312
  and US Attorney, 369
US Export-Import Bank, 392
US Foreign Sovereign Immunities Act, 313
US Global Leadership Coalition Conference, 388
USS *Cole*, 18
U-turn financial transaction, 303, 308

Vardaman, John, 178
Ven digital currency, 396
Venezuela, 304, 371, 374
  and Iran, 309–310, 375
  oil in, 403–405
  and Taliban, 369
Vienna (Austria)
  and Iran, 296, 350
  and North Korea, 220, 233
Vienna Convention for Consular Affairs, 149
Vietnam, 299, 389
Vitol, 337
Vladivostok, 264

Wachovia, 263
Wall Street Journal, 18, 274, 310
Wallerstein, Ryan, 165–167
Wallwork, Anne, 140, 158
Warren, Mary Lee, 142
Washington, D.C. (US), 31, 107, 148, 167, 170, 183, 326, 338
Washington Post, The, 275
Wayne, Tony, 33, 178
weapons of mass destruction (WMD), 29, 111, 213–215
  in Iraq, 171, 173
  proliferation of, 210–211
Wells Fargo, 410
Werner, Bob, 214
Western Union, 30, 96
  in Kabul, 98
White House Situation Room, 41, 58, 232, 267, 299, 329, 345

WikiLeaks, 430
Wilkinson, James R., 263, 267, 291
Williams & Connolly, 26
Willy Wonka and the Chocolate Factory, 254
Wolfe, George, 26
  and Iraq, 174, 178
  and SWIFT, 55
World Bank, 32, 47, 137, 373, 392
  Stolen Asset Recovery (StAR) Initiative of,
    199
World Economic Forum's Global Risks 2008
    report, 411
World War I
  and League of Nations, 4
World War II, 399
  and "The Control," 23–24
  and counterfeiting, 224
  and economic sanctions, 4–5
Wynn, Steve, 226

Yakuza, 376, 381
YBM Magnex, 380
Yemen, 18, 164
  and Al Qaeda in the Arabian Peninsula, 78,
    398
  and cash couriers, 106
  and North Korea, 222
Yeonpyeong Island, 322
Yugoslavia, 148

zakhat (charitable giving), 70, 109
"Zarate-Zubkov" reports, 162
Zelikow, Philip, 291
Zhou Xiaochuan, 241–242
Zhu Guangyao, 389
Zubkov, Viktor, 160–163
Zurich (Switzerland), 106

Photo: Winnie Lee

Juan C. Zarate is a senior adviser at the Center for Strategic and International Studies (CSIS), the senior national security analyst for CBS News, and a visiting lecturer of law at Harvard Law School. Prior to that, he served as the deputy assistant to the president and deputy national security advisor for combating terrorism, and the first ever assistant secretary of the Treasury for terrorist financing and financial crimes. He appears frequently on CBS News programs, PBS's *NewsHour*, NPR, and CNN, and has written for the *New York Times, The Wall Street Journal, Washington Post,* and more. He and his family live in Alexandria, Virginia. Follow him on Twitter: @JCZarate1.